# HOW TO DOUBLE YOUR VOCABULARY

By the Author

The Dictionary of ...

How to Increase ...

**By the Author**

THE COMMAND OF WORDS

HOW TO DOUBLE YOUR VOCABULARY

# HOW TO DOUBLE
# YOUR VOCABULARY

S. Stephenson Smith
*Revised by Herbert B. Greenhouse*

## FUNK AND WAGNALLS
### New York

Funk & Wagnalls Paperback Edition, 1974

Library of Congress Catalog Card No. 73-15092

ISBN 0-308-10099-9

This book is also published in a special edition entitled *The Vocabulary Builder*.

**To Frank Loxley Griffin**

AFTER THIRTY-THREE YEARS

# Publisher's Preface
## To the Second Edition

S. Stephenson Smith knew that words do not exist in a vacuum and that an authoritative book on vocabulary would not be limited to dictionary definitions. Thus, the first edition treated words as dynamic entities and drew heavily upon popular media to show words in action. In the second edition Mr. Greenhouse has added recent examples of word usage from many of the sources mentioned in the first edition, from other printed matter, and from radio and television programs of the '50s and '60s. There are two completely new chapters: one analyzes words used on the air, and the other gives a comprehensive view of new words that have come into the language in the last two decades.

Mr. Smith devoted several chapters to the technical vocabularies of the post-World War II scientific age, which was just gathering momentum in 1947. Mr. Greenhouse has added the new terminology of the Space Age to the special vocabularies of science and technology discussed in the first edition. He has also included recent slang terms and new words used in business, politics, international relations, and other areas of contemporary life.

Because Mr. Smith felt strongly that words help to shape events, he wrote extensively about the "word-hijackers," those who distort the meanings of words for unscrupulous ends. Mr. Greenhouse has cited examples from recent history to illustrate how the adulteration of words creates fear and hatred, and how the ultimate result is violence such as the bombing of churches or the assassination of a President.

The second edition has been updated to include an analysis of current dictionaries and new material on the etymology of words. Full treatment has been given to the classic controversy among lexicographers of the '60s over the definition and labeling of words.

The publisher and Mr. Greenhouse are grateful to Bert A. Gottfried of The Research Institute of America, Inc., for his contribution to the section on business terms in Chapter 11; to Harriet Bachman of *Time* and Robert J. Landry of *Variety* for their helpfulness in explaining the editorial policies of their publications; to Evan Esar, whose *The Humor of Humor* (Horizon Press, Inc.) was a valuable source of material for the chapter on wordplay; to the Clarendon Press, Oxford, for permission to reprint the entry for *character* from the *Concise Oxford Dictionary* and a short excerpt from the introduction of the *Oxford English Dictionary*; and to Carol Schultz, who proved to be a discerning and creative editorial assistant.

# Contents

" . . . language such as men do use."
—Ben Jonson

# 1

# How to Make a Game Out of Building Your Vocabulary

You can double your vocabulary and have fun while you're doing it. Just follow the example of people in the word trades—make a game out of it. Walter Winchell, Earl Wilson, Robert Sylvester, and the bright young phrasemakers of *Time* magazine are constantly playing tricks with words, coining new words and word combinations, sneaking in unusual words and foreign expressions for shock effect. Gag writers make their living with wordplay.

Even lexicographers, those ultraserious compilers of dictionaries, play games with words. Bergen Evans and other word fanciers have a new game called word labels: Is the beatnik term *square* a slang word or should it be labeled standard? Is *lousy* condemned to be a vulgarism or should popular usage raise it to a higher level in word society?

Another popular sport of word scholars is to play detective and find out where words came from. Etymologists like Eric Partridge put on their Sherlock Holmes outfits and ferret out dusty old manuscripts with the object of tracing the history and cultural background of a word. They don't always agree on the ancestry of a word, but they have fun arguing about word origins. Henry L. Mencken in his *American Language* made a game out of watching the behavior of English words transplanted to a new environment during our early history.

## USE THE GAMBLER'S SYSTEM WITH WORDS

Edward L. Thorndike came up with a novel kind of word game; he examined thousands of words in print to find out just how often they turn up, and he based the relative difficulty of words on the number of times they appeared in print. Then he posted odds

1

against the frequency of their occurrence in newspapers and magazines.

A gambler figures odds the same way: in a card game, how often is the ace of spades likely to turn up and what combinations pay off? Thorndike wanted to know which words turn up most often, in the range just beyond the average American's vocabulary. You should ask yourself the same question when you keep running into words that elude your grasp. How often do you see them in print or hear them on the air? Are they worth adding to your stock? Did you try to figure out what ETYMOLOGIST means? And where do these new words fit in, if you want to bring them into play or put them to work? In short, how do you make a game out of words—how do you figure the odds?

In the long run a gambler with a hardheaded system will beat anyone who plays hit-or-miss. The word game can do with a system, too. This holds whether you're playing for fun or money.


## WHAT WORDS CAN DO FOR YOU

Maybe you want a ready, wide, and sure command of words to get ahead in business. Or you would like to travel, first through books, and then in fact, and you feel that out-of-the-way words go with out-of-the-way places. Or perhaps—best reason of all —you want a livelier, wittier, richer vocabulary to increase your enjoyment of life, and your awareness of what is happening in the world.

No matter what your purpose may be for wanting a better vocabulary, this book will tell you the gambling odds on how often words new to you will turn up, and in what kind of reading you're likely to find them. The words printed in SMALL CAPITALS in this book are the utility words just beyond the range of the average American's vocabulary and the less common words used in academic and literary circles. They're the terms you'll need for all-around use, in reading, writing, and talking. Included are many new terms from politics, business, labor, science, and technology.

You'll be surprised to learn how few additional words you'll need in each of these fields, to get along quite well. Where you used to draw a blank on certain words, you'll be able to read right along. Adding the right fifty or a hundred terms will put you at ease with special subjects you've always passed up because you didn't like those four or five blackouts of meaning to a page. Even tough subjects like electronics or astronautics will yield to a little directed homework on technical jargon.

## LEARN THE UNCOMMON WORDS

Keep your eye on the words in SMALL CAPITALS—those used by educated Americans. Make a game out of trying to understand what they mean in context—then test yourself on the many quizzes you'll find in this book. Sharpen your wits on the word games in each chapter; then *score yourself* on the quiz at the end of each chapter from 2 to 11. After you average your total score for these ten chapters, take the Comprehensive Vocabulary-Level Test at the end of Chapter 12 and see what progress you have made. Here is a breakdown of the tests in this book, divided into Practice Quizzes and Scoring Quizzes:

PRACTICE QUIZZES

Word Neophyte's Test—This is a preliminary quiz at the end of this chapter that will test your present vocabulary level.
Word Games—These tests are placed *within* the chapter and are not counted in your total score.

SCORING QUIZZES

Wordplay Quiz—End of Chapter 2.
Working Words Quiz—End of Chapter 3.
Desk Dictionary Words Quiz—End of Chapter 4.
Magazine Words Quiz—End of Chapter 5.
Television Words Quiz—End of Chapter 6.
Classical Words Quiz—End of Chapter 7.
Word Derivation Quiz—End of Chapter 8.
Word Cluster Quiz—End of Chapter 9.
Literary Words Quiz—End of Chapter 10.
Technical Words Quiz—End of Chapter 11.
        Total scores of above ten quizzes to be added, and the average score compared with
Comprehensive Vocabulary-Level Test—End of Chapter 12.

Your goal will be to raise your test score from "substandard" or

3

"average" to the "educated" level. If your progress is rapid, you'll become familiar with the uncommon words known to graduate students and professors. But don't be discouraged if you miss many of these words on the Scoring Quizzes; you'll have another chance when you take the Comprehensive Vocabulary-Level Test. Just keep rereading this book with the help of one of the dictionaries mentioned in Chapter 4 and see how quickly you'll double your vocabulary.

## TRY THESE MEMORY JOGGERS

Seeing the uncommon words *in context* and testing yourself in the word games is one way to fix them in mind. But this is only one of eight methods that you can use to learn new words. Let's look briefly at these memory joggers before we discuss them in detail in subsequent chapters.

### WORD RELATIVES

*Tie many words into one.* When you come across an unfamiliar word, look in a dictionary or a book of SYNONYMY for words that are related to it. You're sure to know at least one word in this group of related words. Center the others on it. Distinguish the fine shades of meaning. In doing so, you'll find you've learned not just one but a whole handful of new words. Take the word ARGOT. In *Webster's Dictionary of Synonyms* this is one of the many words related to the key word *dialect*. Since we'll be referring constantly in this book to *slang, jargon, cant,* etc., we have given you a visual picture of these related words in the accompanying diagram.

### WORD OPPOSITES

*Learn the* ANTONYM *of a new word.* The antonym of a word has an opposite meaning. What is the antonym of ALLEVIATE? VERBOSE? PLIABLE? When you get to Chapter 9 you'll be playing the Word Game of Opposites. Play this game with every new word you meet.

### WORD MECHANICS

*100 will get you 5000.* As a word mechanic you'll take apart uncommon words of classical origin and identify their Latin and Greek roots, prefixes, and suffixes. At the end of the book there's a Word-

**VERNACULAR**
A term applied to the language used by the "man in the street" as opposed to the language of cultivated persons.

**PATOIS**
A form of dialect spoken by the uneducated inhabitants of a provincial area.

**LINGO**
A general term of contempt applied by outsiders to what they consider the unintelligible language of a group.

**PATTER**
Rapid speech such as that of a theatrical performer. Often applied in a contemptuous sense to language that has lost its meaning through repeated use.

**DIALECT**
Language used only in certain districts or regions; not in nationwide use.

**JARGON**
Special vocabulary of members of a profession or cult. This term is used, often in a derogatory sense, by those to whom such vocabulary is unintelligible.

**ARGOT**
Special vocabulary of groups that have developed a peculiar kind of communication not readily understood by outsiders. This term is applied particularly to the language of the underworld.

**CANT**
Trite words or phrases that are part of the special vocabulary of a group. Such terms are intelligible to outsiders but are derided because of their staleness and emptiness of meaning.

Analyzer with 100 word elements that will add 5000 new words to your vocabulary.

WORD PACKAGES

*Tie in one package new words that belong to a given subject.* Word-packaging is one of the functions of *Roget's International Thesaurus.* On page 6 there is a diagram of terms tied together under the heading of ASTRONAUTICS in the new edition.

WORD LABELS

*What kind of word is it?* Is it a standard word that has the dignity of many centuries of usage behind it? Is it a technical word? Is it slang, jargon, dialect? Is it a *colloquialism,* an informal word of good standing not yet admitted to the standard class in the dictionary? Pay particular attention to slang and jargon as language in the making. They're A-1 guides to the way words change meaning, as well as keys to the spirit of your own times. Listen to the jazz buffs, tune in on labor lingo, catch the patter of Pentagonese, read *Variety* for the clip-talk of showbiz. What does *cowboy* mean in the argot of the underworld? How would a policeman define it? What is a *flap*? What would the hipsters call the writer of that overelaborate definition of *square* in *Webster's Third Unabridged*?

And remember—whatever label you put on the word, particularly if it is slang or jargon, a lexicographer might disagree with you. Words sometimes change labels while we're using them.

WORD HISTORIES

*Run down the history of any interesting new word you meet.* Play the game of word detective. Do you know what a GOOGOL is? Or a CHIMERA? Or EXTRAPOLATION? Where is the original BEDLAM? When the girls in the backroom at *Vogue*, the fashion magazine, want to designate a woman's clothes as gaudy and MERETRICIOUS, what term do they use? Should Mayor LaGuardia have sued *Time* for coupling his name with the epithet STEATOPYGOUS? Do you know where the *juke* in *juke-box* comes from? How did the good old English word *talk* come to have a Greek trailer hitched on it to form *talkathon*?

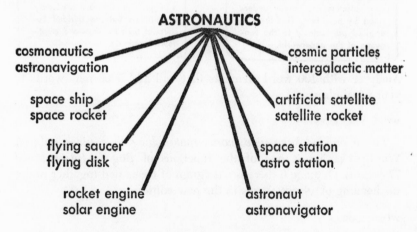

**ASTRONAUTICS**

cosmonautics
astronavigation

cosmic particles
intergalactic matter

space ship
space rocket

artificial satellite
satellite rocket

flying saucer
flying disk

space station
astro station

rocket engine
solar engine

astronaut
astronavigator

This is only a partial list. There are many more related words and phrases in each category (categories are separated by semicolons): *space flight, interplanetary reconnaissance, multistage flight; rocket ship, multistage rocket; UFO; solar battery; micro-instrumentation, magnetometer;* etc.

And how do perfectly proper words—*hot, lit, swell,* BUZZARD, *tomato* —come down in the world, acquiring a slang or vulgar sense? (You'll find the answers later in the book.)

## WORD CLUES

*Look for clues to word meanings.* You'll find them in all kinds of word games. A multiple-choice quiz gives you four guesses at the meaning of a word. The dictionary gives you a straightforward definition, sometimes in clear-cut language, sometimes in circular fashion that brings you right back where you started. (It depends on the dictionary, of course. They're improving in the kind of clues they give to the meaning of a word—but they still play games at times.) There are other clues to word meanings described above, such as related words (synonyms), opposites (antonyms), context, etc.

Don't fail to take all the quizzes in this book.

## WORDPLAY

*Always remember the key word in a new joke.* Notice how comedians play with words on the air, in a nightclub, on recordings. Catch Earl Wilson in the act of INSINUATING a foreign word like *paparazzi* into his column. Notice the shock effect produced by the sudden appearance of a sixty-four-dollar word. By thus getting a humorous association with a new word, you'll fix it in your mind. Learn the tricks and turns of wordplay, and you won't need jokebooks. Above all, study the technique of wordplay used by *Variety, Time,* and the columnists mentioned above.

You're going to find out in the next chapter how to increase your vocabulary with wordplay, but first let's see how you stand wordwise at the present time. How good is your vocabulary? Can you define words easily—and quickly—that would stump an average American? Is your vocabulary level "average," "educated," or "substandard"? Have you ever applied for a job and found out—to your CHAGRIN— that you were word-poor?

### How Good Is Your Vocabulary—under Stress?

Anybody who walks into the PERSONNEL office of a big firm and asks for a job usually confronts—as the first HURDLE—a vocabulary checkup. "If there is time for only one test," says a famous psychologist who conducts placement examinations for such a firm, "I give the applicant a vocabulary test. It's the best single measure." And he doesn't make it easy.

The following test isn't a big enough sample to give any exact measure of your total vocabulary. But it's built on something more than guesswork. Discounting for the shortness and spottiness of the test, you can, if you like, make a rough guess about your vocabulary range. If you get 15 to 20 right, your vocabulary is equal to that of the average American; over 20 puts you in the higher education class; under 15 gives you a substandard rating. If you get all 30 right, you don't have to read any further. If you get fewer than 15, don't fail to do your homework at the end of each chapter.

## Word Neophyte's Test

Place in the brackets the number of the word or phrase closest in meaning to the initial word—for example:

1. [ ] ALLERGIC [1] lazy [2] friendly [3] adverse [4] adversely sensitive to

The right equivalent is [4], so you place that number in the bracket preceding allergic. (A proper use of the word: "The doctor found the patient allergic to egg proteins.")

1. [ ] bone [1] mistake [2] vertebrate [3] horn [4] element of SKELETAL structure
2. [ ] TURBID [1] muddy [2] upset [3] swirling [4] crowded
3. [ ] affect [1] result [2] influence [3] cause [4] shortcoming
4. [ ] accord [1] notes in harmony [2] unit for measuring wood [3] agreement [4] bind up
5. [ ] INORDINATE [1] not working [2] in order [3] excessive [4] ordained
6. [ ] PERFUNCTORY [1] in the manner of [2] official [3] mechanical [4] dying
7. [ ] behavior [1] wickedness [2] way of acting [3] school of PSYCHOLOGY [4] occasion for punishment
8. [ ] ally [1] to state as supposition [2] narrow lane [3] to label as falsehood [4] fellow-BELLIGERENT
9. [ ] affront [1] precede [2] insult [3] ahead [4] beach
10. [ ] FORTUITOUS [1] accidental [2] planned [3] courageous [4] defensive
11. [ ] EDICT [1] banning of sacraments [2] UKASE [3] decision of jury [4] tyranny

8

12. [ ] PROVOST [1] enraging [2] official [3] foresighted [4] a special kind of ceremonial gown
13. [ ] NOISOME [1] clamorous [2] smelly [3] appalling [4] rascal
14. [ ] CANTO [1] half gallop [2] a singer [3] section of a long poem [4] drinking vessel
15. [ ] OVERARCH [1] church POTENTATE [2] a kind of tree [3] meet above in middle [4] COQUETTE
16. [ ] MODULATION [1] shyness [2] temperance [3] method of shifting from one key to another [4] admiration
17. [ ] KINETIC [1] EGOTISTIC [2] wavy [3] pertaining to motion [4] attractive
18. [ ] IMMINENCE [1] quality of being outstanding [2] height [3] state of threatening [4] edge of cliff
19. [ ] SUBTRAHEND [1] lower tendency [2] number to be taken away from another [3] underground stream [4] drift below
20. [ ] ENZYME [1] commissioned officer in Navy [2] flag [3] gland-produced CATALYTIC agent [4] a paste
21. [ ] AMBIVALENT [1] walking [2] tricky [3] double-valued [4] symmetrical
22. [ ] EMPATHY [1] lack of sympathy [2] DIVERGENCE [3] participating in another's feelings [4] roundabout way
23. [ ] BOTULISM [1] turning rods [2] poisoning from bacterially spoiled foods [3] improper canning [4] ALCOHOLISM
24. [ ] CATALYST [1] INVERT [2] one who classifies books [3] stone-throwing device [4] reaction agent itself unchanged
25. [ ] IRREDENTA [1] UNRECLAIMED [2] water-ditch [3] GULLY [4] glittering
26. [ ] NEUTRON [1] impartial [2] of intermediate gender [3] colorless [4] uncharged particle
27. [ ] DYSGENIC [1] noninheritable [2] biologically deficient [3] kingly family [4] REGENERATIVE
28. [ ] ENDOCRINE [1] HERETICAL doctrine [2] DUCTLESS gland [3] salty [4] poisoned
29. [ ] MULTIVERSE [1] kind of TURBINE [2] plural worlds [3] universal screw [4] extra stanza
30. [ ] PASQUINADE [1] volley of shots [2] ornament [3] SATIRIC verse [4] column

| | | | | | |
|---|---|---|---|---|---|
| 1. [4] | 6. [3] | 11. [2] | 16. [3] | 21. [3] | 26. [4] |
| 2. [1] | 7. [2] | 12. [2] | 17. [3] | 22. [3] | 27. [2] |
| 3. [2] | 8. [4] | 13. [2] | 18. [3] | 23. [2] | 28. [2] |
| 4. [3] | 9. [2] | 14. [3] | 19. [2] | 24. [4] | 29. [2] |
| 5. [3] | 10. [1] | 15. [3] | 20. [3] | 25. [1] | 30. [3] |

| | | |
|---|---|---|
| 30 right | Ph.D. | ⎫ |
| 28–29 right | Master's Degree | ⎪ Educated |
| 25–27 right | College Graduate | ⎬ |
| 21–24 right | Above Average | ⎭ |
| 15–20 right | Average | |
| Under 15 right | Substandard | |

(This test doesn't count in your total score—it's just a check on your present vocabulary level. Your official scoring will begin with the Wordplay Quiz at the end of Chapter 2.)

# 2

## How to Increase Your Vocabulary with Wordplay

Wordplay is the spice that gives life and brightness to magazines like *Time* and *Variety*. *Fortune* and *Newsweek* spruce up their copy with ALLITERATION, ONOMATOPOEIA, and other forms of word manipulation. Their primary purpose is to report the news, but the temptation to play with words, to surprise and TITILLATE the reader, is often irresistible. Gagwriters play with words for a living. And even serious-minded statesmen often startle their colleagues with far-out words like TROGLODYTES and ZIZITH.

Those stylists who believe in economy of language, in TERSE, spare, unadorned Saxon words, frown upon such practices and accuse the word players of wrecking the language. But language is DYNAMIC and the style that shocks can tell us something about the temper of the times. And it often sends the reader to the dictionary in search of ENLIGHTENMENT.

### COLUMNISTS COIN WORDS

Language purists bitterly attack word blenders such as Walter Winchell and other columnists who feed us the news about Broadway and Hollywood. But if Winchell takes liberties with the language, he also adds to its stock-in-trade. Mostly he gives currency to his own coinages based on the slang and jargon of the amusement world: theaters, nightclubs, movies, gambling joints, and the divorce courts.

Dealing largely in personal gossip (when he isn't throwing barbs at politicians) Winchell is particularly resourceful in inventing fancy wording for courtship, marriage, and divorce. Couples in love are *breathless* or *on fire;* they *hide-a-woo* or go *goo-gooing* at ocean retreats. Couples out of love *shrug it off*. Disillusioned wives *resign* (go to Reno) and get out of *husbondage*. Winchell is fond of clipped

11

forms: *mag* for magazine; *condish* (condition); *dghtr* (daughter); *showbiz.*

The slanguage of clipped forms started with *Variety,* the chief trade publication of the amusement world. *Variety* uses *pic* for moving picture (the plural is *pix*); *biz,* for business; *exec,* for executive; *prez,* for president; *legit,* for legitimate. Home office is abbreviated as *h.o.*; box office becomes *b.o.*; once over is *o.o.* A headline reads:

> Chi Cool, Pix Hot; "Birdie" Wow 47G,
> "Eagles" Boffo $24,000, "Sam" Fair 17G;
> "Irma" Sockeroo $28,000 in 2d

Translated, this means that cool weather helped the box office in Chicago for *Bye Bye Birdie, A Gathering of Eagles,* and *Irma La Douce* in its second week. *Savage Sam* grossed a modest $17,000.

*Variety* likes lively words for theatrical success: *wow, boffo, sockeroo, lusty, socko, hep, buxom take, smasheroo.* A failure is a *flip* or *fliv,* sometimes a *clambake.* To avoid the stale effect of word repetition, *Variety*'s writers constantly spin out new compounds and clipped forms. Teen-agers are called *juves* or the *soft-drink set;* their weekly allowance for disks (records) is *teen coin.*

An amusing take-off on *Variety* style was heard on the New York nightclub circuit in 1939, when a group called The Revuers used an opening number, half-sung, half-spoken, in which they offered to translate *Variety* jargon: [1]

> Broadway is dead and the theatre's a flop
> Receipts at the box office start to drop
> Deep in despair the theatre is—
> Variety says—Show Bizz Fizz!
>
> You open a show in Buffalo
> You give out passes but business is slow
> You give out more passes till it's full enough—
> Variety says—Buff on Cuff!
>
> An opera opens at popular price
> But popular price does not suffice

[1] Copyright 1939 by The Revuers; quoted by permission. The Revuers: Betty Comden and Adolph Green, coauthors of *The Bells Are Ringing;* Judy Holiday, lead actress in *Born Yesterday;* Al Hammer, deadpan comic in the movies.

The opera decides to close up shop—
Variety says—Pop Op Flop!

You open a picture out of town
The reviews come in—all thumbs down
You open five more but none of them clicks—
Variety says—Hix Nix Six Pix!

*Variety* in the Sixties no longer is addicted to the "hix nix six pix" kind of rhymed clips. Its style sheet stresses "clarity" rather than "cuteness." Its writers are urged not to "strain for supposed Varietyese." Actually, clipped forms came into being as space-savers, and in this respect they should have been acceptable to advocates of economy in language. *Variety* is now trying to get away from self-conscious wordplay but is still using clipped forms to tell the showbiz story. The attitude of its managing editor is PERMISSIVE. If a gifted writer invents a clever turn of phrase, it stays in; but the object is not to add to American slanguage but to reflect the talk of the amusement trade.

Although it is true that magazines like *Variety* and columnists like Winchell add fresh words and phrases to Americanese, they showcase the language of the times more than they contribute to it. From journalistic wordplay the vocabulary-conscious reader can learn much about the slang, argot, and jargon of special groups like theater people, underworld characters, jazz musicians, even dope addicts and streetwalkers. Many of the coined words and clipped forms come into the language and go right out again. But many such words remain as slang or colloquialisms and in time are labeled "standard" in our dictionaries. Shortened forms like *curio* (from *curiosity*) and blends like *motel* (from *motor hotel*) are now standard words. A coined word like *socialite* made its way from *Time* magazine into the standard class in *Webster's Third Unabridged*.

Earl Wilson, who once gave himself the title of saloon editor of the *New York Post,* has a different approach to wordplay. He will slyly insert an unusual word in his column, sometimes with mock self-consciousness, as he did with ENCEPHALOGRAM (which he pretended was an OBSCENITY). The shock effect of having a sixty-four-dollar word blunder in among the nickel variety makes the reader think twice about what the word means.

What the Broadway and Hollywood gossip artists do for diversion, more serious columnists do in earnest by putting unusual words into circulation to convey new meanings. *Time* did this with TYCOON. They took the Japanese word *taikun* (great lord) and altered it slightly to give it its present meaning of "businessman of extraordinary wealth, power, and influence." In this case they found, rather than coined, a word. Keeping a weather eye out for these novel terms is an ideal way to extend your own word range.

### Wordplay in the News

This is your first Word Game. Answers immediately follow the questions.

1. A Vice-President once called some of his conservative opponents TROGLODYTES. Nobody at the press or radio table knew what he meant. Do you?

2. The *New York Herald-Tribune* reported this item in the news:

   President Kennedy's failure to kiss Pope Paul VI's ring or to kneel before him. . . . provoked comment yesterday in Catholic circles. . . . "It was proper PROTOCOL," remarked Auxiliary Bishop James H. Griffiths, Holy See observer at the United Nations. "The President was on a visit in his capacity as President of the United States, as a chief of state."

   Do you know what protocol means?

3. In *Fortune* (July, 1963) an editorial writer says that the Chinese Nationalists on Formosa are prepared to invade Communist China "if they have assurance of LOGISTICAL support from the U.S." What is logistical support? What did the headline writer in the *New York Times* mean when he wrote, "The Logistics Behind a Camping Trip to France?" Does one say logistics *is* or logistics *are?*

4. Ben Hecht wrote in *Theatre Arts:*

   Accepted, also, are the new plays of the absurd and of unintelligible disaster. . . . There are always people willing to endure the most dismal boredom if it enables them to boast of superior perception. It is our old form of hazing for admittance into the INTELLIGENTSIA.

   Who or what are the intelligentsia? For more information about the Theatre of the Absurd, read drama critics Taubman, Kerr, Watts, Chapman, et al.

5. From Leonard Lyons' column in the *New York Post*, there was a squib as follows:

During the preliminary discussions on the forthcoming International Business Conference in which 46 nations will participate, Sylvia Porter, the financial columnist, asked the President of the National Association of Manufacturers: "Mr. Gaylord, would you say that one of the results of this conference will be an agreement on policy toward CARTELS?" . . . "I doubt it," Mr. Gaylord answered. "We'd be lucky if we agree on a definition of the word."

Do *you* know what a cartel is?

6. Comedians sometimes become involved in offstage wordplay. Here's an old story about Zero Mostel, reported in Leonard Lyons' column:

Last time he [Zero Mostel, the comedian] was in Hollywood, the papers extraed about wages being frozen, and according to Zero, a $100,000-a-year man dashed up to him breathlessly and said, "Look, Zero, you're a college man, aren't you?" "Yeah," said Zero. "Well, then, what does FISCAL mean?"

What does fiscal mean?

7. The *New Republic* gives us this clipping about Colonel McCormick, late publisher of the Chicago *Tribune*.

At a rehearsal for WGN's fashion show, the *Tribune*'s Robert R. McCormick dropped by to have a look and promptly censored the word "DÉCOLLETAGE" from the script, saying he'd never heard of it, and "besides, it sounded too foreign."—*Dale Harrison in The Chicago Sun.*

Would you know what décolletage meant if you heard it on the air?

8. The International Business Conference at Rye was snarled for a while, during the discussion on cartels, over the translation into the 51 other languages, of the word "*know-how*." The compromise effected was to substitute, instead of "know-how," the long phrase "technical information and important knowledge designed to etc., etc., . . ." Can you fill out the etceteras? And is *know-how* slang, colloquial, or standard American?

9. In the controversy over *Webster's Third Unabridged*, Dwight Macdonald made this comment in *Dictionaries and* THAT *Dictionary*:

To argue that the excesses of the schoolmarms show that authority is undesirable in language and that "good English" is a CHIMERA is like deducing from the excesses of Judge Jeffreys' "Bloody Assizes" that the

15

English would have been better off if they had had no law or judge at all.

What is a chimera?

10. In the issue of June 21, 1963, *Time* used two PORTMANTEAU (blend) words: *cinemactor* (an old *Time* favorite) and *medicare* (not a *Time* original). Can you give ordinary synonyms for these verbal potpies? In the same issue *Time* also used the following coined words: *denti-perforate, pray-ins, credit-cardsmanship, autosacrifice, cosmonette, cloak-and-suiter, funmaster-in-chief.* Can you sight-read those? *Time* couldn't resist this punplay: "Britain's fastest-rising fallen woman," and followed it with *womanizer* (does *Webster's Third Unabridged* call it slang, colloquial, or standard?); *bawd* (under the alliterative heading, "Bed and Bawd"); *doxies* (is this word obsolete?); *grandes cocottes; strumpetry; tarts;* and *poules.* Do you recognize these saucy native and foreign words from the DEMIMONDE?

WORDPLAY QUIZ KEY

(Don't score yourself. This is just a trial run.)

1. cave dwellers
2. diplomatic etiquette
3. art of organizing and administering service of supply, including headquarters, takes singular verb (is).
4. Those with whom intellect is a passion
5. See page 295.
6. financial (especially pertaining to public finance)
7. How far down the neckline comes
8. See page 291.
9. An imaginary monster with a lion's head, a goat's body, and a serpent's tail; it breathed out fire. Now: any fantastic or absurd idea.
10. *Cinemactor:* movie actor
   *Medicare:* government-sponsored health insurance
   *Denti-perforate:* gap-toothed
   *Pray-ins:* sit-ins who pray
   *Credit-cardsmanship:* art of deferring payment
   *Autosacrifice:* self-mutilation for religious reasons
   *Cosmonette:* girl astronaut
   *Cloak-and-Suiter:* man in the garment industry
   *Funmaster-in-chief:* star comedian

*Womanizer:* girl chaser (standard in *Webster,* informal in *Funk & Wagnalls Standard College Dictionary,* 1963)
*Bawd:* mistress
*Doxies:* prostitutes (not obsolete but it goes back a long way)
*Grandes cocottes:* highborn ladies of easy virtue (another oldie)
*Strumpetry:* the practice of harlotry
*Tarts:* British strumpets
*Poules:* French tarts

## GAGWRITERS AT WORDPLAY

The highest-priced words you hear are written by gag-men who furnish the raw material for stage and screen comedians, television cutups, nightclub favorites, convention m.c.'s, disc jockeys, and performers in other MEDIA. They have a word lore all their own which is worth a close look, if you want to know more about words through wordplay—or if you're part of the forty percent of the population who make their living in the word trades.

Whether the gag is written for a visual medium such as television or for a comedy monologue on a recording, it comes out of a vast reservoir of material that goes back hundreds of years (which should be Bennett Cerf's defense against the charge of gag-pilfering). Comedy writers take the old material, dust it off and refurbish it with time-tested techniques for getting laughs. The gimmick may be ancient but the lingo is contemporary—the breezy, informal style of our fast-moving, fast-talking culture, with an occasional ESOTERIC word thrown in for shock effect.

Although television has stressed the action joke and situation comedy, comedians still have to talk and they still make people laugh by saying the key word at the right time. We still have a Bob Hope who fast-talks his audience with a constant stream of wordplay, a Groucho Marx whose ad lib puns have as much ear appeal as his cigar has eye appeal. Jimmy Durante continues to be a specialist in "murdering" the language. And one of the top stars in the media of movies, stage, and television—Danny Kaye—is a VIRTUOSO at verbal dexterity.

Their technique of wrecking the mother tongue is based on the trickiness of English words, some of which have nineteen different meanings, others which sound alike but differ in sense. If each word in the dictionary had just one meaning, communication might be simpler for natives and foreigners. But we'd miss out on a lot of fun. When an attractive girl once said admiringly to Groucho Marx, "Mr.

17

Marx, you're a man after my own heart," he answered, "That's not all I'm after." *Webster's Third Unabridged* gives five definitions of *after* used as a preposition; Groucho mixed up two of them—"a function word to indicate the object or goal of a stated or implied action (my soul thirsteth after thee)" and "so as to resemble in some respect." If you were to explain to Groucho what he had done, he would merely give you a blank stare or BEMUSE you with another double-meaning gag, which would send you back to *Webster*. But he couldn't deny that the multiple-meaning words give him and others in the comedy business an excellent living.

Milton Berle and other "talking" comedians keep their audiences off balance with rapid-fire multiple-meaning gags. Said Berle of President Eisenhower: "Ike is a great President and we're all glad he's going back to Washington this Friday. Ike back in Washington— well, that's what you would really call a Capital Gain." Evan Esar, in his *The Humor of Humor,* has several illustrations of the pun based on multiple meanings. "The first thing that strikes a stranger in New York is a big car." *Webster Seventh Collegiate Dictionary* lists twenty-four different meanings for the verb "strike" and eleven for the noun. A union may "strike"; the crew of a Broadway play "strikes" a set; a fisherman gets a "strike"; a baseball pitcher throws a "strike." Jokes based on words with multiple meanings can become quite involved.

More raucous laughs come from "murdered" words (see MALAPROP-ISMS on page 21). Danny Thomas calls someone "the most objectional man I ever met." On Jack Benny's program the BUCOLIC Mortimer Snerd talks about an "eaves-dripper." A girl corrects him: "Mortimer, that's dropper." and the gag is concluded by Mortimer with a sly dig at Benny: "Looks more like a drooper." Sam Levenson conjures up a picture of eight squalling infants in a multiple birth when he calls himself and his seven brothers "octuplets."

Words don't have to be "murdered" to get a laugh. If they are uncommon enough, the surprise effect of their appearance gets a response. Sometimes the humor of character adds to the humor of wordplay. Steve Allen, in *The Funny Men,* gives an example from a Sid Caesar sketch. Sid's wife has found a perfumed letter sent to him by another woman (a business associate) and he is trying to stall his way out of it.

*Sid:* You have a nerve! You have the barbaric audacity . . . the SURREP-TITIOUS EFFRONTERY to demand to see this letter?

18

He goes on in this vein. He is using uncommon words and CIRCUM-LOCUTIONS to get himself out of trouble.

Evan Esar in *The Humor of Humor* has an illustration of POLYSYL-LABIC humor in what is called the distortion of "technical jargons like medicalese, legalese, and the like, because imitations of them are clearly recognizable."

A garage owner cut his hand and the next day it became infected. The doctor who examined it explained in high-falutin' medical terminology, quickly treated the wound, and charged him ten dollars. A week later the man's assistant said: "Your doctor's out here with a flat tire." "Diagnose it as an absence of FLATULENCE of the PERIMETER," said the garage owner, "and tell him it's caused by the PENETRATION of a foreign object resulting in the DISSIPATION of the compressed ATMOSPHERIC contents, and see that you charge him accordingly."

Of course, we're pleased to see the doctor get back some of his own in the form of humorous GOBBLEDYGOOK, but with the rates of car mechanics going higher and higher, some gagsmith could reverse the situation and give the doctor the last laugh.

As humor goes up the intellectual scale, uncommon words become more common. PARODY, a type of humor that pokes fun by exagger-rated imitation, offers many examples of polysyllabic wordplay. Here's one in *The Humor of Humor* on "Twinkle, twinkle, little star."

> Scintillate, scintillate, globule vivific,
> Fain would I fathom thy nature specific,
> Loftily poised in ether capacious,
> Strongly resembling a gem carbonaceous.

From your knowledge of the original "twinkle, twinkle" verse, can you guess at the meaning of SCINTILLATE, GLOBULE, VIVIFIC, LOFTILY, CARBONACEOUS? Is *fain* an archaic word? [2]

## GAGWRITERS AT WORK

Just how do the hard-working comedy writers practice their technique of wordplay? Why do we laugh when a sad-eyed little man standing in front of a microphone confuses BIGOTRY with BIGAMY?

[2] Archaic and poetic (*Funk & Wagnalls Standard College Dictionary*, 1963).

ILLITERATE with ILLEGITIMATE? OSCULATION with OSCILLATION? For most of the audience, these fancy terms linger in a twilight zone of meaning. Their use is a deliberate attempt to make everybody feel cozy at hearing big words jumbled up or smacked down.

The comedy writers' trade is a hard one, and they regard it as a serious business. Like many comedians, they are often subdued men in private life, not because they suffer from MELANCHOLIA but because they live in dread of not getting that expected laugh.

For anyone who doesn't have to be funny for a living, it's instructive to go behind the scenes and watch gagwriters at work. Two, three, or four of them get together, loosen up their ties—and consult a master file. Comedy writers do not depend on their own unaided intellects. Next to the Bible on their desk is their Joe Miller joke book and their dictionary. The first modern joke book was put out in 1739 by an Englishman named Joe Miller and he started a trend in the field of gag collection and storage. Some of the most famous files in the industry run to over a million entries, classified by subject. Many of the jokes are finally pegged on a single key word—generally one with multiple meanings or one that stumbles into the wrong context.

Having decided on the general subject they want to play with, the gagmen fish a few jokes out of the file. With luck, one of these will furnish the skeleton structure for a new gag. Given this start, they begin batting the topic around. They try to put a new rattle on the old wheeze. Or they look for a "gimmick," the "twist" or "wrinkle" that will be the turning point of the joke. A gimmick, originally a magician's prop, is the device that will make the old gag new. It may be a dodge that will turn a piece of wordplay into an action gag. Any one of these shifts by which they work the transformation is called a "switch."

George Q. Lewis, who trains writers for the wordplay business in his Comedy Workshop, points up the gagwriter's (and the comedian's) dilemma in this excerpt from his *Humor Exchange Newsletter:*

. . . How long can a comic use the same piece of material? Smith and Dale have used their Dr. Kronkeit sketch for more than 50 years. It's a classic. But must Mort Sahl change his material—and up-date it—every time out? If you put material on record, the comic will find the audience doing the lines with him. But if you don't—how long can a comic use the same piece of material???

When a piece of material does go stale, when Joe Miller fails to inspire, our gagwriter reaches for the dictionary. There are 450,000 entries in *Webster's Third Unabridged,* and a good percentage of them can provide the key word for a joke. Each word used this way is put in a different category of humor, and it is rewarding for the student of vocabulary to examine the various techniques of wordplay. They will add to his stock of words and deepen the meaning of words he already knows.

## TIME-TESTED TECHNIQUES OF HUMOR

The fact is that humor and the developed techniques of humor come, like words, out of the culture itself. Canon Spooner of Oxford solemnly reads "conquering kings" as "kinkering congs" and the SPOONERISM is born. A professor tells his student, "You hissed my mystery lectures" and the file on spoonerisms begins to build up.[3] The *London Globe* writes (involuntarily, we hope) that "the inhabitants of London suffer from a high rate of *morality.*" Then the playwright Sheridan in his *The Rivals* invents a character named Mrs. Malaprop who cheerfully "murders" words. From this point on when someone uses ACRIMONY in place of MATRIMONY, we call the mistake a malapropism.

Gradually the file expands. A very young scholar writes: "At this time King Henry VIII walked with difficulty, having an abbess on his knee," and we have a new entry—schoolboy boners. Meanwhile foreigners eager to learn English INADVERTENTLY speak in two (sometimes three) languages at once, and the gag label man comes up with another category: MACARONIC lingo.

In addition to malapropisms, spoonerisms, schoolboy boners, and macaronic lingo, there are other categories of humor based on word manipulation: doubletalk, Goldwynisms, wellerisms, parkerisms, and the much-maligned common *pun.* Let's examine some of them.

## MALAPROPISMS: MURDER IN POLYSYLLABLES

Evan Esar calls a malapropism a "polysyllabic blunder." He tells this story in *The Humor of Humor:*

[3] The spoonerisms quoted are from Evan Esar's *The Humor of Humor.*

. . . A chairwoman . . . noticed that the guest of honor was not touching her food. "You must feel like I do," she said, "just too nervous to eat. When it's over, I'm sure we'll both be ravished. I know I'll have a wonderful appetite for anything that comes along."

An industrious German, Heinz Stallman, went through the whole body of English plays in print, from the beginnings to 1800, to collect all the malapropisms he could find. He got a good harvest, nearly three hundred. English is a punning language, and no mistake; it's probably richer in wordplay than any other, partly because it's so loose, rambling and ill-defined that it lends itself to comic effects; also it's fuller of HOMOPHONES than any other language except Chinese.

It wasn't until Sheridan's Mrs. Malaprop that the trick had a name, but there were plenty of malapropisms before her, and there have been plenty since—as witness the great ACCUMULATION of Goldwynisms, most of which have been FOBBED off on Sam Goldwyn. The best malapropisms belie their name. For even if in theory they are "ill-befitting" (*mal à propos*) words, they actually have a kind of "shock logic" of their own, in that the PERPETRATOR, while he uses the wrong word, works it into a combination that makes a kind of gifted nonsense. So when Mrs. Malaprop speaks of the "contagious" countries (she means CONTIGUOUS) we chuckle over those Typhoid Mary areas, at the same time we relish the PRETENTIOUS DOWAGER's overambitious flight. When she says "INDUCTION" for SEDUCTION, "ILLEGIBLE" for INELIGIBLE, transforms HYSTERICS into "HYDROSTATICS," VERNACULAR into "ORACULAR," we feel these are PROVIDENTIAL errors. Mrs. Malaprop is always TEETERING on the verge of a really colossal slip into INDECORUM, and her minor verbal INDISCRETIONS fill us with hope.

## A Malapropian Word Game

Which five of the following malapropisms do you think the funniest?

| | By mistake for | Source |
|---|---|---|
| LACONICALLY | IRONICALLY | Sheridan—*The Rivals* |
| ILLITERATE | obliterate | *The Rivals* |
| canary | QUANDARY | Shakespeare—*The Merry Wives of Windsor* |
| FELICITY | velocity | *The Rivals* |
| PUTREFACTION | PETRIFACTION | *The Rivals* |
| COMMONTY (form of "community") | comedy | Shakespeare—*The Taming of the Shrew* |

| | By mistake for | Source |
|---|---|---|
| perpendiculars | particulars | *The Rivals* |
| INEFFECTUAL | intellectual | *The Rivals* |
| LECHERY | LETHARGY | Shakespeare—*Twelfth Night* |
| extrumpery | EXTEMPORE | Rychardes—*Misogonus* |
| SUBTRACTORS | DETRACTORS | *Twelfth Night* |
| upstantial | substantial | Jonson—*Tale of a Tub* |
| honeysuckle | HOMICIDAL | Shakespeare—2 *Henry IV* |

You can go on making your own wordplay on these themes. A "honeysuckle" maniac would put any "commonty" writer in a decided "canary"—and it wouldn't be the wine from the Canary Islands that went into Falstaff's sack, either. Leonard Bacon may have been UN-CONSCIOUSLY recalling one of these malapropisms when he described a character in his *Ph.D.'s* as a "pale, ineffectual, Christian intellectual." Certainly we all have heard speakers whose content and delivery alike are wonderfully described by "extrumpery." And next time you hear about an "upstanding" and "substantial" young man, just substitute Ben Jonson's "upstantial," and you can sit through the after-dinner speeches in a better humor.

## BONERS: ACADEMIC MALAPROPISMS

A special form of malapropism is the schoolboy boner—or "howler," as the British call it. For example:

> A CAUCUS is a dead animal.
> An OCTOPUS is a person who hopes for the best.
> A PLAGIARIST is a writer of plays.
> A RUMINANT is an animal that chaws its cub.

Jokebooks have been compiled from these "boners," supposedly made by high school and college students who misunderstood or misused words. *It apparently never occurs to anyone that the examiner, teacher, or school board should come in for part of the laughter.* Actually, the pupils are giving them away. Somebody made a mistake before the student slipped up. Examiner and student are engaged in the game of cross questions and crazy answers. The crazy answers are funny enough but they also have an IRONICAL aspect.

*Before a student pies up his words, somebody has slipped in es-*

23

*timating his* COMPREHENSION *and his word range.* Often the student, not knowing what the word means, fuses it in his mind with a word he happens to know—or he confounds it with a word very like the original. But the error is not all his. *Some educational doctor made the wrong* DIAGNOSIS *and there was no way to bury his error.*

Our democratic DOGMA which insists on exposing all students to miscellaneous verbal learning should also come in for a little DERISIVE laughter. In fact, when we laugh at boners we should also reflect somewhat soberly, Who's stupid now?

The case is different with contrived verbal slips.

## SPOONERISMS: SLIPS OF THE TONGUE

The spoonerism, which takes it name from Canon Spooner of Oxford, is a TRANSPOSITION of the initial consonants of two words: a special case of what is called METATHESIS, which involves altering the order of consonants anywhere in a word—as *calvary* for *cavalry*, ANENOME (pronounced like "an enemy") for *anemone.* But the spoonerism differs from an ordinary slip in that the pied-up combination usually makes a kind of NONSENSICAL sense.

According to legend Canon Spooner became addicted to these slips of the tongue, dictated by a SUBCONSCIOUS QUIRK with a logic all its own. After "kinkering congs" there was no stopping him. Once he greeted some undergraduates whom he had invited to tea, by telling them, "Gentlemen, I feel a half-warmed fish within my bosom."

From these small beginnings a regular industry of manufacturing spoonerisms grew up in England. Volumes are still published, and the more nonsensical sense the initial metathesis makes, the better readers like it. In this country, radio and television announcers talk always in fear of making an unintentional spoonerism that will also be an IMPROPRIETY.

## HOLLYWOOD'S MR. MALAPROP

A Goldwynism hardly needs definition for Americans. It's a piece of "shock logic," based on wrenching English idiom, at the same time using a twist of phrase that is decidedly outlandish. Probably the only Goldwynism Goldwyn ever used was "Include me out,"

24

but even this is suspect, according to Earl Wilson (*New York Post,* July 19, 1963) who attributes the expression to Howard Dietz. But since the "Include me out" got around, all the ODDITIES of speech perpetrated by Hollywood characters are charged to Sam Goldwyn. Actually, Goldwyn is a shrewd-spoken man, whose capacity for critical THEORIZING is well indicated in his famous APHORISM, "Sleep's a form of criticism, ain't it?"

## FOLK ETYMOLOGY

Another PERENNIAL source of amusement to the SOPHISTI-CATES is the havoc played with certain words by what is called *folk* ETYMOLOGY: a fanciful DERIVATION is invented to account for a word, and in accord with this homemade etymology the difficult term is approximated to some simple, understandable phrase or verbal compound—ASPARAGUS is transformed into "sparrow grass," or the battleship BELLEROPHON becomes "Belly Ruffian."

Sometimes a foreign word sounds so much like an English word that Americans change the spelling and the meaning to what they think it should be. This was the fate of the Chinook *hiu muckamuck,* which became *high-muck-a-muck.* Originally it meant "plenty to eat." Now it refers to a "higher-up" or "big shot."

Our tongue exhibits a good many examples of folk etymology in the course of real translation. *Coleslaw* is from the Dutch *koolsla,* "cabbage salad." *Woodchuck* has nothing to do with either *wood* or *chuck:* it's the pioneer's way of naturalizing the Algonquin word for the creature: *wejack.* The principle of folk etymology is often facetiously applied, and we hear of Hume Bogo, whose stories came to be called HUMBUG; or of Mr. Monk, inventor of the monkey wrench.

Sometimes one part of the imported word is snipped off and tacked on to an English standard or slang word, and a new kind of word may come in vogue. Stuart Flexner describes how this can happen in his *Dictionary of American Slang:*

Due to modern communications a foreign word can suddenly be presented to the dominant culture any morning in its newspapers or on its radio and television programs. *Sputnik* was introduced directly without the help of immigrants, soldiers, or travelers: immediately thereafter were evolved a group of words taking the Russian–*nik* ending, as *beatnik.* Such direct borrowing of words and word elements will probably increase in the future.

Folk etymology illustrates once again how wordplay, conscious or unconscious, often starts with the general public and is then taken over by those in the word trades. By understanding the ITINERARY of a word and tracing the way it changes, the student of words has another tool to help him expand his vocabulary.

## MACARONIC LINGO

Some real verbal stews turn up when a writer, speaker, or singer deliberately mixes two languages. DUO-LINGUAL verse of this type is called *macaronic*—deriving from the Italian for "hash." The term seems a handy one to cover also prose mish-mash in two languages. In Pennsylvania Dutch (which is actually Low German and not Hollander at all) you can savor:

Nix commen aus to the Deitcher's house, when the Deitcher is nix zu housa. Have you the light gedoused and the cat outgeput?

Evan Esar, who calls macaronic lingo a "multilingual mixture," gives a literary example in which English and Latin are mixed for humorous effect:

He who praises in praesentia
And dispraises in absentia
May he get the pestilentia!
or
I sometimes think I have au fond
A penchant for the demi-monde.

Do you recall the use of demimonde in connection with *Time's* article about the British scandal? (See page 16)

## DOUBLETALK: TONGUE-TRIPPERS

Orthodox language is left behind when we come to doubletalk, made famous by Danny Kaye, whose tongue-trippers conveyed a squirrely kind of sense, aided by gestures and acting. It is the ultimate term of the patter song which Gilbert built up to such a high

26

point in the Savoy operas. The classic example of the single double-talk word in English is, of course, the psuedo-Latin that Shakespeare put in Holofernes the schoolmaster's mouth in *Love's Labors Lost: Honorificabilitudinitatibus,* which the Baconians, regarding as a cryptogram, unscramble into

Hi   ludi   Fr. Bacono nati         se         tuiti
(These plays, born of Francis Bacon, are their own protection.)

## PUNS: PROPER AND IMPROPER

In the realm of the pun proper, the best ones are IM-PROMPTUS fathered by experts in patter-song lingo. W. S. Gilbert got off some good ones, usually out of RANCOR. Among his many aversions was Sir Charles Alexander, a well-known theatrical producer. Once in the newspaper room of his club, Gilbert came on an advertisement of Alexander's newest show, featuring strongly the charms of the leading lady with whom Alexander was generally supposed to have set up light-housekeeping arrangements. "Hm," Gilbert snorted, "Alexander is blowing his own strumpet." (See *strumpetry* page 16.)

Joyce's *Ulysses* is full of pied-up proverbs and puns, most of them heavily charged with SARDONIC commentary:

God made the country, man the tune.

Lawn Tennyson, gentleman poet.

If others have their will, Ann hath a way . . .
She put the comether on him, sweet and twenty-six.

Whether these be sins or virtues, old
Nobodaddy will tell us at doomsday leet.

Artful craftsmen can even achieve notable effects by translating a proverb from one language to another. The Chinese sage Wu Ting Fang, when he was Minister to England, was invited for the weekend to the country house of the Duchess of Norfolk. When he came to leave, the Duchess asked him to write in her guest book.

"What shall I write?" asked Minister Wu.

"Oh, just some proverb or other," said the Duchess, "and sign your name."

27

"Proverb," said Wu, "what is a proverb?"

"Why, it's a TRADITIONAL saying, like 'penny wise, pound foolish,'" the Duchess told him.

Wu made some elaborate Chinese HIEROGLYPHICS, and left.

A month later the Duchess had as her guest the Keeper of the Chinese manuscript room at the British Museum. As he was signing the guest book on his departure, the Duchess said, "Now, Sir Frederick, you can tell me what Minister Wu wrote." Sir Frederick screwed his MONOCLE into his eye and as soon as he saw Wu's Chinese characters his jaw dropped.

"How did he come to write anything so extraordinary?"

"Oh," said the Duchess, "I just asked him to write some proverb or other like 'penny wise, pound foolish.'"

"Ah," Sir Frederick said, "that explains it. He has written the Chinese equivalent of 'penny wise, pound foolish': 'What profiteth it a man if he go to bed early to save candlelight and beget twins?'"

Who would have the heart to apply to that anecdote (a true one) De Quincey's PETULANT GROWSING?

Of all the bores whom heaven in its merciful kindness and man in his utter folly have foreborne to hang, the teller of good stories is the worst.

If De Quincey's drastic remedy were to be carried out, most Americans would be hanged higher than HAMAN. But luckily there is little chance that anything could make Americans stop telling stories or enjoying wordplay.

## A Word-Twister's Word Game

Here's another word game to play with. It won't count in your overall score; it's a way to learn how to paste labels on different kinds of comic manipulation you come across in print or on the air.

Each word-twister is one of the following: a malapropism, a schoolboy boner, a spoonerism, folk etymology, macaronic mixture, doubletalk, a pun, an ordinary gag, portmanteau word manufacture, jocose use of learned words.

1. In a murder mystery by Craig Rice, *Home Sweet Homicide*, the children who play detective are considering burning a lot of clippings and

letters that had been used by the murdered woman for blackmailing purposes. The little boy speaks:

"Let's have a bonfire," Archie said. "It's no fun burning stuff in the—*insinuator*."

2. *The Smiling Ghost*, said the advertisement, is *mystorical*.
3. A *bamboo* is an Italian baby.
4. His hair waved a little like the statue of the *dinkus* thrower in the Vatican at Rome.—O. Henry.
5. A *census taker* is a man who goes from house to house increasing the population.
6. And I follows, like Delilah when she set the *Philip Steins* on Samson.—O. Henry.
7. A CRITERION is a most savage animal.
8. The bee-what of the tee-mother of the trotharooroo.—A. Huxley, *Point Counterpoint*.
9. An *epicure* is a poet who writes epics.
10. "Andy," says I, "the boys ought to have *dromedaries*. All colleges have 'em."

   "What's that?" says Andy.

   "Why something to sleep in, of course," says I.—O. Henry.
11. A Gael is a storm at sea. There was a gael in Shakespeare's *Tempest*.
12. The *horse-peculator* said, "This ain't no *debile* or *eleemosynary* business, though it's carried on at *vespertine* hours, and it's likely to lead to an *epicedian* fate via the rope."—Manufactured from O. Henry's elevated vocabulary.
13. God's Own Country is Heaven.
14. Strong drink is an adder and a *subtractor*, too.—O. Henry.
15. GORILLA warfare means when the sides get up to monkey tricks.
16. "Have you ever drunk from the fountain of this immortal poet, TASSO's, lines, Mr. Thacher?"

   "Not even a demi-Tasso."—O. Henry.
17. An IBEX is where you look at the back of the book to find out anything you want.
18. "I ain't particular," says Andy, "I'm equally good and VARICOSE on all subjects."—O. Henry.
19. ICONS are what you fatten pigs on under oak trees.
20. A MILLENNIUM is something like a CENTENNIAL, only it has more legs.
21. *Love's Last Shift*, by Colley Cibber, means, said the Frenchman, "La dernière *chemise* de l'amour."
22. Adagio is a kind of ANESTHETIC dancing.
23. "You say my boy is *illiterate*," Mrs. Shaughnessy said to the social worker. "It's a lie. I married his father three weeks before the lad was born."

24. An INCINERATOR is a person who hints bad things instead of coming right out and telling you.
25. I can't read nor write, and I see no reason why I ain't *illegible* for office. —O. Henry.
26. What disease did Oliver Goldsmith die of? The book said that he died of PECUNIARY embarrassment.
27. He was outwardly decent, and preserved his AQUARIUM, but inside he was IMPROMPTU and full of unexpectedness.—O. Henry.
28. A *lyric* is something written to be sung by a liar.
29. Odysseus tried to rescue his men from the *lettuce-eaters.*—O. Henry.
30. The Macedonian *phenolax* went straight through the Persian Army.
31. Pope wrote principally in heroic *cutlets*.
32. Wells' *Outline of History* is a veritable MILLSTONE on the road to learning.
33. "You catchee me one piecee Johnny Walker three dollar?" "Can do."
34. I had an *ample* teacher last term. He taught us to do three things. First how to write briefs and then to *exaggerate* them; second how to extract substances from novels, and last how to *interrupt* poetry.
35. Panurge tried to find out if he should marry or not by consulting the *virginal* lots.
36. Louis XIV had two wives and six *mattresses*.
37. Figurative language is when you mean a rooster and say CHANDELIER.
38. We had a lot of tinned food served on the *table d'goat.*—after O. Henry.
39. In quintessential triviality the shesoul dwelt . . .
    she-souls, he-souls, she-souls.—Joyce, *Ulysses*
40. The equator is a MENAGERIE lion running round the earth and through Africa.
41. Abracadadabra zib-zab-sum, tigna bina sesquipedalia, sesame, sedamy, Shadrach, Mashach and Abedwego.
42. The cuckoo is a bird that lays other bird's eggs in its own nest and "VIVA VOCE."
43. Persian cats is the chief industry of Persia, hence the word "purr."
44. Sound is a rapid series of ESCULATIONS.
45. The prevailing religion of England is HYPOCRISY.
46. Letters in sloping type are in HYSTERICS.
47. "Marden me, padam, you are occupewing the wrong pie. May I sew you to a new sheet?"
    "Cheautiful birch you have here."
    "Many thinkle peep so."
48. The boss was in *circumference* when the insurance agent came. Don Parker—*New York Daily Mirror*, January 21, 1933.
49. "In the last bundle, one rag failed.—Fritz Rundl, Ph.D." (A Swiss

recently come to an American university as an instructor, notifies his laundry driver that something was missing.)

50. Go climb a tree up, and around chase yourself.

ANSWERS

| | | | |
|---|---|---|---|
| 1. malapropism | 13. boner | 27. malapropism | 38. folk etymol- |
| 2. portmanteau | 14. pun | 28. boner | ogy |
| 3. boner | 15. boner | 29. folk etymol- | 39. doubletalk |
| 4. malapropism, | 16. pun | ogy | 40. folk etymol- |
| folk etymol- | 17. boner | 30. folk etymol- | ogy, boner |
| ogy | 18. malapropism | ogy, boner | 41. doubletalk |
| 5. boner | 19. boner | 31. folk etymol- | 42. boner |
| 6. malapropism | 20. boner | ogy, boner | 43. boner |
| 7. boner | 21. pun | 32. boner, pun | 44. malapropism |
| 8. doubletalk | 22. boner | 33. macaronic | 45. boner |
| 9. boner | 23. malapropism | 34. boners | 46. boner |
| 10. malapropism | 24. boner, mala- | 35. boner | 47. spoonerism |
| 11. boner | propism | 36. boner | 48. Goldwynism, |
| 12. jocuse use | 25. malapropism | 37. boner | malapropism |
| of learned | 26. boner | | 49. Goldwynism |
| words | | | 50. macaronic |

Notice that many of the gags depend for their effect on "confusion" words that have widely different meanings: those that are similar in spelling and sound (incinerator-insinuator, bamboo-bambino, milestone-millstone) and those that are identical in sound (Gael-gale, liar-lyre). Wordplay of this kind can help you separate such words and thereby increase your vocabulary. In the next chapter there is a discussion of HOMONYMS, HOMOGRAPHS, and HOMOPHONES that will help you recognize the look-alikes and sound-alikes.

## FOR THE SERIOUS STUDENT OF HUMOR

For a more detailed study of the categories of humor, Evan Esar's *The Humor of Humor* is invaluable. Among other kinds of comedy he lists the wellerism ("After you," as the glass of water said to the pill); the parkerism (a rhyming epigram, started by Dorothy Parker with "Men seldom make passes at girls who wear glasses" and parodied by Ogden Nash with an added dash of blendage—"A girl who is spectacled don't often get her nectacled"); and the fooltown, described by Esar as "an absurd story . . . heightened by crediting it to an inhabitant of a town noted for numbskullery."

A thriving town would ridicule a neighboring backwoods village and give the locality an EPITHET for ASININITY. . . . Typical of the tales told about these places is the one about a man from Cumae who, traveling on an ass, passed a fig orchard. One of the branches of a tree, heavy-laden with fruit, extended near the road, so he grasped it with both hands. The animal continued on, leaving him suspended. Just then the farmer approached and demanded what he was doing there. The Cumaean replied: "I fell off my ass."

Another kind of joke mentioned by Esar is the ANTONYMISM, which uses a word along with a word of opposite meaning for comedy effect. An example was *Time*'s "Britain's fastest-rising fallen woman."

Currently we have the Tom Swifties, the Elephant stories, and many more kinds of wordplay.


## THE PACK RAT METHOD

For the student of vocabulary, all this wordplay adds up to a story. Packaged up in words we find the history of our own times and of far-off times and places, of characters real and imagined. The Spooners and the Wellers, the schoolboys and the imitators of Mrs. Malaprop bring the uncommon words to our attention and point up the confusions in the language. Words filter in from foreign sources and are twisted into new forms through folk etymology. Walter Winchell and other columnists keep their ears tuned for the slang and jargon of our day and add their coinages. New words that come from the humor of the underworld or from teen talk make their way into the language and give us the "feel" of the period we've just lived through. Sometimes these words creep in by the slang route, more often from the jargon of the various trades.

Many of these words we pick up as we read or watch television programs. But if we want to bring a little art to the aid of nature, and extend our word range faster, there's a good deal to be said for bringing a certain amount of system into the business, for tackling words actively as well as absorbing them passively. There are ways of improving on the pack rat method, of gathering only shiny odds and ends, and piling them up in a miscellaneous heap.

One of the systems in this book is to introduce the less common words in SMALL CAPITALS. If you glance back, you will see that many of the words beyond the ten-thousand level are found in the workouts on "Wordplay in the News" and "Word-Twister's Word Game." Be aggressive with these words; knit your brows when you see them and figure out a TENTATIVE definition. Then test yourself by taking the first scoring quiz at the end of the chapter.

If you read fairly rapidly for two hours a day, in a wide range of material, you would encounter the less frequent of these words—say, those in the eighteenth or nineteenth thousands—less than five times a year.[4] This is not often enough to learn them by OSMOSIS—or SEEPAGE. Reading all kinds of literature from the daily newspapers to the classics is certainly a valuable way to increase your vocabulary. But to speed up the process, you'll have to seek words out and make a frontal attack.

Subsequent chapters will help you plan your campaign strategy. You have already examined words at play; this is the pleasurable way of meeting new words—the frosting on the cake. The next step is to see how people in the word trades make words work for them. When you've learned how reporters, rewrite men, stenographers, and researchers meet a word head on and subdue it, you'll be able to do the same. You'll find that words are working for you—and you'll have a larger active vocabulary.

[4] Since this statement was written in 1947, the popular magazines such as *Time* and *Newsweek* have been using more uncommon words in their appeal to the educated reader. Faithful reading of these magazines and of *Harper's, The Atlantic,* and other "highbrow" periodicals will add many words to one's vocabulary.

## Wordplay Quiz

Most of the words in this test are from Chapter 2; some of them are from Chapter 1, including the Word Neophyte's Test. Make your choice from the Word List that follows the questions.

1. She's a *tart* in England, a *poule* in France, a *doxy* in the nineteenth century. You could call her a *harlot*, but the word is _____.
2. What word resembles the last name of Cleopatra's lover but is defined as a "word of opposite meaning"?
3. What word reminds you of spaghetti but refers to a mixture of two or more languages, a "verbal stew"?
4. If your friend should announce that he has found a way to make a million dollars in the stock market, you would call this fanciful notion a _____.
5. In nuclear physics, what is the uncharged particle in the atom?
6. The literal meaning of this word is "cave-dweller." A politician once used it as wordplay to confound an opponent. What is the word?
7. What is a more learned word for "twinkle"?
8. In order to change key while playing, a pianist must _____.
9. "The spoonerism, which takes its name from Canon Spooner of Oxford, is a transposition of the initial consonants of two words; a special case of what is called _____."
10. What word means "composed of many syllables"?
11. What is a more dignified word for "word detective"?
12. _____ is exaggerated imitation of someone's style of writing or speaking.
13. What word in the cluster that includes "dialect" is defined as the "special vocabulary of the underworld"?
14. What is a word from the Word Neophyte's Test that means "smelly"?
15. What do you call talk that goes around in a circle?
16. When you do something quietly and without wanting to be noticed, you do it _____.
17. What are "murdered" words?
18. A blend word is also called a _____ word.
19. A word taken from Japanese that means "businessman of great wealth and influence" is _____.
20. A _____ hypothesis is one that a scientist will accept temporarily until he can prove or disprove it.
21. Substitute a word for the one in italics: The audience was *bewildered* by the magician's tricks.
22. He had the _____ to swagger into the room and insult his host.

23. Girls from the _____ are frowned upon by respectable ladies.
24. When you want an answer to a perplexing political, economic, philosophical, or literary question, the _____ will always have several at your disposal.
25. Many columnists amuse and _____ their readers with wordplay.
26. An _____ is a concise statement of a truth.
27. The managing editor's attitude toward his writers was intelligently _____; he allowed them a great deal of latitude in their choice of words.
28. Danny Kaye is a _____ at verbal dexterity.
29. Canon Spooner had an idiosyncrasy or peculiar trait that could also be called a _____.
30. Here's one from the Word Neophyte's Test: What is a word that means "reaction agent itself unchanged"?

WORD LIST

| | | | |
|---|---|---|---|
| hallucination | strumpet | noisome | lackadaisical |
| titillate | odor | chimera | malapropisms |
| metathesis | reprise | diatribes | surreptitiously |
| critique | demimonde | welded | versification |
| neutron | disturb | fornication | intelligentsia |
| vixen | coinage | flatter | aphorism |
| hierarchy | argot | definitive | catalyst |
| effrontery | shine | permissive | quirk |
| caesura | satire | virtuoso | neurosis |
| diversified | dinosaur | entomologist | macaronic |
| ravioli | polysyllabic | etymologist | impetus |
| scintillate | antonym | circumlocution | exurbs |
| cautiously | kabuya | portmanteau | pasquinade |
| modulate | bemused | tycoon | meticulously |
| parody | tentative | troglodyte | tyro |

ANSWERS

1. strumpet
2. antonym
3. macaronic
4. chimera
5. neutron
6. troglodyte
7. scintillate
8. modulate
9. metathesis
10. polysyllabic
11. etymologist
12. parody
13. argot
14. noisome
15. circumlocution
16. surreptitiously
17. malapropisms
18. portmanteau
19. tycoon
20. tentative
21. bemused
22. effrontery
23. demimonde
24. intelligentsia

35

## SCORING KEY

30 right—Ph.D.
27–29 right—Master's degree
23–26 right—College graduate
18–22 right—Above average
12–17 right—Average
Under 12 right—Substandard

SCORE: _____

# 3 ~

## How to Make Words Work for You

~~~ Words have personalities; like people, they can be tricky and ELUSIVE. They are often difficult to pin down; they are two- and sometimes three-faced. If you regard them as fixed and unchanging, they'll slip away from you. But if you play the word game well and watch a word as you would a CHAMELEON, you have a chance to come out on top. Instead of being mastered by words, you'll make them do your bidding.

Tricky words can be a source of fun, as we've seen in wordplay. But it's another story when you want them to stop playing and go to work for you. People in the word trades, who must make words work for them, are constantly on guard against the confusion words, many of which we met in the last chapter—the look-alikes, the sound-alikes, the nearly-alikes. Multiple-choice quizmakers are particularly fond of the nearly-alikes, words that resemble one another but are widely separated in meaning. Your first Word-Game Quiz gives you an example in No. 14 (page 9). The right definition for CANTO is "a section of a long poem." A half-gallop is a CANTER, a singer may be a CANTOR, and a drinking vessel is a CANTEEN.

Even trickier are words that are identical in appearance and sound, the look-and-sound-alikes. What does a word like JIBE mean? *Jeer, agree,* or *flip a sail?* It means all three. There are three different words, all spelled and pronounced alike. They look like identical triplets. But they are not related at all. Unlike the multiple-meaning words whose definitions are listed under one parent word, jibe has three separate listings in the dictionary.

The Mets fans jibed at the visiting team. ("jeered")

For once, a politician's actions jibed with his words. ("agreed")

We jibed to the north, and ducked the sail. (Here *jibed* means "shifted course so that the sail flipped over." Samuel Eliot Morrison, in his life of Columbus, *Admiral of the Ocean Sea,* spelled it "gybbed," pronouncing it evidently with the short "i" sound.)

37

Take another example. Pan was the Greek god, half-man and half-goat, who played the flute and represented universal nature. His name also gives us the prefix *pan-*, meaning "all," as in the compound *Pan-American*. There is another word *pan*, meaning "a container or dish," quite unrelated to the Greek god. Associated by derivation with this *pan*, but differing widely in meaning, is the *pan* that means "to abuse vigorously" (probably coming from the harsh scouring involved in gold-mining). The slang sense of *pan*, meaning "face" (as in the compound "deadpan") is also distantly related to the "container or dish" *pan*.

When a television camera is rotated to take in more details of a scene, this is called a "pan shot." Although it has a separate listing in *Webster's Seventh Collegiate Dictionary*, with a distinct meaning of its own, this *pan* is related to PANORAMA and hence to the prefix *pan* meaning "all."

Westerners learning Chinese complain that a single word spoken in that language may have five different meanings, depending on a slight variation in the pitch. *Pan* has six different meanings in English,[1] without any pitch difference at all!

These words, spelled and pronounced alike but with different meanings, are called HOMONYMS. They are also called HOMOGRAPHS whenever they are spelled alike and HOMOPHONES whenever they sound

|  | HOMONYMS (same spellling, same sound) | HOMOGRAPHS (same spelling) | HOMOPHONES (same sound) |
|---|---|---|---|
| pan (6 meanings) jibe (3 meanings) | YES | YES | YES |
| pan, pän | NO | YES | NO |
| cite, sight, site | NO | NO | YES |

[1] There are several more entries for *pan* in *Webster's Third Unabridged*, but they occur only rarely in print.

alike. For example, the six *pan* words discussed are homonyms because they look and sound the same; but they are also homographs in their spelling and homophones in their sounds. In this way all three labels overlap. But there is another *pan* word (pän) meaning "betel leaf," which is not pronounced like other *pan* words. It therefore is a homograph with the other *pan* words. *Cite, sight,* and *site* are homophones.

The multiple-meaning words, words with split personalities like "strike" (which has twenty-four definitions under its verb form in the dictionary) [2] are so numerous that it is pointless to put them in a separate category. Just knowing that the English language is made up of words that are acquiring new meanings will keep you on the alert.

## OFFICE MALAPROPS AT WORK

One good way to increase your vocabulary is to take a job as a stenographer and be ready to pounce on words as they jump out of your typewriter. Stenos make mistakes, but unless they are hopelessly malapropian, they learn from their errors. It is the confusion words particularly that give them the most trouble.

Not long ago, in one of the top sales organizations of the country, a house organ publication was sent out to encourage the women secretaries in the divisional offices. One sentence read: "The ideal secretary should *compliment* the work of the sales manager." No doubt telling the boss how good he is may be ADROIT secretarial strategy. But what the vice-president in charge of sales had dictated was *complement.*

That sort of error comes easy when two words sound alike (homophones). There's no way of telling from a shorthand PHONETIC character which word is meant—except from the sense.

### A Quiz for Stenos—and Bosses

Here's a test for stenographers and others whose ear and eye for words may deceive them from time to time. Pick the right words in the following examples.

[2] *Webster's Seventh Collegiate Dictionary.* There are, however, sixty-three numbered meanings for the verb and twenty-four for the noun in *Webster's Third Unabridged.*

1. ANNALIST or ANALYST? He was an _____ with the Du Pont Company.
2. AURICLE or oracle? The Delphic _____ was in the heart of Greece.
3. Bass or base? Purcell liked a firm ground _____.
4. BOLL, BOLE, or bowl? The dry-rot was in the _____ of the tree.
5. Borough, burrow, or BURRO? Somebody beat up the _____ COUNCILLOR.
6. CARAT, CARET, or carrot? He marked the insert with a _____.
7. QUIRE or choir? They sold music paper by the _____.
8. Crews, cruise, or CRUSE? They brought in the _____ of holy oil.
9. Faker or FAKIR? This _____ was a holy man.
10. FANE, feign, or fain? How could he _____ illness well enough to fool a doctor?
11. Idol, idle, or IDYL? Their romance was a summer _____.
12. Literal or LITTORAL? They postponed attack on the Adriatic _____.
13. Raise, raze, or rays? They will _____ the fort on the island after capturing it.
14. Right, write, rite, or -wright? It was a solemn _____.
15. LICHEN or liken? A _____ is similar to moss.
16. Vial, vile, or VIOL? He put the perfume in a small _____.

### ANSWERS

| | | | |
|---|---|---|---|
| 1. analyst | 5. borough | 9. fakir | 13. raze |
| 2. oracle | 6. caret | 10. feign | 14. rite |
| 3. bass | 7. quire | 11. idyl | 15. lichen |
| 4. bole | 8. cruse | 12. littoral | 16. vial |

Then, to add to the PITFALLS, there are words that look or sound very much alike, though one of the vowels may be different. *Affect* and *effect* are the stock pair—but there are many others that are easily misread from shorthand notes.

### Which Word Was Meant?

1. Adapt, adept, adopt. He was so _____ they called him in to _____ the play for the movies.
2. ALLUSIVE, ELUSIVE, ILLUSIVE. I found the meaning very _____ because the writing was highly _____.
3. Ballad, BALLET, ballot. Let me write the _____ of a country, and I care not who casts its _____.

4. BAZAAR, BIZARRE. There were a good many _____ hats donated to the church _____.
5. Cannon, CANON, and canyon. They fired the salute according to the _____ of military etiquette.
6. COMA, COMMA. He fell into a _____ from which he did not recover.
7. Consul, council, counsel. The American _____ gave him good _____ to get out fast.
8. Decent, descent, dissent. The motion was passed without_____.
9. Eminent, imminent, IMMANENT. An explosion was _____.
10. EPIGRAM, EPIGRAPH, epitaph. They took an impression of the _____, which proved to be an _____ in the form of an _____.
11. HYPERCRITICAL, HYPOCRITICAL. The book reviewer had no time to be _____.
12. MAGNATE, magnet, maggot. He was a great iron _____.
13. Spacious, SPECIOUS. He gave a _____ reason.
14. Surplus, SURPLICE. They had an extra _____ for the visiting cleric.
15. VENAL, VENIAL. It does not pay a politician to be openly _____.

ANSWERS

| | | | |
|---|---|---|---|
| 1. adept, adapt | 5. canons | 9. imminent | 12. magnate |
| 2. elusive, allusive | 6. coma | 10. epigraph, epi- | 13. specious |
| 3. ballads, ballots | 7. consul, counsel | taph, epigram | 14. surplice |
| 4. bizarre, bazaar | 8. dissent | 11. hypercritical | 15. venal |

A really topflight stenographer who wants to graduate into the secretary class must be able to mop up UNOBTRUSIVELY on the boss's errors, particularly if she is working for an executive in the amusement business. It's no MYTH that they are given to outdoing Mrs. Malaprop at PERPETRATING malapropisms.

Here's a collection, lovingly gathered over many years, of words confounded by one or another of these MOGULS dictating over his head. The sentences given opposite are to test your ability to discriminate between the words. They're not the sentences in which the word was butchered.

### Put the Right Word in the Right Slot

A
1. The law provided for _____ prices for basic crops.

PARODY

2. He wrote a _____ of a famous song.  PARAGON
3. A very _____ of fashion.  PARADOX
4. A most ingenious _____.  PARITY

### B
1. The choir sang a well-known _____.  canter
2. The horses went at a fast _____.  CANTATA
3. The _____ sang the Kol Nidre.  CANTO
4. He talked a very smug _____.  cantor
5. He took a drink from the _____.  CANT
6. The third _____ of a Renaissance epic.  canteen

### C
1. They sang a well-known sea _____.  CHANTRY
2. It was a _____ venture altogether.  chant
3. Masses for the departed were sung in the  CHANTEY
_____.
4. A solemn Gregorian _____ was sung.  CHANCY

### D
1. The _____ inhabitants were Indians.  abdominal
2. It was a severe _____ wound.  HEBDOMADAL
3. Hydrogen sulfide has an _____ smell.  ABORIGINAL
4. A meeting of the _____ Council was held.  abominable

### E
1. The Civil War _____ Exhibition.  sentiment
2. Poe was interested in theories of vegetable  SENTENTIOUS
_____.
3. Richardson wrote _____ novels.  SENTIENT
4. Polonius uttered _____ remarks.  sentimental
5. He stood _____ duty before the palace.  SENTIENCE
6. A _____ being will respond to stimulus.  sentinel
7. Clarissa was a woman of _____.  CENTENNIAL

### F
1. An exhaustive _____ showed no arsenic.  ANACHRONISM
2. There was one bad _____ in that history.  ANALOGY
3. Reasoning from _____ often errs.  analysis
4. First aid work calls for some knowledge of  anatomy
_____.

### G
1. He computed the _____ between the extremes.  medium
2. They invited him to _____ between the con-  MEDIATE
flicting claims.
3. Trial by ordeal was a _____ custom.  MEDIAN

42

4. Water is a good _____ for transmitting sound.  MEDIEVAL
5. Fewer persons now _____ upon their sins.  meditate
6. NATUROPATHS do not _____ as a rule.  MEDICATE

### H

1. They brought out a _____ horse for the child.  gentile
2. A _____ approach to the problem will show the various stages of development.  genial
3. _____ is the possessive case.  gentle
4. Help-wanted ads no longer specify that _____s only need apply.  GENETIC
5. A _____ instance is more conclusive than an ATYPICAL one.  GENERIC
6. His manner was bland and _____.  GENITIVE

### I

1. We flushed a _____ of partridges.  cover
2. He gave her a _____ glance.  COVEY
3. Put back the _____ on the jar.  COVERT

### J

1. The canoe made a swift _____ down the rapids.  decent
2. He was inclined to _____ fully on his trip.  DESCANT
3. It happened in the last _____ of the century.  descent
4. He told him to _____ four LITRES of the fluid.  DECANT
5. Everything was done in _____ and orderly style.  decade
6. The motion was passed without _____.  dissent

### K

1. He expressed a _____ opinion.  DISSOLUTE
2. He tried to _____ himself from his party on questions of national defense.  dissipate
3. MODERNIST music abounds in _____ phrases.  DISSONANT
4. He told them to _____ the CADAVER.  DISSOCIATE
5. It is unwise to _____ one's energies before a match, by too much practice play.  dissenting
6. A thoroughly _____ wretch.  dissect

### L

1. They quietly arranged a _____ of his duties.  RESURGENCE
2. The _____ was due to a revival of interest in the classics.  resurrection
3. There was a _____ of interest in the relics.  RENAISSANCE
4. The _____ of Lazarus was thought a miracle.  RESUMPTION

43

### M

1. The emperor had a magnificent _____.     RETENTION
2. His _____ proved of great aid in diplomacy.     RETICENCE
3. The lawyer accepted a large _____.     retinue
4. His memory showed unusual powers of _____.     RETAINER

### N

1. One _____ of the front was weak.     SECTIONAL
2. The fanatic was an extreme _____.     SECTOR
3. The _____ of the United Nations.     secular
4. He was _____ even for a diplomat.     SECTARIAN
5. The _____ dispute between North and South.     SECRETARIAT
6. The dispute was over _____, not religious issues.     SECRETIVE

## ANSWERS

| A | B | C | D | E |
|---|---|---|---|---|
| 1. parity | 1. cantata | 1. chantey | 1. aboriginal | 1. centennial |
| 2. parody | 2. canter | 2. chancy | 2. abdominal | 2. sentience |
| 3. paragon | 3. cantor | 3. chantry | 3. abominable | 3. sentimental |
| 4. paradox | 4. cant | 4. chant | 4. hebdomadal | 4. sententious |
| | 5. canteen | | | 5. sentinel |
| | 6. canto | | | 6. sentient |
| | | | | 7. sentiment |

| F | G | H | I | J |
|---|---|---|---|---|
| 1. analysis | 1. median | 1. gentle | 1. covey | 1. descent |
| 2. anachronism | 2. mediate | 2. genetic | 2. covert | 2. descant |
| 3. analogy | 3. medieval | 3. genitive | 3. cover | 3. decade |
| 4. anatomy | 4. medium | 4. gentile | | 4. decant |
| | 5. meditate | 5. generic | | 5. decent |
| | 6. medicate | 6. genial | | 6. dissent |

| K | L | M | N |
|---|---|---|---|
| 1. dissenting | 1. resumption | 1. retinue | 1. sector |
| 2. dissociate | 2. Renaissance | 2. reticence | 2. sectarian |
| 3. dissonant | 3. resurgence | 3. retainer | 3. secretariat |
| 4. dissect | 4. resurrection | 4. retention | 4. secretive |
| 5. dissipate | | | 5. sectional |
| 6. dissolute | | | 6. secular |

## OVERWORKED WORDS

Next to the hazard of using the wrong word, comes a menace that haunts everybody in the word trades: the danger of overworking one word. It's not only your friends who will tell you about it. The rewrite man will protest, the copy desk will yell, the news editor will tell you to find a new word for it, the SCRIPT-producer will claim you're getting into a rut, and you'll begin to feel like a PARIAH. That's why everyone who works with words is on the alert for synonyms.

## HURRY-UP HEADLINES

When a headline writer needs a synonym, he has to have it in a hurry. He has no time to look it up. His problem is severely practical. He has to have a word to fit a fixed space. How would you like to CUDGEL your wits to find a three-letter word meaning "depression," or a five-letter one for "consolidate"? You'd be as STYMIED as a poet trying to find a rhyme for "orange"—until you picked up the knack. The old hand at the game can usually shuffle around the words in the headline, if he has to. He knows the usable equivalents for most words that turn up often in the news. His synonym-finder has to be inside his head; and it had better work at adding-machine speed.

### Headline Synonyms

These words occurred in the key passages of newspaper stories. The headline writer in each case wanted to use the word to convey the core of the story, but found he needed a shorter term. How fast can you furnish in each case the needed headline synonym, with the number of letters specified in the middle column?

| Key Word in Story | Number of Letters in Synonym | Synonym? | Key Word in Story | Number of Letters in Synonym | Synonym? |
|---|---|---|---|---|---|
| 1. ALLEGATION | 5 | | 14. level | 4 | |
| 2. catastrophe | 5 | | 15. JEOPARDIZE | 4 | |
| 3. IMPLICATE | 7 | | 16. narrative | 5 | |
| 4. VINDICATE | 5 | | 17. CONFLAGRA- TION | 4 | |
| 5. EXONERATE | 5 | | 18. congregate | 6 | |
| 6. acknowledge | 5 | | 19. diminish | 6 | |
| 7. facilitate | 5 | | 20. reduction | 4 | |
| 8. irritate | 4 | | 21. HOLOCAUST | 5 | |
| 9. EULOGIZE | 6 | | 22. INUNDATION | 5 | |
| 10. apprehend | 5 | | 23. APPORTION | 5 | |
| 11. ASPERSION | 4 | | 24. contribute | 4 | |
| 12. DISCRIMINA- TION | 4 | | 25. SCRUTINIZE | 4 | |
| 13. OSTENTATION | 7 | | | | |

| | | | | |
|---|---|---|---|---|
| 1. claim | 6. admit | 11. slur | 16. story | 21. blaze |
| 2. smash | 7. speed | 12. bias | 17. fire | 22. flood |
| 3. involve | 8. fret | 13. display | 18. gather | 23. share |
| 4. clear | 9. praise | 14. raze | 19. lessen | 24. give |
| 5. clear | 10. catch | 15. risk | 20. drop | 25. scan |

## More Headline Synonyms

Often the headline writer wants a more vigorous or telling synonym, even when he is not so cramped for space. Give short, expressive synonyms for each of the following 25 words found in the news:

| | | | |
|---|---|---|---|
| 1. admonish | 7. endowment | 14. congregate | 20. consolidate |
| 2. SUCCUMB | 8. SWELTER | 15. EXPATRIATE | 21. transaction |
| 3. GAINSAY | 9. secrete | 16. REPUDIATE | 22. PIGEONHOLE |
| 4. DONATE | 10. COMMANDEER | 17. upbraid | 23. conspiracy |
| 5. ALLOCATE | 11. government | 18. outlaw | 24. postponement |
| 6. investigation | 12. surrender | 19. SCHISM | 25. CATECHIZE |
| | 13. ASSEMBLAGE | | |

| | | | | |
|---|---|---|---|---|
| 1. warn | 6. inquiry | 11. regime | 17. scold | 22. bury (in |
| 2. die | 7. gift | 12. yield | 18. ban | committee) |
| 3. deny | 8. bake | 13. meeting | 19. split | 23. plot |
| 4. give | 9. hide | 14. meet | 20. merge | 24. delay |
| 5. allot | 10. seize, take | 15. exile | 21. deal | 25. question |
| | | 16. disown | | |

## Long Words for Short in Headlines

Sometimes a headline writer needs a longer word to fill out a line. What are long synonyms for the following:

| | | | | |
|---|---|---|---|---|
| 1. question | 6. charge | 11. scare | 16. revolt | 21. fret |
| 2. end | 7. hint | 12. end | 17. fray | 22. tight |
| 3. ease | 8. show | 13. outcome | 18. beat | 23. build |
| 4. lessen | 9. start | 14. levy | 19. unfair | 24. burst |
| 5. bid | 10. steal | 15. rush | 20. dried | 25. rate |

| | | | |
|---|---|---|---|
| 1. interrogate | 7. intimation | 14. assessment | 20. dehydrated |
| 2. abolish | 8. demonstrate | 15. stampede | 21. bother |
| 3. alleviate | 9. inception | 16. rebellion | 22. constricted |
| 4. mitigate | 10. defalcate | 17. fracas | 23. construct |
| 5. invitation | 11. frighten | 18. overwhelm | 24. explode |
| 6. allegation | 12. terminate | 19. inequitable | 25. estimate |
| | 13. denouement | | |

## WORD DOCTOR AT THE REWRITE DESK

A rewrite man on a newspaper or magazine has one chief duty: to make copy more readable. He's the sworn enemy of blackouts of meaning. Whatever will jar on a reader, or slow him down, the rewrite man must eliminate. This includes any harping on a single word, which is as bad as a MONOTONE in singing.

To avoid this stumbling block to easy and effortless reading, a rewrite man needs a ready command of synonyms for words that turn up often in a given type of news. Otherwise the reader will be

47

JUSTIFIABLY annoyed at the repetition, and will suspect Gertrude Stein's influence at work.

On a business page, for example, price rises and falls have figured every day for years. In talking of prices, rewrite men have hit on a number of equivalents for the word *increase*. It's a *hike, boost,* or *up*. These three synonyms are both verbs and nouns. If an "up" in price sounds barbarous to the ear (and the language purists have objected vehemently to the tendency to make adverbs and adjectives do the work of nouns and verbs) put it down to two factors: the EXIGENCIES of rewrite, and the ready INTERCHANGEABILITY of parts of speech in our language. A preposition is first transformed into a verb—"The manufacturer 'upped' the price of shirts"—then into a noun: "an 'up' in prices."

Another part of the rewrite job is to open war on fancy phrases and complicated sentences. The rewrite man, out to give time off to overworked words, follows the DICTUM of Thoreau: Simplify! In recasting sentences that get lost in a maze, he resolves much of the trouble by substituting plain words for PRETENTIOUS ones.

A standing grievance at the rewrite desk is that copy turned in by feature writers with their own by-lines is not to be "improved." It must stand as written.

Pitts Sanborn, the music critic on the *New York World-Telegram* in the old days, once wrote:

The evening's only other magic issued from the leader's NECROMANTIC hands, whose BATON-less paired sweep would have brushed back desk and score into the void immense, had such mediocre IMPEDIMENTA ENCUM-BERED the PODIUM.

No rewrite man was allowed to touch this piece of fancy VERBIAGE. Had he been turned loose on it, his first impulse would have been to throw it out—lock, stock, and barrel. With capital punishment barred, he would probably have recast it to read:

Conducting without a baton or score, the leader waved his hands around so that he would have knocked the music desk off the podium—if there had been a desk, which there wasn't. As it was, he had enough magic in his hands to raise the dead.

Making words work too hard is often motivated by reluctance to come to the point. Sometimes the writer is aware of what he is

48

doing; other times he is not. Stock-market analysts are particularly cagey about calling a spade a spade. They hedge; they beat about the bush; they obscure the issue. Here is an excerpt from the financial page of the *New York World-Telegram* (June 19, 1963):

A significant portion of the recent sluggish market action reflects the probability that the buoyant economic strength being experienced in the second quarter will give way to leveling tendencies during the final six months of 1963.

(In other words, we really don't know what's going to happen, but we don't want you to know that we don't know.)

This is an example of EQUIVOCATION (a form of doubletalk). Another kind of overelaborate language is the result of falling in love with the jargon of one's trade or profession, which happens often in governmental and educational circles. Maury Maverick coined an American name for it: GOBBLEDYGOOK.


## WORD-HAPPY SCHOLARS

Nowhere do words work harder and with less result than in the lingo of PEDAGOGY. This jargon is full of moral EXHORTATION and runs to wise saws as self-evident and boring as those of Polonius. But fortunately the sternest criticism of the professional educators comes from the campus itself. Here's an item from *Time:*

*Gobbledygook Gagged*

Back from three years in the Army, a New York University instructor named William Brickman took a look at the educational periodicals he used to write for. "The world," he found, "may indeed move, as Galileo once insisted, but educational writers . . . do not." To show what he meant, he wrote a paragraph for *School and Society:*

"The schools continue *to serve pupil and community needs.* The teachers *revitalize* the old methods, *stimulate interest* in the new program, and *implement the recommendations* of the curriculum experts. The latter envision a wider adoption of *vitalized* method and content, and are always striving after the *coordination of program* for the schools in transition. Under the *enriched curricula,* it will be possible for pupils *to achieve self-realization by meeting real situations, by being weaned from blind conformity to authority,* and by being *confronted with thought-provoking problems.* Above all, the school must be intent upon harnessing and *integrating the social and cultural forces* within the structural framework of modern society. It is only through *pooling the resources* that the nation will be enabled to enjoy a generation of youth equipped with the desirable social behavior for this complex world."

First, what new meanings have the pedagogues run into the italicized words? Take the terms one by one, jot down their meaning in ordinary talk or writing. Then try to figure out what these pedagogical exhortations signify in the field of action. What is it they really mean to do?

2. By way of contrast to the ASBESTOS-gray texture of modern pedagogese, listen to a great Renaissance teacher:

> To the illustrious Vice-Chancellor, professors, masters and doctors of the University of Oxford, greetings from Jordanus Bruno of Nola, doctor of a nobler divinity, professor of a purer and more harmless wisdom, the QUELLER of VAUNTING and kicking ignorance, feared and hated by POETASTERS, CRITICASTERS and all pretenders to learning! I do challenge you singly or all together in friendly fashion to a debate, upon any subject of your own choosing.

Which teacher would you rather try to learn from? Bruno was a follower of the old HUMANISM, which believed, in the words of his near-namesake Lionardo Bruni, that the young should study human nature in the great books of the ancients *and* in life around them. Humanists also believed a class was better off if it had two professors before it, of DIAMETRICALLY opposed views. Then truth and the student would have some chance!

### Short Words for Long

Evidently space and speed are of little consequence in academic circles; but people in the word trades cannot afford the luxury of writing gobbledygook. Put yourself on the rewrite desk and see what you can do with the following list of long words that may slow up your copy. Give a short synonym for each one:

| | | | |
|---|---|---|---|
| 1. precipitous | 7. abominate | 14. RELICT | 20. DENIGRATE |
| 2. collapse | 8. SOMNOLENT | 15. PEDESTRIAN | 21. INCULCATION |
| 3. commotion | 9. LOQUACIOUS | 16. DEFUNCT | 22. INDURATED |
| 4. EMACIATED | 10. ERUBESCENCE | 17. PERSPICUOUS | 23. ANATHEMA |
| 5. CONTORTED | 11. DOMICILE | 18. CALIBRATION | 24. BENEFACTION |
| 6. SCINTILLATE | 12. EXPECTORATE | 19. INTERROGATION | 25. insinuate |
| | 13. LIBIDINOUS | | |

| | | | | |
|---|---|---|---|---|
| 1. steep | 6. sparkle | 11. house | 16. dead | 21. implanting |
| 2. fold | 7. despise | 12. spit | 17. clear | 22. hardened |
| 3. stir | 8. sleepy | 13. lewd | 18. scaling | 23. curse |
| 4. thin | 9. talkative | 14. widow | 19. question | 24. aid |
| 5. twisted | 10. blush | 15. walker | 20. blacken | 25. hint |

## Plain Words for Learned

Magazines which reprint in condensed form articles from other sources, or which offer their readers cut-down versions of best sellers, must boil down the material to the indispensable minimum. Generally, they can't change any of the language, but they can step up the pace by eliminating sections that move too slowly and wordily for their readers.

Other magazines, such as *Science Digest,* that reprint technical articles for the laymen not only condense these articles but often substitute words in the under-ten-thousand range and just beyond for words that only a scientist might understand. Anyone translating into this simpler English needs a ready command of synonyms.

We won't ask you to find equivalents for the more difficult technical terms; that's a professional's job. But try your hand at suggesting plain synonyms for the following learned words.

| | | | |
|---|---|---|---|
| 1. CONCATENATION | 8. EMULATION | 14. HERCULEAN | 19. VITUPERATION |
| 2. CONCUSSION | 9. EXPOSTULATE | 15. OPTIMISTIC | 20. VOLATILITY |
| 3. DISINTEGRATE | 10. PROGNOSTICATE | 16. SPORADIC | 21. RESILIENCE |
| 4. DEHYDRATE | 11. MERETRICIOUS | 17. ARTICULATION | 22. CIRCUMSCRIBE |
| 5. CIRCUITOUS | 12. GRATUITY | 18. ERUDITION | 23. LOCUM TENENS |
| 6. CORPOREAL | 13. GARGANTUAN | | 24. MUTATION |
| 7. ADULATION | | | 25. APPELLATION |

| | | | |
|---|---|---|---|
| 1. chain | 8. rivalry | 13. huge | 20. lightness |
| 2. shock | 9. object | 14. difficult | 21. bounce |
| 3. break up | 10. foretell | 15. hopeful | 22. limit |
| 4. dry | 11. false or fake (lit. harlotlike) | 16. rare | 23. substitute ("stand-in") |
| 5. roundabout | 12. gift (idiomatically, "tip") | 17. joint | 24. change |
| 6. bodily | | 18. learning | 25. name |
| 7. flattery | | 19. cursing | |

Immediate practical work with synonyms leads, sooner or later, to a strong interest in the theory of the subject: how do synonymous words come to develop fine shades of difference in meaning? You'll find this question answered at length in Chapter 9. But there are a good many tricks of the word trades that are needed, to appreciate fully the finer points of synonym study. The problem of meaning is central—how words change meaning, and why. One way to lead up to this is to look closely at new words—which are not yet encrusted with history.

## CHECKING ON EVERY WORD

To make words work efficiently for you, you have to know as much as possible about them, what kind of words they are, where they came from, what family of words they belong to—their brother-words, sister-words, cousin-words—and how they are labeled by dictionaries. In many cases, they may be so new to the language or held in such poor esteem by lexicographers that there is no place for them in the dictionary. The popular magazines like *Time* and *Newsweek* have research departments that dig up material about a doubtful word, in addition to checking the facts that go into a story.

Not only do proper names and place names call for the researcher's constant vigilance; with new terms constantly turning up in science and TECHNOLOGY, and new coinages coming in from politics and business, they often have their work cut out for them in AUTHENTICAT-ING new TERMINOLOGY. The editors of *Time* are INSISTENT that any new term that's to keep its place in the copy shall be explained, even if it takes a footnote. Preferably it should be translated in the story, as unobtrusively as *Time*-style permits.

But above all, it must be correct, and the researcher must have the authority ready to prove it. If the word is too new to have found its way into the dictionaries or encyclopedias, he must do some concentrated detective work. And even if the dictionary has grudgingly admitted it, labeling it slang, cant, or technical, the entry often isn't full enough to give the feel, flavor, and history of the word, so the researcher must turn to other sources.

Language changes faster than it can be fully recorded by the dictionary, and new words are springing into the news that have no written precedents. Often writers will send in stories directly from places like Cape Kennedy and use terms that have been born in the technical talk of ground crews. *Time's* home office will then wire back for more information about the word's environment; it will not get past the copy desk until it has been completely authenticated.

If you had access to the researchers' file entries on new words checked since *Time* began, you'd have pretty good clues to the history of the Jazz Age 20's, the troubled 30's, the stormy 40's, the bland 50's, and the uncertain 60's (Earl Wilson calls them the "Sick, Sick, Sick Sixties"). Here are some samples of the type they check, with ANNO-TATIONS (not in *Time*-style).

*Ad lib,* verb and adverb. Polite equivalent: "to IMPROVISE"—to speak, sing, or play without a SCRIPT. This may have been used in theater circles before radio got going in the early 20's, but it had no wide currency. Once a slang word, it is now standard in *Webster's Third Unabridged;* [3] it is evidently here to stay.

*Agit-prop,* theater cant. Bobtailed form of AGITATION-PROPAGANDA, a compound formed on analogy with the Russian phrase. It is short-hand for a play—or theater—used as a vehicle for spreading propaganda. Originating in the 20's, it conjures up the Russian Revolution, the Group Theater of Clurman and Odets, some of Brecht's early plays, or any play that agitates for social change.

*Moppet,* an archaic word that was revived during the 30's. *Time* took it out of the literary ARCHIVES, dusted it off, and made it an active journalistic term. In its older senses it meant "an endearing appellation for a baby, a girl, etc. . . . also used contemptuously for a gaily dressed or frivolous woman . . . a rag doll . . . a wooly variety of dog. . ." [4] When the glorification of toddlers started with the Shirley Temple craze in the 30's, moppet was given the specific meaning of "a little child or young girl."

*Pizzazz,* a term first used by Danny Kaye in *Lady in the Dark* (a Kurt Weill musical of the 40's). It meant "chic" or "stylish" in its context in the play. The term faded out, but in the 50's the word *bazazz,* meaning push or effort ("the old bazazz") came into vogue. One of *Time's* copy editors suspects that there's a connection between the original word and what may be its reincarnation, but the word detectives will have to settle the issue, if an issue like this is ever settled.

*Hep,* a slang term in use since the 20's. For reasons they haven't

---

[3] Listed as "Informal" in *Funk & Wagnalls Standard College Dictionary* (1963).

[4] *Oxford English Dictionary* (1933).

53

made public, the beatniks modified *hep* to *hip* when they arrived on the scene in the 50's. In 1938 Cab Calloway came out with his *Catalogue: A Hepster's Dictionary. Hep* and *hepster* are now obsolete, replaced by *hip* and *hipster.*

*Time* magazine, in addition to popularizing new words like *pizzazz* and bringing back archaic ones like *moppet,* has altered the language in other ways. *Tycoon* is one example. Others are the coined and blend words that used to break out like a rash over *Time*'s pages. Most of these words never got past *Time*'s files, but some blend words like SOCIALITE finally made it into the dictionary. A coined word with an interesting history is ECDYSIAST, a variation of ECDYSIS. *Webster's Third Unabridged* defines ecdysis as "the act of molting or shedding an outer corticular layer (as in insects and crustaceans)." A *Time* writer, probably inspired by watching a stripteaser in action, pinned the new word on Sally Rand and her "molting" partners. (Or was it H. L. Mencken who first coined the word? He is given credit in the ADDENDA of *Webster's Second Unabridged.* Again, we'll turn the matter over to the etymologists.) Ecdysiast may well be a useless word, but it is permanently enshrined in *Webster's Third Unabridged.*

### GETTING WORD-WISE

What this all adds up to is that anybody working in the word trades—stenographer, journalist, rewrite man, ad, script, or gag writer, editor, or researcher—needs a ready, wide, and sure command of words. Ready, because he's usually working against a deadline and has to be able to summon up the needed words fast. Wide, for the sake of variety and fitness—the right word in the right place. Sure, to dodge the pitfalls offered by tricky words in the language.

For the student of vocabulary, acquiring this command of language means keeping on the trail of new words, and clearing up the meaning of those only half-known. Clearly it's an advantage to tackle words in a practical situation, as those working in the word trades do of necessity. They learn them on the site, in relation to an immediate need. That way they don't forget them. Further, they acquire a feeling for the word, and a sense of what company it belongs in.

You don't have to be a stenographer, headline writer, rewrite man,

54

or researcher to make words work for you. Just follow their lead—actively pursue words and enlarge your vocabulary by

1. spotting and labeling the tricky ones,
2. tracing words back to their source,
3. hunting for synonyms,
4. haunting the dictionary.

You are employed as a rewrite man, and you have deadlines to meet. Think quickly; your Word List will help you recall the words you need. Your salary is $150; take off $5 for every wrong answer.

1. You need a longer word for "dried." Hurry.
2. How about a shorter word for "vindicate"?
3. "Commandeer" is too long; find a shorter word.
4. "Claim" has been repeated too many times in an article; get a longer synonym.
5. "Precipitous" is too highfalutin for your *Daily News* readers. Give them a one-syllable word.
6. Try a polysyllabic word in place of "to ease."
7. The reporter couldn't think of the one word that means "split in the church." Help him out.
8. A high religious authority has pronounced a solemn curse. The word is _____.
9. The tyro reviewer wrote about the "outcome" of the play, but you know a more exact word.
10. The playwright thought the reviewer was too harsh in his criticism; he accused the reviewer of being _____.
11. The television comedian did a playlet that was a _____ of a Broadway hit.
12. You come across "cantor" used in the sense of a "half-gallop." Should you change the spelling? (Not in Word List)
13. I had the (allusive, illusive, elusive) word on the tip of my tongue. (Not in Word List)
14. You would like to titillate your *New York Times* readers with a more pretentious word than "steep."
15. "Eulogize" has already been used; find a shorter word.
16. He was deeply (affected, effected) by the tragedy. (Not in Word List)
17. It was announced that enemy troops were only a few miles away. Disaster was (immanent, imminent, eminent). (Not in Word List)
18. A rewrite man resolves much of the trouble caused by overworked words when he substitutes plain words for _____ ones.
19. The psychiatrist explained that although the accused murderer Othello loved his deceased wife Desdemona, he had _____ feelings toward her.
20. What word did the science editor use that means "gland-produced catalytic agent"?

21. Perry Mason is always given a large _____, a lawyer's fee paid in advance to pre-empt his services.
22. What did the literary editor mean when he said the poet's verses had the quality of "perspicuity"?
23. The stenographer typed "meat" instead of "mete." You are well aware that these words are homo_____s.
24. He was (adapt, adept) at many lines of work. (Not in Word List)
25. The feature writer, who had had one too many at the wedding, wrote about the "erubescent" bride. Find the equivalent in your Word List.
26. What did Perry Mason do when he "interrogated" the witness?
27. She neither smoked nor drank; she would neither listen to evil nor speak ill of others. She was a _____ of virtue.
28. The composer's ATONAL composition was full of _____.
29. He was accused, euphemistically, of "expectorating" on the sidewalk. What word (past tense) describes what he did?
30. A piece of "verbiage" comes across your desk, written by a professor of sociology. If the writer were trying to avoid coming to the point, he would be guilty of "equivocation." It could be called an example of "circumlocution," since the writer is going around in verbal circles. There is another word coined by the late Maury Maverick that is a fitting label.

The socioeconomic factors that could conceivably be said to be determinants in the overall pattern of community attitudes that motivate juvenile behavior in its aberrant forms have been spawned by the vast complex of interacting forces resulting from every level of psychological activity in the area of interpersonal relations.

WORD LIST

| | | | |
|---|---|---|---|
| blushing | hormone | praise | hypocritical |
| bonus | parity | retainer | anathema |
| peripety | schism | homonyms | homophones |
| ambivalent | emaciated | cantilevered | inebriated |
| loitered | clear | order | steep |
| ease | comfort | redundant | denouement |
| elongated | accuse | gobbledygook | seize |
| separation | dehydrated | paragon | alleviate |
| allegation | parody | dissonances | questioned |
| homographs | spat | deposition | ambidextrous |
| bulldozed | crawled | conciliate | high |
| précis | pariah | disclaimer | perspicacity |
| precipitous | consonance | tawdry | hypercritical |
| climax | pretentious | enzyme | concise |
| clarity | euphemism | unadulterated | tergiversation |

| | | |
|---|---|---|
| 1. dehydrated | 11. parody | 21. retainer |
| 2. clear | 12. canter | 22. clarity |
| 3. seize | 13. elusive | 23. homophones |
| 4. allegation | 14. precipitous | 24. adept |
| 5. steep | 15. praise | 25. blushing |
| 6. alleviate | 16. affected | 26. questioned |
| 7. schism | 17. imminent | 27. paragon |
| 8. anathema | 18. pretentious | 28. dissonances |
| 9. denouement | 19. ambivalent | 29. spat |
| 10. hypercritical | 20. enzyme | 30. gobbledygook |

## SCORING KEY

30 right—You're promoted
27–29 right—You're a master at your trade
23–26 right—You've graduated from the ranks
18–22 right—You're better than average at your job
12–17 right—You're just getting by
Under 12 right—You're fired

SCORE: _____

58

# 4 〜

# How to Choose and Use a Dictionary

〜 A good dictionary is not a dull book. Many a hot argument
has gone into making it, and there are just as many word battles
among lexicographers as there are among politicians and baseball
fans. One of the all-time classic controversies followed the appearance
in 1961 of *Webster's Third Unabridged.* The free-for-all among the
wordmen (which will be described later) centered not only on what
words should be in the dictionary but also on how they should be
labeled.

There has always been a difference of opinion in dictionary circles
about slang. When does a word like *jazz* cease to be slang? Is the
beatnik term *square* still slang or is it respectably standard? Is *highbrow* slang or has it now become good formal English? Are the dictionaries in agreement on the labeling of a *stretch* (in jail)?

Take the case of *razz* and *razzberry.* Earl Wilson wrote (*New
York Post,* July 22, 1963): "Now I know how an umpire feels. Arlene
Francis started razzberrying me—about the Miss Universe title going
to Miss Brazil." In *Webster's Third Unabridged* the raspberry has
moved up in class to standard, although some other dictionaries would
disagree.[1] *Razz,* however, is a house divided in that *to razz* is now
standard, but *the razz* is still slang in the big Webster.[2]

How lexicographers are able to split the personality of *razz* is a
trade secret. *The razz* may be a bit too caustic for them. But *to razz*
is acceptable, at least to Webster's editors, possibly because it became
part of White House English when Franklin Delano Roosevelt used
it twice in campaign speeches. It may be that a presidential blessing
conferred upon a word removes any stigma that attaches to it. When
President Eisenhower said, "Somebody made a goof," the noun *goof*
was received with honors in *Webster's Third Unabridged* and dig-

---

[1] *Funk & Wagnalls Standard College Dictionary* and the *American College
Dictionary* list it as slang.
[2] The Webster house itself is divided on the labeling of *the razz.* It is listed as
standard in *Webster's Seventh New Collegiate Dictionary.*

nified with the quotation from Eisenhower. One of *goof*'s verb forms, however,—"to idle or loaf"—remains slang and waits upon a public utterance by a future president or movie star for a change of label.

Words labeled slang in the dictionary are at the halfway point. They may keep this label indefinitely, or they may go up in class as *raspberry, razz,* and *goof* have done. They may be considered slang in one sense and standard in another: *racket* is slang in *Webster's Third Unabridged* when it means "occupation or business"; in its other senses, even that of a "fraudulent scheme," it is standard. There may be disagreements among dictionaries: *jalopy* is standard in *Webster's Third Unabridged* and informal in *Funk & Wagnalls Standard College Dictionary. Heel* is standard in Webster and colloquial in the *American College Dictionary.* A *tart* is respectably standard in *Webster's Seventh New Collegiate Dictionary,* but she is labeled in the *American College Dictionary* as *"Chiefly Brit. Slang." Swell,* considered slang in *Webster's Second Unabridged,* made the grade to standard in *Webster's Third Unabridged,* but it is still labeled as slang in *Webster's New World Dictionary.*

## SLANG FILLS A NEED

At least the above terms have gained entry into the dictionary. Many slang terms never get that far; rather they wither on the vine. But expressive, colorful, short words that fill a real need persist in getting into print, thanks to Damon Runyan, Walter Winchell, sports writers, radio and television, the movies, and novelists with an ear for spoken American; and when they have appeared in mass media a number of times, they are duly recorded by the dictionary editors as slang in nationwide use. If such a word maintains its vogue, it may eventually graduate into the colloquial or informal class—the halfway house between slang and standard English. Sometimes a word like *heel* will make the grade in one jump. Not listed in *Webster's Second Unabridged,* it is standard in *Webster's Third.* Perhaps Webster's editors COGITATED awhile about such borderline cases, since it no longer uses the "colloquial" label, substituting "substandard" or "nonstandard" for words of doubtful status. *Kook,* which didn't get into the big Webster this time, may be in standard use when Webster's *Fourth* is unveiled. Or it may go into the dustbin along with other current slang terms.

60

Gelett Burgess' coined word BLURB, to describe the puff that a publisher prints on the jacket of a new book, has now, after fifty-six years, finally had its dictionary label changed from informal (*Webster's Second Unabridged*) to standard (*Webster's Third Unabridged*). This is the route it took:

**1907**          **1934**          **1961**

**BLURB** ➡ slang ➡ informal ➡ standard
(colloquial)

Actually, the term "standard" is implied and not written; when a dictionary puts no label after a word, it indicates by silence that the word is in general and current use (standard) and will pass muster in formal writing and speaking.

But if you don't think there are many borderline cases like *heel, goof,* and *pitch* (standard in *Webster's Third Unabridged* but slang in *Funk & Wagnalls Standard College Dictionary*) that stir up argument whenever lexicographers gather to talk shop, try your hand at sorting out a job lot of words used in a single issue of a current magazine.

### Slang Guessing Game

Of the following words from *Time*, June 21, 1963, which are slang and which standard in *Webster's Third Unabridged?* The big Webster has long been considered the final authority for word definitions and word labels, but you don't have to agree with it; many writers and lexicographers don't. This is just a guessing game. Check √ for slang, √√ for standard.

1. potboiler
2. heel (we gave that one away)
3. pep up
4. flop (fail)
5. guts
6. mec (a French word)
7. flic (also French)
8. rally
9. square (one not in the know)
10. flatfoot
11. foil
12. belly laughs
13. eyesore
14. boom
15. brag
16. conk (hit on the head)
17. heckles
18. upstart
19. clincher
20. racket
21. ploy
22. the heat (the pressure)
23. date (to make a date)
24. the twist (dance)
25. the left (political)
26. rabble-rousing
27. catcall
28. boo
29. a fix (a deal)
30. stretch (in jail)

| | | |
|---|---|---|
| 31. fallen (woman) | 36. bistro | 42. liner (baseball) |
| 32. pad (apartment) | 37. feds (short for fed- | 43. sea dog |
| 33. scanties | eral officers) | 44. offbeat |
| 34. rubberneckers | 38. sprung (from jail) | 45. bounced (checks) |
| 35. bitch (said of a | 39. gimmick | 46. hit-and-run |
| woman) | 40. put the finger on | 47. call girl |
| | 41. goof-offs | |

The only ones listed as slang in *Webster's Third Unabridged* are 10, 16, 20, 22, 32, and 38. *Mec* (a "guy") and *flic* (a "cop") are French slang terms. It may surprise you that the big Webster designates *stretch* (30), *bounced* (45) and *square* (9) as standard. This dictionary's definition of *square* reads: "a person who is an outsider or adversary because of the conventionality, conservatism, or respectability of his taste, behavior, or way of life: one who is not in the know." Other lexicographers have objected to labeling *square* as standard; [3] beatniks who read this definition would call the writer of it a "square." For that matter, beatniks themselves are considered standard by Webster, a label they would bitterly resent. (More of the controversy over word labels later—in Chapter 9.)


## WARNING SIGNALS

Dictionary makers have a good many other special labels for words, besides "slang" and "informal." They run up warning signals for words that are in some way limited in their use:

Archaic —Found only in older English literature but occasionally used in a special context. Examples are *jowke* (rest); *limbeck* (a pinch); *wonner* (for *dweller, inhabitant*).

Obsolete —No longer in common use, out of date; not in the fashion of our time: *laxy* (for lax); *witcrack* (Shakespearean for "wisecrack"—it should be revived).

Poetic —Used only in poetry—hence barred from present-day prose as out of place: *eftsoons, aye* (for "always"), *yore, fain.*

Dialect —Used only in certain districts or regions; not in nation-wide use; *beasties, shindy* (a dance, noisy gathering, or

[3] The new *Funk & Wagnalls Standard College Dictionary* prefers the "slang" label.

a fight), *briggle-diggle* (to putter around, procrastinate).

*U.S.* —Used only in the United States; *graft* (illicit rake-off in connection with public business) is marked *U.S. Colloq.* by the Concise Oxford.

*Brit.* —Used only in Great Britain: *dustbin* (garbage can).

*Scot.* —Of Scottish origin: *loch* (lake).

*Lat.* —Latin. See also *Fr.* (French) *Germ.*, etc.

*Technical* —Properly used only in scientific or technical connections. Some dictionaries subdivide this category into *Geog.* (Geography), *Geol.*, *Chem.*, *Math.*, *Electr.*, *Naval*, *Mil.*, *Med.*, etc.

There are, in addition, such status labels as "vulgar," "profane," "illiterate," "erroneous," "obscene"; other special designations are "humorous," "rare," "figurative." The use of these labels depends on the preference of a dictionary's editors. The editors of *Webster's Third Unabridged* have eliminated many of the older labels, including "poetic." They prefer not to attach specific labels to words, nor to brand a word too harshly; hence the use of "substandard" and "nonstandard":

*Substandard* —Exists "throughout the American language community but differs in choice of word or form from that of the prestige group." (An example is *ain't*, which is standard in its sense of "are not," "am not," but substandard when it replaces "have not," "has not.")

*Nonstandard* —A word that "can hardly stand without some status label" but is "too widely current in reputable context to be labeled substandard." (Webster puts *irregardless* in this category.)

The labeling of technical words is always a problem to dictionary editors; these words are continually shuttling into wider use, in senses derived from their technical meaning. How soon are these FIGURATIVE and DERIVATIVE senses recognized as standard? ALLERGIC is a banner example. It is in common use in "I'm allergic to rock 'n' roll . . . singing commercials . . . soap operas." It is now recognized as proper speaking and writing English (*Webster's Third Unabridged*),[4] yet it is so overworked that it's setting up an allergy against itself.

---

[4] Listed as informal in *Funk & Wagnalls Standard College Dictionary.*

# PRONUNCIATION IS IMPORTANT, TOO

Stenographers, proofreaders, printers, writers, and all the rest of us, when in doubt about the spelling of a word—or when we wonder how it's to be divided by a hyphen—turn to the dictionary. And we rely on it to settle arguments over pronunciation.

Now that radio, television, the movies, and recordings have brought the spoken word into such sharp relief, these arguments are apt to be hot and heavy. The major networks employ speech consultants to cope with the problem. The *NBC Handbook of Pronunciation* [5] is the result of careful inquiry into the actual problems of announcers and newscasters in dealing with disputed words. It deals also with the pronunciation of proper and place names in the news—especially foreign ones.

The British Broadcasting Corporation has a Pronunciation Unit, consisting of four members of the BBC staff, with the OCTOGENARIAN Daniel Jones, the PHONETICIAN, as outside Linguistic Adviser. The BBC at one time circulated recordings of the preferred pronunciation of words; now, however, it is permissive in its attitude toward pronunciation and issues no DOGMATIC DIRECTIVES on speech.

### Words Announcers Must Know

Here's a select list of words from the new *NBC Handbook of Pronunciation*. While you're guessing how to say them, bear in mind that you might hear them almost any day on radio or television; they are keys to current events and personalities. First time through, cover up the right hand column, giving the key to pronunciation,[6] and see

[5] 3rd Edition (1964) revised by Thomas Lee Crowell, Jr., and published by Thomas Y. Crowell Company.

[6] Here is the pronunciation key, based on the actual sound patterns of American speech.

| KEY WORD | RESPELLING | KEY WORD | RESPELLING | KEY WORD | RESPELLING |
|---|---|---|---|---|---|
| at | at | do | doo: | hurt | hert |
| ah | ah | elm | elm | is | iz |
| air | air | eel | eel | high | high |
| awful | AW fuhl | server | SER ver | jet | jet |
| say | say | server | SER ver | kiss | kis |
| back | bak | fit | fit | lamb | lam |
| chair | chair | go | goh | my | migh |

how you score. Second time through, see how many of the words you can define. You're going to meet most of these words in subsequent chapters. By the time you've finished this book, they'll be old friends.

| KEY WORD | RESPELLING | KEY WORD | RESPELLING |
|---|---|---|---|
| ABERRATION | a buh RAY shun | conjure | KAHN jer |
| AGORAPHOBIA | a guh ruh FOH bi uh | CRITERIA | krigh TI ri uh |
| | | CRITIQUE | kri TEEK |
| AMOROUS | A muh ruhs | DEPRECATE | DE pruh kayt |
| AMORPHOUS | uh MAWR fuhs | DIALECTICS | digh uh LEK tiks |
| ANTIQUATED | AN ti kway tid | DIATRIBE | DIGH uh trighb |
| ANTONYM | AN tuh nim | EBULLIENT | i BUH lyuhnt |
| APARTHEID | uh PAHRT hight | ECDYSIAST | ek DI zi ast |
| ASCENSION | uh SEN shuhn | ECHELON | E shuh lahn |
| AUTOBIOGRAPHI-CAL | aw tuh bigh uh GRA fi kuhl | ECLECTIC | i KLEK tik |
| | | ELECTROCARDIO-GRAM | i lek troh KAHR di uh gram |
| AVANT-GARDE | ah vahnt GAHRD | ENCLAVE | EN klayv |
| BALLISTIC | buh LI stik | epoch | E puhk |
| BIZARRE | bi ZAHR | ERUDITE | AI ryoo dight |
| BONA FIDE | BOH nuh FIGHD | EUPHEMISM | YOO fuh mi zuhm |
| BOURGEOIS | boor ZHWAH | EUTHANASIA | yoo thuh NAY zhuh |
| CABAL | kuh BAL | | |
| CACOPHONY | kuh KAH fuh ni | EXCORIATE | ik SKAW ri ayt |
| CALUMNIATE | kuh LUHM ni ayt | EXPOSTULATE | ik SPAHS chuh layt |
| CANTILEVER | KAN tuh le ver | EXTANT | EK stuhnt |
| CASTIGATE | KA stuh gayt | EXTRASENSORY | ek struh SEN suh ri |
| CASUIST | KA zhoo ist | FASCES | FA seez |
| CAUSTIC | KAW stik | FEMME FATALE | fem fa TAL |
| CEREBELLUM | se ruh BE luhm | FISSIONABLE | FI shuh nuh buhl |
| CHARGÉ D'AF-FAIRES | shahr ZHAY da FAIR | FLUOROSCOPE | FLOO ruh skohp |
| CHAUVINISM | SHOH vi ni zuhm | GERONTOLOGY | je ruhn TAH luh ji |
| CHICHI | SHEE shee | GERRYMANDER | GE ri man der |
| CHIMERA | kuh MI ruh | GHERKIN | GER kin |
| CLIMACTIC | kligh MAK tik | HARPSICHORD | HAHRP si kawrd |
| COERCE | koh ERS | HEMOGLOBIN | hee muh GLOH bin |
| CONCOMITANT | kahn KAH muh tuhnt | HEMOPHILIA | hee muh FI li uh |
| CONFABULATE | kuhn FA byoo layt | HEPARIN | HE puh rin |

| KEY WORD | RESPELLING | KEY WORD | RESPELLING | KEY WORD | RESPELLING |
|---|---|---|---|---|---|
| nice | nighs | pie | pigh | above | uh BUHV |
| sing | sing | ray | ray | vine | vighn |
| oh | oh | so | soh | wine | wighn |
| oil | oil | shall | shal | whine | hwighn |
| foot | foot | to | too: | you | yoo: |
| food | foo:d | thin | thin | zoo | zoo: |
| how | how | then | th:en | rouge | roo:zh |
| | | above | uh BUHV | | |

65

| | | | |
|---|---|---|---|
| HETEROGENEOUS | he tuh ruh JEE ni uhs | PALAZZO | pah LAHT soh |
| HOLOCAUST | HAH luh kawst | PANORAMA | pa nuh RA muh |
| HOMOPHONE | HAH muh fohn | PARODY | PA ruh di |
| HUMANITARIAN | hyoo ma nuh TAI ri uhn | PATOIS | PA twah |
| | | PAVAN | PA vuhn |
| | | peremptory | puh REMP tuh ri |
| HYDROPHOBIA | high druh FOH bi uh | PERFUNCTORY | per FUHNGK tuh ri |
| HYDROPONIC | high druh PAH nik | PERIGEE | PE ruh jee |
| HYPERBOLE | high PER buh li | PERIPATETIC | per ri puh TE tik |
| IMPECCABLE | im PE kuh buhl | PHILOLOGY | fi LAH luh ji |
| IMPRESARIO | im pri SAH ri oh | PHONEME | FOH neem |
| IN ABSENTIA | in ab SEN shi uh | PLETHORA | PLE thuh ruh |
| INGENUE | an zhi NOO: | PLEXIGLAS | PLEK si glas |
| INTELLIGENTSIA | in te luh JENT si uh | POLTERGEIST | POHL ter gighst |
| | | POLYGLOT | PAH li glaht |
| INTERNECINE | in ter NEE sin | POLYPHONY | puh LI fuh ni |
| ITINERANT | igh TI nuh ruhnt | POLYSYLLABIC | pah lis si LA bik |
| JEU D'ESPRIT | zher de SPREE | PORNOGRAPHY | pawr NAH gruh fi |
| JUDICIARY | joo: DI shi ai ri | POSITRON | PAH zuh trahn |
| KENOTRON | KE nuh trahn | PRESTISSIMO | pre STI suh moh |
| KLYSTRON | KLI struhn | PSYCHIATRIST | sigh KIGH uh trist |
| LAISSEZ FAIRE | le say FAIR | PUNCTILIO | puhngk TI li oh |
| LIAISON | LEE uh zahn | QUADRANT | KWAH druhnt |
| LICHEE | LEE chee | RACONTEUR | ra kahn TER |
| MACABRE | muh KAH ber | RADIONICS | ray di AH niks |
| MACADAM | muh KA duhm | RAPPROCHEMENT | ra prawsh MAHN |
| MACARONIC | ma kuh RAH nik | RECONNAISSANCE | ri KAH nuh suhns |
| MAGNETOMETER | mag nuh TAH muh ter | REGIME | ri ZHEEM |
| | | SECRETARIAT | se kruh TAI ri it |
| MATZOTH | MAHT sohth | SESQUIPEDALIAN | SE skwi puh DAY li uhn |
| MELANCHOLIA | me luhn KOH li uh | | |
| METATHESIS | muh TA thuh sis | SOLILOQUIZE | suh LI luh kwighz |
| MODUS VIVENDI | MOH duhs vi VEN digh | STACCATO | stuh KAH toh |
| | | STRONTIUM | STRAHN shi uhm |
| MORDANT | MAWR duhnt | SUPERCILIOUS | soo: per SI li uhs |
| MYSTIQUE | mi STEEK | SYCOPHANT | SI kuh fuhnt |
| NARCISSISM | nahr SI si zuhm | THERMONUCLEAR | ther moh NOO: kli er |
| NEGATRON | NE guh trahn | | |
| NEPOTISM | NE puh ti zuhm | VIRAGO | vi RAY goh |
| NIRVANA | ner VA nuh | VIRTUOSO | VER choo OH soh |
| NUCLEONICS | noo: kli AH niks | VULPINE | VUHL pighn |
| OBSCENITY | uhb SE nuh ti | XENOPHOBIA | ze nuh FOH bi uh |
| OMNIBUS | AHM nuh buhs | | |

# Names from the Past and Present

Names make news, and news makes history. Here's another list of terms from the same source, of proper names you've seen in the newspapers, heard on the airwaves, or remembered from school or from your general reading. Follow the same procedure as you did with the previous test. Do you know who Nkrumah is? Bourguiba? Who was Desdemona? Scarlatti?

| | | | |
|---|---|---|---|
| Bach | bahk | Malthusian | mal THOO: shuhn |
| Bayreuth | bigh ROIT | Modigliani | maw deel YAH nee |
| Beowulf | BAY uh woolf | Monteverdi | mawn te VAIR dee |
| Bergson, Henri | BAIRG suhn, AHN ree | Mozart | MOHT sahrt |
| | | Nabokov, | NAH boh kuhf, |
| Bourguiba, Habib | boo:r GEE bah, hah BEEB | Vladimir | VLAH duh meer |
| | | Ngo Dinh Diem | uhng O DIN zi EM |
| Brandeis | BRAN dighs | Nigeria | nigh JI ri uh |
| Brecht, Bertolt | brekt, BER tawlt | Nkrumah, | uhn KROO: mah, |
| Brobdingnagian | brahb ding NA gi uhn | Kwame | KWAH me |
| | | O'Casey, Sean | oh KAY si, |
| Candida | KAN di duh | | SHAWN |
| Carlsbad | KAHRLZ bad | Othello | uh THE loh |
| Cro-Magnon | kroh MAG nahn | Pakistan | PA ki stan |
| Dalai Lama | dah LIGH LAH mugh | Palestrina | pa luh STREE nuh |
| | | Pauling, Linus | PAW ling, LIGH nuhs |
| Desdemona | dez duh MOH nuh | | |
| Don Giovanni | dahn joh VAH ni | Rimski-Korsakov | RIM ski KAWR suh kawf |
| Dürrenmatt, | DOO: ruhn maht, | | |
| Friedrich | FREE drish | Scarlatti | skahr LAH ti |
| Endymion | en DI mi uhn | Senegalese | se ni gaw LEEZ |
| Fermi | FAIR mee | Spinoza | spi NOH zuh |
| Franck, César | frahngk, say ZAHR | Stanislavsky | sta ni SLAHF ski |
| Francophobe | FRANG kuh fohb | Sudanese | soo: duh NEEZ |
| Galileo | ga luh LEE oh | Talmudic | tal MUH dik |
| Ghana | GAH nuh | Thant, U | TAHNT, OO |
| Hayakawa, | hah yah KAH wah, | Titanic | tigh TA nik |
| Sessue | SAY shoo: | Tomalbaye, | toh mahl BIGH, |
| Helmholtz | HELM hohlts | Francois | frahn SWAH |
| Holinshed | HAH linz hed | Toynbee | TOIN bi |
| Jekyll | JEE kuhl | Tshombe, Moise | CHAHM bay, maw EES |
| Kamchatka | kam CHAT kuh | | |
| Kanchenjunga | kahn chuhn JOONG guh | Van Dyck | van DIGHK |
| | | Xanadu | ZA nuh doo: |
| Kuomintang | KWOH min TAHNG | | |

# MAPPING THE DICTIONARY MAZE

The chief role of a dictionary is to serve as a storehouse of word meanings. Anyone can open it. But it's an odd kind of DEPOSITORY, for it's only after you've opened it, that you need the combination: the code in which a dictionary tells the story of each word. You must note the key to pronunciation; the method for showing the breaks between syllables, if you have to HYPHENATE the word; the abbreviations employed to give the facts about it; and the system for showing its PEDIGREE or derivation—etymology is the technical term. And as a matter of prime concern, what aid is offered for determining the right meaning of a word in a given situation? For you often have to pick out, from the dictionary entry, the particular meaning which fits.

You've already heard about the "confusion" words, about homophones, homographs, homonyms, multiple-meaning words. A casual glance at any page in the dictionary will show that one out of every four or five English words has anywhere from two to fifty meanings —and some keep adding more.[7] This gives gagwriters and columnists a vast file of material for wordplay, but it often causes other persons in the word trades to tear out their hair.

An item from a recent newspaper article reads: "The *tenor* of the talks could be read in the shrill POLEMICAL battle carried on publicly all week by Moscow and Peking." A quick check will show you that *tenor* in this context refers to the "drift" or "general purport" of the bitter exchanges between the two communist giants, not to the shrillness of the polemical battles. Besides, the other kind of tenors are heard and not read (though they are often shrill). Homophones such as these can cause confusion if you are not alert to the problem of multiple meanings.

There's a story about an editor of the defunct *Daily Worker* who pulled a yard of copy off the TELETYPE and threw it across the desk to his newest cub, saying, "Here, boy, class-*angle* these stories and, mind you, hew to the *line.*"

The *angle* here is not "the space between two intersecting lines or planes"; nor is it the "number of degrees of opening." And the *line* intended is not the "MATHEMATICAL track made by a moving point."

[7] *Strike*, for example. See footnote 2, page 39.

What the editor is saying, spelled out, is "Re-slant these stories according to MARXIAN doctrines of class conflict, and keep to the present 'party line' in rewriting them."

You'll note, of course, that *tenor, angle,* and *line* are relatively simple cases of dual or triple meanings, which you can sight-read. But they point up the fact that the same words can often be made to mean different things. Since there are now many "party lines" heard in the squabbling among the communist countries, language must be giving Marxian journalists throughout the world as many headaches as our rewrite men suffer daily.

## WORDS APE PEOPLE

Words describing some aspect of human nature are likely to roll up a whole bundle of complex meanings. Take, for instance, the word *character.* Here is its entry in the *Concise Oxford Dictionary:*

**character** (k-), n. & v.t. Distinctive mark; (pl.) inscribed letters or figures; national writing-symbols (*in the German c.*) person's handwriting; characteristic (esp. of species &c. in Nat. Hist.); collective peculiarities, sort, style; person's or race's idiosyncracy, mental or moral nature; moral strength, backbone; reputation, good reputation; description of person's qualities; testimonial; status; known person (usu. *public c.*); imaginary person created by novelist or dramatist; actor's or hypocrite's part (*in, out of, c.,* appropriate to those or not, also more widely of actions that are in accord or not with person's c.); eccentric person (*c. actor,* who devotes himself to eccentricities). (Vb. poetic & archaic) inscribe; describe. [f. F. caractère f. L. f. Gk *kharaktēr* stamp (*kharattō* engrave)].

It's not hard to tell which meaning is involved in the lines

> Firm *character'd* in antique gold
> The head of Alexander, King of Macedon . . .

Here it is the literal, primary sense of the word: *stamped* or *engraved.* The head of the King is stamped on the old Greek coin—with perhaps a double meaning implied, that his temperament is revealed by the face. When Jeremy Taylor says in one of his sermons

God hath writ His Commandements in so large *characters* . . .

69

he means "letters" or "symbols,"—which in the days of writing on wax, clay or stone, were stamped, INCISED, or carved. We carry this meaning over to describe any alphabet or set of symbols, written or printed. And *character* may also mean the "style of handwriting peculiar to an individual," since it was possible to recognize from his single letter strokes the CHIROGRAPHY of a particular scribe or copyist. Again, in a sense derived from this, *character* is used to mean a cipher or secret mode of writing peculiar to one man. All these meanings are pretty close to the literal.

In the stock phrase "inheritance of acquired *characters*" the word means "the distinguishing features of a species or GENUS,"—the "characteristics." In Macaulay's use of it in the following,

He now tried to give to the war the *character* of a crusade . . .

it means "essential peculiarity or nature."

When we find a historian writing of Henry VIII

Thorough selfishness formed the basis of Henry's *character* . . .

we recognize the principal present-day meaning of the word: "the sum of the mental and moral qualities which distinguish an individual or a race." This is the *stamp* of a man, the *brand* or IMPRINT left upon his nature by that sovereign instrument for marking, life itself. Derived from this is the common use of the word to mean "moral FIBER," as in "a man of strong *character*."

In the passage

Henry James wrote a *character* for his servant in a style so elaborate that neither she nor any of her prospective employers could make out what it meant . . .

the meaning is "a formal TESTIMONIAL from an employer as to the reputation and efficiency of one who has been in his employ."

Familiar enough is the use of the word to mean "a person in a play or novel." From this use also comes the phrase "out of *character*," meaning acting "contrary to the personality which an actor has assumed in the play." And the meaning "an odd or eccentric person" is at once clear to us in Goldsmith's lines

A very impudent fellow this, but he's a
*character* and I'll humor him . . .

From this use perhaps comes the recent DEROGATORY slang sense, found in "Are you bringing those *characters* to dinner again?"

These examples do not by any means exhaust the possibilities of the term. The *Oxford English Dictionary* gives twenty-four different meanings for *character*, nineteen as a noun and five as a verb; some of them are subdivided. And its latest citation is dated 1888. Many new shades of meaning have come in through the immense development of PSYCHOLOGY in the nearly seventy-five years that have elapsed.

It is doubtful, in fact, if even the main meaning of the word, quoted above, will fully convey the sense of the term as it is used in discussions of the PSYCHOLOGICAL novel and drama, in the phrase "development of *character*." Since Goethe and Coleridge first called attention to the extraordinary significance of *the growth of character* in the modern scheme of things, the word has taken on great richness of meaning. Character, in this sense, connotes more than the *stamp* of a man. The time factor comes in. What a man has been is taken as predicting what he is likely to become in the future. His "character" in this sense is a growing process. The term hints also at the judgment others form of his make-up. It includes his motives and probable future acts. *Character in this sense varies with time and the observer.* It becomes a matter of interpretation. How many readings there have been of the "character" of Hamlet!

## Pick the Right Meaning

The following words dealing with aspects of human nature have a long history behind them. While they may not all have piled up as many meanings as *character*, each one can be taken in a good many different senses. For each of the sentences containing the word, jot down your notion of the meaning as it is used in this particular instance. Then check your definitions with the dictionary entry.

### A. WIT

1. She relied on her mother*wit* to get her out of a tight spot.
2. He kept his *wits* about him.
3. True *wit* is Nature to advantage dressed,
   What oft was thought but ne'er so well expressed.
4. "We ought to get together. I'm a *wit* myself." "Half—or three-quarters?" (Does it have the same sense in the implied *half-wit?*)
5. "I am not only witty in myself, but the cause that *wit* is in other men." —Falstaff.

### B. Humor

1. Every Man in His *Humour*. (British spelling in this title.)
2. She was in a very bad *humor*.
3. A very happy mixture of the *humors*.
4. "Better *humor* him, Mac. He's a bad actor when he's lit."
5. Fred Allen's *humor*, while often including laughter at himself, was tempered by wit—and the wit was always at somebody else's expense, his favorite targets being the imbecilities of other radio programs. Jack Benny, on the other hand, is usually on the receiving end of the *humor* and wit in the jibes contrived by his own gagmen.

### C. Temper

1. His *temper* got the better of him.
2. The Mayans were of more civilized *temper* than the Aztecs and Toltecs.
3. It takes vanadium alloy to give steel the right *temper* for the purpose.
4. *Temper* the wind to the shorn lamb.

### D. Heart

1. "I have the body of a weak woman, but the *heart* and stomach of a prince."—Queen Elizabeth. (And what does *stomach* mean here?)
2. He went straight to the *heart* of the matter.
3. "Have a *heart*, bud, and give me one more beer."
4. The electrocardiogram showed grave irregularities in *heart* action.
5. Mackinder the Englishman anticipated the doctrines of Dr. Haushofer as to the importance of the *Heart*land of Eurasia; in fact, geopolitics may be said to be of British invention, not German.

### E. Mind

1. "*Mind* the baby while I go to the attic, will you?"
2. He didn't *mind* the hubbub, in fact he was used to it from batting out his copy in the infernal din of a newspaper city room.
3. The splendid shadowy caverns of the *mind*,
   Illumined by the very fires of spirit.
4. Neurologists and experimental psychologists seem determined to break down the boundaries between *mind* and matter.
5. "I felt as if I were going out of my *mind*." "How could you tell?"
6. Do you think clairvoyance, clairaudience, telepathy, precognition, and similar phenomena of parapsychology are matters of *mind* or of the senses? Or are both involved?
7. Time out of *mind*. (This is a tricky one.)
8. "I've spoken my *mind* too fully out."—Browning, *Soul's Progress*, i.207.
9. She knows her own *mind*—such as it is. (Double talk here.)
10. "The Papacy, under the guidance of her greatest *minds* . . ." Bryce.
11. He never saw that treasure except in his *mind's* eye, clouded over with the fumes of alcohol.

72

12. He went to a psychoanalyst for a *mind*-cure at twenty-five dollars a visit, when what he needed was some hard exercise and a good dose of physic.

13. "The blacksmith said to me the other day, that his 'prentice had no *mind* to his trade.' "—George Eliot, *Daniel Deronda,* lviii.

It pays to buckle down to the dictionary. It's not enough to consult it on the run. A few sessions of INTENSIVE use will convince you that *you can double your effective vocabulary by clearing up the meanings of words you only half know.* For this purpose you need to own a dictionary.

## CHOOSING YOUR DICTIONARY

For handy desk use there are several good dictionaries on the market, each with certain distinctive features.[8] You can't go wrong with the ones we're going to mention, but you can make a more intelligent choice if you have certain CRITERIA with which to evaluate them:

*Revision* —How recently has it been revised and re-edited?

*Entries* —What is the total number of words defined, including new words and phrases?

*Definitions* —How complete are the definitions? Are all possible meanings included? In what order are the definitions given?

*Clarity* —Are the defining words simpler than the word they define? Do they make the meaning clear or more obscure?

*Synonyms and Antonyms* —Does it give several synonyms and antonyms for the word defined? Does it discuss the fine shades of meaning that distinguish related words?

*Pronunciation* —Is the pronunciation key easy to follow? Where there are two or more pronuncia-

---

[8] Desk dictionaries are so called because of their size or because they are ABRIDGED works of unabridged dictionaries such as *Webster's Third International.* Desk dictionaries are practical for home, school, and office use. Pocket dictionaries are more compact in size.

tions of a word, are they listed in order
of preference?

*Etymology* —Does it give the history and origin of
words?

*Spelling* —Does it give VARIANT spellings?

*Symbols* —Are the abbreviations and labels clear?

*Typography* —Is the type and makeup easy to read?


## SIX DESK DICTIONARIES

The latest revised desk dictionary is the *Funk & Wagnalls
Standard College Dictionary* (1963), with over 150,000 entries, a record for dictionaries in this category. Most desk dictionaries have made
progress in completeness and clarity of definitions, number of entries, DISCRIMINATION of synonymous words, and inclusion of ENCY-
CLOPEDIC material. The trend to greater size and extra features is
ANALOGOUS to the progress in low-priced automobiles, with the Fords
and Chevrolets taking on the luxurious look of the Cadillacs and
Lincolns.

*Funk & Wagnalls Standard College Dictionary,* although not necessarily superior to other desk dictionaries, does have the advantage
of recent revision and the consequent updating in new words and new
word meanings. The TYPOGRAPHY is restful to the eyes, with good
white space between words and letters and with a variety of type
styles: the synonymy (with the synonyms in italics) is set apart in
smaller type under the definitions. This dictionary, in addition to being hospitable to new words and phrases, including special and technical vocabularies, also gives full coverage on slang and informal
language.

*Webster's Seventh New Collegiate Dictionary* (G. & C. Merriam
Company, 1963) is the next most recently revised desk dictionary. It
is based on *Webster's Third Unabridged,* which came out in 1961.
Although the definitions are both SUCCINCT and comprehensive, given
with logical rigor and precision, the print is small and difficult to read.
One of our researchers complained bitterly that "the smallish, rather
pale type is conducive to sudden, frightening cries on the part of the
reader, for bifocals." Yet she prefers this desk dictionary because of
the completeness of its definitions, which, though often more aloof
and abstract than those of the other desk dictionaries, would stand up

74

in a court of law or before a tribunal of scholars. *Webster's Seventh New Collegiate Dictionary* has 130,000 entries, culled from the 450,000 words in the unabridged parent work.

Another good desk dictionary is the *American College Dictionary* (Random House, Inc.), which adds new words yearly. It has 132,000 entries, defined in simple, straightforward language. Each main entry is in enlarged, bold-faced type, setting it off clearly from its definitions. This dictionary has a distinguished staff of consultants, including the well-known lexicographer, C. L. Barnhart, Editor-in-Chief; Dr. Kemp Malone, who prepared the authoritative etymologies; and W. Cabell Greet, an expert on pronunciation.

*Webster's New World Dictionary* (College Edition),[9] which made its debut in 1951, follows the policy of the *American College Dictionary* in adding new words each year but not changing the main body of words. It is a fairly bulky work but is second to the *Funk & Wagnalls* in number of entries: 142,000. The type is pleasing, with a large and darkened main entry and well-proportioned definition type. The definitions are clear and complete, and special attention has been given to etymologies.

A handy-sized dictionary is the *Winston Dictionary* (Holt, Rinehart & Winston, Inc.). It has fewer entries than the other works previously mentioned, but the definitions are simple and readily understandable and the type is easy on the eyes. Holt, Rinehart & Winston puts out different school editions of varying size and level of difficulty, the advanced editions including more technical terms.

The *Thorndike-Barnhart Comprehensive Desk Dictionary* (Doubleday & Company, Inc.) is comparable in size, readability, number of entries, and INTELLIGIBILITY of definitions to the *Winston Dictionary* and is also put out in several school editions.


## ORDER OF DEFINITIONS

It is advisable to consult the introductory notes in a dictionary before looking up the word in the text. Dictionaries differ in their order of meanings for each entry, their placement of etymologies,

[9] This dictionary is published by the World Publishing Company of Cleveland and should not be confused with *Webster's Seventh New Collegiate Dictionary* or *Webster's Third International* (referred to in this book as *Webster's Third Unabridged*), which are put out by G. & C. Merriam Company, of Springfield, Mass.

their handling of synonymy, and their use of labels. *Webster's Seventh New Collegiate Dictionary*, for example, follows the policy of *Webster's Third Unabridged* in giving the definitions of a word in historical order: the oldest meaning first and so on down to the most recent meaning. *Webster's New World Dictionary* gives definitions in this order: (a) recent meanings that follow historically from the etymology; (b) meanings that are obsolete, archaic, colloquial, etc.; (c) technical senses. *American College Dictionary* gives the central (most common) meaning first, then the figurative, special, and general senses in which a word may be used, followed by the rare or obsolete meanings, if any. *Funk & Wagnalls, Winston,* and *Thorndike-Barnhart* give first the most common meaning of a word and then the other meanings in descending order of frequency.

## LABELS

The desk dictionaries differ widely in their choice of labels. *Webster's Seventh New Collegiate Dictionary* follows the example of the parent work in eliminating "colloquial" and "informal." It tends also to ignore technical labels that would DIFFERENTIATE the special senses in which words are used in science, business, etc. The definitions are admirable and complete, and there is often an italicized mention of the special field to which a word belongs; the absence of clear-cut labels, however, prevents the reader from making sharp distinctions. The meanings are differentiated in the definitions, but they are blurred by the appearance of a solid block of words.

*Funk & Wagnalls Standard College Dictionary* uses field labels (Aeronautics, Physics, Law, etc.) and usage labels (Slang, Informal, Dial., Illit., Poetic, Archaic, Obsolete, Rare, U.S., Brit., etc.). *Webster's New World Dictionary* prefers the conventional labels of the past: Colloquial, Slang, Obsolete, Archaic, Poetic, Dialect, etc. The *American College Dictionary* uses such labels as Slang, Colloquial, Humorous, Obsolete, Archaic, Rare. The *Winston Dictionary* and the *Thorndike-Barnhart Comprehensive Desk Dictionary* use traditional labels. There are also regional labels in most dictionaries, indicating how words are used in other countries and in specific areas of this country.

76

## ETYMOLOGY AND SYNONYMY

The desk dictionaries place the etymology of a word either before or after the definitions. In *Webster's Seventh New Collegiate Dictionary, Webster's New World Dictionary*, and the *Winston Dictionary*, the etymology precedes the definitions. It is placed after the definitions in the *American College Dictionary*, the *Funk & Wagnalls Standard College Dictionary*, and the *Thorndike-Barnhart Comprehensive Desk Dictionary*.

The newer desk dictionaries include more complete discriminations of synonyms, following the practice of *Webster's Dictionary of Synonyms* (see Chapter 9). Rather than merely listing the synonyms of a word, they devote whole paragraphs in many cases to a careful explanation of the way in which synonymous words differ in their shades of meaning. These paragraphs are placed, along with synonyms and antonyms, after the definitions of the main word entry.

## A SAMPLING OF EACH

In the final analysis, number of entries, completeness and clarity of definitions, and recency of revision are the most important criteria of a good dictionary. Entries from four of the dictionaries mentioned are reproduced on the next two pages. You will refer to them later in Chapter 6. This sample is by no means conclusive, of course, in making a decision in favor of any one dictionary. None of them has a clear-cut advantage over the others.

## LITERARY DESK DICTIONARIES

The *Concise Oxford Dictionary*, an abridgement of the great *Oxford English Dictionary*, is enlivened now and then by the quiet, SARDONIC wit of the Fowler brothers, who made the CONDENSATION. Even though there is a special American edition, there was no way to edit out the British flavor. Again, the work is longer on the literary and historical side than on the technical and scientific, in line with

**the·o·ry** (thē'ə rĭ, thĭr'ĭ), *n., pl.* **-ries.** **1.** a coherent group of general propositions used as principles of explanation for a class of phenomena: *Newton's theory of gravitation.* **2.** a proposed explanation whose status is still conjectural, in contrast to well-established propositions that are regarded as reporting matters of actual fact. **3.** *Math.* a body of principles, theorems, or the like, belonging to one subject: *number theory.* **4.** that department of a science or art which deals with its principles or methods, as distinguished from the practice of it. **5.** a particular conception or view of something to be done or of the method of doing it; a system of rules or principles. **6.** contemplation or mental view. [t. LL: m.s. *theōria,* t. Gk.: contemplation, theory] —**Syn. 1.** THEORY, HYPOTHESIS are both often used colloquially to mean an untested idea or opinion. A THEORY properly is a more or less verified or established explanation accounting for known facts or phenomena: *the theory of relativity.* A HYPOTHESIS is a conjecture put forth as a possible explanation of certain phenomena or relations, which serves as a basis of argument or experimentation by which to reach the truth: *this idea is offered only as an hypothesis.* —**Ant. 1.** principle, axiom, law.

From the *American College Dictionary,* © copyright 1947, 1963 by Random House, Inc. Reprinted by permission.

**hy·poth·e·sis** \hī-'päth-ə-səs\ *n, pl* **hy·poth·e·ses** \-ə-,sēz\ [Gk, fr. *hypotithenai* to put under, suppose, fr. *hypo-* + *tithenai* to put — more at DO] **1 :** a tentative assumption made in order to draw out and test its logical or empirical consequences **2 a :** an assumption or concession made for the sake of argument **b :** an interpretation of a practical situation or condition taken as the ground for action

**syn** HYPOTHESIS, THEORY, LAW mean a formula derived by inference from scientific data that explains a principle operating in nature. HYPOTHESIS implies insufficiency of presently attainable evidence and therefore a tentative explanation; THEORY implies a greater range of evidence and greater likelihood of truth; LAW implies a statement of order and relation in nature that has been found to be invariable under the same conditions

By permission. From *Webster's Seventh New Collegiate Dictionary,* copyright © 1963 by G. & C. Merriam Company, publishers of the Merriam-Webster Dictionaries.

**hy·poth·e·sis** (hĭ·poth'ə·sis, hi-) *n. pl.* **·ses** (-sēz) **1.** An unproved scientific conclusion drawn from known facts and used as a basis for further investigation or experimentation. **2.** An assumption or set of assumptions provisionally accepted as a basis for reasoning or argument. **3.** *Logic* A conditional proposition. *Abbr.* hyp., hypoth. [< NL < Gk., foundation, supposition < *hypotithenai* to put under < *hypo-* under + *tithenia* to put] —**Syn.** *Hypothesis, theory, supposition, assumption,* and *conjecture* are compared as they denote an unproved assertion about reality. In science, a *hypothesis* is a proposition advanced as possibly true, and consistent with known data, but requiring further investigation; a *theory* is a *hypothesis* so well substantiated as to be generally accepted: the nebular *hypothesis* of the origin of the solar system, the atomic *theory* of Dalton. *Supposition* and *assumption* are propositions accepted with less assurance than a *hypothesis;* their acceptance facilitates investigation, but the investigation may quickly show them to be untrue. A *conjecture* is a conclusion drawn from admittedly insufficient data; it differs from a guess only in not being wholly random and uninformed. Compare GUESS.

Used by permission of Funk & Wagnalls Company, Inc., publishers of the *Standard College Dictionary.*

78

**the·o·ry** (thē′ə-ri), *n.* [*pl.* THEORIES (-riz)], [< Fr. or LL.; Fr. *théorie;* LL. *theoria;* Gr. *theōria,* a looking at, contemplation, speculation, theory < *theōrein,* to look at], *1.* originally, a mental viewing; contemplation. *2.* an idea or mental plan of the way to do something; hence, *3.* a systematic statement of principles involved: as, the *theory* of equations in mathematics. *4.* a formulation of apparent relationships or underlying principles of certain observed phenomena which has been verified to some degree: distinguished from *hypothesis. 5.* that branch of an art or science consisting in a knowledge of its principles and methods rather than in its practice; pure, as opposed to applied, science, etc. *6.* popularly, a mere hypothesis, conjecture, or guess: as, my *theory* is that he's lying. *SYN.*—theory, as compared here, implies considerable evidence in support of a formulated general principle explaining the operation of certain phenomena (the *theory* of evolution); hypothesis implies an inadequacy of evidence in support of an explanation that is tentatively inferred, often as a basis for further experimentation (the nebular *hypothesis*); law implies an exact formulation of the principle operating in a sequence of events in nature observed to occur with unvarying uniformity under the same conditions (the *law* of the conservation of energy).

From *Webster's New World Dictionary of the American Language,* College Edition, copyright © 1964, by The World Publishing Company.

the Fowlers' conviction that a dictionary is concerned with words and word usage, not with the things and processes for which words stand. They did not believe in making a LEXICON encyclopedic. But they created the *Concise Oxford* style, and once the user learns to watch for their higher mischief he enjoys a good deal of quiet amusement.

Of the pocket dictionaries, one worth owning is also the work of the Fowlers: the *Pocket Oxford Dictionary of Current English,* revised for American use by George Santvoord. Its 1050 close-packed but easily readable pages, 3½ inches by 6, contain a lot in small compass. The preface is a noble specimen of the Fowlers' wit. Here's one example:

. . . the reader . . . may fairly expect to be told not only the meaning of an ox, an icosahedron . . . a major-general . . . but also what are the words for the ox of various ages and sexes, and for *the other regular solids, army officers* . . . and so forth.

If you don't think the Fowlers intended that juxtaposition of army officers and other regular solids, ask some of our boys who have done a stint in the army. The Fowlers had just come out of the British Army when they wrote these lines.

Their *Pocket Oxford* also contains a valuable appendix giving pronunciations of foreign words and phrases, including both the usual

Anglo-American APPROXIMATION and the actual pronunciation in the foreign language, indicated by the International PHONETIC Alphabet. Another appendix gives words that came into the language during the first three decades of this century and new meanings and uses of words listed in the main body of the lexicon. While the Fowlers say that this pocket work is not, like their *Concise Oxford*, intended for those who enjoy reading the dictionary straight through, don't believe them. They have slipped in some quiet wit in this one, too.

### Suppose You Were Writing a Dictionary

Just for fun, see how you'd make out COMPILING dictionary entries for the following words, all of which have multiple meanings. If you want to do it right, and start a collection for word games and word quizzes, make your entries on cards 4 x 6 inches. Put the word under treatment in the upper left-hand corner, and jot down the definitions for the different meanings in numbered order. Then check them with your desk dictionary. Keep the cards in alphabetical order, and as you run into the word in your reading, copy down the sentence in which it occurs—particularly if you find a lively or humorous use of the word.

Take, for example, the word CAISSON (pronounced, in America, "kaysen," in England "kassoon," with the accent on the "soon.") You'll think at once of the line from the song, "The caissons went rolling along." Here it means "a vehicle to carry ammunition." Then you think of men working under water, tunneling, who get the "bends" if they come out of the caissons too quickly, without DEPRESSURIZING gradually. In this use, a caisson is "an airtight pressure chamber permitting men to work under water." Evidently sentences illustrating the word's use are very helpful in giving a full and precise sense of its varied meanings.

Try your hand at dictionary entries for these words:

| | | | |
|---|---|---|---|
| 1. ABSTRACT | 6. CORRELATION | 11. DYNAMICS | 16. LEACH |
| 2. ANTECEDENT | 7. COSMOS | 12. ENSEMBLE | 17. MANIPULATE |
| 3. CAPITALISM | 8. DEDUCTION | 13. EQUINOCTIAL | 18. MEDIAN |
| 4. ANALOGOUS | 9. DUCTILE | 14. INDUCTION | 19. mode |
| 5. EXTRASENSORY | 10. DYNAMIC | 15. JARGON | 20. MOLLIFY |

# Fortune-Telling with a Dictionary

Here's a parlor game invented by a sardonic wit who said the one excuse for bridge is that it ends free speech for MORONS. His favorite type of word quiz is based on a method of fortune-telling that was in vogue in the late Middle Ages and the early RENAISSANCE. The person who wanted to know his future was blindfolded, and handed a small pointer or STYLUS. He was then led to a table or LECTERN on which lay a copy of Vergil's *Aeneid*. He was expected to open it at random, and bring the pointer to rest on one line of the poem. The expert fortune-teller then interpreted this verse for him, as revealing his future destiny. This was called consulting the Vergilian lots, or STICHOMANCY.

Try this method, using a dictionary instead of Vergil. When the word has been selected, go round the circle until you find someone who can define it correctly, not necessarily in the exact words of the dictionary, but near enough to convey the sense—or senses—of the term. A pleasant variation is to ask that the definer also use the word in a sentence, humorously if possible—with an added point for every laugh. (Serious players will promptly develop frozen faces.)

Keep score, devise appropriate penalties and rewards—and if anyone wants to gamble on his word prowess, let his conscience be his guide.

It is to be made clear from the start that the words picked by the blindfolded person, taken in sequence as long as he does the picking, will be interpreted as his fortune by the most expert word doctor in the room, as shown by the score.

This method of DIVINATION is no worse than any other. At a house party recently a professor turned up *faculty*, a politician came up with INAUGURATION, and an AVID baseball fan picked *pennant* (but his team finished last in the standings). A successful businessman, however, pointed to *unemployed*, while a free-lance writer, just getting by financially, chose BONANZA. Any way you look at the game, at least it gives faster action than a Ouija board, and it's more fun than ANAGRAMS or the various modern variants of *bouts rimés*. And it makes the dictionary seem more sociable.

# WORD COURT OF LAST RESORT

Anybody, however, who wants to get primed for such games by reading a page of the lexicon every day, and learning the words which amuse him, should not rest content with a desk or pocket dictionary. A work is available that is much richer reading.

The greatest venture in the history of LEXICOGRAPHY is the *Oxford English Dictionary* (OED)—sometimes called the New English Dictionary, or Murray's, from its first editor. Begun in 1857, and completed only in 1933, this work treats words on historical principles. For each entry, instances of the use of the word were gathered, including wherever FEASIBLE its earliest use, and TRAVERSING its history through all its subsequent changes of meaning. Five million quotations in all were collected, of which two million were finally used in the thirteen huge folio volumes. So for each of the 215,000 main words, and the 200,000 subordinate word- and phrase-entries, not only are there definitions which show all the meanings that the word has had, but examples of the use in each sense are given.

The OED is therefore a great treasury of sentences from English literature, beginning with the eighth century, and coming down, in the last volume, to 1930. These illustrations, which give the word in CONTEXT—on the site where it was found, so to speak—are the best revelations of the actual significance which the word has had at different periods. To trace the successive meanings and uses of the word *humor,* or of the word *wit,* as recorded in the OED, is an exercise that will uncover much of the history of the English mind and of English social life during a thousand years.

A *Dictionary of American English* (DAE) was made on the same principles, but the ILLUSTRATIVE sentences are predominantly from American literature before 1900, and slang is not treated at all. These limitations rule out the bulk of the saltier and more CHARACTERISTICALLY American expressions, so the DAE, useful though it is, is not nearly as entertaining reading as the OED.

Take, for example, the OED entry on the word *lousy.* It shows that the word was used as a VULGARISM as early as 1386. In this sense the OED defines lousy as

dirty, filthy, obscene. Also as a general term of abuse: Mean, scurvy, sorry, vile, contemptible.

Then follows the annotation: *Now rare*—which was true only when it was written. But the really amusing part of the entry under *lousy* comes with the examples from the best authors:

1663 DRYDEN *Wild Gallant* 1 i And to discredit me before strangers, for a lousy, paltry sum of money?
1708 *Brit. Apollo* No. 38 2/1 Wicked Rhimes . . . sung to lowsey Tunes.
1893 STEVENSON *Catriona* 65 The lousiest, lowest, story to hand down to your namesakes in the future.

All these examples from standard authors made *lousy* a slang vulgarism in the past; but in *Webster's Third Unabridged* it is now a respectable standard word.[10]

One of the most admirable features of the OED is the introductory article on the vocabulary of the English language. It contains one REVELATORY passage that brings into place with a sudden click that huge, KALEIDOSCOPIC collection of words which the dictionary offers. In a flash we see an ordered picture of the English vocabulary, marked by strong and sure design:

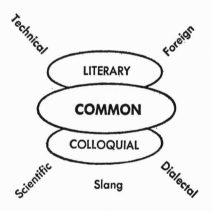

The center is occupied by the common words, in which literary and colloquial words meet. "Scientific" and "foreign" words enter the common language through literature; "slang" words ascend through colloquial use; the

[10]*Funk & Wagnalls Standard College Dictionary* still regards *lousy* as slang. *Webster's Third Unabridged* and *Webster's Seventh New Collegiate Dictionary* differ radically with the other dictionaries in their labeling of slang terms. Since *Funk & Wagnalls Standard College Dictionary* is the most recently revised work (1963) it is cited frequently in this book for the purpose of comparison.

"technical" terms of crafts and processes, and the "dialect" words, blend with the common language both in speech and literature. Slang also touches on one side the technical vocabulary of trades and occupations, as in "nautical slang," "Public School slang," "the slang of the Stock Exchange," and on another passes into true dialect. Dialects, similarly, pass into foreign languages. Scientific terminology passes on one side into purely foreign words, on another it blends with the technical vocabulary of art and manufactures. It is not possible to fix the points at which the "English Language" stops, along any of these diverging lines.—OED, I, xxvii, note. (Quoted by permission of the Oxford University Press.)

### Desk Dictionary Words Quiz

Most of the questions below are based on the material about current desk dictionaries in Chapter 4. A few questions are about words in Chapters 1, 2, and 3.

1. One who compiles a dictionary is called a _____.
2. An _____ word is one found only in older English literature but occasionally used in a special context.
3. A _____ word is used only in certain districts or regions; it is not in nationwide use.
4. A _____ is one of two or more words spelled the same but differing in sound or meaning.
5. The size and arrangement of letters on a page is known as the _____.
6. Definitions that are compact and to the point may be called _____.
7. Distinguishing the fine shades of meaning between a word and other words close to it in meaning is called _____ of synonyms.
8. The Fowlers in their *Pocket Dictionary of Current English* compare "army officers" with "other regular solids." Placing two items side by side in this fashion is called _____.
9. What word is defined as "the special vocabulary of members of a profession or cult; a term used, often in a derogatory sense, by those to whom such vocabulary is unintelligible"?
10. Fortune-telling with a dictionary is a form of _____.
11. A word that means "satiric verse" is _____.
12. A note added to a script for extra comment is an _____.
13. A coarse word, generally not used in polite society, is a _____.
14. Daniel Jones, who is in his eighties, is an _____.
15. An expert in the subject of speech sounds is called a _____.
16. Cases of alleged extrasensory perception are studied by those interested in the science of _____.
17. A dictionary that contains information on a wide variety of subjects in addition to definitions is said to be _____.
18. *Webster's Seventh New Collegiate Dictionary* is an _____ of *Webster's Third New International*.
19. What word is defined as "poisoning from bacterially spoiled foods"?
20. What is the term for that branch of military art covering transport and supply?
21. What is the plural form of a word that means "a standard upon which to base a judgment"?
22. A fantastic notion is a _____.

23. A beginner in a new discipline is a "tyro." He may also be called a _____.
24. A person who appears to be saying two things at once without actually saying either is guilty of _____.
25. Something that is unwholesome, offensive, disgusting, smelly could be called _____.
26. What is a "word of opposite meaning"?
27. What's a highfalutin synonym for "cave-dweller"?
28. A_____ agreement to a proposition means that it will be subject to certain conditions not yet fulfilled or clarified.
29. Writing that is clear, logical, easy to understand has the quality of _____.
30. A word spelled and pronounced like another word but differing in meaning is a _____.

## WORD LIST

| | | | |
|---|---|---|---|
| botulism | criticism | lexicographer | perspicacity |
| acronym | succinct | annotation | vulgarism |
| abstract | divination | equivocation | phonetician |
| noisome | abridgment | hallucination | discrimination |
| toxicity | etymological | troglodyte | dialectical |
| typology | colloquial | primitive | typography |
| lexicographical | asseveration | tendentious | encyclopedic |
| antonym | compendium | perspicuity | homonym |
| psychosomatics | neophyte | necromancy | parapsychology |
| archaic | tentative | gobbledygook | semanticist |
| chimera | homograph | jargon | homophone |
| neologist | pasquinade | octoroon | logistics |
| random-tandem | passacaglia | parody | anachronistic |
| cryptic | obsolete | octogenarian | septuagenarian |
| synonym | criteria | juxtaposition | matériel |

## ANSWERS

1. lexicographer
2. archaic
3. dialectical
4. homograph
5. typography
6. succinct
7. discrimination
8. juxtaposition
9. jargon
10. divination
11. pasquinade
12. annotation
13. vulgarism
14. octogenarian
15. phonetician
16. parapsychology
17. encyclopedic
18. abridgment
19. botulism
20. logistics
21. criteria
22. chimera
23. neophyte
24. equivocation
25. noisome
26. antonym
27. troglodyte
28. tentative
29. perspicuity
30. homonym

30 right—Ph.D. in lexicography
27–29 right—You know your dictionaries.
23–26 right—You've done your homework
18–22 right—Just ahead of the pack
12–17 right—Still around the 50th percentile
Under 12 right—Time's a-wasting

SCORE: _____

# 5 ~

## How to Analyze Words in Print

~~~ There are 450,000 entries in *Webster's Third Unabridged* —words of every class and description—standard, substandard, non-standard,[1] slang, archaic, obsolete, dialectical, technical, etc. Webster's editors collected 10,000,000 citation slips, with information about how words were used by writers, well-known personalities, ETHNIC and regional groups, special groups like musicians and underworld characters, and the general public. Then they made their judgments about whether the word should be included, how it should be defined, and how it should be labeled.

Lexicographers are a patient lot; they spend years examining words in all their aspects, carefully tracing the linguistic background of a word and determining the variations of meaning that have arisen in the course of its history. They check to see which is the most commonly used meaning, the next most common meaning, and so on down to the least common, possibly archaic sense in which the word is or has been used.

But it remained for a psychologist to come up with the most novel approach to a word. In E. L. Thorndike's survey to see how often words turn up in print, his staff counted ten million words in books and magazines most widely read at grade, high school, and adult levels, to find out how often each word occurred (frequency) and in how many different kinds of material it appeared (range). Taking account of these two CRITERIA, they grouped words by thousands, from the thousand most commonly and widely found (1) and so on up to the twentieth thousand (20) containing mostly long, hard words used now and then in highbrow writing. According to this system, the *higher the frequency number* (1–20 and 20 plus) *the rarer the word.* Most of the words over ten thousand are above the vocabulary level

[1] Webster no longer uses the designations "colloquial," "informal," "vulgar," "illiterate," "erroneous." The new *Funk & Wagnalls Standard College Dictionary* (1963) has also dropped the "colloquial" label but uses "informal" and "illiterate." The terminology in a dictionary depends on its editors and their philosophy of word labeling.

of the average American. If you have been watching the less common (11-20) and the uncommon (20 plus) words in small capitals, and doing the Scoring Quizzes at the end of each chapter, you're on your way to adding 10,000 or more new words to your vocabulary.

The count was made only of words *in print*. So occasionally a word that frequently turns up in speeches or on the air may not be included, or it will have quite a high number because it is not often written. BOTCH, for example, is a word every farm boy knows and uses. But it seems to find its way into print rather rarely, maybe because it sounds slangy—though it is indicated as standard English in the dictionaries. When the New York *Herald Tribune* reported that "The Italian police seem really to have botched their job while President Kennedy was in Rome," this was one of the rare occurrences of the word in print.

There are not too many examples of words like "botch," words common in speech but infrequent in print, that are bracketed with more difficult terms in the Thorndike count. For the most part, the words in the lower brackets are easy, and the words in the higher thousands are hard, hence less apt to be familiar to the listener or reader with an average vocabulary.

*Van, substantial, perpetual, fluid,* and *novelty* are typical words in the fourth thousand, according to the Thorndike system. When you reach the ninth thousand, some of the words are tougher going: *similitude, conjugate, inscrutable, inert, magnanimous, malign, retinue.*

The words in the fourteenth thousand are distinctly not the familiar: OBDURATE, TURBID, VERNACULAR, FRUITION, MISAPPREHENSION, SYLLOGISM are a few. However, you will also find in this range TAXICAB, QUOTA, and SCRIPT—all words which everybody knows. Apparently they were not so often found in print when Thorndike made his count.

## FLAWS IN THE FINDINGS

Many words listed have come into wider use since the expanded count was first made in the 30's.[2] World War II and the Korean War have made a difference. Advances in science and TECHNOLOGY, new TERMINOLOGY in ECONOMICS and SOCIOLOGY have increased the

[2] In 1944 Thorndike and Lorge published *The Teacher's Word Book of 30,000 Words,* based on a newer count of 18,000,000 words in print. The numerical rating of the words in small capitals is taken from this book.

frequency of words in print like SEGREGATION, DISCRIMINATION, NUCLEAR (over 20 in the original count), IDEOLOGY, and RADIATION. Radio and television have shifted the word-SPECTRUM, making colloquial or informal language more important—and it's on this side that Thorndike's count is admittedly weakest. The movement to write as you speak, SPEARHEADED by Rudolph Flesch, has increased the frequency of informal words in print.

Some of the words in wider use have taken on specialized meanings —MEDIA, APPEASEMENT, RECESSION. And there are many strictly new terms from PSYCHIATRY, ELECTRONICS, ASTRONAUTICS, labor, and business: *tranquillizer, escalation, automation, bubblebath, mystique, laser, cybernetics, megalopolis, turbo-prop.*

### Try These Way-Out Words

Many of the words in the original count and the 1944 count are now seen less frequently in print. Without benefit of statistics, and purely on the basis of one man's fancy, here are some candidates picked from the list that could well be replaced. The picker knew only thirty-two of them. How many do you know?

| | | | | |
|---|---|---|---|---|
| TRIVET | FIEF | GROAT | probably a | SILESIA |
| FELLOE | FILLIP | GYVE | misprint) | SPLAY |
| FERRET | FINESSE | MESSALINE | PIMPERNEL | STANCHION |
| FERRULE | FITCH | MOIL | PLUMULE | STEAPSIN |
| DARNEL | FLAGON | MULLEIN | PURSUIVANT | STIPULE |
| DACE | FLITCH | JUSTLE | PYX | STOMA |
| COLE | FUNK | KIBE | RACEME | STOMATE |
| COLLOP | FURBELOW | LAPPET | RAVIN | TENDANCE |
| CARPEL | GALENA | LIBBARD | RIVE | THALLUS |
| AGARIC | GALLEON | LORN | ROOD | THRID |
| FRONTLET | GARBLE | LOUR | RUNNEL | THRUM |
| HATCHMENT | GHOUL | MARQUISETTE | SEBACEOUS | TRICOTINE |
| FUSTIAN | GIBBER | NARD | SELVAGE | TRYPSIN |
| ALEXANDRINE | GLOZE | PALID (*sic,* | SHENT | TUSSAH |
| FITTLE | | | | XYLEM |

### A ROUGH-AND-READY GAUGE

After making all discounts and allowances, however, Thorndike's grouping of words by thousands is still a good rough-and-ready guide in estimating the difficulty of a word. If it's in the first 10,000, the chances are the average reader will know it, though he may have to infer the meaning if it's used in a special, novel, or extended sense. If it's over ten, he may or may not know it.

To be sure, some of the words in the higher brackets are derived from shorter, easier words—which is lucky, because we can usually sight-read these, even if we haven't seen them before. But the bulk of the words above the 10,000-line are part of the learned vocabulary. Most of them are needed by anyone who wants to be a thoroughly literate reader or writer; and many of them are among the more expressive words in English.

For vocabulary-building, there is a question of practical interest involved. How many of these high-bracket words turn up per hundred thousand words you read?

To get down to cases, it is interesting to see how Thorndike's count applies in this respect to *Newsweek* and *Time,* which together run about a hundred thousand words a week.

In the main, *Newsweek* is written in the commonest 10,000 words in the language. In the last twenty years, however, more words in the upper brackets have been appearing in both *Time* and *Newsweek* as they cater to educated readers who want a deeper interpretation of the news than they can get in the daily newspapers or on television. The number of less common and uncommon words varies with the department and the kind of material. Neither *Time* nor *Newsweek* prescribes what kind of language to use, except that it should be bright and interesting and that the facts should be accurate. As in the case of *Variety,* if a writer shows a flair for words, he is given *carte blanche* to write as he pleases. You will note in the following *Newsweek* examples that the "Books," "Movies," and "Theater" sections are marked by a flowing, polysyllabic style. And since the language of many of the departments is informal, an occasional slang or coined word will appear, but these are rare.

### Have You a Middlebrow Vocabulary?

WORDS BEYOND THE COMMONEST 10,000 IN *Newsweek,* JULY 1, 1963

The number in parentheses after each word so marked indicates in which of Thorndike's thousands it occurs.
(20 plus) means beyond the 20,000 level.

(not in T) means not in Thorndike and Lorge's *The Teacher's Word Book of 30,000 Words*.

(tech.) technical term.

(inf.) means informal or colloquial, according to the consensus of current dictionary opinion.

(slang) means a word so designated by *Webster's Third Unabridged* (1961) or *Funk & Wagnalls Standard College Dictionary* (1963).

Check each word you can define in the various departments of *Newsweek*:

*The Periscope:*

SPATE (20 plus)
INFRINGEMENT (14)
JITTERY (20 plus)
SEGREGATION (14—but now in wider use)
INFRARED (20 plus)

TUNERS (tech.)
COOL (slang)
CONTROVERSIAL (16)
MYTHICAL (19)
CLARITY (20)
CONFRONTATION (not in T)

APARTHEID (not in T)
REACTOR (tech.)
JAMMING (a common word now having a special use in radio terminology)

"The Periscope" gives inside information and forecasts trends. It is right about 88 percent of the time, a high score for any prophet. The eight words over the 10,000 level indicate what is most in the news: the civil rights controversy, astronautics, the test-ban treaty, the United Nations, atomic energy, and politics. *Apartheid* is a borrowed word from South Africa. *Cool* is the only informal or slang term used. An absolute figure cannot be given for *confrontation*—but it is rare enough to be considered over the 10,000 level.

*National Affairs:*

STRICTURE (20 plus)
ELECTORATE (20 plus)
CONCILIATORY (15)
ACTIVIST (not in T)
BEMUSED (20 plus)
AVOWAL (14)
PARLIAMENTARY (12)
DISCRIMINATION (14—now in wider use)
DESEGREGATION (not in T)
CLOTURE (20 plus)
COMMITMENTS (20 plus)

INTEGRATION (20 plus)
SEPARATISM (20 plus)
BACKBITING (20 plus)
CALDRON (12)
MANEUVER (11)
DIVISIVENESS (not in T)
AGITATOR (11)
MUGGY (20 plus—unless the summers are hotter than they used to be)
FACADES (12)
MARKETABLE (20 plus)
OMNIBUS (12)

RABBLE-ROUSING (not in T)
INFLUX (14)
DISENFRANCHISED (20 plus)
MORATORIUM (20 plus)
IDEOLOGY (20 plus)
EXEMPTION (12)
BONA FIDE (20 plus)
MENTORS (20 plus)
FALLOUT (not in T)
PROPAGANDISTS (20 plus)
FISCAL (12)

| | | |
|---|---|---|
| INDOCTRINATE (20 plus) | UNDERMINE (12) | ELOQUENT (16) |
| DEFINITIVE (13) | COGNIZANCE (15) | SUCCUMBED (14) |
| AUTOMOTIVATED (coined—may be broadly considered an informal word) | MINIMIZED (15) | NAÏVETÉ (20 plus) |
| | MARITAL (19) | CAPABILITIES (11) |
| | LIAISON (15) | INSTANTANEOUS (20 plus) |
| | RATIONALIZATIONS (20 plus) | |
| ULTIMATELY (18) | | DEBRIS (11) |
| CANDOR (12) | BURDENSOME (13) | INGENUOUS (14) |
| CONDESCENSION (12) | VISIBILITY (20) | IDEALIST (18) |
| RANCOR (15) | MEDIAN (13) | EXPLICIT (15) |

"National Affairs" is one of the largest departments in *Newsweek,* hence the long list of less common words. The words used to report the news are themselves a key to the era we live in; *divisiveness, propagandists, rancor, discrimination, separatism, agitator* suggest the conflicts between various groups and ideologies. There are a host of 20-plus words in this section, an indication that *Newsweek* believes its readers have a better-than-average vocabulary. *Automotivated* is a rare instance of a coined word in *Newsweek*—a blend of meanings from *automotive* and *motivation.* Its writers, as well as those of *Time* and *Variety,* are all too human; they like occasional wordplay.

*Washington:*

| | | |
|---|---|---|
| POLEMICS (20 plus) | COERCE (11) | TACTICS (10) |
| MILITANCY (14) | COERCIVE (20 plus) | TACTICAL (20 plus) |
| INTERVENTION (12) | HEAT (slang) | IMMUNE (16) |
| | ALIENATE (11) | |

Kenneth Crawford tells the Washington story in a straightforword style. Two pairs of words—*coerce-coercive* and *tactics-tactical*—illustrate how a word may be more common as one part of speech than as another. The adjectives *coercive* and *tactical* are less common than the verb *coerce* and the noun *tactics.*

*International:*

| | | |
|---|---|---|
| CUMULATIVE (16) | used in diplomacy) | ESPIONAGE (18) |
| HIGHFALUTIN (inf.) | MANEUVERED (11) | KIBBUTZ (Israeli word) |
| OSTENSIBLY (20 plus) | BACCHANALIS (20 plus) | INTEGRATE (20 plus) |
| IDEOLOGICAL (20 plus) | VOYEURS (not in T) | STOCKPILE (not in T) |
| POLEMICS (20 plus) | PROTÉGÉE (17) | REDEPLOY (20 plus) |
| PUTATIVE (not in T) | VITUPERATION (20 plus) | DEVASTATION (14) |
| PLENUM (not in T) | EXACERBATE (20 plus) | IRONIC (13) |
| JAMMED (radio) | SCHIZOPHRENIC (not in T) | MARGINAL (13) |
| DÉTENTE (a borrowed word from French | | MANDATE (11) |
| | TACTICIAN (20 plus) | INTERIM (12) |

Two of the 20-plus words are part of a quotation from Tass, an example of the doubletalking DIALECTICAL exchanges between the Kremlin and China. "To publish the text [of China's attack on Russia]," said Tass, "would be to exacerbate the polemics." When the international news is reported, you'll frequently see words such as *ideological, mandate, détente,* and *stockpile. Highfalutin* (in the headline) is a bit of wordplay.

*The Americas:*

| | | |
|---|---|---|
| SPARSELY (15) | FACSIMILE (20 plus) | CONTROVERSIAL (16) |
| RAMSHACKLE (20 plus) | SNOWBALLING (not in | MONITORING (12) |
| DEVASTATION (14) | T) | HOAX (20 plus) |
| | INFILTRATION (20 plus) | |

Words such as *infiltration, devastation, controversial,* and *monitoring* suggest Cuba and the explosive situation in the Caribbean. *Snowball* is listed as 13 in Thorndike but evidently as a noun and not in its extended sense of "to increase, accumulate, expand, or multiply at a rapidly accelerating rate."

*Newsmakers:*

| | | |
|---|---|---|
| SOCIALITE (not in T— the blend word from *Time*) | (not in T—a bit of wordplay) | plus) |
| BOGUS (19) | DISCLAIMER (20 plus) | FLAMENCO (not in T) |
| CHORTLE (20 plus) | INCOGNITO (20 plus) | WELSHING (more word-play) |
| WOOSOME TWOSOME | CACOPHONY (not in T —but it should be 20 | BOGUS-POCUS (word-play) |

This section has more of the gossipy tone of a Winchell column. The informal style peppered with wordplay stems from the material —international amours, leisure moments of great ladies (Jacqueline Kennedy), newsworthy children (Caroline), and other feature events in the news. The caption-maker waxes poetic: "Froth for a Troth," "Lark in the Park," "Irish Mist" (about Playwright Brendan Behan, who left the hospital with "his tales wagging behind him"). *Chortle,* by the way, is a blend word from way back. Lewis Carroll dreamed it up in *Alice in Wonderland* when he combined *chuckle* and *snort.*

*Press:*

| | |
|---|---|
| PRIME MOVER (extended use of U.S. Army tech. phrase) | GOURMET (not in T) |
| JAZZ BUFFS (inf.) | EVOLVED (14) |
| | EMASCULATED (20 plus) |

94

This section deals with shop talk about newspapers and magazines. The style is breezier than you'll find in some of the other departments. There are fewer uncommon words.

*Religion:*

| | | |
|---|---|---|
| PONTIFICATE (20 plus) | CRAZY-QUILT (not in T) | form of high fidelity) |
| TONSURES (20 plus) | HIERARCHY (15) | OSTENSIBLY (20 plus) |
| COLONNADE (12) | AUTOCRATIC (15) | FORTHRIGHTNESS (20 |
| CONCLAVE (14) | PATRICIAN (14) | plus) |
| ARBITER (11) | SEMINARIAN (14) | COMPREHENSION (20 |
| JUBILATION (20 plus) | ATTACHÉ (20 plus) | plus) |
| TRADITIONALIST (not in | NUNCIATURE (not in T) | AUGURY (20 plus) |
| T) | APOSTOLATE (not in T) | DESICCATED (not in T— |
| ASCETIC (17) | AUSTERITY (14) | should be over 20) |
| DECIBEL (tech.) | CATACOMB (20 plus) | AMBIGUOUS (12) |
| ARCHDIOCESE (not in T) | BILLETED (12) | COORDINATION (15) |
| DEFERENTIAL (15) | RENOVATED (13) | SWIRLED (11) |
| ENTOURAGE (20 plus) | CLEMENCY (12) | DISPIRITING (11) |
| ECUMENICAL (not in T) | HI-FI (inf.—shortened | TWIST (the dance) |

Many of the above terms belong to the language of special vocabularies—*seminarian, pontificate, archdiocese, ecumenical, nunciature.* Some of them apply particularly to the Catholic Church, which was very much in the news with the death of John XXIII and the ASCENSION of Paul VI to the papacy. The aura of solemnity that surrounds these words is COUNTERBALANCED, however, by the wordplayful tone of "A mighty whoop drowned the rest"; "Even Montini's personal traits make a crazy-quilt pattern"; ". . . the Pontiff's 10-year-old niece, Elisabetta . . . hailed his elevation by breaking into the twist." A word is borrowed from PHYSICS when "the crowd gave back the responses with a decibel force." The mixture of 20-plus words with homier expressions may derive from the humanity of Pope John XXIII, who gave a touch of warmth and simplicity to the somewhat aloof and intellectualized Church HIERARCHY.

*Space and the Atom:*

| | | |
|---|---|---|
| COSMONAUTS (not in T) | tronomy—20 plus) | JET JOCKEYS (horse- |
| TANDEM (20 plus) | LAMENTABLE (12) | play) |
| RENDEZVOUS (11) | THRUST (tech.) | IMPERIOUS (14) |
| PERIGEE (not in T— | ASTRONAUTS (not in T) | TEMPO (13) |
| tech. word from as- | WEIGHTLESSNESS (tech.) | INNATE (15) |

95

*Newsweek* regards space flight and atomic energy as important enough to deserve a section of their own, apart from the general "Science" section. New terms from astronautics are *weightlessness, thrust, astronauts,* and *cosmonauts.* Such words are clear in meaning to all readers; there is no attempt to mystify them with too technical language. But even astronautics has its gay, wordplay side for *Newsweek* writers, who speak of "jet jockeys" and quote Soviet press references to Valentina Tereshkova and Valery Bykovsky as the "Cosmic Couple."

*Education:*

| | | |
|---|---|---|
| INVOCATION (13) | EXEMPTIONS (13) | HACKLES (20 plus) |
| IRONY (12) | PERFUNCTORY (20 plus) | DICTUM (17) |
| GAINSAID (12) | DESEGREGATE (not in T) | INOCULATED (13) |
| DISSENTER (11) | MANDATORY (20 plus) | HUMBUG (15) |

In discussing the Supreme Court decision against school prayers, *Newsweek's* writer told a semidramatic story, comparing Justice Clark to "a Texas uncle kindly explaining why he is doing something that may seem puzzling." The story form built slowly, then dissolved into wordplay at the end: ". . . a high school . . . took the final step in separating church and state: it removed a praying mantis from its biology collection."

*Transition:*

| | |
|---|---|
| EUPHEMISM (20 plus) | COMMANDEERED (20 plus) |

"Transition" is *Newsweek's* column about names in the news: deaths, marriages, births, and ODDITIES. Apparently it takes few highbrow words to tell these stories of real life.

*Business Trends:*

| | | |
|---|---|---|
| EBULLIENT (not in T—should be 20 plus) | GRILL (12) | DISPARITIES (15) |
| | DEFICIT (16) | PORTFOLIO (11) |
| LIQUIDATION (18) | | INVENTORIES (11) |

Terms like liquidation, deficit, inventories, and portfolio (of stocks) are technical business terms (see Chapter 11) but are understandable to the average reader of *Newsweek.*

*Spotlight on Business:*

TAUT (18)
JUBILATION (20 plus)
AUTOMATE (not in T—
a new word from
technology)
AUTOMATION (the noun

form of automate)
DECENTRALIZATION (20
plus)
FRAGMENTIZED (20
plus)

FEATHERBEDDING (a
term from labor-
management rela-
tions)
ARBITRATORS (11)
SYNONYM (11)

*Automate* and *automation* (in *Webster's Third Unabridged* but not
in the *Second*) form a word cluster with *featherbedding* and *arbitrators.* They suggest technological unemployment, the threat of strikes
and possible government intervention. *Featherbedding* is an old word
that has given headaches to both labor and management; it will be
described at length in Chapter 11.

A recurring theme in *Newsweek* is the use of words like *jubilation:*
"The general jubilation [in Washington] over the steel settlement";
"From Washington . . . came *cries of* official *joy.*" In the previous
section, "automakers" were "ebullient" about the demand for new
cars. The reader gets the feeling that our business leaders and politicos are really little children at heart, ready to dance the twist when
they get past an economic HURDLE.

*Business Tides:*
PROGRESSION (18)
DISCRIMINATORY (not in T)

Henry Hazlitt's column is written in a serious vein, with no lapse
into LEVITY such as we've seen in other sections. Perhaps a discussion
of taxes is too grim for any wordplay. Most of the language is in the
under-10,000 bracket.

*Theater:*

IMPRESARIOS (20 plus)
DOUGHTY (13)
CORNCRIB (not in T)
INNOCUOUSNESS (15)
INGÉNUE (20 plus)

PHOENIXLIKE (13)
ORNATE (12)
APOGEE (20 plus—tech.
—astronomy)
SLOSHED (not in T)

ROISTERING (20 plus)
BEDEVILS (20 plus)
AFFIRMATION (15)
DARKLING (20 plus)
INCONGRUOUS (14)

Although there is no obvious stage lingo here, the writer takes off
on a flight of fancy wordplay in describing a summer theater:
"phoenixlike glow . . . a doughty set of battlers . . . . inevitably
spooked each Sunday driver who spied its mansard turrets. . . ."

Notice the extended use of an astronomical term: "But that was the Old Vic at apogee. . . ." There is a faintly ARCHAIC air about some of the words used to describe Shakespeare's plays: *roistering, bedevils, darkling.*

## Medicine:

MEDICARE (a new blend word)    IMMUNE (16—tech.)

TRANSPLANTATION (20 plus)    ANTIBODY (20 plus—tech.)

Very few technical terms are used here, and they don't have to be explained to most readers.

## Sports:

This section is written so that even a non-sports enthusiast can understand it. *Newsweek* wants its readers to peruse each issue from cover to cover.

## Music:

RESTAURATEUR (borrowed from    ROCKABILLY (rock 'n' roll term)

French)

There is a welcome absence of technical jargon that can spoil music reviews for the non-musical reader in this department.

## Life and Leisure:

BEAT MOVEMENT (inf.)    SUBURBIA (not in T)    AMBIGUOUS (12)

BEAT (inf.)    PAD (slang)    HIPPER (slang)

HITCHED (inf.)

The style here is relaxed and informal. There is much wordplay used to describe police sirens. "In Paris they *honk*, in Berlin they *howl*. . . ." The U.S. has a *wailer*. Then there is the *yip-yip*. The other article is about the marriage of a beatnik. No over-10,000-level words here.

## Science:

PAYLOAD (tech.)    NOMINAL (12)    SOPHISTICATED (12)

AERODYNAMIC (tech.)    CHURNING (12)    TURBULENT (tech.)

SUPERSONIC (tech.)    FRICTION DRAG (tech.)

There are, of necessity, more technical terms in this section than you'll find elsewhere in the magazine. Try to find synonyms to replace them and you will realize that technical writing, even though meant for the general reader, requires a good many special words. They are carefully explained by the use of similes: ". . . 'friction drag,' which is akin to the churning of a wave across a beach . . ."; "The wings on the X-21A have hundreds of long, thin, slots cut along their length, like pinstripes on a man's suit."

## Art:

| | | |
|---|---|---|
| SQUALID (15) | SURREALISM (not in T) | METICULOUSLY (20 plus) |
| PARAPHERNALIA (19) | PREOCCUPATIONS (20 plus) | COMPLACENCY (12) |
| AUTHENTICITY (15) | REPERTORY (20 plus) | DELECTABLE (12) |
| SHUNTING (15) | SATURATED (11) | STOLID (17) |
| TEPID (12) | FLUOROSCOPE (not in T) | CONFAB (shortened form of confabula- |
| RECOUPMENT (20 plus) | EXPLICITLY (15) | tion—20 plus) |
| BOURGEOIS (12) | NOSTALGIA (20 plus) | EXORCISE (20 plus) |
| IMAGERY (11) | METEOROLOGISTS (20 plus) | |
| SYMBOLIC (18) | | |

Evidently the art CONNOISSEURS who read this section have close to 20-plus vocabularies and can follow such highfalutin wordplay as "symbolic fluoroscope," "landscape becomes mindscape," and "the squalid paraphernalia of neglected genius." Since the writer is describing a surrealist painting, he may be excused for his LINGUISTIC ABSTRACTIONISM.

## Movies:

| | | |
|---|---|---|
| MYTHICAL (19) | IRRELEVANT (15) | MAWKISHNESS (20 plus) |
| BUMBLED (Thorndike missed this one) | EXOTIC (14) | INDECOROUSLY (20 plus) |
| | AUSPICIOUS (11) | IDEOLOGICAL (20 plus) |
| OENOLOGICAL (too rare even for Thorndike) | CAR-NAPPERS (coined) | DEFTNESS (17) |
| | TRITENESS (16) | SLUDGE (20 plus) |

The style of this section is lively and LITERATE. The sudden *thrust* of "oenological"[3] ("Professor Kokintz . . . will not confine himself to his oenological investigations. . . .") is a form of polysyllabic wordplay. *Ideological* (a 20-plus word in Thorndike's day) seems to be a word-of-all-work in areas other than politics and diplomacy. Here the writer calls a soldier in a movie "an ideological mascot." Familiarity with an uncommon word enables one to use it not only in its diction-

[3] *Webster's Third Unabridged* lists it as an adjectival form of *oenology*, a variation of *enology*—"science that treats of wine and making wine."

ary sense but in many extended senses. The writer of this section moves easily in the rarefied atmosphere of 20-plus words.

The caption-writers of *Newsweek*, it should be noted, are ADDICTED to ALLITERATION. Heading up the movie articles are "Lunar Lunacy," "Sweet Sadness," and "Sellers Straight." The wordplay caption over an article about a Japanese rock 'n' roll singer is "Rising Son." You'll find an ANTONYMISM in "Ads Subtracted." An item about an attorney named Gerdes is boldfaced "Gerdes for the Battle." Whatever restraint the writers show in their yearning for wordplay is tossed overboard when the headlines are written.

*Books:*

EQUANIMITY (16)  
BALEFUL (15)  
ADULATION (14)  
PREDATORILY (15)  
SONAR (tech.)  
NARCISSISTIC (12)  
DETERMINISTS (20 plus)  
FLORID (14)  
BIZARRE (17)  
EBULLIENT (not in T)  

GENEALOGICAL (20 plus)  
EXISTENTIALIST (not in Thorndike's time)  
ACIDULOUS (20 plus)  
PROTEAN (not in T)  
SUMMARY (12)  
EXPOSTULATING (13)  
FORENSIC (20 plus)  

DURANCE VILE (borrowed from Latin)  
VOLUNTARIST (not in T but 20 plus)  
CENTRIFUGAL (13)  
SEMANTICS (post-Thorndike)  
MISCELLANY (12)  
ENTHRALLING (14)  
SCHISM (14)  

Once again we meet *ebullient* in a book review: ". . . the ebullient background of Tudor England." Its closest relative in Thorndike is *ebullition,* which is at the 16,000 level. Some magazines and writers are fond of using certain words; by seeing the word in several different contexts in the same issue, you'll have a pretty good idea what it means when you put down the magazine. The "Books" section of *Newsweek* is a good one to browse around in if you want to add to your stock of uncommon words.

*Perspective:*

PERIPHERY (20 plus)  
BASTIONS (14)  

AMORPHOUS (18)  
IRREPARABLE (15)  

Raymond Moley is a sober observer of the political scene who does not indulge in wordplay. There is a sprinkling of words above the 10,000 level but no slang or informal language.

*Emmet John Hughes:*

DILEMMA (13)  
PERFUNCTORY (20 plus)  
INALIENABLE (16)  

COERCION (16)  
INERADICABLE (20 plus)  
NONCONFORMIST (14)  
INTRINSIC (12)  

JUDICIARY (16)  
IRONY (12)  
CHAPLAINCY (20 plus)

Columnist Hughes brings his own literate style and knowledge of politics to his commentary in *Newsweek*. There are more uncommon words than in other *Newsweek* departments.

*Top of the Week:*

ASCETIC (17)　　　　MILITANT (14)　　　　PROFILE (12)

This department SUMMARIZES the outstanding news events of the week and whets the reader's appetite for the articles that follow.

## ANSWERS

*The Periscope:*

spate—sudden outburst
infringement—trespass on a right or privilege
jittery—jumpy
segregation—separation of racial groups
infrared—invisible rays beyond the red of the spectrum
tuners—tuning device on radio or television receiver
cool—unemotional

controversial—debatable
mythical—imaginary
clarity—clearness of thought and expression
confrontation—face-to-face meeting
apartheid—racial segregation
reactor—machine for generation and control of atomic energy
jamming—electronic interference with radio broadcast

*National Affairs:*

stricture—something that limits
electorate—body of voters
conciliatory—tending to please and win over
activist—one who is active in a cause
bemused—bewildered, stupefied
avowal—open declaration
parliamentary—pertaining to rules of governing bodies
discrimination—bias
desegregation—elimination of racial segregation
cloture—limitation of debate
commitments—pledges to future action
integration—bringing racial groups together as equals

separatism—belief in segregation of races
backbiting—knifing in the back
caldron—mixture of seething elements
maneuver—strategic action
divisiveness—dissension
agitator—one who incites
muggy—hot and humid
facades—false or artificial fronts
marketable—saleable
omnibus—pertaining to a collection of miscellaneous items
rabble-rousing—inciting crowds by appealing to emotions of hate and fear
influx—a flowing in

disenfranchised—deprived of a chartered right

moratorium—legal grace period

ideology—system of ideas for a political or social program

exemption—immunity from an obligation

bona fide—in good faith

mentors—teachers

fallout—radioactive particles

propagandists—persuaders

fiscal—financial

indoctrinate—to teach partisan dogmas

definitive—conclusive

automotivated—influenced by association with automobile industry

ultimately—finally

candor—forthright expression

condescension—patronizing attitude

rancor—deep-seated enmity

undermine—cut the ground from under

## Washington:

polemics—art of argumentation

militancy—fighting spirit

intervention—coming between

coerce—use pressure tactics on

coercive—intended to apply force or pressure tactics

## International:

cumulative—steadily increasing

highfalutin—highflown, pretentious

ostensibly—apparently

ideological—pertaining to the way ideas influence political and social actions

polemics—see Washington

putative—reputed, supposed

plenum—full or fullness

jammed—interfered with (radio)

détente—lessening of tension between nations

cognizance—awareness

minimized—cut down to smallest degree in size and importance

marital—pertaining to marriage

liaison—close contact

rationalizations—plausible but inaccurate explanations for one's conduct

burdensome—imposing a hardship

visibility—possibility of being seen

median—middle

eloquent—vividly expressive

succumbed—yielded

naïveté—artless simplicity

capabilities—latent abilities that can be developed

instantaneous—immediate

debris—fragments resulting from destruction

ingenuous—naïvely frank

idealist—one who believes in high standards

explicit—clearly expressed

heat—pressure (slang)

alienate—to cause estrangement

tactics—art of maneuvering

tactical—pertaining to tactics

immune—exempt; protected

maneuvered—see "maneuver" above

bacchanalis—orgy

voyeurs—peeping Toms

protégée—career girl under the protecting wing of a patron

vituperation—bitter condemnation

exacerbate—aggravate; irritate

schizophrenic—withdrawn from reality

tactician—an "operator"

espionage—spying

kibbutz—Israeli collective farm
integrate—to make whole
stockpile—storage of essential materials
redeploy—transfer
devastation—destruction

*The Americas:*
sparsely—meagerly
ramshackle—tumbledown
devastation—destruction
facsimile—exact copy
snowballing—rapid increase and accumulation
infiltration—in a military sense, to

*Newsmakers:*
socialite—socially prominent person
bogus—counterfeit
chortle—chuckle
woosome twosome—lovers
disclaimer—denial of claim
incognito—disguised

*Press:*
prime mover—original cause or force
jazz buffs—jazz fans

*Religion:*
pontificate—pontiff's term of office
tonsures—shaven patches on heads of clerics
colonnade—row of columns
conclave—private meeting or assembly
arbiter—judge
jubilation—rejoicing
traditionalist—one who believes in established customs
ascetic—austere in living
decibel—unit of sound measurement
archdiocese—archbishop's area of ecclesiastical authority

ironic—having a meaning contrary to what is expressed
marginal—just getting by (business)
mandate—authoritative command
interim—intervening period

filter unobtrusively through enemy lines
controversial—see *The Periscope*
monitoring—observing something for a special purpose
hoax—deception

cacophony—dissonance
flamenco—spirited style of Spanish dance
welshing—cheating by avoiding payment
bogus-pocus—phoney boloney

gourmet—good judge of food and drink
evolved—developed
emasculated—deprived of virility

deferential—respectful
entourage—group of attendants or followers
ecumenical—universal in scope, particularly applied to the church
crazy-quilt—patchwork
hierarchy—higher echelons
autocratic—absolute
patrician—aristocratic
seminarian—clergyman-in-training
attaché—diplomat
nunciature—nuncio's term of office
apostolate—office of the Pope
austerity—severity of outlook

catacomb—underground burial place
billeted—ordered to lodge and feed troops
renovated—made over
clemency—mercy
hi-fi—high fidelity sound equipment
ostensibly—apparently
forthrightness—directness
comprehension—understanding

augury—omen
desiccated—dried up
ambiguous—unclear
coordination—integrated action
swirled—whirled
dispiriting—discouraging
twist—popular American dance marked by vigorous vibration of torso

## Space and the Atom:
cosmonauts—space travelers
tandem—group of two or more, one following the other
rendezvous—meeting place
perigee—satellite's nearest point to earth
lamentable—regrettable
thrust—driving force

astronauts—space travelers
weightlessness—state of lacking gravitational pull
jet jockeys—airplane pilots
imperious—arrogant
tempo—rate of movement
innate—inborn

## Education:
invocation—opening prayer
irony—see *International*
gainsaid—denied
dissenter—one who disagrees with the majority
exemptions—amounts allowed as deductions from gross income
perfunctory—in a mechanical manner

desegregate—to eliminate segregation
mandatory—obligatory
hackles—hairs on back of dog's neck that rise in anger (generally used in a figurative sense)
dictum—authoritative statement
inoculated—mentally prepared
humbug—hogwash

## Transition:
euphemism—see page 188

commandeered—seized for military or public use

## Business Trends:
ebullient—joyful
liquidation—abolishment
grill—to cross-examine
deficit—loss

disparities—inequalities
portfolio—list of stocks and bonds
inventories—goods on hand

## Spotlight on Business:
taut—pulled tight
jubilation—rejoicing

automate—to mechanize
automation—see page 300

decentralization—dispersal from a center to several points

fragmentized—broken off

featherbedding—see page 300

*Business Tides:*

progression—sequence or series (applied here to graduated income tax)

*Theater:*

impresarios—entertainment managers

doughty—brave and bold

corncrib—crib for storing corn

innocuousness—state of being harmless

ingénue—young actress

phoenixlike—immortal

ornate—very fancy

*Medicine:*

medicare—see page 16

transplantation—transference of portion of tissue to another part of body or to another individual

*Music:*

restaurateur—proprietor of restaurant

*Life and Leisure:*

beat movement—cult of the beatniks

beat—hipster

suburbia—residential outskirts of city

*Science:*

payload—warhead or cargo of missiles

aerodynamics—science that studies the interaction between air and bodies in motion

supersonic—beyond range of human hearing

arbitrators—those chosen to decide disputes

synonym—word having nearly the same meaning as another word

discriminatory—used here as "discrimination" against persons in high income bracket

apogee—culmination

sloshed—splashed

roistering—carousing

bedevils—drives to distraction

affirmation—positive assertion

darkling—belonging to night or darkness

incongruous—out of place

immune—see *Washington*

antibody—infection-resisting protein produced in the body

rockabilly—style of popular music

pad—apartment

hitched—married

ambiguous—not clear

hipper—sharper

nominal—insignificant

churning—continuous agitation

sophisticated—worldly-wise

turbulent—tumultuous

friction drag—wind resistance caused by airplane in flight

### Art:

squalid—wretched
paraphernalia—personal belongings
authenticity—validity
shunting—turning aside
tepid—lukewarm
recoupment—recovery of losses
bourgeois—middle class
imagery—creation of mental images
symbolic—pertaining to an idea or object that stands for something else
surrealism—artistic expression through dreamlike images
preoccupations—engrossing interests

repertory—literally, a collection (a repertory theater presents several plays in one season)
saturated—filled to capacity
fluoroscope—x-ray instrument
explicitly—clearly
nostalgia—wistful yearning
meteorologists—weather watchers
meticulously—scrupulously attentive to detail
complacency—self-satisfaction
delectable—pleasing
stolid—impassive
confab—chat
exorcise—expel evil spirit

### Movies:

mythical—see *The Periscope*
bumbled—botched
oenological—pertaining to wine making
irrelevant—not applicable
exotic—fascinating, foreign
auspicious—having a favorable aura
car-nappers—auto thieves

triteness—staleness
mawkishness—overdone sentimentality
indecorously—improperly
ideological—see *International*
deftness—skill in manipulation
sludge—muddy deposit

### Books:

equanimity—calmness of mind
baleful—deadly
adulation—adoration
predatorily—in a plundering manner
sonar—device that detects submerged object by sound waves
narcissistic—excessively self-regarding
determinists—those who believe there is no free will in human actions
florid—flowery in style
bizarre—grotesque
ebullient—see *Business Trends*
genealogical—pertaining to family tree

existentialist—pertaining to philosophy expressing the importance of human actions
acidulous—caustic in taste or manner
protean—able to assume many roles
summary—giving a condensed version
expostulating—earnestly protesting
forensic—rhetorical
durance vile—imprisonment
voluntarist—believer in the dominance of free will in human experience
centrifugal—moving away from the center
semantics—study of how people

react to word meanings
miscellany—assortment
enthralling—captivating

schism—division within a religious
group

*Perspective:*
periphery—external boundary line
of an area
bastions—bulwarks

amorphous—shapeless
irreparable—beyond repair

*Emmet John Hughes:*
dilemma—problem involving two
equally unsatisfactory choices
perfunctory—in a mechanical manner
inalienable—incapable of being
taken away (as an "inalienable
right")
coercion—see "coerce" or "coercive" above

ineradicable—impossible to destroy
nonconformist—social or intellectual rebel
intrinsic—essential
judiciary—pertaining to courts of
law
irony—see *International*
chaplaincy—chaplain's office

*Top of the Week:*
ascetic—austere in living
militant—combative

profile—outline

Run back through the *Newsweek* word list and count the number
you checked which you could define, including the words not in Thorndike. Multiple this figure by 30, add 10,000 to it, and you'll have a
rough and ready measure of your total vocabulary up to this page.


### TIME-TICS

*Time* has always prided itself on a style at once colloquial
and condensed. Its present managing editor stresses "brevity and
brightness." Brevity, as we have seen in the case of *Variety's* clipped
forms, is part of our fast-moving American scene. *Time's* blend words
(*cinemagnate, musicomedienne, socialite*) had as their object space-
saving as well as cleverness, but the magazine is gradually getting
away from the "cuteness" of this style of writing. Although *Time*
uses fewer blend words than it did a generation ago, it still coins

words, again with brevity and brightness as the object. A word such as "credit-cardmanship," for example, packs a wealth of social commentary into one word and adds ZEST to the writing.

*Time* is not going conservative. It still TITILLATES the reader with "poules," "grandes cocottes," and "funmaster-in-chief." It scoffs at the movie "Cleopatra" with such comments as "Burton staggers around looking ghastly and spouting IRRELEVANCE." It ribs Hollywood PREMIÈRES: "10,000 rubberneckers milled on the MACADAM . . . smiles popping like flashbulbs . . . scarlet letters volted with excitement . . ." But aside from occasional pen-pricking social criticism, the magazine is not as flippant as it was a number of years ago when one of its writers called Mayor LaGuardia STEATOPYGOUS (duck bottomed).

A close reading of *Time* (as of *Newsweek*) will show not one but several styles of writing, depending on the department of news. And the editors aren't afraid to use learned words when they need to, e.g., in reviewing a critical work on Dylan Thomas or a volume by Toynbee. They're equally bold in tackling the jargon of science and technology and do a good job of translating it.

*Time* editors believe in keeping the reader on the jump, though perhaps they wouldn't go quite as far as the advertising agency head who used to greet his staff every morning with the slogan, "Boys, hit 'em in the eye, nose, and throat."

*Time* has a great deal to offer the student of vocabulary. Anybody who can do a BREAKDOWN of its DICTION can be sure he's going pretty well above the 10,000-word range. If he reads each issue from cover to cover, he's on his way up to Cloud Nine—above the 20-plus level.

### Have You a Highbrow Vocabulary?

This is a tougher test than the one you just took; we're going to include only the words above the 20,000 level. This doesn't mean that *Time* is more highbrow than *Newsweek*, but we'll assume you've sharpened up on the less common words in the *Newsweek* test and you're ready for the region inhabited by the Ph.D's. You're headed there eventually, so you might as well get a whiff of the air they breathe. The following words are taken from the June 21, 1963, issue of *Time*:

108

## The Nation:
RAUCOUS
CORTEGE
IMPINGE
FARCICAL
FRAGMENTED
COMPENSATORY

## Defense:
STUBBY
ATTACHÉ

## Labor:
DISSIDENTS

## The Congress:
CANTANKEROUS

## Elections:
INCLUSION
ANACHRONISM
INORDINATE
RIGMAROLE
ABERRATIONS
GERRYMANDER

## The World:
SACROSANCT
BAWD (you
   should know
   this one)
DISGRUNTLED
CERTITUDE
FORNICATION
SLEAZINESS

PUNGENCY
MASSEUSES
PREEMPTED
PIROGUES
PROMISCUITY
PORNOGRAPHY
STRUMPETRY
TANDEM
TREK
ETHNIC
NIRVANA
SQUALOR

## People:
ANEMIA
TÊTE-À-TÊTE

## The Hemisphere:
TERRORISTS
TRUNCATED
ARCHEOLOGISTS
OBSIDIAN

## Medicine:
LEATHERY
CUTANEOUS
FADDIST
METABOLIC

## The Press:
OBSCENITY
CAPTION
TURGID
FRILLY
CLIENTELE

CRUSTY
APOCRYPHAL

## Music:
CREDO
MATZOTH
MYOPIC

## Science:
ANTIMONY
INFRARED
ELECTROSTATIC

## Modern Living:
KIOSK
CANTILEVER
INEPT
ARMADILLO

## U.S. Business:
DISBURSEMENT
BEFUDDLED
NUANCES

## World Business:
STRATEGICALLY
LITERATE
ATTACHÉ

## Cinema:
TRIUMVIRATE
ASP
ECSTATICALLY
RAFFISHLY
CANTILEVERED
FLAMBOYANT
PIMP

PRURIENCE
FOPPISH
FATUOUS
DROLLERY
LAMPOON

## Books:
ESTHETIC
IDYLLIC
POLARITIES
HUMANISTIC
EVOCATION
GRUBBY
FRAGMENTARY
SPATE

## Education:
DOCTORATE
ELITE
ARBITRARILY

## Kudos:
ECCLESIOLOGY
COHESIVENESS

## Art:
PASTEL
PROTAGONIST
SUFFUSION

## Religion:
ONTOLOGICAL
HISTORIOGRAPHY
EXTRAPOLATION
EXISTENTIALIST
HUMANIST

## ANSWERS

## The Nation:
raucous—harsh-sounding
cortege—train of attendants
impinge—to come into close contact
farcical—pertaining to exaggerated
comedy
fragmented—broken up
compensatory—serving to make up
for a loss

*Defense:*
stubby—stocky

attaché—see *Religion* (*Newsweek*)

*Labor:*
dissidents—dissenters

*The Congress:*
cantankerous—cranky

*Elections:*
inclusion—something contained within something else
anachronism—something that is out of its time
inordinate—excessive
rigmarole—incoherent talk

aberrations—deviations from the norm
gerrymander—to juggle election districts for political advantage (see page 302 )

*The World:*
sacrosanct—sacred
bawd—prostitute
disgruntled—grumpy
certitude—certainty
fornication—sexual intercourse not legally sanctioned by marriage
sleaziness—slackness
pungency—sharpness
masseuses—women whose work is massaging
preempted—taken over to the exclusion of others
pirogues—canoe-shaped boat

promiscuity—free-wheeling in choice of sex partners
pornography—pictures or writing intended to cause sexual excitement
strumpetry—harlotry
tandem—single file
trek—slow journey
ethnic—pertaining to groups whose members have same racial traits and customs
nirvana—mystical state of oblivion
squalor—wretchedness

*People:*
anemia—deficiency of red blood cells

tête-à-tête—private personal conversation

*The Hemisphere:*
terrorists—those who use terror to enforce their will
truncated—cut short
archaeologists—those who study an-

cient cultures through objects buried in the earth
obsidian—black volcanic glass

*Medicine:*
leathery—having the appearance and flexibility of leather
cutaneous—pertaining to the skin
faddist—one given to fads

*The Press:*
obscenity—something offensive to decency
caption—heading
turgid—bombastic
frilly—showy
clientele—customers of a person or institution that renders professional service
crusty—harsh in appearance or manner
apocryphal—not genuine

*Music:*
credo—belief
matzoth—unleavened bread
myopic—shortsighted

*Science:*
antimony—metalloid element
infrared—see *The Periscope (Newsweek)*
electrostatic—pertaining to static electricity

*Modern Living:*
kiosk—small structure with open sides
cantilever—projecting beam anchored at one end
inept—clumsy
armadillo—burrowing animal with tough shell

*U.S. Business:*
disbursement—expenditure
befuddled—mixed up
nuances—subtle distinctions

*World Business:*
strategically—skillfully maneuvering
literate—able to read and write
attaché—see *Religion (Newsweek)*

*Cinema:*
triumvirate—trio
asp—small poisonous Egyptian snake
ecstatically—rapturously
raffishly—vulgarly
cantilevered—projected outward from a supporting base (used here with "bust")
flamboyant—showy
pimp—procurer
prurience—lewdness
foppish—vain
fatuous—foolish
drollery—whimsical humor
lampoon—satire

*Books:*

esthetic—artistic
idyllic—having a pastoral quality
polarities—direct opposites
humanistic—concerned with people
evocation—calling forth

grubby—crummy
fragmentary—incomplete, piecemeal
spate—see *The Periscope*

*Education:*

doctorate—degree earned by Ph.D.
elite—upper crust

arbitrarily—wilfully

*Kudos:*

ecclesiology—study of church art

cohesiveness—sticking together

*Art:*

pastel—soft, pale color
protagonist—leader; in literature,

one who forces the action
suffusion—state of spreading over

*Religion:*

ontological—of the nature of being
historiography—the writing of history
extrapolation—prediction based on

present knowledge
existentialist—see *Books* (*Newsweek*)
humanist—see *Books* (*Time*)

Now multiply your number of right answers by 200. If you had all of them right, your vocabulary is at least at the 20,000 level and beyond. In that case, you can put this book down and go fishing. Actually, this is the kind of test you should take after you've mastered the contents of this book; but it does no harm to probe the outer reaches of the vocabulary COSMOS.

It is no mere coincidence that the issues of *Time* and *Newsweek* just analyzed had the same number of 20-plus words. The better weekly news magazines are slanting their stories to those in the "educated class" who are not glued to the chairs in front of their television sets. For the student of vocabulary this is a hint to read his *Newsweek* and *Time* copies with SCHOLARLY devotion.

Does this mean that you should give away your television set or leave it permanently in the children's room? Not necessarily, unless you've done so since starting this book. Television has some surprises which we will discover in Chapter 6. Among the WELTER of lowbrow words that fill the airwaves, there are many middlebrow and a few choice highbrow ones for a DISCRIMINATING audience. When we've finished analyzing words-on-the-air, you'll know where to find them.

The first fifteen sentences that follow appeared in the July 1, 1963, issue of *Newsweek*, and the last fifteen in the June 21, 1963, issue of *Time*. In some cases the definition of the missing word is given in brackets.

1. There are the presumed determinists . . . giving an indeterminate beating to the self-styled _____ [believers in free will]. . . .
2. Although he [Montini] was the first prelate whom Pope John elevated to cardinal, the uncomplicated John apparently had _____ feelings about the intellectual Montini.
3. During recent years, when summer-theatre _____ [entertainment managers] were eying every unguarded corncrib, the Goodspeed Opera House . . . stood a-mouldering by the Connecticut River. . . .
4. To thwart the immune reaction, the patient is now receiving doses of . . . an anticancer drug which suppresses _____ production.
5. . . . this has narrowed down to the Oxford School's concentration on _____, or linguistic philosophy.
6. . . . the Chinese have responded with shrewd probing attacks on Soviet policies . . . public vituperation against Nikita S. Khrushchev, subtly calculated appeals to _____ [supposed] Stalinists in Russia and elsewhere. . . .
7. Yet, even President Kennedy seemed to take _____ of the Negro leadership split.
8. At the other extreme are the Black Muslims, the much-publicized but little supported nationalist sect that seeks Negro _____.
9. Nizer then proceeds to defend mass judgment with deft _____ [debating] skill.
10. Neither the House nor Senate can be _____; both can be impressed. Any suggestion of urgency will be called coercive by the Southern diehards. . . .
11. Once on the floor of the Senate, the bill probably will be amended to add that _____ [something that limits] but limiting it to large private establishments.
12. Thus _____ [deprived of a chartered right], Washington's Negroes—and whites—have never developed strong political leadership within the community.
13. Brown's request for a four-year _____ [legal grace period] on the death penalty was turned down in committee.
14. If a _____ [conclusive] clue to the cause of the disaster is ever to be found, it will have to come from the hull of the lost ship.

113

15. No one could foretell how long the decision to stop_____ Western broadcasts would remain in force. . . .

16. . . . Oregon's _____ [cranky] Democratic Senator Wayne Morse announced that he may stage a one-man talkathon of his own against the Administration's $4.5 billion foreign aid request.

17. When the _____ [dissenters] met, bullets whizzed warningly past their meeting place.

18. Kennedy's plan would perpetuate the system, but tidy it up a bit, getting rid of the rituals and forestalling such _____ [deviations] as the South's unpledged elector movement.

19. But it does call renewed attention to a widespread feeling that the U.S. electoral college system . . . is an _____.

20. His plan, says Mundt, would diminish "the present _____ [excessive] power of organized pressure groups."

21. . . . at last only a pair of massive, _____ [cut short] pyramids and a few mounds remained to mark the city's grave.

22. The martyr is usually considered a holy man so close to _____ [mystical state of oblivion] that he is unaffected by pain.

23. At the river landing there are only _____, crude dugout canoes, the one type of river ambulance Schweitzer will use.

24. "The visible _____ [pertaining to the skin] changes usually interpreted as aging," says the report, "are apparently due largely, if not entirely, to sunlight."

25. One possibly _____ [not genuine] story tells of a speech Markel gave to the *Time*'s Washington Bureau.

26. . . . circulation between levels will be by elevators, escalators or stairs enclosed in glass _____ [small structures with open sides].

27. . . . neo-Orthodoxy soon surrendered before Paul Tillich's _____ [of the nature of being] theology and the method of Scriptural study known as Form Criticism.

28. This oral tradition consisted almost exclusively of Jesus' sayings; thus his actions as recounted in the Gospels, and the geographical circumstances of his words . . . were almost exclusively the additions, based on _____ or invention, of a later tradition. . . .

29. Deprived of its link with the historical Jesus, Christianity might end up as some kind of _____ philosophy, of which Christ was little more than a mythological symbol.

30. Other theologians complain that in place of the _____ [concerned with people] Jesus produced by the old quest, the new quest is shaping an existentialist one.

## WORD LIST

| | | | |
|---|---|---|---|
| sentimental | generic | anachronism | antibody |
| truncated | voluntarists | amputated | existentialist |
| disparate | extension | pessimistic | ontological |
| separatists | nirvana | dilatory | apocryphal |
| nihilism | stoicism | epistemological | entrepreneurs |
| cloture | extrapolation | aberrations | determinists |
| cantilever | humanist | circulatory | ambivalent |
| nihilistic | epidermis | separatism | linguistics |
| stricture | cantankerous | evolutionary | putative |
| kiosks | coerced | kayaks | disenfranchised |
| cutaneous | neoclassicists | forensic | pirogues |
| incorrigible | cognizance | integration | ingenious |
| chartered | moratorium | debunking | enfranchised |
| commandeered | jamming | impresarios | dissidents |
| semantics | iconoclasts | definitive | inordinate |

## ANSWERS

| | | | |
|---|---|---|---|
| 1. voluntarists | 11. stricture | 21. truncated | |
| 2. ambivalent | 12. disenfranchised | 22. nirvana | |
| 3. impresarios | 13. moratorium | 23. pirogues | |
| 4. antibody | 14. definitive | 24. cutaneous | |
| 5. semantics | 15. jamming | 25. apocryphal | |
| 6. putative | 16. cantankerous | 26. kiosks | |
| 7. cognizance | 17. dissidents | 27. ontological | |
| 8. separatism | 18. aberrations | 28. extrapolation | |
| 9. forensic | 19. anachronism | 29. existentialist | |
| 10. coerced | 20. inordinate | 30. humanist | |

## SCORING KEY

30 right—Ph.D. in cultural history
27–29 right—Master's degree in current events
23–26 right—College graduate—well-read
18–22 right—Above average reader
12–17 right—Average reader
Under 12 right—Substandard reader

SCORE: _____

115

# 6

## How to Analyze Words on the Air

Do you know what FOSSICK means? LIANA? RANDEM? DROMOND? These words were puzzlers in a game on a BBC radio program; [1] the object of the game was to stump experts who had vocabularies on the Ph.D. level. But the experts would not be stumped. *Fossick* was correctly defined as "to mosey around looking for something of profit"—a term that goes back to gold mining. A *dromond* was a medieval ship of war. A *liana* is a tropical climbing plant. And *random* comes from *randem-tandem;* it describes three horses harnessed in single file.

These words occur only rarely in print; using them on a radio program was a form of wordplay. Both the studio audience and the home audience could enjoy the program and at the same time gain some insight into unusual words and their histories. And if it would send some of the listeners to an etymological dictionary to trace words back to their source, the program had more than mere entertainment value.

### DID YOUR EARS DECEIVE YOU?

If you think 20-plus words come only from highbrow radio programs or from the ERUDITE atmosphere of English literary circles, take a look at the following list of words that were on the airwaves. Do you remember hearing any of them? Did they come only from highfalutin highbrow programs? Can you define them?

| | | |
|---|---|---|
| CRYPTO-COMMUNIST | PERFUNCTORY | MICROCOSM |
| INORDINATELY | INTERNECINE | ETHNOLOGICAL |
| JUXTAPOSE | PAVAN | ANTIDISESTABLISH- |
| HETEROGENEITY | GENOCIDAL | MENTARIANISM |
| MEGALOPOLIS | PRISTINE | ABERRATIONS |
| AUTHORITARIAN | BACCHANALIS | EUTHANASIA |
| PHYLACTERIES | GRANDILOQUENT | HIPPOCRATIC |
| CEREBELLUM | IDYLLIC | NIHILISTIC |
| | HYGROMETER | |

[1] *My Word.*

116

These words are from American television and radio programs. Some of them were used wordplayfully. Arthur Godfrey, in commenting on a chess tournament, said RUEFULLY that he didn't have the CEREBELLUM needed by a champion chess player. Martha Raye, mentally transformed by the wave of a fairy's wand, correctly defined HYGROMETER as "an instrument for measuring the moisture content of the air." Jackie Gleason, about to compete in a quiz show, was taken down a peg when his wife on *The Honeymooners* asked him to define ANTIDISESTABLISHMENTARIANISM. This jawbreaker is always good for a laugh.

Moving up a notch from the lowbrow comedy programs, we find that David Brinkley referred humorously to his friendly rivalry with Walter Cronkite as INTERNECINE warfare. This word has been used to describe the conflict between North and South that tore the United States apart in the Civil War, a bloody battle between members of the same national family that prompted Abraham Lincoln to speak of "binding up the nation's wounds." *Internecine* may refer also to nonviolent conflict within a group related by family, geographical, artistic, or ideological ties. It is often used now as wordplay, in the sense that Brinkley used it.

The other words on the list, all 20-plus, were on middlebrow and highbrow programs. Some of them belong to special and technical vocabularies. PHYLACTERIES [2] are defined by *Webster's Seventh New Collegiate Dictionary* as "leather boxes containing slips inscribed with scriptural passages . . . worn on the left arm and forehead by Jewish men during morning weekday prayers." The problem of EUTHANASIA comes up in a dramatic series when a nurse allows her fiancé to die when she cannot bear to watch him suffer. A PAVAN is music written for a sixteenth-century dance.

Other words on the list belong to the general vocabulary of educated persons: INORDINATELY (more than usually); JUXTAPOSE (to place side by side); ABERRATIONS (deviations from the NORM); PERFUNCTORY (in a mechanical manner). These are capsule definitions; to get the true "feel" of words like these when you hear them on radio or television, try to grasp them in context just as you do the words in SMALL CAPITALS.

[2] From Paddy Chayefsky's television play *Holiday Song*.

# WORDPLAY ON THE AIR

Lowbrow scripts are those that appeal to a wide audience who want to relax and be entertained. It is rare, therefore, to find an uncommon word in a soap opera, western, or sports program. Comedy shows, however, often use such a word to get a laugh; it sticks out because it has wandered into the wrong social circle. But—like all wordplay—it's an effective way to add to your vocabulary.

Fred Allen once said to a visitor on his radio program, a man whose business it was to catch worms: "They tell me . . . you have made a profession of snaring the ELUSIVE (17) and legless INVERTEBRATE (13)." Surely in this context, *elusive* and *invertebrate* would not create a block for any listener. This is the old minstrel show technique, using long and flossy words for FARCICAL purposes. It is the mock ponderous style.

Wordplay on radio moved at a leisurely pace; on television the pace has been stepped up. The words go by faster, since this medium stresses movement and plot action in its comedy shows. But the less common and uncommon words do crop up in television wordplay, and their meaning is generally as clear in their context as Fred Allen's "legless invertebrate."

A television audience was startled and amused recently at hearing the following words on a comedy program: NIHILISTIC, GENERALIST, IRREPARABLE, HYPOTHESES, KINETIC, PATINA, BOURGEOISIE, and PERCENTILE. These words have the aura of the classroom. *Nihilistic* is a PHILOSOPHICAL term; it refers to the view that existence is meaningless. An *irreparable* situation is an ADVERSE one that cannot be changed; for example, an irreparable loss is one that cannot be made good. *Hypotheses* are conjectures or TENTATIVE assumptions that are made in science or other areas about the truth of a proposition. A *generalist* is a person who is VERSATILE in many fields. *Kinetic* is the adjectival form of KINETICS, a science that studies the way objects move as a result of the forces that act upon them. An interesting word that derives from it is TELEKINESIS, coined in the laboratories of Duke University, where experiments were conducted to see if mental energy could make dice come up with the desired "sevens" and "elevens."

*Patina* is the ornamental film that covers copper and bronze through the effect of oxidation. Of the desk dictionaries discussed in Chapter

4, only *Webster's Seventh New Collegiate Dictionary* gives the extended senses of patina: "a surface appearance of something grown beautiful esp. with age or use . . . an appearance or aura that is derived from association, habit, or established character."[3]

*Bourgeoisie* belongs to the terminology of communist dialectic; it refers to the cake-eating capitalists and their nonproductive SYCOPHANTS who neither toil nor spin but live off the labor of the "working class." According to Marx, members of this group get their COMEUPPANCE when the DOWNTRODDEN PROLETARIAT rises in wrathful vengeance. There have been revolutions of this kind, but somehow the "proletariat" gets lost during the shooting and winds up where it was before, often in a worse state of subjection.

*Percentile* is defined in *Webster's Seventh New Collegiate Dictionary* as "the value of the statistical variable that marks the boundary between any two consecutive intervals in a distribution of 100 intervals each containing one percent of the total population."[4] This is one instance where a dictionary definition is practically useless for the layman.

Actually, *percentile* is a term used in statistical measurements. For example, if you should answer every question correctly on your tests, you will be at the 100th percentile, which is Ph.D. level. If your score matches that of the average American, you are at the 50th percentile, or just above or below it. The "substandard" category is well under the 50th percentile. Most scores are in the "average" category, grouped around the 50th percentile, with fewer persons in each percentile group that is closer to 100 or 1. If we rated you according to this system, you would be in one of 100 percentile groups; for practical purposes you are placed in one of three categories in the tests.

All this may seem heavy going for a lowbrow comedy show about a teen-ager who goes to high school and uses expressions such as "kookie," "man!", "square," "buzz," and "crazy!" Through a mistake the girl is thought to be a mental genius by a smug "egghead," who spouts the uncommon words. The context in which the words are used, however, sheds some light on their meaning. Visual effects, such as an electric computer that goes haywire while it is testing the

[3] From *Webster's Seventh New Collegiate Dictionary*. (By permission. Copyright © 1963 by G. & C. Merriam Co., publishers of the Merriam-Webster Dictionaries.)
[4] From *Webster's Seventh New Collegiate Dictionary*. (By permission. Copyright © 1963 by G. & C. Merriam Co., publishers of the Merriam-Webster Dictionaries.)

girl, add horseplay to wordplay and bring the abstract terms down to earth, closer to the COMPREHENSION of the audience.

Can you add to your vocabulary by watching this kind of program? If you enjoy wordplay, the way-out words will make an impression on you; this is the passive way to learn. But you can also keep a notebook and dictionary handy; jot down the unusual words and look them up after the program is over. If the comedy situation is fresh in your mind, you can tie it in with the dictionary definition. Thereafter, keep watching for the word in new contexts, whether in print or on the air.

## WORKING WORDS ON THE AIR

Suppose, while you are in your study late at night looking up an uncommon word in the dictionary, a GENIE appears and presents you with Aladdin's lamp and the power to make one wish come true. You rub the lamp and ask to have a film projected on your wall, showing a scene that illustrates the uncommon word in action; accompanying the film is the voice that uses the word in an ILLUSTRATIVE sentence. Now you see and hear how a word behaves when it leaves the dictionary and goes out working.

This kind of AUDIOVISUAL instruction is available on your television screen. In a script from the OMNIBUS series, the narrator speaks:

> England's Lloyd George was
> humorously cavalier about the
> impossible task they faced.

The filmed scene and speech that follow DRAMATIZE the meaning of CAVALIER.

> LLOYD GEORGE:
> Please refresh my memory. Is it
> Upper Silesia or Lower Silesia
> we are giving away? [5]

Now you turn to *cavalier* in *Webster's Seventh New Collegiate Dictionary* and find that it means "given to offhand dismissal of important

[5] This example is taken from Erik Barnouw's *The Television Writer* (Hill & Wang, Inc.).

matters." Lloyd George is "humorously" cavalier. The full context of the word, a context possible only in a visual medium such as films and television, is made up of the words of the narrator, the words and vocal nuances of Lloyd George's speech, and the Prime Minister's gestures and facial expression.

A television program of this kind is called a DOCUMENTARY—the dramatization of actual events, with a running commentary by a narrator. As a key to contemporary life, television documentaries and news programs perform the same function as newspapers and magazines; the difference is that television gives words a larger context with the help of film clips. The subject matter of these programs is prepared by people in the word trades, and a good deal of the language used is composed of "working words" that belong to special areas such as politics, sociology, science, etc. When you hear a "working word" on the air, jot it down in your notebook and assign it to its special field.

Here are some words taken from a variety of news programs that belong to special vocabularies. Which of them could be used in other senses as well?

| | |
|---|---|
| LIAISON | politics |
| DESEGREGATION | civil rights |
| COALITION | international affairs |
| SPLICE | photography |
| PONTIFICATE | religion |
| ORBITING | astronautics |
| TRACKING | radar |
| HABEAS CORPUS | law |
| MICROWAVE | television |
| MICROFILM | photography |

In the following list there are twelve categories of words heard recently on television that belong to special and technical vocabularies. See if you can place them. Cover up the right-hand column while you are making your guesses; then check your answers.

| | | |
|---|---|---|
| 1. | HARPSICHORD | music |
| 2. | COMMON MARKET | economics |
| 3. | ECUMENICAL | religion |
| 4. | FREUDIAN | psychiatry |
| 5. | NEUROSURGEON | medicine |
| 6. | FISCAL | economics |
| 7. | COLLAPSIBLES | navigation |

| | |
|---|---|
| 8. ESCALATOR CLAUSE | labor |
| 9. TORTS | law |
| 10. DEVELOPER | photography |
| 11. EMBOLISM | medicine |
| 12. ETHNIC | sociology |
| 13. FELONY | law |
| 14. COUNTERPOINT | music |
| 15. COLONIALISM | international relations |
| 16. DEFICITS | economics |
| 17. STEAM WINCHES | navigation |
| 18. INTESTATE | law |

## LITERARY WORDS ON THE AIR

In addition to "working words" and wordplay, another kind of word is a frequent visitor on the airwaves, on both television and radio. Adaptations of plays, readings of poetry and prose, and discussions on literature are valuable sources for names from cultural history, both real and imaginary. Such names sometimes become the symbols for traits in human nature and are incorporated into the general vocabulary of educated persons. Hearing them on the air might stimulate you to investigate their backgrounds, if only to fill the gaps in your knowledge of literature.

It is not only the strictly highbrow programs that make reference to names of writers, titles of their books, and the characters they have created. The BBC program mentioned earlier, which makes a game out of springing unusual words, combines wordplay with erudition. Some of the words are so rare that they are impractical for ordinary use; but they often take the listener back to former times and to literary PERSONAGES. A JANEITE, for example, was described (in the British manner) as "Someone absolutely mad about the author Jane Austen." WERTHERISM was correctly defined as "morbid sentimentality," a quality ascribed to GOETHE's hero in the *Sorrows of Werther*.

Here is a list of words heard on the air recently that includes names of writers and fictitious characters, and titles of books, poems, and plays. Can you identify them?

| | |
|---|---|
| 1. Macbeth | 4. Iago |
| 2. Desdemona | 5. Dostoevsky |
| 3. Othello | 6. Tolstoy |

7. Minotaur
8. Aldous Huxley
9. George Orwell
10. Archibald MacLeish
11. Captain Ahab
12. Moby Dick
13. Endymion

14. Orpheus
15. Voltaire
16. Eudora Welty
17. Camelot
18. Christopher Marlowe
19. Peter Pan
20. Spengler

1. Chief character in Shakespeare's play *Macbeth*
2,3,4. Characters in Shakespeare's *Othello*
5,6. Russian novelists
7. Monster in Greek mythology
8,9. English novelists
10. American poet
11,12. Leading characters in Herman Melville's *Moby Dick*

13. Poem by John Keats
14. Character in Greek mythology
15. French writer
16. American novelist
17. Musical comedy
18. Elizabethan playwright
19. Play by James Barrie
20. German historian

Literature is part of cultural history, which also gives us many words that are clues to what has happened in science, philosophy, psychology, music, painting, and other areas of knowledge. Try this list of terms from cultural history, heard on a variety of radio and television programs ranging from lowbrow to highbrow.

1. Michelangelo
2. Van Dyke
3. Don Giovanni
4. Copernicus
5. Newton
6. Pericles
7. Leonardo da Vinci
8. Wanda Landowska
9. Archimedes
10. Buddhist

11. Scarlatti
12. Thomas Paine
13. Patrick Henry
14. Einstein
15. Parthenon
16. Ghengis Khan
17. Hippocratic oath
18. The Medicis
19. Machiavelli
20. Plato

1. Italian painter
2. Flemish painter
3. Opera by Mozart

4. Astronomer who said the earth revolved around the sun

5. Scientist who FORMULATED the theory of GRAVITATION
6. Greek statesman during the Golden Age of Greece
7. Italian painter and generalist
8. Harpsichordist
9. Greek mathematician
10. Follower of Buddhist religion
11. Composer
12. Patriot of Revolutionary days
13. Same

14. Scientist who formulated theory of relativity
15. Greek temple
16. Mongol conqueror
17. Referring to Hippocrates, the "Father of Medicine"
18. Family of Italian rulers during Renaissance
19. See page 253
20. Greek philosopher

## A "HYPOTHETICAL" CASE

How are you going to trap the less common and the uncommon words: the "working words" from special and technical vocabularies, the words from cultural history that fly by so quickly on your television programs? We suggested before that you keep a pencil and notebook in your hand and be ready to go into action. Often, however, it is not practical either during or after a program to start tracking down the meaning of a word. Even though you are making a game out of every opportunity to add to your vocabulary, your family may think you are flaunting your knowledge. Vocabulary building is, for the most part, a solitary occupation.

You might try the CUMULATIVE method of letting the word IMPINGE on your consciousness several times until you get the "feel" of it; then let the dictionary do the rest. Let's go back to the word *hypothesis*. You are having a discussion with a friend about whether it is better for children to be disciplined or indulged. Your friend says, "Let's take a hypothetical case," and he tells you about an imaginary child who receives a severe upbringing and becomes a mean and uncooperative adult. You look up *hypothetical* in *Webster's New World Dictionary*, which defines it as "based on, involving, or having the nature of, a hypothesis; assumed; supposed." Memory stirs; you recall that you heard *hypothesis* on the teen-ager comedy show. At the time you had an INKLING of what it meant, but you went out for a beer after the program and forgot about it.

The use of the word on the program, your friend's mention of *hypothetical*, and the dictionary definition have given you a deeper understanding of *hypothesis*. You mentally file the word for future

124

reference. Later you are watching another television program about the great English mathematician Sir Isaac Newton. An actor portraying Newton is shown on film conducting an experiment to test the rate of ACCELERATION of a falling object. The narrator says that Newton arrived at a "working hypothesis" that finally led to his theory of gravitation.

You think you understand the word now—almost, but not quite. Why does a "hypothesis" lead to a "theory"? Don't they mean the same thing? You recall something about "discrimination of synonyms" (see dictionary entries on pages 78–79); the *American College Dictionary* tells you that they have the common meaning of "an untested idea or opinion," but that a theory is a "more or less verified or established explanation accounting for known facts or phenomena," whereas a hypothesis is a "conjecture put forth as a possible explanation of certain phenomena . . . which serve as a basis of argument or experimentation by which to reach the truth." Now you know that "hypothesis" is "conjecture" and that "theory" is closer to the truth as being "more or less VERIFIED."

You begin to ask questions: Isn't Newton's theory of gravitation "verified" or "established"? How about Einstein's theory of RELATIVITY? You know that a "law" in science admits of no doubt; it is verified and established. In the *American College Dictionary's* discrimination of synonyms nothing is said about "law" except that it is an antonym. This gives you a clue; "hypothesis" and "theory" are not synonymous with "law"; they are word relatives.

Being a determined word detective, you examine the discrimination of synonyms in *Webster's Seventh New Collegiate Dictionary;* "hypothesis," "theory," and "law" are listed as synonyms. All three words suggest degrees of verification in science; "law" applies to a phenomenon in nature that is "invariable under the same conditions."

Now you're in pretty good shape; you're certain you know what "hypothesis" means, and in your zeal at finding out, you have insight into two other words that belong to the same CONCEPT. Your appetite is whetted for more; you turn to *Funk & Wagnalls Standard College Dictionary* and discover that three more terms are grouped in a cluster with "theory" and "hypothesis": SUPPOSITION, ASSUMPTION, and CONJECTURE. These are defined as propositions based on less certain data than are the first two terms. "Law" is missing from this cluster, but you already know that it applies to observations accepted by science as fact.

From this exploration into word meanings, you now know that it is possible to learn about a word by comparing it with other words that are close in meaning. (This subject will be expanded in Chapter 9).

## ANOTHER KIND OF WORD GAME

Did you get the aura of the word cluster built around "hypothesis"? It would be quite possible for all of these words to be part of the "working words" vocabulary of a television program on a scientific subject. On a program about Newton, for example, it might be explained that he started out with an "assumption" or "conjecture" about gravity, and after patient experimentation, developed his "hypothesis" and finally his "theory," which was later accepted as a "law" of nature.

Most programs have words that form a cluster and create an aura. We've devised a new kind of word game; you'll see several word clusters, each from a particular radio or television program. The "atmosphere" of the words should give you some idea about what type of program they come from—comedy, drama, news, etc. This is a tricky game, however, because some of the words may not seem related.

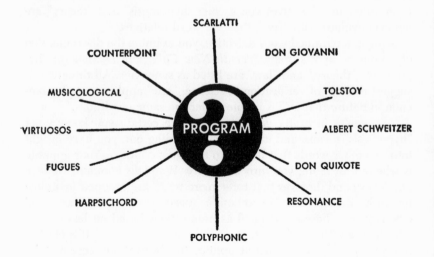

Most of the terms relate to music, of course; they were spoken by Agnes Moorehead on a program devoted to the REMINISCENCES of Wanda Landowska. The HARPSICHORD is a keyboard instrument, the FORERUNNER of the piano. MUSICOLOGICAL refers to research in the field of music (musicology). VIRTUOSOS are accomplished performers. COUNTERPOINT is the art of weaving CONCURRENT melodies into a composition; music of this kind is said to be POLYPHONIC (many-voiced). RESONANCE is the richness of echoing sound. SCARLATTI was a composer of the PIANOFORTE. DON GIOVANNI is the name of an opera written by MOZART.

So far, the word cluster is consistent. But how did the novelist Tolstoy and the humanitarian Schweitzer get into this musical circle? Schweitzer, in addition to his work as a doctor among the African tribes, is an accomplished musician. And Tolstoy was a lover of music; Mme. Landowska tells how ENRAPTURED he was when she performed for him.

Now try another cluster:

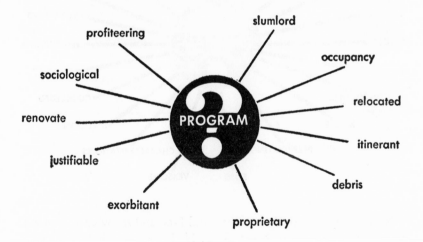

The aura of these words should not be difficult to figure out. They were heard on a documentary program called *Eye on Housing*, about the Harlem slums. *Slumlord* is a coined word that tells its own story. RENOVATE (13) is used often now with "building" or "apartment."

JUSTIFIABLE (14) is an abstract word involving a judgment. EXORBI-TANT (16) means "excessive" and applies to rent in this context. PROPRIETARY (17) refers to the rights of ownership and is a reference in the context to the ABSENTEE landlord. PROFITEERING (15) almost speaks for itself. OCCUPANCY (19) refers simply to the percentage of apartments rented. ITINERANT, a 20-plus word in Thorndike's count, now is in wider use in such combinations as "itinerant worker," "itin-erant population." Its greater frequency in print and on the air tells the story of a restless, MOBILE people.

This cluster may be more difficult to place:

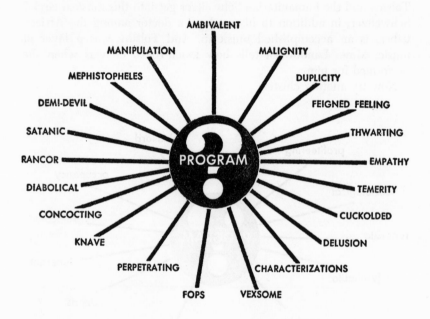

AMBIVALENT
MANIPULATION
MALIGNITY
MEPHISTOPHELES
DUPLICITY
DEMI-DEVIL
FEIGNED FEELING
SATANIC
THWARTING
RANCOR
PROGRAM
EMPATHY
DIABOLICAL
TEMERITY
CONCOCTING
CUCKOLDED
KNAVE
DELUSION
PERPETRATING
CHARACTERIZATIONS
FOPS
VEXSOME

Now add OTHELLO, DESDEMONA, and IAGO and see what you've got. If you didn't know anything about Shakespeare's play, you might make a guess as to its contents from the aura of this word cluster: MEPHISTOPHELES (20 plus—agent of the Devil); SATANIC (20 plus); DIABOLICAL (18—fiendish); DUPLICITY (17—double-dealing); MALIG-NITY (12—evil); MANIPULATION (15—skillful maneuvering); DEMI-DEVIL (not in Thorndike but it refers to Iago as one who is aping the Devil in his MACHINATIONS); CONCOCTING (13—used here in the sense of scheming); PERPETRATING (13—another word with the connotation of evildoing). These less common and uncommon words are tied in with the more common *knave* and *feigned feeling;* they describe Iago, the cunning protagonist of the play *Othello,* who by DEVIOUS manipulation of the other characters in the play, brings about the final tragedy: Othello, torn by his AMBIVALENT feelings of love and hate, murders Desdemona.

These are not words from the play itself. They are taken from a radio speech in which the character of Iago is discussed. Other words from the cluster—*fops* and *cuckolded*—have the air of the sixteenth century, although they are not yet labeled as archaic.

## INFORMAL WORDS ON THE AIR

Words in print and words on the air generally differ in style. Written material is for the most part formal in manner and uses more multisyllabic words of classical origin. Speech, even when Ph.D.s are involved, is more informal; unless a professor is hopelessly academic or ENMESHED in the toils of gobbledygook, he will throw in some slang and colloquial terms along with the uncommon and less common words.

Informal language, therefore, is not confined to sports and comedy programs. On a recent panel of professors, the words *crummy* and *guy* were INTERSPERSED with such top-level words as PATERNALISTIC, HETEROGENEITY, MEGALOPOLIS, RESTRUCTURING, and AUTHORITARIAN. These uncommon words were used in a discussion of city planning, and as such are a key to one aspect of our culture, the area of overcrowded and underfinanced cities. But there is no uncommon word that has quite the aura of "crummy." It would not appear in print in a SOCIOLOGICAL tract, but on the air a professor may feel the urge to let down his hair and use the informal word that gives vent to his feelings.

The lowbrow programs, particularly the comedy shows, have the highest proportion of slang and colloquial terms, but informal language is scattered throughout the spectrum of radio and television shows. *Lousy, gimp, crumb,* and *nut* were heard on a recent hospital show, along with such 20-plus words as *authoritarian* and technical phrases such as *speech center, behavior pattern,* and *cranial fracture.* In a serious discussion about the MORES of our times, Dr. Albert Burke

spoke of *guts, rackets,* and *oddballs,* along with CONCEPT (15), COM-
PATIBLE (15), BIGOTRY (15), and PHILANTHROPIC (18). At one point
he held up a pamphlet sent to college students by an oil corporation
warning against unpopular opinions. Instead of using a word of classical origin to describe the pamphlet (and there were many to choose
from), he called it a "thing," a generalized term used in a specifically
DEROGATORY sense (see page 176).

Informal language on the air is of particular interest to the student
of words as a key to the culture of the present and the past. By
closely following radio and television programs from year to year, it
is possible to record the way that language changes, particularly in
the area of slang. Here is a list which includes informal terms from
recent television shows and some from a Jack Benny program of
twenty years ago. Can you pick out the older terms? Are any of them
still current?

| | | |
|---|---|---|
| 1. kook | 12. top dog | 22. wet blanket |
| 2. deep-freeze | 13. cop a plea | 23. it's a cinch |
| 3. junkie | 14. hooked | 24. show-off |
| 4. the pay-off | 15. butt in | 25. you've got a nerve |
| 5. burn her | 16. sick (in the head) | 26. nut |
| 6. welcher | 17. on the button | 27. rackets |
| 7. sure-fire | 18. no kiddin' | 28. big deal |
| 8. gimp | 19. oddballs | 29. come off it |
| 9. square | 20. yeah | 30. beatnik |
| 10. lousy crumb | 21. ratted | 31. our licks |
| 11. get lost | | 32. guts |

Benny's show used 4, 6, 7, 14, 15, 18, 20, 24, and 25. If you couldn't
pick them out of the list, you can be sure that many slang terms do not
give up the ghost so easily. Some of these terms, such as "it's a cinch,"
ANTEDATE this century.

## SHAW WRITING AND SPEAKING

The last word about words on the air (and in print) should
belong to that master of language and ideas, George Bernard Shaw.
Shaw moves easily in the atmosphere of 20-plus words, polysyllabic
words of classical origin, and just as easily among the words that
make up the bones and sinews of English—earthy, everyday terms

130

that are mostly from Anglo-Saxon. There is a wealth of wordplay and informal language in Shaw and many words from cultural history. And for him all words are working words; they are not ends in themselves but the media for ideas.

Yet Shaw did recognize the difference between language written for the prefaces to his plays and the words he used on a radio or television broadcast. The direct, conversational style is still apparent in the prefaces because it stemmed from Shaw's personality; he lived in no ivory tower peopled with abstractions. But he used more one- and two-syllable words when he talked than when he wrote. Twenty-plus and Latinized words do appear among his spoken words when they are needed to describe or explain a complex idea; but in general there is a difference in style.

Let's make a comparison between a paragraph from the preface to one of his plays and an address Shaw gave over BBC radio:

### PREFATORY TO "THE SIX OF CALAIS" [6]

The most amusing thing about the first performance of this little play was the exposure it elicited of the quaint ILLITERACY of our modern London JOURNALISTS. Their only notion of a king was a pleasant and highly respectable gentleman in a bowler hat and VICTORIAN beard, shaking hands affably with a blushing football team. To them a queen was a dignified lady, also Victorian as to her COIFFURE, graciously receiving bouquets from excessively washed children in beautiful new clothes. . . .

### WHITHER BRITAIN? [7]

Whither Britain? Now, what a question. Even if I knew, and you know very well that I don't know, could I tell you in half an hour? Put a reasonable question, say, a little bit of the big question. Is Britain heading straight for war? That's what you want to know, isn't it?

Well, at present Britain is not heading straight for anywhere. She is a ship without a pilot, driving before the winds of circumstances, and—as such—she is as likely to drift into war as into anything else, provided somebody else starts the war.

The first example would not sound out of place on radio or television; it brings up concrete pictures. But it does not have the con-

---

[6] From *The Shorter Plays of Bernard Shaw* (Dodd, Mead & Company. Apollo edition).
[7] First broadcast on February 6, 1934. Rebroadcast on October 28, 1947.

versational punch of the radio address. Of the two examples, which are about the same length, the first has sixteen words of more than two syllables, the second has four. The PREFATORY material has twenty-three words of classical origin; the radio address has twelve ("question" occurs three times). There are fifty words of Anglo-Saxon origin in the written example and eighty-two in the radio speech (excluding "London" and "bowler," which started as a trade name).

There are four over-10 words in the first example: *illiteracy* (17), *journalists* (17), *coiffure* (20-plus), and *Victorian* (12). The radio address has no over-10 words, but some occur later in the broadcast, such as HETEROGENEITY.

## MAKE A GAME OUT OF IT

Shaw was quite serious about everything he said and wrote; but he enjoyed the game he was playing, of making governments and people realize how absurd they were. Learning as well as teaching should be done in a relaxed atmosphere, and this can apply to increasing one's vocabulary as well as to any other activity.

You don't have to tune out your favorite programs; listening for the unusual word can increase rather than interfere with your enjoyment. Even what are called lowbrow programs can be a source of pleasure and surprise if you are ready for the unusual word that may wander in. You can laugh at words and often at "eggheads" who use them INDISCRIMINATELY; but you can also note them in context, and reach for the dictionary.

While you don't have to forego your favorite comedy show, western, or sports program, there are a large number of radio and television broadcasts that will reward you not only with new words but with new ideas. You may have to get up early in the morning to catch a professor in the act of DISSEMINATING culture, but your vocabulary is bound to profit if you do so. And you can bring a little system into the business, too—by noting the distinct aura of words that form word clusters on a given program; by separating words on the air into their various categories of wordplay, informal language, working words, literary words, and other terms from cultural history; and by studying how polysyllabic words, the long, hard words of classical origin, are used to express fine shades of meaning in the realm of ideas.

## Television Words Quiz

Although most of the words you will be asked to recall are from this chapter, some of them go back to previous chapters. If you miss a word, reread the section where it appears in small caps. This procedure will fix it firmly in your mind.

1. A news commentator referred to his friendly rivalry with another commentator as _____ warfare.
2. What word used by President Kennedy at a press conference means "deviations from the norm"?
3. What word used as wordplay on a comedy show is the adjectival form of the "science that studies the way objects move as a result of the forces that act upon them"?
4. The _____ was the PRECURSOR of the piano.
5. Who are the two leading characters in Melville's *Moby Dick* (one is a whale)?
6. Who was the "Father of Medicine"?
7. Does *hypothesis* mean the same as *law*? (Not in Word List)
8. Is a "theory" a proposition that is more verifiable than a "hypothesis" or less? (Not in Word List)
9. What is another word for "satanic"?
10. Othello had _____ feelings toward Desdemona.
11. He performed his tasks in a _____ (mechanical) manner.
12. What is a philosophical term that refers to the belief that existence is meaningless?
13. What word mentioned on a comedy show is used in statistical measurements?
14. When two pieces of film are connected, they are _____.
15. Name a Russian novelist who was mentioned on the air.
16. Who was the scientist who formulated the theory of gravitation?
17. "Excessively" or "more than usually" may be defined as _____.
18. What is the term applied to a person who is adept in many fields?
19. Supply the missing word: "Cake-eating capitalists and their nonproductive _____ (fawning followers)."
20. The "economically-deprived lower classes who must live by the sweat of their brows" were called the _____ by Karl Marx.
21. What is the adjective meaning "given to offhand dismissal of important matters"?
22. To what special vocabulary does "counterpoint" belong?
23. Persons who are learned may be called _____.
24. Who wrote *The Sorrows of Werther*?

25. Who or what is *Don Giovanni?*
26. The four desk dictionaries mentioned discussed "hypothesis," "theory," "law," and other related words, differentiating their shades of meaning. This is called _____ of synonyms.
27. What do "fugue" and "polyphonic" have in common? (Not in Word List)
28. When two objects are placed side by side, they are _____.
29. Television is an _____ (sight and sound) medium.
30. What is a word used in connection with Iago that suggests his "evil" nature?

## WORD LIST

| | | | |
|---|---|---|---|
| telegenic | randem-tandem | discrimination | Glinka |
| cunning | spliced | proletariat | auditory |
| Werfel | generalist | music | organ |
| sycophants | Newton | ambitious | welded |
| Ahab | Dostoevski | erudite | colleagues |
| Moby Dick | mobile | juxtaposed | ambivalent |
| Hippocrates | internecine | nihilistic | pedantic |
| combat | audio-visual | programmatic | nothingness |
| anarchistic | perquisites | malignity | Dick Whittington |
| diabolical | capitalists | operator | percentile |
| humorous | inordinately | Prokofiev | philosophy |
| cavalier | Archimedes | Spanish king | dilatory |
| Goethe | rapaciously | opera by Mozart | supercilious |
| etymology | kinetic | ambidextrous | aberrations |
| definition | perfunctory | Bacon | harpsichord |

## ANSWERS

| | | |
|---|---|---|
| 30. malignity | 20. proletariat | 10. ambivalent |
| 29. audio-visual | 19. sycophants | 9. diabolical |
| 28. juxtaposed | 18. generalist | 8. more |
| 27. musical terms | 17. inordinately | 7. no |
| 26. discrimination | 16. Newton | 6. Hippocrates |
| 25. opera by Mozart | 15. Dostoevski | 5. Ahab, Moby Dick |
| 24. Goethe | 14. spliced | 4. harpsichord |
| 23. erudite | 13. percentile | 3. kinetic |
| 22. music | 12. nihilistic | 2. aberrations |
| 21. cavalier | 11. perfunctory | 1. internecine |

30 right—Highbrow level
27–29 right—Working on your doctorate
23–26 right—Alert to new words on the air
18–22 right—Middlebrow
12–17 right—You can do better
Under 12 right—Tune out the westerns

Score: _____

# 7

## How to Learn 5000 New Words from 100 Latin and Greek Roots

There is a case for long, hard words. You will not often hear it argued. The contrary doctrine is more fashionable: keep to short, simple Saxon. Ever since Herbert Spencer, set this half-truth going, it has snowballed in the way that half-truths usually do. It is sound advice as far as it goes. You cannot help using a PREPONDERANCE of Saxon, since the small change of the language and most of its connective tissue (*the, of, an, to,* etc.) come from that source. But there are at least six COGENT reasons why some of the long, difficult words are needed, though they should be used sparingly.

First, one such word can sometimes do the work of ten. It just looks long, but it's actually a time- and space-saver. The rate of increase of a moving or falling object is ACCELERATION. The capacity to adjust to changes in environment by altering responses or habits is ADAPTABILITY. Mixing in a cheaper and less EFFICACIOUS substance in some food or chemical is ADULTERATION. An index or small number written above and to the right of an ALGEBRAIC symbol or quantity to show how many times the symbol or quantity is to be used as a factor is an EXPONENT. Think what a nuisance it would always be to go around Robin Hood's barn by using the long phrase when we wanted to express the meaning in such words as these. The long word is really verbal shorthand.

Such words may be needed as synonyms, for variety as well as COMPACTNESS. If two DISPUTANTS are so far apart that they cannot patch up their quarrel, it helps a reporter if he can say—at the second mention of the fact—that they're IRRECONCILABLE or UNCOMPROMISING. If graft is involved, it is handy to know about "squeeze" and "loot," but sometimes the polite or euphemistic term is also useful: PERQUISITES. If you have to call somebody *stingy* three times, PARSIMONIOUS and *tight-fisted* suggest themselves.

Again, the long or unusual word may be needed to express an exact shade of meaning. There is only one possible word for a time scheme covering a series of events or a succession of DYNASTIES: CHRONOLOGY. And the curve traversed by a PROJECTILE is its TRAJECTORY. The case is still stronger if descriptive words are involved. Shaw somewhere talks of *"breath-bereaving* insolence." Just try expressing that any other way.

In the world of diplomacy there is a need for euphemistic terms to cover up the fact that nations are out for the best bargain they can get. We read daily about UNILATERAL and BILATERAL agreements; somehow *one-sided* and *two-sided* sound harsh and suggest schoolboy quarrels. Instead of a showdown we have CONFRONTATIONS. Words of classical origin have subtle CONNOTATIONS that may relieve tension in a world where blunt words may trigger a war. The text of Article 33 of the United Nations Charter reads:

. . . The parties to any dispute, the continuance of which is likely to endanger the maintenance of international peace and security, shall . . . seek a solution by negotiation, ENQUIRY, MEDIATION, CONCILIATION, ARBITRATION, JUDICIAL settlement, resort to REGIONAL agencies or arrangements, or other peaceful means of their own choice. . . .

The exchange of long, hard words in the chambers of the United Nations does let off steam that might go into armed conflict. It takes energy to speak at length in the language of diplomacy.

In specialized fields the need for precise terms that can be taken in only one sense accounts for extensive borrowing directly from Latin and Greek. New words that are necessary to describe scientific or technical gadgets, substances or processes are coined from Latin and Greek elements. This type of term that must convey a specific technical sense cannot well be replaced by any simple Saxonism. That is a fifth reason justifying long, hard words.

And the older words from classical sources, those that make up the bulk of the 450,000 entries in *Webster's Third Unabridged,* are words that every literate person needs to know. These are words that have been in the language unchanged (except for spelling) since the sixteenth century; they are keys to CULTURAL history—politics, ECONOMICS, literature, religion, philosophy, and other fundamental subjects.

# CLASSICAL WORD

| COMPACTNESS<br>(one word in<br>place of many) | ACCELERATION<br>(the rate of increase of<br>a moving or falling body) |
|---|---|
| EXACTNESS<br>(exact shade of<br>meaning) | TRAJECTORY<br>(the curve traversed by<br>a projectile) |
| VARIETY<br>(synonyms) | stingy ⟶ PARSIMONIOUS<br><br>can't patch }<br>up a quarrel } IRRECONCILABLE,<br>UNCOMPROMISING |
| TACT and DIPLOMACY<br>(polite terms for<br>harsh ones) | graft, loot ⟶ PERQUISITES<br><br>wrangle, tiff, }<br>squabble, fight } ARBITRATE,<br>MEDIATE,<br>ADJUDICATE |
| SCIENTIFIC<br>PRECISION<br>(words coined<br>from Latin and<br>Greek elements) | SPECTROSCOPE<br>spectro — (from spectrum, "image")<br>scope —— (from skopos, "to look")<br>(instrument used to<br>study light waves) |
| CULTURE<br>(terms used in liter-<br>ature, philosophy,<br>economics, etc.) | philosophy ⟶ EXISTENTIAL,<br>TRANSCENDENTAL<br>politics ⟶ DEMOCRACY, SOCIALISM<br>literature ⟶ PROTAGONIST,<br>PERIPETY |

## What's the One Long Word for It?

What single word conveys the meaning for each of the following?

1. Familiar with many languages.
2. Refers to a political party formed in 1891 which advocated wider distribution of land, AGRARIAN reform, cheap money, etc.
3. Latent power or capacity, as opposed to ACTUALIZED achievement.
4. Being first in rank, order, or importance.
5. Custom or law that devolves inheritance or title on the eldest son.
6. Act or process of spreading out from a center.
7. Greedy grabbiness.

8. Mutual exchange, especially of trade privileges and concessions between two countries.
9. Sufficient to keep alive.
10. To EVADE immediate action, in order to gain time or avoid trouble.

1. polyglot
2. populist
3. potentiality
4. primacy

5. primogeniture
6. radiation
7. rapacity

8. reciprocity
9. subsistence
10. temporize

## What's Another Word for It?

What's an alternative word, to give variety, for each of the following?

1. peppery (of somebody's disposition)
2. roundabout
3. mercy

4. clotting (of the blood)
5. smugness
6. QUALM

7. accompanying
8. dictionary
9. doubletalk
10. blot out

1. choleric
2. circuitous
3. clemency
4. coagulation

5. complacency
6. compunction
7. concomitant

8. lexicon
9. equivocation
10. expunge

## What's the Exact Word for It?

How many times somebody says, "I have the idea, but I can't think of the word for it." For each of the following ideas or definitions, four possibilities are offered. Only one is right. Pick the right one in each case:

1. To destroy completely:
   (a) ANNOTATE   (b) INCARCERATE   (c) annihilate   (d) PETRIFY

2. Government in which a privileged upper class rules; that class is a:
   (a) TIMOCRACY   (b) MOBOCRACY   (c) aristocracy   (d) tyranny

3. Hired murderer:
   (a) BLACKGUARD   (b) assassin   (c) THUG   (d) bandit

4. Making up for a wrong, loss, sin, or injury:
   (a) SCAPEGOAT   (b) agony   (c) atonement   (d) redemption

5. To declare frankly and openly:
   (a) ASSEVERATE   (b) AVOW        (c) protest      (d) ACCLIMATE

6. Officer of court who has charge of prisoners in the courtroom:
   (a) CHANCELLOR   (b) prosecutor   (c) BAILIFF      (d) COUNCILLOR

7. Having to do with public finances or treasury matters:
   (a) FIDUCIARY    (b) trusting     (c) FISCAL       (d) MONOPOLIS-
                                                          TIC

8. Tool for boring holes in wood, or in the earth:
   (a) TERMITE      (b) gear         (c) AUGER        (d) plane

9. Soldier or sailor who has been wounded, killed, or lost:
   (a) CASTAWAY     (b) CASUALTY     (c) STOWAWAY     (d) CATALYST

10. Stand or rack for seasoning bottles:
   (a) slot         (b) CASTOR       (c) ANTIMACAS-   (d) DOILY
                                         SAR

11. Condition of having an evil and unwholesome character:
   (a) DELIQUES-    (b) MALTREAT-    (c) DEVIATION    (d) DEGENERACY
       CENCE            MENT

12. To bend or turn aside:
   (a) slip         (b) DEFLECT      (c) REGRESS      (d) encircle

13. To trace the outline of:
   (a) CIRCUMNAVI-  (b) traverse     (c) survey       (d) DELINEATE
       GATE

14. Condition of having become worse; or the process of worsening:
   (a) DETERIORA-   (b) ENCOMIUM     (c) PROFANATION  (d) DETONATION
       TION

15. To disregard the sacredness of:
   (a) DISINTEGRATE (b) DESECRATE    (c) disfigure    (d) ICONOCLASM

16. Having many shapes:
   (a) POLYGONAL    (b) MULTIFORM    (c) MORPHOLOGY   (d) ELUSIVE

17. All-devouring:
   (a) ESURIENT     (b) OMNIVOROUS   (c) CARNIVOROUS  (d) RUMINANT

18. Act or process of swinging back and forth:
   (a) DEVIATION    (b) dependency   (c) OSCILLATION  (d) OSCULATION

19. Established by long usage or custom:
   (a) insured      (b) TABOOED      (c) PRESCRIPTIVE (d) MANDATORY

20. Circular tower, building, or pit in which green food for farm animals is
    stored:
   (a) bin          (b) SILO         (c) elevator     (d) CHUTE

21. Sudden outrush of troops from a besieged fort or town, to attack the besiegers:
    (a) ONSLAUGHT   (b) SORTIE   (c) breach   (d) CATAPULT

22. Very loud or powerful in sound:
    (a) RAUCOUS   (b) explosive   (c) STENTORIAN   (d) MNEMONIC

23. Harsh-sounding, creaking, or grating:
    (a) RACHITIC   (b) STRIDENT   (c) DETONATING   (d) BANSHEE

24. To come as something additional or interrupting:
    (a) AGGRANDIZE   (b) SUPERSEDE   (c) DEVIATE   (d) SUPERVENE

25. Solution of plot or story—the outcome:
    (a) suspense   (b) climax   (c) DENOUEMENT   (d) disaster

ANSWERS

| 1. (c) | 6. (c) | 10. (b) | 14. (a) | 18. (c) | 22. (c) |
| 2. (c) | 7. (c) | 11. (d) | 15. (b) | 19. (c) | 23. (b) |
| 3. (b) | 8. (c) | 12. (b) | 16. (b) | 20. (b) | 24. (d) |
| 4. (c) | 9. (b) | 13. (d) | 17. (b) | 21. (b) | 25. (c) |
| 5. (b) | | | | | |

## DOUBLING YOUR WORD SCORE

What the NUMEROLOGY of words keeps turning up is just this fact: *standard words in Thorndike's second 10,000 are, in the main, of classical origin.* A Chinese MANDARIN had to know 30,000 separate picture-characters to read his classics. Luckily most books, magazines, and newspapers in English can be read easily by anybody who has a vocabulary of 20,000 words. And while some of our learned phrase patterns and allusions are as complex as Chinese picture-writing, ours still are made up of combinations of twenty-six letters. So it's not so hard to double a vocabulary in English.

*The master key to the problem of acquiring these long, abstract words is the fact that the great majority of them are derived from Greek and Latin—5000 of them from seventy Latin and thirty Greek roots, with special twists of meaning given by prefixes or* SUFFIXES *from the same source.* It may seem odd to bring two dead languages into the picture to speed up learning new words in English. But once you know these few key roots, prefixes, and suffixes, you can take a lot of long words apart without any trouble, when you meet them, and make a good guess at their primary or literal meaning.

Actually you already know a lot of these roots, whether you're consciously aware of it or not. And learning the rest is no great trick. A beginner in a foreign language does well to master a thousand new words in a year, learning them all three ways: for reading, writing, and speaking. It should not be such a heavy chore to acquire a hundred basic Greek and Latin stems, *for recognition purposes only.* It's a prize shortcut that will pay big dividends in extending the command of words. And it will help make the other shortcuts shorter.

## A FEW PHOBIAS

A generation ago we got along with only one PHOBIA. That was HYDROPHOBIA, the fear of water. Now, since Freud and Jung, we have a whole flock of phobias, mysterious HOBGOBLINS of the mind which may be lurking in anyone's SUBCONSCIOUS, ready to jump out any time. Here's a partial list from the PSYCHOANALYST's repertory, all manufactured out of Greek stems grafted onto *phobia:*

| | | |
|---|---|---|
| ACROPHOBIA | acro-, high place | fear of heights |
| AGORAPHOBIA | agora-, marketplace | fear of open spaces |
| ALGOPHOBIA | algo-, pain | fear of pain |
| ASTROPHOBIA | astro-, star | fear of thunder and lightning |
| CLAUSTROPHOBIA | claustro-, closed | fear of closed places |
| COPROPHOBIA | copro-, filth | fear of filth |
| HEMATOPHOBIA | hemato-, blood | fear of blood |
| GLOSSOPHOBIA | glossa-, tongue | fear of speaking |
| MYSOPHOBIA | myso-, dirt | fear of contamination |
| NECROPHOBIA | necro-, dead | fear of dead bodies |
| NYCTOPHOBIA | nycto-, night | fear of darkness |
| PATHOPHOBIA | patho-, suffering | fear of suffering |
| PHONOPHOBIA | phono-, sound | fear of speaking aloud |
| PHOTOPHOBIA | photo-, light | fear of light |
| SITOPHOBIA | sito-, food | fear of eating |
| TAPHOPHOBIA | tapho-, burial | fear of being buried alive |
| THANATOPHOBIA | thanato-, death | fear of death |
| TOXOPHOBIA | toxo-, poison | fear of being poisoned |
| XENOPHOBIA | xeno-, stranger | fear of strangers |
| ZOOPHOBIA | zoo-, animal | fear of animals |

Is there anybody in the house who didn't already know phobia? And of the Greek stems combining with it to describe these PATHOLOG-

ICAL forms of fear, it's an even bet that you also knew *claustro-, phono-, photo-, thanato-, patho-,* and *xeno-* for "foreigner."

The *New York Times* travel section described Kabul, Afghanistan, as the "seat of a strongly XENOPHOBIC monarchy." You can spot xenophobes every time—people who are suspicious and fearful of strangers who do not belong to their tribe, race, class, or city block. Compounds like ANGLOPHOBE and RUSSOPHOBE are familiar. Here the fear gets mixed up with hate. You can make up similar compounds if you're annoyed with anyone. Just hitch *-phobe* onto the name—FRANCOPHOBE, for instance. Already this adds up to twenty-five words from one, *phobos,* fear. And it's still open for return engagements.

So far nobody has coined a single word for "fear of atomic bombs." This unnamed and most rational of fears brings to mind the SPELEOLOGICAL Society of America, whose members, nicknamed "spelunkers," met for the NOSTALGIC purpose of exploring our scenic SUBTERRANEAN wonders, such as the Mammoth Caves of Kentucky and the Carlsbad Caverns of New Mexico. Our contemporary spelunkers are digging backyard shelters and underground caves in the hope that the A- or H-Bomb will politely detour around them if it is dropped.

"Spelunkers" comes from the Latin *spelunca,* a cave, which in turn is first cousin to the Greek word, *spelunke.* SPELEOLOGY means the "science of caves." Coiners of the term took the combining form *speleo-,* from *speleum,* Latinized spelling of Greek *spelaion,* cave, and added *-logy,* from *logos,* word. Because words play such a large part in reasoning, *logos* came also to mean in Greek "reasoning," and finally "study" or "science."

Undoubtedly you've long known about "-ologies," and heard irreverent persons joke about them, sometimes with reason. But the jokers might have more respect for *logos* if they knew that it enters into at least 156 words in English. Here's a partial collection. Remember that the stem can mean either "word," "reasoning," "study (of)," or "science (of)."

## How Many -Ologies Do You Know by Name?

1. ANALOGY
2. ANGELOLOGY
3. ANTHOLOGY
4. ANTHROPOLOGY
5. APOLOGUE
6. APOLOGY
7. ARCHEOLOGY
8. ASTROLOGY
9. BACTERIOLOGY
10. biology
11. CATALOGUE
12. CHRONOLOGY
13. CONCHOLOGY
14. COSMOLOGY
15. CRIMINOLOGY
16. DECALOGUE

| | | | |
|---|---|---|---|
| 17. DEMONOL-OGY | 27. GENEALOGY | 39. MONOLOGUE | 49. PHYSIOLOGY |
| 18. DIALOGUE | 28. geology | 40. MORPHOL-OGY | 50. PSYCHOLOGY |
| 19. DOXOLOGY | 29. HISTOLOGY | | 51. PROLOGUE |
| 20. ECLOGUE | 30. ILLOGICAL | 41. MYTHOLOGY | 52. TAUTOLOGY |
| 21. ENTOMOL-OGY | 31. LOGARITHMS | 42. NEOLOGISM | 53. TECHNOLOGY |
| | 32. logic | 43. ORNITHOL-OGY | 54. TERMINOL-OGY |
| 22. EPILOGUE | 33. LOGISTICS | | |
| 23. ESCHATOL-OGY | 34. LOGOGRAM | 44. OSTEOLOGY | 55. TETRALOGY |
| | 35. LOGOTYPE | 45. PATHOLOGY | 56. theology |
| 24. ETHNOLOGY | 36. LOGOGRAPH | 46. PHILOLOGY | 57. TRAVELOGUE |
| | 37. METEOROL-OGY | 47. PHRASEOL-OGY | 58. TRILOGY |
| 25. ETYMOLOGY | | | 59. ZOOLOGY |
| 26. EULOGY | 38. MINERALOGY | 48. PHRENOLOGY | 60. DENDROLOGY |

Similarly, if we take the stem *graph-* from the Greek *grapho*, to write, we find that a great many English words derive from it. You've already met *homograph*, a word spelled exactly like another word but differing in sound and meaning. How many more *-graph* words can you define?

| | | | |
|---|---|---|---|
| 1. AUTOGRAPH | 8. COSMOGRA-PHY | 15. LEXICOGRA-PHER | 22. PHOTOGRA-PHER |
| 2. BIBLIOGRAPHY | | | |
| 3. BIOGRAPHER | 9. DICTOGRAPH | 16. LITHOGRAPH | 23. PYROGRAPHY |
| 4. CALLIGRAPHY | 10. DIGRAPH | 17. LOGOGRAPH | 24. SEISMO-GRAPH |
| 5. CEROGRAPH | 11. geography | 18. MONOGRAPH | |
| 6. CHIROGRA-PHY | 12. GRAPHIC | 19. MULTIGRAPH | 25. STENOGRA-PHER |
| | 13. GRAPHITE | 20. ORTHOGRA-PHY | |
| 7. CINEMATO-GRAPH | 14. HOLOGRAPH | | 26. STYLOGRAPH |
| | | 21. paragraph | 27. TELEGRAPH |
| | | | 28. TYPOGRAPHY |

This is just a small sample of the Greek you've been using, even if you didn't know it for Greek. Much of this Greek element came into English through the Latin. The Romans were the great TRANSMITTERS of HELLENIC culture to Western Europe and England.

What we call the *romance* element in English comes either direct from Greek and Latin, or through the French. It makes up three-fifths of the words in the total English vocabulary, so it deserves a close look. Since it is so MASSIVE and RAMIFYING a collection, we need to pick out the key exhibits so we'll know our way around the museum.

# LATIN IN THE HEADLINES

Luckily most readers know a lot of Latin even if they aren't aware of it. Check through the 20,000 commonest words in English and you'll find 261 have come over absolutely unchanged from Latin, spelling and all, as against only 89 from the Greek—a third as many. Of the 261 Latin imports, nearly all are in the higher brackets. They are learned words to us, even those that were household words to the Romans. Besides these Latin words that have been thoroughly DO-MESTICATED in English, there are many others that can on occasion be used in everyday writing.

A headline in *Time* runs: *Jus, Imperium, Pax.* The story is about the 2000th anniversary of Julius Caesar's landing in Britain. It's pegged on an editorial in the *London Times*, which admits it may be fanciful to imagine. . . .

that by any MYSTICAL communion a spark of the VIRGILIAN light of empire was tended through the centuries in Merlin's cave. Yet somehow the grand ideals of Roman dominion have not been lost in the modern world: *jus*, the conception of a law that should TRANSCEND the limitations of the small people who first conceived it, and become at last the GUARANTOR of justice to all sorts and conditions of men; *imperium*, the principle of a dominion that can enable all manner of races, languages and faiths to live together within the bounds of a single system of ordered rule, and of a citizenship that, though it may begin as the privilege of a governing race, will gradually be extended until it is enjoyed by all; and *pax*, the product of the other two, the belief in the mission of imperial government, based evenly upon the foundations of justice and national authority, to bring in the golden age when war shall cease from the earth.

*Jus Romanum, Imperium Romanum, Pax Romana*—by changing the adjective Britain has given to each of them a changed flavor and connotation. But that is only because the tradition at the heart of them is a living thing, and grows continually. After two thousand years an imperial people can with a clear title claim its spiritual ANCESTRY.

*Jus Britannicum, Imperium Britannicum,* and *Pax Britannica* have an organ tone that *British law, British Empire,* and *British peace* could not equal. There are many historic Latin expressions like these, just as there are borrowed words and phrases from other countries, for which there are no equivalents in English. They enrich the language beyond measure.

You'll see many of these old standbys in *Time* and *Newsweek*. In the same week these magazines used the Latin phrases "de facto," "quid pro quo," "deus ex machina," "in absentia," "magna cum laude," and "modus vivendi." They may not have quite the majesty of "Jus Britannicum" and "Imperium Britannicum," but they make us realize that Latin is far from a dead language; it appears constantly in print side by side with its English derivatives.

Here are two sentences from *Time*'s music section (June 21, 1963):

Pianists Malcolm Frager and Vladimir Ashkenazy have been fast friends ever since 1958, when Ashkenazy made his American DEBUT. Frager was introduced as a *magna cum laude* Russian student at Columbia, and shy Ashkenazy greeted him like a *deus ex machina* friend.

Does the context of these Latin phrases tell you more about them?

### When We Talk Roman

A good many of the Latin words that have come over into English unchanged are concerned with diplomacy, politics, or law. How many of the following forty can you define?

| | | | |
|---|---|---|---|
| ALIAS | LEX | PROCURATOR | "whispering |
| ARBITER | LICTOR | PROPAGANDA | campaign") |
| BONUS | MEDIATOR | QUAESTOR | sanctum |
| CAUCUS | MODERATOR | QUORUM | solicitor |
| COADJUTOR | orator | QUOTA | SPONSOR |
| DICTATOR | PERPETRATOR | REFERENDUM | STATUS |
| DICTUM | PERSECUTOR | REGIMEN | superior |
| ELECTOR | PLEBS | ROSTRUM | TESTATOR |
| FIAT | PRAETOR | rumor (cf. "rumor | TOGA |
| GENS | PROCONSUL | factory" and | TRANSGRESSOR |
| INTERREGNUM | PROCTOR | | TRIUMVIR |

### Medical Latin That's Also Common English

Most of our everyday words for parts of the body, common complaints, and remedies come from Anglo-Saxon. Since these terms are not precise enough for medical use, doctors have continued to employ the Latin (and Greek) terms which they once used exclusively when all physicians wrote and lectured in Latin (and when they wrote prescriptions in abbreviated PHARMACIST's Latin rather than trade names). Of these medical Latin terms, 50 have SHUTTLED into

146

the 20,000 commonest words in the language. How many of them do you know well enough to convince a doctor?

| | | | |
|---|---|---|---|
| ANEMIA | HORMONES | PLEXUS | SINUS |
| ANTIHISTAMINE | INCISOR | RECTUM | SPUTUM |
| AORTA | INSOMNIA | REFLUX | STERNUM |
| CAESARIAN | IRIS | REGIMEN | STUPOR |
| CANCER (liter- | LAUDANUM | REJUVENATOR | TETANUS |
| ally, a crab) | LEUKEMIA | RETINA | THALLUS |
| CEREBRUM | MANIA | SALIVA | THROMBOSIS |
| CEREBELLUM | MATRIX | SANITARIUM | THYMUS |
| CORNEA | MEDULLA | SERUM (news to the | TIBIA |
| CORTEX | NAUSEA | Romans, in the | TUMOR |
| CRANIUM | OPIUM | modern medical | TYMPANUM |
| DELIRIUM | OVUM | sense; in Latin it | TYPHUS |
| FEMUR | PALLOR | means "whey" or | ULCER |
| FUNGI | PELVIS | "watery fluid") | VACCINE |

Besides these forty words from politics and fifty from medicine, the remaining 180-odd that have come over from Latin unchanged are mostly words that express a single specific meaning (see page 157). They are single-shot terms.

## THE ROMANS WERE LONG ON ACTION

To locate the Latin words that have fathered a flock of DERIVATIVES in English, we have to look elsewhere. Among those that have been most PROLIFIC are certain words expressing action, which was the thing the Romans were best at. And each of these Latin verbs may figure in English in any one of several forms, so you have to know not only the stem form, but its main changes. But you soon learn to detect these mild disguises.

One Latin stem, *fac-*, from the verb *facio*, means both "do" and "make." This one stem yields sixty-five English words, without exhausting its possibilities. The last eighteen are beyond the commonest 10,000.

### Using Words That Come from FAC

In the words which follow, *fac* enters in one of its various forms: *fac, fic, fact, fect, fict, factur*, etc.

| fact | facility | counterfeit | defect | imperfect |
|------|----------|-------------|--------|-----------|
| perfect | factor | efficacy | faculty | certificate |
| difficult | feature | efficient | affectation | edifice |
| effect | manufacture | infection | artifice | faction |
| fashion | sacrifice | affection | benefactor | fashionable |
| affair | affect | defeat | efficiency | facilitate |
| benefit | factory | difficulty | facile | forfeiture |
| deficiency | official | perfection | feat | surfeit |
| defective | sufficient | artificial | forfeit | unaffected |
| effective | beneficial | | | |

| IMPERFEC-TION | CONFECTION | UNIFICATION | VERSIFICA-TION |
|---------------|------------|-------------|----------------|
| PROFICIENT | AFFECTED | BENEFICIARY | EXEMPLIFI-CATION |
| FEASIBLE | DISAFFEC-TION | PONTIFICAL | COMFIT |
| INEFFICIENCY | MANUFAC-TORY | PUTREFAC-TION | FACSIMILE |
| SUFFICIENCY | | REFECTION | |

Taking the group from IMPERFECTION down to the end, which is the right word to fill in the blank in each of the following sentences?

1. The meat was far gone in _____.
2. A poet needs to know the rules of _____ and when to break them.
3. The troops were in a state of _____.
4. It was an admirable _____ of democratic methods.
5. He gave Araminta a _____ box for her birthday, and acquired great merit in her eyes, since she loved sweet things.
6. He was the chief _____ under the will.
7. She had a MINCING and _____ manner.
8. He wrote in a TOPLOFTY and _____ style.
9. The Presidium fired the top officials in the COSMETICS industry, because of their _____.
10. The process of _____ is not yet complete in the new African countries.

ANSWERS

| | | |
|---|---|---|
| 1. putrefaction | 5. comfit | 8. pontifical |
| 2. versification | 6. beneficiary | 9. inefficiency |
| 3. disaffection | 7. affected | 10. unification |
| 4. exemplification | | |

Taking the stem pon-, from ponere, to put or place, we find that it also gives a big yield: 35 DERIVATIVES. Omitting those in the common-

148

est 10,000, as already familiar in meaning, we find a sizable number remaining in the higher brackets.

## Spotting Words Derived from PON

The combining forms for *pon* include also *pos, posit*. Choosing among its derivatives, can you put the right word in each sentence blank?

| | | |
|---|---|---|
| DEPOSITION | INTERPOSI- | APPOSITE |
| COMPOSITE | TION | EXPOSITOR |
| DECOMPOSI- | COMPOST | PROPOUND |
| TION | JUXTAPOSI- | POSITIVIST |
| EXPONENT | TION | TRANSPOSI- |
| DEPOSITORY | IMPOST | TION |

1. The picture was a _____ photograph.
2. _____ duties are never popular, but are any taxes?
3. It was an _____ quotation.
4. The judge ordered that a _____ be taken, since the witness was BEDRIDDEN and could not come to court.
5. Dean Inge was a notable _____ of ANGLICAN views.
6. A long spell of hot sun following the rain speeded up the _____ of the _____ heap.
7. The pianist had mastered the difficult tricks of _____.
8. The _____ of the two diagrams caused the confusion in interpretation.
9. A Swiss bank was picked as a _____ for the funds.
10. Averill Harriman went to Russia to _____ the American view.

### ANSWERS

1. composite
2. impost
3. apposite
4. deposition
5. exponent
6. decomposition, compost
7. transposition
8. juxtaposition
9. depository
10. propound

Leadership was a Roman specialty and the stem *duc*, from *ducere*, "to lead," has gone on playing a strong role in English. In fact, via the Italian, it gave us a new loan word of unhappy memory, *Il Duce*, closely tied in with FASCISM, from the *fasces*, or bundle of rods carried by the LICTORS who guarded Roman CONSULS.

## Forty Words from One

Here are forty derivatives from *duc, duct:*

| | | | | |
|---|---|---|---|---|
| produce | production | conduit | VIADUCT | DUCHY |
| conduct | educate | dukedom | DUCAL | ABDUCT |
| education | introduction | CONDUCE | SEDUCTIVE | INDUCTION |
| introduce | seduce | DEDUCE | DUCAT | ABDUCTION |
| reduce | duchess | DEDUCT | ADDUCE | CONDUCIBLE |
| duke | reproduce | AQUEDUCT | DUCTIBLE | DEDUCIBLE |
| induce | reproduction | CONDUCIVE | EDUCE | INDUCT |
| conductor | productive | DEDUCTION | TRADUCE | SEDUCTION |

Fill in the blank with the right word, drawing on the derivatives of *duc* from CONDUCE to the end:

1. His record did not _____ to confidence.
2. He was able to _____ very good reasons for the move.
3. An _____ from the SERAGLIO was not easy to contrive.
4. The conclusion was _____ from the premises.
5. The lawyer tried to _____ his opponent.
6. He had not taken all the _____s which the tax law permitted.
7. Reasoning by _____ cannot give the certainty possible in _____ logic, since it is not possible to exhaust the instances.
8. Da Vinci did not find the _____ service wholly to his taste.
9. Khrushchev's tone was not _____ to the best feeling.
10. _____ is under some circumstances punishable as a crime.

ANSWERS

1. conduce
2. adduce
3. abduction
4. deducible
5. traduce
6. deduction
7. induction, deductive
8. ducal
9. conducive
10. seduction

The Romans had a handy system for building up a flock of verbs from a single basic stem. The Latin word for "write" is *scribere.* Its combining forms are *scrib, script.* Take a close look at the string of derivatives we have from it:

| | | | |
|---|---|---|---|
| ASCRIBE | prescribe | SUPERSCRIBE | are verbs) |
| CIRCUMSCRIBE | PROSCRIBE | TRANSCRIBE | CONSCRIPT |
| INSCRIBE | subscribe | (all of above | description |

| | | | |
|---|---|---|---|
| inscription | NONDESCRIPT | subscriber | scribble |
| manuscript | prescription | SUPERSCRIPTION | script |
| indescribable | RESCRIPT | scribe | scripture |

The first eight describe certain special types of writing, by putting a prefix on the basic stem *scrib*. In Saxon English we say "write him down as one to be killed in the purge." The Romans used the one word, *proscribere*, which meant to "write forth" or "publish" a name on the condemned list. We have borrowed this word practically unchanged, to express the same meaning. *Prescribere* was "to give advance directions, to write beforehand (*prae*)." *Where we tend to hitch* DIRECTIVE *words loosely to the far end of a verb, the Romans put theirs in front, and glued them to the main stem.* Instead of saying "sail around" they said *circumnavigare*, from which we get *circumnavigate*. Rather than asking a man to "write his name under" a petition, they said *subscribere*, from which we get *subscriber* and *subscription*.

## ROMAN SMALL CHANGE STILL CIRCULATING

Many of these classical prefixes—and suffixes, too, such as the *-able* in *indescribable*—are still in active use in English. Using *ante*, the Latin prefix meaning "before," "in front of," we make new words quite freely, writing ANTEDILUVIAN, or ANTEDATE, or ANTE-CHAMBER, without any worry over the fact that such words did not exist in classical Latin. Similarly we use *post*, "after," when we speak of *postwar* legislation, just as we use the opposite prefix *pr(a)e*, "before," in PRENATAL or *pre-war*. Co-, and *con*, combining forms of *cum*, "with," provides us with *corespondent*, "one jointly answerable with another," now specialized to mean the "other man" or "other woman" in a divorce suit. We have *coed*, a COLLOQUIAL abbreviation of *coeducational student* (feminine gender).

The prefix *re*, meaning "back" or "again" we use almost recklessly. We even add to it a Latin word which arrived in our language already equipped with it, and *re-refer* something to a committee.

Of the suffixes hitched on at the end of words, *-able* or *-ible*, from the Latin *-abilis*, *-ibilis*, meaning "able to be" or "causing," is found in INNUMERABLE English words. So with *il*, *-ile*, from Latin *ilis*, *ile*, "belonging to," as in SERVILE "belonging to a slave" and hence "submissive" or "CRINGING." A very common one is *-ive*, from Latin *-ivus*,

151

*-ivum,* "relating to" or "involving," as in the instances *fugitive,* "relating to flight," CURSIVE, "involving running," as a cursive hand, referring to the difference between a running and a printed script. *-Ion,* meaning "act of," or "state of," is also in widespread use.


## GREEK IS AN EXACT LANGUAGE

Greek prefixes and suffixes, fewer in number, are mostly used in exact, fixed, and unvarying senses. *Anti,* meaning "against," is one of the most common. In fact, we use it colloquially to mean just a plain "anti"—an "againster." A man may be anti-Civil Rights legislation, anti-New Frontier, anti-Russian, or, like the cartoon character in the DEFUNCT humorous magazine *Life, Old Anti-Everything.* The Greek prefixes:

| | | | | | |
|---|---|---|---|---|---|
| *a, an,* | not | *ec, ek,* | out of | *meta,* | beyond, after |
| *apo,* | from | *hyper,* | over | *peri,* | around |
| *cata, kata,* | down | *hypo,* | under | *syn,* | with |
| *dia,* | through | | | | |

are still employed in compounding words the Greeks never heard of. DIATHERMY, a "heating through," by deep heat which warms the tissues beneath the skin, without heating the surface, is drawn from a word coined out of Greek in 1833 by an Italian physicist, Melloni. *Diathermy* itself first appeared in print around 1910.

When it comes to Greek suffixes, there are only a few in common use, but they are hard-worked. *-Ism* is hitched onto all sorts of words, to a degree that leads us to speak of "isms" when we mean doctrines that are much discussed, such as COMMUNISM, CAPITALISM, FASCISM, and EXISTENTIALISM. By changing the ending to *-ist,* we get the suffix that distinguishes the ADHERENT of any of these "isms." Sidney Hook, reviewing *The Essential Lippmann* in the *New York Times,* writes about EMPIRICISTS, SECULARISTS, NATURALISTS, POSITIVISTS, and PRAGMATISTS.

*-Ism* and *-ist* are used as labeling devices in politics and diplomacy. If you don't like a man's or a nation's ideas, you pick out a derogatory term and tack either suffix onto it. The Chinese accuse Khrushchev of "adventurism," "capitulationism," "great power chauvinism," "revisionism," and "splittism." Just as there are overworked words, *-ism* and *-ist* are now in the category of overworked suffixes.

The Greek *-ize,* meaning "make" or "make like," is another overactive suffix. It forms such compounds as SYSTEMATIZE, "to make systematic"; automatize, "to make automatic"; URBANIZE, "to give the characteristics of a city." [1] In recent years, with a push from Madison Avenue, we have overworked this suffix to the point of exhaustion. FINALIZE, "to put in final or finished form," is one of the words that set up two armed camps in the controversy over *Webster's Third Unabridged*. It has received the blessing of two presidents—a fact that only further infuriates the language purists.

## THE SPLITTING PROCESS

Besides these authentic Greek suffixes, parts of Greek words are sometimes split off and used as if they were suffixes. *Talkathon*, made by analogy with MARATHON, is one instance. *Talk* is a good Anglo-Saxon word, and to hang onto it the tail end of a Greek word, *-athon*, which is in no sense a suffix, is a triumph of language manufacture by the Greekless.

Another kidnapping of this kind occurred in the case of ELECTRON. It's been split, too. An even half of it, *-tron*, has been treated as if it were a suffix, and hitched on to form the tail end of trade names for various types of electronic tubes: KENOTRON, THYRATRON, KLYSTRON —all of which have Greek stems to start with; but one huge tube has been labeled IGNITRON, thus adorning the Latin word for "fire" with a Greek suffix that is strictly homemade. At least the Berkeley BEVATRON and the Brookhaven COSMOTRON, new research instruments that are probing ANTIMATTER, are strictly Greek in their wedding of word elements, but the splitting process is still there.

Talking about "splitting," we would have jarred another Greek philosopher with our popular term, *atom-splitting*. Literally, this means "splitting the UNSPLITTABLE." (Remember the gag about unscrewing the INSCRUTABLE?) Democritus deliberately labeled what he surmised to be the smallest particle of matter *atomos*, from *a*, "not," and *tomein*, "to cut": that which cannot be cut, split, or divided is an atom. With new knowledge about the VOLATILE behavior of electrons and protons in an atom, science may find ways to split more unsplittable particles of matter. Thus the term *atom* poses a PARADOX—

[1] Since SUBURBIA has become a sociological ENTITY on its own, the word *suburbanize* has been added to the dictionary. Beyond the suburbs are the EXURBS, or SUPER-suburbia, a gilt-bordered area inhabited by the "elite" who presumably read *Fortune*. A word of the near future may be *exurbanize* unless cities, suburbs, and exurbs are incorporated into one huge MEGALOPOLIS.

it is both splittable and unsplittable. Maybe that's why the physicists prefer to speak of "NUCLEAR FISSION."

Aside from the HYBRID words, however, and the changes that science has wrought in words like *atomos*, the Latin and Greek roots, prefixes, and suffixes still in circulation can help you learn an amazing number of new words which may be just beyond your reach. All you have to do is break hard words down into their component parts and make a good stab at the literal meaning. You'll be able to sight-read

| *male* | *dict* | *ion* |
|--------|--------|-------|
| evil | spoken | that which |

which reshuffles into "that evil which is spoken"—or "a curse."

The basic Greek and Latin stems thus indicate clearly the main families of classical words in English, while the prefixes and suffixes mark relationships of meaning within each clan group of derivatives. There is a Word-Analyzer in the last chapter which we'll tell you about later, that will simplify the process of learning the mechanics of word derivation.

## GREEK WORDS WITH MANY DERIVATIVES

Derivatives from the following Greek words are mostly technical. Many of these words will turn up again in the section on technical vocabularies (Chapter 11). Notice that most of them have highly specific, DELIMITED meanings. You either know them or you don't.

*Aer, Aeros,* air—AERODYNAMIC, AEROSPACE, AEROEMBOLISM, AEROPAUSE, AEROPLANE, AEROSOL, AERONAUTICS, AERONEUROSIS, AERIAL, AERATE, AEROBALLISTICS, AERODUCT.

*Agon,* a contest—PROTAGONIST, agonizing, agony, ANTAGONIST.

*Allos,* another—ALLOTROPE, ALLOMORPH, ALLOPATHY, ALLOPHANE, ALLEGORY.

*Arche,* beginning, rule, chief—ARCHANGEL, ANARCHY, ARCHIVES, ARCHETYPE, ARCHDUKE, architect, ARCHIPELAGO, ARCHITRAVE, HIERARCHY, monarchy, OLIGARCHY, PATRIARCH.

*Aster, Astron,* a star—ASTER, ASTERISK, ASTRAL, ASTROLABE, disaster, ASTEROID, ASTROLOGY, ASTRONOMY, ASTRIONICS, ASTROGATION, ASTRONAUT, ASTRONAUTICS, ASTROPHYSICS.

*Biblos* or *Biblion,* a book—BIBLIOPHILE, BIBLIOGRAPHY, BIBLICAL, BIBLIOMANCY, Bible, BIBLIOMANIA.

154

*Demos,* the people—democracy, epidemic, DEMOS, DEMOTIC, democrat, demagogue.

*Drao,* I do, act—DRAMATURGY, dramatics, MELODRAMATIC, dramatize, drama.

*Dunamis,* power—DYNAMICS, dynamite, HYDRODYNAMICS, AERODYNAMICS, DYNAMOMETER, DYNAMO, DYNE.

*Eidos,* form—KALEIDOSCOPE, SPHEROID, GEODE, CYCLOID, ANTHROPOID.

*Electron,* amber—electricity, ELECTRON, ELECTRONICS, ELECTROLYSIS, DIELECTRIC, ELECTROJET, ELECTROSTATIC.

*Ergon,* work—energy, METALLURGY, ALLERGY, ERG, ERGOMETER.

*Ge,* the earth—geography, geology, geometry, GEOMORPHOLOGY, GEODESY, GEODETIC, GEOID, GEODE, GEOCENTRIC, GEOCOSMIC, GEOPHYSICS.

*Homos,* the same—HOMOGRAPH, HOMOLOGUE, HOMONYM, HOMOMORPHY, HOMOLOGOUS, HOMOGENEOUS.

*Hydro,* water—hydraulic, hydrogen, HYDROPHOBIA, HYDRO, HYDROSTATIC, HYDRANT, DEHYDRATE, HYDROPONICS.

*Idios,* one's own, peculiar—IDIOM, IDIOSYNCRASY, idiot, IDIOCY, IDIOMORPHIC, IDIOCRACY, IDIOMATIC.

*Isos,* equal—ISOCHRONOUS, ISOSCELES, ISOTHERM, ISOSTASY, ISOGONAL, ISOCLINE, ISOBAR, ISOTOPE.

*K(C)linein,* to bend, slant, lean—CLINIC, DECLINATION, recline.

*K(C)ryptos,* hidden—CRYPTOGRAM, CRYPTIC, CRYPTOGRAPHY.

*Metron,* a measure—ANEMOMETER, BAROMETER, diameter, "FOOLOMETER" (Sydney Smith), GASOMETER, geometry, HEXAMETER, HYDROMETER, meter, PENTAMETER, PERIMETER, SYMMETRY, thermometer, TRIGONOMETRY.

*Monos,* alone—monarch, monastery, MONOSYLLABLE, MONOGAMY, MONOLITH, MONOMANIA, MONOGRAPH, MONOGRAM, MONOCLE, monotony.

*Neos,* new—NEOLOGY, NEOPHYTE, Neocene, NEON, NEOLITHIC, NEOLOGISM, NEOPLASM.

*Philos,* loving, fond of—PHILOLOGY, philosophy, PHILANTHROPY, PHILHARMONIC.

*Phone,* a sound—ANTIPHON, EUPHONY, EUPHONIOUS, PHONETICS, PHONIC, phonograph, POLYPHONIC, PHONOLOGY, symphony.

*Phos,* light—PHOSPHORUS, photograph, PHOTOMETER, PHOSPHATE, PHOTOSYNTHESIS, PHOTOSTAT.

*Phusis,* nature—PHYSIOGNOMY, PHYSIOGRAPHY, physic, PHYSICIST, METAPHYSICS, physician, physiology.

*Protos,* first—PROTONOTARY, PROTOCOL, PROTOMARTYR, protoplasm, PROTON, PROTOTYPE.

*Psyche,* soul, mind—PSYCHIATRY, PSYCHOANALYSIS, METEMPSYCHOSIS, PSYCHOSIS, PSYCHOTHERAPY, PSYCHOSOMATIC, PSYCHOSURGERY, PSYCHODRAMA.

*Skopeo,* I see—bishop, episcopal, KALEIDOSCOPE, microscope, SKEPTIC, telescope, STEREOSCOPE, STETHOSCOPE, SPECTROSCOPE.

*Topos,* a place—topic, TOPOGRAPHY, TOPONYM, TOPICAL, TOPARCHY.

*Zoon,* an animal—zoology, ZOOPHYTE, ZODIAC, EPIZOOTIC, PROTOZOAN, AZOIC, AZOTE, ZOON, ZOOTOMY (and at least 200 others in the OED).

## WHAT ENGLISH WORDS COULD PLINY SIGHT-READ?

Among these words of classical origin that make up three-fifths of our total stock, there are a surprising number that have come into English unchanged, even in spelling. The Greeks and Romans would not in some cases get the same meaning from one of these words as we do, if they could come back to life and see it in print. Caesar would know that *tractor* means something that draws something else along, a "puller"; but he could hardly be expected to identify it as a caterpillar tractor, powered with a gasoline engine. The Roman scientist Pliny, however, who knew his Greek as well, would spot a good many of the Greek words in something close to our sense, because he was the first to use them in that way: *naphtha* for crude oil, for example, and *pyrites* in our sense. ASBESTOS he knew was unburnable but he thought it a plant fiber. CINEMA (Gk. *kinema*) would stump him completely. He would know it meant "motion," but he couldn't realize that our word is shortened from CINEMATOGRAPH, which is literally motion picture.

If you want to check on your knowledge of cultural history, you might amuse yourself by guessing which of the following 260 Latin words resurrected Romans would understand in the same sense we do; and how many of the subsequent 85 Greek words Pliny the Elder (A.D. 23–79) could sight-read. We'd have to print them in capitals for him, since he wouldn't know our lower-case type.

Where Greek words have come to us through the Latin, and where it's the Roman spelling that persists in English, I have for the most part included these immigrants in the Latin list, marking the clue word (Gk.) to distinguish them. I have also included many Late Latin and MEDIEVAL Latin words; but not those which since 1700 have been formed on analogy with ancient rules from Greek or Latin stems by scientists or trade name inventors.

### Latin Words Taken into English Unchanged

Some of these you have already met, on p. 146 *et seq.* As you will note from the fact that they're printed in small capitals, and have high frequency numbers, most of these words belong to the range between 11 and 20 thousand. You should know them if you want to have a thorough command of English. Since they come about midway in the book, it seems like a good idea to use them also as a comprehensive check on your vocabulary range. For each group of ten, match the key word with its right meaning in the second column. For 17 [    ] cancer, below, the right meaning in the second column is [j] malignant tumor, so you put "j" in space in BRACKETS after 17.

| | | |
|---|---|---|
| 1. [   ] ALIAS (16) | [a] | Roman living room |
| 2. [   ] ALMA MATER (20+) | [b] | halo; visible emanation |
| 3. [   ] ALUMNI (13) | [c] | MEDIATOR plus; also arbiter |
| 4. [   ] ANTIPODES (16) | [d] | sharpest-pointed tip |
| 5. [   ] AORTA (14) | [e] | graduates |
| 6. [   ] APEX (12) | [f] | fake name |
| 7. [   ] ARBITRATOR (11) | [g] | the great artery (Gk.) |
| 8. [   ] ATRIUM (20) | [h] | foster mother |
| 9. [   ] AURA (17) | [i] | extra pay |
| 10. [   ] BONUS (12) | [j] | exactly opposite points on earth (Gk.) |

| | | |
|---|---|---|
| 11. [   ] CAESURA (19) | [a] | husk; SEPALS of flower (Gk.) |
| 12. [   ] CALCULUS (17) | [b] | just under the bark |
| 13. [   ] CALIBER (16) | [c] | top brain |
| 14. [   ] calyx (10) | [d] | taker |
| 15. [   ] CAMBIUM (12) | [e] | fluxions |
| 16. [   ] camera (8) | [f] | diameter; quality |
| 17. [   ] cancer (7) | [g] | pause |
| 18. [   ] CAPTOR (17) | [h] | vote-fixing powwow |
| 19. [   ] CAUCUS (13) | [i] | picture-taking device |
| 20. [   ] CEREBRUM (14) | [j] | malignant tumor |

| | | |
|---|---|---|
| 21. [   ] CEREBELLUM (17) | [a] | digest |
| 22. [   ] circus (5) | [b] | outer coat of eye |
| 23. [   ] COADJUTOR (15) | [c] | body |
| 24. [   ] COLOSSUS (17) | [d] | brain case |
| 25. [   ] COMPENDIUM (20+) | [e] | muscle-control center |
| 26. [   ] CORNEA (20) | [f] | big tent show |
| 27. [   ] CORPUS (15) | [g] | sun's AURA |
| 28. [   ] CORTEX (12) | [h] | first aide (esp. to bishop) |
| 29. [   ] CRANIUM (14) | [i] | giant statue |
| 30. [   ] CORONÁ (19) | [j] | gray matter (lit., bark) |

| | | |
|---|---|---|
| 31. [ ] CRUX (19) | [a] | keeper |
| 32. [ ] CUMULUS (20+) | [b] | raving frenzy |
| 33. [ ] CURATOR (16) | [c] | propriety |
| 34. [ ] CURRICULUM (14) | [d] | something sought after |
| 35. [ ] CYCLOPEDIA (17) | [e] | worn-off particles |
| 36. [ ] DECORUM (11) | [f] | course of study |
| 37. [ ] DELIRIUM (12) | [g] | all (?) about everything (Gk.) |
| 38. [ ] DESIDERATUM (17) | [h] | aut Caesar aut Khrushchev |
| 39. [ ] DETRITUS (19) | [i] | main point (lit., cross) |
| 40. [ ] DICTATOR (11) | [j] | rounded cloud |

| | | |
|---|---|---|
| 41. [ ] DICTUM (17) | [a] | balance |
| 42. [ ] DOLOR (15) | [b] | expounder |
| 43. [ ] elector (8) | [c] | on the spur of the moment |
| 44. [ ] EQUILIBRIUM (13) | [d] | do-it-all |
| 45. [ ] EQUINOX (14) | [e] | voter |
| 46. [ ] error (2) | [f] | thighbone |
| 47. [ ] EXPOSITOR (19) | [g] | pronouncement |
| 48. [ ] EXTEMPORE (16) | [h] | night equals day |
| 49. [ ] FACTOTUM (20) | [i] | grief |
| 50. [ ] FEMUR (20) | [j] | mistake |

| | | |
|---|---|---|
| 51. [ ] FIAT (15) | [a] | molds |
| 52. [ ] FLAMEN (19) | [b] | clan; tribe |
| 53. [ ] focus (7) | [c] | dynamo; begetter |
| 54. [ ] FULCRUM (13) | [d] | where rays meet at a point |
| 55. [ ] FUNGI (14) | [e] | spirits |
| 56. [ ] GALENA (20) | [f] | priest serving one god |
| 57. [ ] GENERATOR (15) | [g] | let there be; ukase |
| 58. [ ] GENII (16) | [h] | supreme natural endowment |
| 59. [ ] genius (4) | [i] | lever rests on it |
| 60. [ ] GENS (20) | [j] | lead SULPHIDE ore |

| | | |
|---|---|---|
| 61. [ ] GENUS (11) | [a] | gap |
| 62. [ ] GLADIATOR (11) | [b] | (army) baggage (including baggages) |
| 63. [ ] GLADIOLUS (18) | [c] | earth |
| 64. [ ] GYPSUM (20) | [d] | CATEGORY between species and family |
| 65. [ ] HIATUS (20) | [e] | Roman arena fighter |
| 66. [ ] HUMUS (14) | [f] | species of iris |
| 67. [ ] IMPEDIMENTA (20+) | [g] | front tooth |
| 68. [ ] IMPETUS (11) | [h] | books printed before 1500 A.D. |
| 69. [ ] INCISOR (14) | [i] | HYDRATED CALCIUM |
| 70. [ ] INCUNABULA (20+) | [j] | forward drive |

71. [ ] index (6)
72. [ ] INCUBATOR (11)
73. [ ] INCUBUS (16)
74. [ ] INERTIA (15)
75. [ ] INFLUX (14)
76. [ ] INSIGNIA (13)
77. [ ] INSOMNIA (13)
78. [ ] instructor (8)
79. [ ] INTERIM (12)

80. [ ] INTERIOR (12)

[a] inflowing
[b] sleeplessness
[c] teacher
[d] meanwhile
[e] non-hen egg-hatcher
[f] emblems
[g] key to contents
[h] inside
[i] tendency to stay put or keep moving
[j] burden

81. [ ] INTERREGNUM (16)
82. [ ] inventor (10)
83. [ ] INVESTIGATOR (11)
84. [ ] INVESTOR (14)
85. [ ] isthmus (3)
86. [ ] janitor (9)
87. [ ] junior (5)
88. [ ] LABOR (1)
89. [ ] LABURNUM (18)
90. [ ] LACUNA (20+)

[a] work
[b] younger
[c] gap (esp. in MS.)
[d] yellow-flowered shrub
[e] first maker of something new
[f] a breather between kings
[g] one who digs up the facts
[h] one who puts up money
[i] narrow land-bridge (Gk.)
[j] caretaker who also cleans

91. [ ] LANGUOR (11)
92. [ ] LAUDANUM (16)
93. [ ] LEX (16)
94. [ ] LICTOR (16)
95. [ ] liquor (4)
96. [ ] LUBRICATOR (14)
97. [ ] major (4)
98. [ ] MANIA (16)

99. [ ] MANIPULATOR (20)
100. [ ] MATRIX (17)

[a] slick handler
[b] greasing device; grease monkey
[c] more important (than a captain)
[d] madness
[e] law
[f] he carried the fasces
[g] mold for casting
[h] any liquid (esp. over 30% $C_2H_5OH$)
[i] opium in alcohol
[j] weariness

101. [ ] mediator (10)
102. [ ] medium (4)
103. [ ] MEDULLA (18)
104. [ ] MILLENNIUM (18)
105. [ ] minimum (8)
106. [ ] minister (2)
107. [ ] minus (10)
108. [ ] MINUTIAE (20)
109. [ ] miser (5)
110. [ ] MODERATOR (16)

[a] one who hoards and gloats
[b] brain switchboard
[c] go-between
[d] spiritual guide
[e] trifling details
[f] midway between extremes
[g] presiding officer
[h] less
[i] 1000 years
[j] least

159

111. [ ] MODICUM (19)     [a] that seasick feeling (Gk.)
112. [ ] MOMENTUM (15)     [b] he plots the ship's course
113. [ ] museum (4)     [c] many in the Milky Way
114. [ ] NAUSEA (15)     [d] saltpeter
115. [ ] nautilus (10)     [e] pearly-shelled cephalopod
116. [ ] navigator (8)     [f] treasure house of art, etc.
117. [ ] NEBULA (16)     [g] nothing
118. [ ] NIL (20+)     [h] what keeps it rolling
119. [ ] NEUTER (12)     [i] pinch; small amount
120. [ ] NITER (14)     [j] neither masculine nor feminine

121. [ ] NOSTRUM (15)     [a] pain-easing poppy extract
122. [ ] nucleus (7)     [b] HARBINGER
123. [ ] OCTOPUS (15)     [c] smell
124. [ ] ODIUM (20)     [d] quack remedy
125. [ ] odor (3)     [e] Carmen is one
126. [ ] omen (8)     [f] hatred
127. [ ] opera (4)     [g] one who bears down hard
128. [ ] operator (8)     [h] eight-armed sea mollusk (Gk.)
129. [ ] opium (7)     [i] one who runs the works
130. [ ] oppressor (8)     [j] central core

131. [ ] OPPROBRIUM (20)     [a] egg
132. [ ] orator (6)     [b] one of the conic section curves (Gk.)
133. [ ] OVUM (15)     [c] paleness
134. [ ] PALLADIUM (17)     [d] cure-all
135. [ ] PALLOR (16)     [e] tiny nipplelike projection
136. [ ] PANACEA (17)     [f] equal
137. [ ] PAPILLA (14)     [g] severe reproach
138. [ ] PAR (17)     [h] Cicero was one; so's Dirksen
139. [ ] PARABOLA (15)     [i] one who takes a share
140. [ ] PARTICIPATOR (20+)     [j] safeguard (Gk.)

141. [ ] pastor (5)     [a] the HOI POLLOI; the common folks
142. [ ] PAX (19)     [b] where hipbones and spine meet
143. [ ] PELVIS (17)     [c] oil
144. [ ] peninsula (5)     [d] peace
145. [ ] per (2)     [e] clergyman
146. [ ] PER CAPITA (17)     [f] each
147. [ ] PERPETRATOR (17)     [g] relentless annoyer
148. [ ] PERSECUTOR (13)     [h] so much apiece
149. [ ] petroleum (6)     [i] the man whodunit
150. [ ] PLEBS (19)     [j] next thing to an island

151. [ ] PLEXUS (20) [a] extra inducement
152. [ ] plus (8) [b] teacher
153. [ ] PRAETOR (16) [c] forerunner
154. [ ] PRECEPTOR (15) [d] MacArthur was one
155. [ ] PRECURSOR (17) [e] Roman judge
156. [ ] premium (7) [f] long snout; trunk (Gk.)
157. [ ] prior (7) [g] more; and; added to
158. [ ] PROBOSCIS (12) [h] balled-up mass of nerves, etc.
159. [ ] PROCONSUL (15) [i] before; one which takes precedence
160. [ ] PROCTOR (19) [j] university moral policeman


161. [ ] PROCURATOR (16) [a] Roman public treasurer
162. [ ] progenitor (9) [b] usually found in cocoon
163. [ ] projector (10) [c] ore-hunter; now after uranium
164. [ ] PROLIX (20+) [d] spreading opinions
165. [ ] PROPAGANDA (11) [e] tax-extractor for a Roman province
166. [ ] PROSPECTOR (15) [f] we run film through it
167. [ ] pupa (8) [g] wordy
168. [ ] QUAESTOR (17) [h] halfway; seeming; as if
169. [ ] QUASI (16) [i] COMEUPPANCE; finishing stroke
170. [ ] QUIETUS (17) [j] forefather


171. [ ] QUONDAM (16) [a] relative magnitude
172. [ ] QUORUM (17) [b] extreme hatred
173. [ ] QUOTA (14) [c] referring legislature's act to people
174. [ ] radius (8) [d] onetime
175. [ ] RANCOR (15) [e] Episcopal parish clergyman
176. [ ] ratio (7) [f] backflow
177. [ ] rector (9) [g] end of large intestine
178. [ ] RECTUM (17) [h] distance from center to rim
179. [ ] REFERENDUM (11) [i] number needed to do business
180. [ ] REFLUX (15) [j] share of total

181. [　] REGIMEN (13)　　　　　[a] holy place for refuge
182. [　] register (3)　　　　　　[b] speaker's platform
183. [　] REJUVENATOR (18)　　　[c] eye's sensitive image-receiver
184. [　] REPLICA (19)　　　　　[d] late December celebration
185. [　] RETINA (11)　　　　　　[e] spit
186. [　] ROSTRUM (13)　　　　　[f] airborne gossip
187. [　] rumor (4)　　　　　　　[g] exact reproduction
188. [　] saliva (8)　　　　　　　[h] youth-restorer
189. [　] SANCTUM (17)　　　　　[i] list for record
190. [　] SATURNALIA (20)　　　[j] the doctor lays it down

191. [　] SECTOR (16)　　　　　[a] expressed comparison
192. [　] SEMI (20)　　　　　　[b] fancy word for a menial
193. [　] SEPULCHER (7)　　　　[c] sequence
194. [　] series (4)　　　　　　[d] part of military area
195. [　] SERUM (11)　　　　　　[e] bone cavity
196. [　] SERVITOR (13)　　　　[f] sun
197. [　] SILVA (18)　　　　　　[g] half
198. [　] simile (8)　　　　　　[h] forest
199. [　] SINUS (15)　　　　　　[i] tomb
200. [　] SOL (14)　　　　　　　[j] ANTITOXIN is one

201. [　] solicitor (8)　　　　　[a] endurance; staying power
202. [　] spectator (7)　　　　　[b] stock-gambler: bull or bear
203. [　] SPECULATOR (17)　　　[c] magnificent show
204. [　] splendor (4)　　　　　[d] he drums up business
205. [　] SPONSOR (18)　　　　　[e] he looks on
206. [　] SPUTUM (20)　　　　　[f] to blame for soap opera; god-
　　　　　　　　　　　　　　　　　parent
207. [　] STADIUM (16)　　　　　[g] coughed-up spit
208. [　] stamen (9)　　　　　　[h] pollen-carrying ANTHER
209. [　] STAMINA (15)　　　　　[i] condition
210. [　] STATUS (11)　　　　　　[j] AMPHITHEATER for games

211. [　] STERNUM (20)　　　　　[a] overseer (of slaves or teachers)
212. [　] stimulus (8)　　　　　[b] one who outlives others
213. [　] STRATA (13)　　　　　　[c] above
214. [　] STUPOR (13)　　　　　　[d] Greek drink-and-talkfest (Gk.)
215. [　] SUBSTRATUM (12)　　　[e] daze
216. [　] SUPER (20)　　　　　　[f] above average; man over you
　　　　　　　　　　　　　　　　　you
217. [　] superior (2)　　　　　[g] underlayer
218. [　] supervisor (9)　　　　[h] breastbone
219. [　] survivor (7)　　　　　[i] layers
220. [　] SYMPOSIUM (18)　　　　[j] it stirs or excites action

221. [　] TANTALUS (17)
222. [　] TAURUS (19)
223. [　] TEDIUM (18)
224. [　] TESTATOR (16)

225. [　] TETANUS (13)
226. [　] THALLUS (19)
227. [　] THYMUS (19)
228. [　] TIARA (13)
229. [　] TIBIA (16)
230. [　] TOGA (19)

[a] thicker lower leg bone
[b] muscular spasm (Gk.)
[c] jeweled headdress or crown
[d] he couldn't reach the grapes (Gk.)
[e] sign of the bull; a constellation
[f] maker of a will
[g] boredom
[h] Roman gentleman's outer robe
[i] gland in neck (Gk.)
[j] a mushroom is one (Gk.)

231. [　] TORPOR (18)
232. [　] tractor (9)
233. [　] TRANSGRESSOR (12)
234. [　] TRANSLATOR (16)
235. [　] TRIUMVIR (16)
236. [　] tuber (10)
237. [　] TUMOR (11)
238. [　] tutor (5)
239. [　] TYMPANUM (14)
240. [　] TYPHUS (18)

[a] a potato is one
[b] necessary since BABEL
[c] pestilential fever
[d] one of three men ruling
[e] sluggish state
[f] heavy puller
[g] sinner; he steps over
[h] drum
[i] teaches one student at a time
[j] swelling growth

241. [　] ulcer (10)
242. [　] ULTERIOR (18)
243. [　] ULTRA (18)
244. [　] UTERUS (18)
245. [　] vapor (3)
246. [　] VELLUM (14)
247. [　] VERSUS (20)
248. [　] VERTEBRA (14)
249. [　] VERTEX (17)
250. [　] vesper (9)

[a] highest point
[b] against
[c] evening song or service
[d] backbone
[e] finest parchment
[f] womb
[g] steam; fog
[h] pus-discharging sore
[i] hidden
[j] beyond

251. [　] veto (10)
252. [　] via (10)
253. [　] vice- (3)
254. [　] victor (10)
255. [　] vigor (3)
256. [　] villa (9)
257. [　] VIRUS (17)
258. [　] VISCERA (17)
259. [　] VORTEX (15)
260. [　] vox (20+)

[a] whirlpool; WHORL
[b] the "innards"
[c] strength
[d] voice
[e] to "nix" a bill or act
[f] winner
[g] suburban mansion
[h] by way of
[i] in place of: No. 2 man
[j] FILTERABLE infectious substance

| | | | | | | |
|---|---|---|---|---|---|---|
| 1. [f] | 11. [g] | 21. [e] | 31. [i] | 41. [g] | 51. [g] | 61. [d] |
| 2. [h] | 12. [e] | 22. [f] | 32. [j] | 42. [i] | 52. [f] | 62. [e] |
| 3. [e] | 13. [f] | 23. [h] | 33. [a] | 43. [e] | 53. [d] | 63. [f] |
| 4. [j] | 14. [a] | 24. [i] | 34. [f] | 44. [a] | 54. [i] | 64. [i] |
| 5. [g] | 15. [b] | 25. [a] | 35. [g] | 45. [h] | 55. [a] | 65. [a] |
| 6. [d] | 16. [i] | 26. [b] | 36. [c] | 46. [j] | 56. [j] | 66. [c] |
| 7. [c] | 17. [j] | 27. [c] | 37. [b] | 47. [b] | 57. [c] | 67. [b] |
| 8. [a] | 18. [d] | 28. [j] | 38. [d] | 48. [c] | 58. [e] | 68. [j] |
| 9. [b] | 19. [h] | 29. [d] | 39. [e] | 49. [d] | 59. [h] | 69. [g] |
| 10. [i] | 20. [c] | 30. [g] | 40. [h] | 50. [f] | 60. [b] | 70. [h] |

| | | | | | | |
|---|---|---|---|---|---|---|
| 71. [g] | 81. [f] | 91. [j] | 101. [c] | 111. [i] | 121. [d] | 131. [g] |
| 72. [e] | 82. [e] | 92. [i] | 102. [f] | 112. [h] | 122. [j] | 132. [h] |
| 73. [j] | 83. [g] | 93. [e] | 103. [b] | 113. [f] | 123. [h] | 133. [a] |
| 74. [i] | 84. [h] | 94. [f] | 104. [i] | 114. [a] | 124. [f] | 134. [j] |
| 75. [a] | 85. [i] | 95. [h] | 105. [j] | 115. [e] | 125. [c] | 135. [c] |
| 76. [f] | 86. [j] | 96. [b] | 106. [d] | 116. [b] | 126. [b] | 136. [d] |
| 77. [b] | 87. [b] | 97. [c] | 107. [h] | 117. [c] | 127. [e] | 137. [e] |
| 78. [c] | 88. [a] | 98. [d] | 108. [e] | 118. [g] | 128. [i] | 138. [f] |
| 79. [d] | 89. [d] | 99. [a] | 109. [a] | 119. [j] | 129. [a] | 139. [b] |
| 80. [h] | 90. [c] | 100. [g] | 110. [g] | 120. [d] | 130. [g] | 140. [i] |

| | | | | | | |
|---|---|---|---|---|---|---|
| 141. [e] | 151. [h] | 161. [e] | 171. [d] | 181. [j] | 191. [d] | 201. [d] |
| 142. [d] | 152. [g] | 162. [j] | 172. [i] | 182. [i] | 192. [g] | 202. [e] |
| 143. [b] | 153. [e] | 163. [f] | 173. [j] | 183. [h] | 193. [i] | 203. [b] |
| 144. [j] | 154. [b] | 164. [g] | 174. [h] | 184. [g] | 194. [c] | 204. [c] |
| 145. [f] | 155. [c] | 165. [d] | 175. [b] | 185. [c] | 195. [j] | 205. [f] |
| 146. [h] | 156. [a] | 166. [c] | 176. [a] | 186. [b] | 196. [b] | 206. [g] |
| 147. [i] | 157. [i] | 167. [b] | 177. [e] | 187. [f] | 197. [h] | 207. [j] |
| 148. [g] | 158. [f] | 168. [a] | 178. [g] | 188. [e] | 198. [a] | 208. [h] |
| 149. [c] | 159. [d] | 169. [h] | 179. [c] | 189. [a] | 199. [e] | 209. [a] |
| 150. [a] | 160. [j] | 170. [i] | 180. [f] | 190. [d] | 200. [f] | 210. [i] |

| | | | | |
|---|---|---|---|---|
| 211. [h] | 221. [d] | 231. [e] | 241. [h] | 251. [e] |
| 212. [j] | 222. [e] | 232. [f] | 242. [i] | 252. [h] |
| 213. [i] | 223. [g] | 233. [g] | 243. [j] | 253. [i] |
| 214. [e] | 224. [f] | 234. [b] | 244. [f] | 254. [f] |
| 215. [g] | 225. [b] | 235. [d] | 245. [g] | 255. [c] |
| 216. [c] | 226. [j] | 236. [a] | 246. [e] | 256. [g] |
| 217. [f] | 227. [i] | 237. [j] | 247. [b] | 257. [j] |
| 218. [a] | 228. [c] | 238. [i] | 248. [d] | 258. [b] |
| 219. [b] | 229. [a] | 239. [h] | 249. [a] | 259. [a] |
| 220. [d] | 230. [h] | 240. [c] | 250. [c] | 260. [d] |

Subtract your error score from 160. Multiply the resulting figure by 62 and add 10,000. This should be a conservative estimate of your vocabulary within the 20,000-word range. Of the 260 words above, 71 are in the first 10,000 for FREQUENCY and range—hence, by our assumption, you should undoubtedly know them; 29 are in the range 20,000 to 30,000—so a hundred words are arbitrarily discounted. Many of the 260 are semitechnical, hence they are probably harder nuts to crack than many of the words that belong in the same frequency groups with them. However, you have an advantage here that you would not have if you came on the words in your reading. Clues are given, in scrambled lists to be sure, but these afford something of the same advantage that the clues do in a crossword puzzle. You can arrive at some meanings by guesswork and the method of RESIDUES; and in other cases the clue synonym, definition, or catch phrase CRYSTALLIZES a connection that was very vague indeed until you ran down the column of ten possible meanings and finally hit on one that clicked in your mind. Balancing off the PROS and CONS, this is therefore probably a relatively fair measure of what proportion you know of the "highbrow" words in the 20,000 commonest.

### Greek Words Taken into English Unchanged

Follow the same procedure as you used for the Latin words above.

1. [ ] ACME (13)
2. [ ] AETHER (17)
3. [ ] ALPHA (20)
4. [ ] AMBROSIA (14)
5. [ ] analysis (8)
6. [ ] ANTITHESIS (16)
7. [ ] APOTHEOSIS (18)

8. [ ] ASBESTOS (11)
9. [ ] CATHETER (19)
10. [ ] CHAMELEON (13)

[a] food of the gods
[b] first letter of Greek alphabet
[c] color-changing lizard
[d] slender tube for body orifices
[e] upper air
[f] high point (of a quality)
[g] breaking it up; in statistics, a breakdown
[h] unburnable
[i] glorification
[j] direct opposite

165

11. [　] chaos (6)　　　　　　　　　[a] basis for judging
12. [　] character (2)　　　　　　　[b] disease due to liver DYSFUNC-
　　　　　　　　　　　　　　　　　　　　TION
13. [　] CHIMERA (16)　　　　　　　[c] wild fancy
14. [　] CHOLER (17)　　　　　　　　[d] movie
15. [　] CINEMA (18)　　　　　　　　[e] anger
16. [　] COSMOS (13)　　　　　　　　[f] world order; universe
17. [　] CRATER (13)　　　　　　　　[g] nature; makeup
18. [　] CRITERION (15)　　　　　　[h] bowl-shaped hole in volcano
19. [　] delta (6)　　　　　　　　　[i] ultimate in disorder
20. [　] DIABETES (13)　　　　　　　[j] area around river mouth

21. [　] DIAGNOSIS (15)　　　　　　[a] puzzle
22. [　] DIAPASON (15)　　　　　　　[b] gullet
23. [　] DILEMMA (13)　　　　　　　[c] I have found it
24. [　] DOGMA (11)　　　　　　　　[d] unit minus electrical charge
25. [　] drama (5)　　　　　　　　　[e] swelling musical sound
26. [　] ENIGMA (12)　　　　　　　　[f] naming the disease from the
　　　　　　　　　　　　　　　　　　　　symptoms
27. [　] EPITOME (14)　　　　　　　[g] brief version
28. [　] ESOPHAGUS (18)　　　　　　[h] a play
29. [　] EUREKA (20+)　　　　　　　[i] AUTHORITARIAN doctrine
30. [　] ELECTRON (20)　　　　　　　[j] either way, you're stuck

31. [　] EXODUS (13)　　　　　　　　[a] dictionary
32. [　] GANGLION (13)　　　　　　　[b] EXAGGERATION for effect
33. [　] HALCYON (16)　　　　　　　[c] laughing or crying fit
34. [　] HYPERBOLE (15)　　　　　　[d] nerve cluster
35. [　] HYSTERIA (19)　　　　　　　[e] a going out
36. [　] ICHNEUMON (20+)　　　　　[f] jot; "i" was smallest letter
37. [　] idea (2)　　　　　　　　　[g] MONGOOSE-like animal
38. [　] IOTA (20)　　　　　　　　　[h] happy and peaceful
39. [　] ISOSCELES (20)　　　　　　[i] something conceived in the
　　　　　　　　　　　　　　　　　　　　mind
40. [　] LEXICON (16)　　　　　　　[j] with two sides equal

41. [　] metamorphosis (8)　　　　[a] goddess of RETRIBUTION
42. [　] metropolis (7)　　　　　　[b] musicians or where they sit
43. [　] MYRMIDON (16)　　　　　　　[c] henchman
44. [　] NAPHTHA (14)　　　　　　　[d] chief city
45. [　] NEMESIS (15)　　　　　　　[e] change of form
46. [　] oasis (7)　　　　　　　　　[f] inflammable volatile liquid
47. [　] OMEGA (17)　　　　　　　　[g] fertile spot in desert
48. [　] ONYX (16)　　　　　　　　　[h] ornamental stone
49. [　] OPHTHALMIA (20+)　　　　　[i] last letter of Gk. alphabet
50. [　] orchestra (5)　　　　　　　[j] eye infection

51. [ ] osmosis (10)
52. [ ] PAPYRUS (17)
53. [ ] PARALLAX (20+)
54. [ ] PARALYSIS (11)
55. [ ] PATHOS (12)

56. [ ] PHAETON (19)
57. [ ] PHALANX (11)

58. [ ] PHARYNX (12)
59. [ ] PARENTHESIS (20)

60. [ ] PHENOMENA (16)

[a] curved lines used to set off insert
[b] light carriage
[c] observable things
[d] sadness
[e] two-way SEEPAGE through porous membrane
[f] paper from pith
[g] angle change in direction as eye shifts
[h] back of mouth
[i] wedge-shaped fighting group with locked shields
[j] palsy


61. [ ] phenomenon (7)
62. [ ] PHOENIX (13)
63. [ ] plasma (10)

64. [ ] POLYGAMY (15)
65. [ ] POLYGON (19)

66. [ ] PRESBYTER (15)
67. [ ] prism (7)
68. [ ] PSALTER (16)

69. [ ] PSYCHE (11)
70. [ ] PYRITES (19)

[a] Cupid's girl friend; the soul
[b] iron SULFIDES
[c] plural marriage; POLYGYNY or POLYANDRY
[d] elder
[e] a glass that breaks up white light
[f] Book of Psalms
[g] liquid part of blood
[h] plane figure with more than four sides
[i] it's unusual
[j] it rose from its own ashes


71. [ ] PYTHON (19)
72. [ ] PYX (20+)
73. [ ] SARCOPHAGUS (17)
74. [ ] satyr (8)
75. [ ] SPERMATOZOON (20+)
76. [ ] STIGMA (17)
77. [ ] STOMA (17)
78. [ ] STROPHE (17)
79. [ ] SYNOPSIS (18)
80. [ ] SYNTHESIS (11)

[a] goat-footed nymph-chasing god
[b] stone coffin
[c] male reproductive cell
[d] big snake; a constrictor
[e] mark of disgrace
[f] bird's-eye view; summary
[g] combining parts into whole
[h] stanza
[i] mouth
[j] container for Host

81. [   ] THERMOS (17)      [a] figure of speech
82. [   ] THESIS (12)       [b] beginner; raw recruit
83. [   ] THORAX (11)       [c] chest
84. [   ] TROPE (14)        [d] essay submitted for degree
85. [   ] TYRO (18)         [e] heat-conserver

| | | | | | | |
|---|---|---|---|---|---|---|
| 1. [f] | 11. [i] | 21. [f] | 31. [e] | 41. [e] | 51. [e] | 61. [i] |
| 2. [e] | 12. [g] | 22. [e] | 32. [d] | 42. [d] | 52. [f] | 62. [j] |
| 3. [b] | 13. [c] | 23. [j] | 33. [h] | 43. [c] | 53. [g] | 63. [g] |
| 4. [a] | 14. [e] | 24. [i] | 34. [b] | 44. [f] | 54. [j] | 64. [c] |
| 5. [g] | 15. [d] | 25. [h] | 35. [c] | 45. [a] | 55. [d] | 65. [h] |
| 6. [j] | 16. [f] | 26. [a] | 36. [g] | 46. [g] | 56. [b] | 66. [d] |
| 7. [i] | 17. [h] | 27. [g] | 37. [i] | 47. [i] | 57. [i] | 67. [e] |
| 8. [h] | 18. [a] | 28. [b] | 38. [f] | 48. [h] | 58. [h] | 68. [f] |
| 9. [d] | 19. [j] | 29. [c] | 39. [j] | 49. [j] | 59. [a] | 69. [a] |
| 10. [c] | 20. [b] | 30. [d] | 40. [a] | 50. [b] | 60. [c] | 70. [b] |

| | | |
|---|---|---|
| 71. [d] | 76. [e] | 81. [e] |
| 72. [j] | 77. [i] | 82. [d] |
| 73. [b] | 78. [h] | 83. [c] |
| 74. [a] | 79. [f] | 84. [a] |
| 75. [c] | 80. [g] | 85. [b] |

Subtract your error score from 85. Multiply the resulting figure by 117 and add 10,000 to it, to get another estimate of your vocabulary score on the Greek refugees compared with the luck you had with the Roman fugitives.


## HOW TO BE A WORD MECHANIC

Learning to distinguish the main types of building material in the classical lumberyard takes a little time; and to be a good word mechanic and find out how the Greeks and Romans put the joints together, takes still more. Also, many word carpenters have worked over the old antiques in France, Italy, Spain, England, and the United

States. Some of them were good craftsmen, who knew the rules and period styles. Others were quite clumsy artisans, and they achieved some weird combinations, putting Greek prefixes on Latin stems— *amoral*, for example. At worst, such VERBAL MONSTROSITIES as *talkathon* and *walkathon* have been manufactured by BOBTAILING off the last half of *marathon* and hanging it on the Old English words *talk* and *walk*.

Luckily in the standard vocabulary there are not too many of these hybrids, and in any case it's amusing to crack them apart. But it is also possible to get off the track, even if the word started as an authentic Latin word which one has never encountered.

As an example, take the word ANFRACTUOSITIES. If interpreted too literally, it might be taken to mean "rough edges," which would hurt anybody who ran into them. If you thought of *fracture* or FRACTIOUS, you might analyze it thus:

| an | fractu | os | ity |
|---------|--------|---------|-------|
| against | break | full of | state |

or "state of being full of breaks against." By consulting *Webster's Dictionary of Synonyms* (1951) you will learn that the word really refers to SINUOSITIES—windings or quirks. By correcting the one mistake in your breakdown, you will arrive at the correct analysis:

| an | fractu | os | ity |
|----|--------|----|-----|

or "state of being full of breaks around." The prefix *an* is here a combining form of *ambo-*, around. A "break around" something implies a "curve,"—a bend, not a break. Actually, therefore, the word means "state of being full of curves" (but don't ever tell a girl she has an ANFRACTUOUS figure unless you have your *Webster* along). The OED defines it as "tortuous crevices, channels, or passages," hence, figuratively, "OBLIQUITY" or "INTRICACY." What looks like a rough break is really a curve.

Not many derivatives are as tricky as *anfractuosity*. And in spite of the hazards, it's worth a gamble to try your luck at sight-reading meanings on the basis of a knowledge of the main Greek and Latin combining forms, plus the AFFIXES that go with them.

## THE WORD-ANALYZER

As a memory device for tying many new words to one, there is a Word-Analyzer in the last chapter, presenting in a compact table the prefixes and suffixes needed, and a summary list of the 100 main Greek and Latin stems that have yielded a good many derivatives. Start to study the stems, and the words derived from them, at the rate of five stems a day. Take plenty of time to look up in the dictionary all the words of which you have the least doubt, after you've made your best guess. Spread out the work over several weeks while you are continuing with the rest of this book and the Word-Game Quizzes. When you feel confident that you know the roots and their derivatives, take the Word Matching Tests before going on to the Comprehensive Vocabulary-Level Test. Daily study of the 100 stems in the Word-Analyzer should add 5000 new words to your vocabulary. Careful rereading of this book will give you 5000 more. That makes 10,000 new words or double the vocabulary of the average American.

The Word-Analyzer will usually enable you to arrive at the literal sense of the word.[2] Remember, though, that the literal sense of a word is just the beginning, the door-opener. To arrive at the present significance of a word in actual use, you need to find out how words change meaning. Put aside your mechanic's tools and get your microscope; you're about to become a word detective.

[2] Before going on to the next chapter, turn to the Word-Analyzer on pages 360–361 and study the first five Latin stems ( ag, act to aud, audit) and their derivatives.

# Classical Words Quiz

Are you keeping a record of your scores on the quizzes following each chapter? You'll total them before taking the Comprehensive Vocabulary-Level Test at the end of Chapter 12.

1. What does the Greek stem *phobe* mean?
2. Give four equivalents for *ology*. (These are not in your Word List.)
3. What does *graph* mean?
4. Combine *graph* and *lexicon* into a word that means "compiler of dictionaries."
5. Give five words that are derived from *fac* and its variant forms *fic, fact, fect, factur.* (Not in Word List.)
6. What is the word derived from *pon* that means "to place side by side"?
7. To outlaw is to _____scribe.
8. What are the Greek prefixes for "over," "under," "beyond," "around," and "with"? (Not in Word List.)
9. What is the suffix that distinguishes the adherents of an *ism*?
10. Give five words derived from the Greek *arch*. (Not in Word List.)
11. The ____AGON____ in a play is the chief character or the one who forces the action.
12. What is the word derived from the Greek *skopeo* that refers to an instrument used to analyze light patterns?
13. "Cryptic" comes from the Greek *cryptos*. They both mean _____.
14. What is the muscle-control center of the brain?
15. What is a word derived from Greek that means "wild fancy" or "fantastic notion"?
16. What is a word that means "beginner" or "raw recruit"?
17. What is a word that literally means "state of being full of curves"?
18. The rate of increase of a moving or falling object is _____.
19. The capacity to adjust to changes in environment by altering responses or habits is _____.
20. What is the polite or euphemistic term for "graft" or "loot"?
21. _____ is a synonym for "stingy" or "tight-fisted."
22. The curve traversed by a projectile is its _____.
23. A word that conveys the meaning of "familiar with many languages" is _____.
24. The custom of law that devolves inheritance or title on the eldest son is _____.
25. To evade immediate action, in order to gain time or avoid trouble is to _____.
26. Something that accompanies something else is _____ with it.
27. The act or process of swinging back and forth is _____.

28. What are the exact opposite points of earth?
29. What is a word meaning "having to do with public finances"?
30. A ruling body consisting of three men is a _____.

## WORD LIST

| | | | |
|---|---|---|---|
| booty | chimera | antipodes | cerebrum |
| *prescribe* | fear | polarization | *proscribe* |
| triumvir | to write | triumvirate | anfractuous |
| tyro | to read | line-of-sight | acceleration |
| polyglot | deceleration | protagonist | articulation |
| love | tangential | hidden | antipodes |
| troglodyte | juxtapose | inheritance | spectroscope |
| fiscal | embryo | oscillation | medulla |
| *or* | adaptability | stereoscope | adept |
| lexicographical | parsimonious | synapse | trajectory |
| *ist* | perquisites | concomitant | cryptogram |
| temporize | primogeniture | fiduciary | ideology |
| antagonist | primordial | osculation | genetic |
| opponent | component | cerebellum | clear |
| poser | lexicographer | caustic | stereophonic |

## ANSWERS

| | | |
|---|---|---|
| 21. parsimonious | 11. protagonist | 1. fear |
| 22. trajectory | 12. spectroscope | 2. see page 143 |
| 23. polyglot | 13. hidden | 3. to write (or "written") |
| 24. primogeniture | 14. cerebellum | 4. lexicographer |
| 25. temporize | 15. chimera | 5. see page 147 |
| 26. concomitant | 16. tyro | 6. juxtapose |
| 27. oscillation | 17. anfractuous | 7. proscribe |
| 28. antipodes | 18. acceleration | 8. see page 152 |
| 29. fiscal | 19. adaptability | 9. *ist* |
| 30. triumvirate | 20. perquisites | 10. see page 154 |

## SCORING KEY

30 right—Ph.D. in Latin and Greek stems
27–29 right—Master word mechanic
23–26 right—College graduate in classical words
18–22 right—You've passed the "tyro" stage
12–17 right—Study the long, hard words
Under 12 right—Reread this chapter

SCORE: _____

# 8

## How to Be a Word Detective by Watching Words Change Meaning

The long, hard words of classical origin were born of Latin and Greek roots, prefixes, and suffixes. Other words in our language—*bog, girth, squat,* SHARD—came from the workaday words of our Anglo-Saxon ancestors. Foreign terms like *sputnik, apartheid,* and *aperitif* were taken directly into the language because we had no precise equivalents for them. But no matter where words come from, they are in a fluid state; they keep traveling and they keep changing both in form and in meaning. They have their histories from the time of conception to maturity and often decline. Sometimes they retain their old meaning as they add new ones; often they lose their original meaning and take on new identities. Meanings are extended, stretched, shrunk, adulterated, radiated, degraded.

When a dictionary is compiled, the history or etymology of a word is telescoped into a brief explanation, generally in brackets before the definitions.[1] But the meanings and the labels attached to a word, which are a dictionary's primary concern, become fixed until the next edition is published. A good word detective, however, is not satisfied with words in a fixed state nor with etymologies that are too sketchy. He wants to observe words closely as they evolved in the past and as they are changing in the present. The Sherlock Holmeses of the lexicography trade—the Skeats, the Partridges, the Shipleys, the Evanses—make a game of tracing the etymology of a word. And they often disagree, coming to verbal blows to defend their findings.

Take the case of *juke-box.* One school of etymologists claims that the word came from an OBSOLETE Middle English word, *jouk,* which was kept alive in the Appalachian hills by the descendants of the Scotch and English settlers who went west in the early 1800's. The word was applied to a tavern as a *juke-joint,* but this was a dialect

[1] See Chapter 4 for an explanation of how dictionaries handle etymologies.

173

localism until the juke-box came along. Why the spelling of *jouk* was modified to *juke* no one seems to know.

Another group of word watchers argues that *juke* is the descendant of the West African *dzug* or *dzugu*, which meant wicked and disorderly. In the Gullah dialect of the South Carolina Negroes, the word was changed to *juke* and *joog*.

One would think that two opposing points of view would be enough. But there is a further split among the followers of the *jouk* → *juke* theory. Here are two versions:

Version 1—from the files of the *New York Times:*

The *jouk* in question, says the *Times*, means "rest" or "roost." It occurs in Chaucer, but did not make the grade further for literary use. However, it crossed the ocean and was COLONIZED, as noted. Roadside taverns in the Southern uplands were called *juke-houses*, meaning "resting-places," and when coin-operated phonographs were installed, the patrons naturally enough labeled these devices *juke-boxes* and the nickname came into national use in spite of opposition from the manufacturers of the canned-music device.

Version 2—by a professional etymologist:

The *jouk* in question, says dissenting Professor Joseph Shipley in his *Dictionary of Word Origins*, "to dodge, to move quickly, was applied to the places where liquor was sold, in prohibition times; hence, any cheap drinking place. . . ."

It is possible that neither version of "jouk" is strictly accurate. Here is Version 3, an entry under *jouk* or *jook* ("dodge") in the OED:

III. A place into which one may dart for shelter; a shelter from a blow, a storm, etc. Mod(ern) Sc(ottish) 1808–18 in Jamieson (Scottish Dictionary).

Maybe a jook-joint was a "shelter-joint," a place you dodged into before its owner and patrons started "dodging out" of it during prohibition days.

Let's get back to the *dzug-joog* camp, which says that the *juke-joint* or *juke-house* as a disorderly place, a place of sin and iniquity, derives its meaning naturally from the original "wicked life" of *dzug*. To bring some order out of confusion, we'll chart this controversy and see what we have (page 175).

This instance shows that you can't always depend on etymology to give you the true history of a word. In its travels a word may acquire many aliases, change its meaning several times, and wind

174

# JUKE-BOX

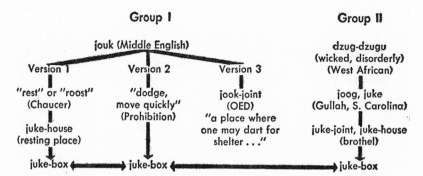

Group I

jouk (Middle English)

| Version 1 | Version 2 | Version 3 |
|---|---|---|
| "rest" or "roost" (Chaucer) | "dodge, move quickly" (Prohibition) | jook-joint (OED) "a place where one may dart for shelter . . ." |
| juke-house (resting place) | | |
| juke-box ⟷ | juke-box ⟵ | |

Group II

dzug-dzugu (wicked, disorderly) (West African)

joog, juke (Gullah, S. Carolina)

juke-joint, juke-house (brothel)

juke-box

up with a far different sense. Then, when you think you have it cornered, ticketed, and labeled, off it goes looking for a new context.

Luckily not many words undergo such a complete shift as *jouk* or *dzug* (take your pick), nor do many have homophones that fit in PLAUSIBLY to account for the meaning when the word is suddenly revived. *Jouk* is such a tricky example that it virtually provides a pit for all but the most ASTUTE etymologists to fall into.

As a rule, once words make their way into the standard language, they may add meanings, but they usually do so in accordance with processes that are pretty well defined. Once you know how the shifts happen, it's usually easy to sight-read a new sense.

## WORD-SHUTTLE SERVICE

Two main processes by which meaning-changes occur are so closely allied that they have to be considered together. One is *stretching*, the other is *shrinking* of meaning. Experts use the terms of Latin origin: GENERALIZATION for stretching, and SPECIALIZATION for shrinking. These twin processes work back and forth, like a SHUTTLE which now pulls the threads TAUT and thin, and now FLARES them out wide and loose on the spindle. When the threads are CONSTRICTED in a taut line, the meaning is specific; when they are spread out spindlewise, the word covers a large area of meaning, and so becomes generalized.

If you're reading an old Icelandic SAGA, and come on the line:

Gunnar's case was brought before the September meeting of the *Thing,* with Old Njal sitting in the judgment seat. . . .

you're encountering the word *Thing* used in its narrow, original sense: "a political or JUDICIAL assembly." Any case, matter, or cause brought before the *Thing* came to be referred to also as a *thing;* and eventually this meaning of "matter" was extended to cover any "affair" or "business," whether before a court or not. Next the meaning was further widened to cover "anything done," or "whatever is to be done." From that it was generalized to mean "anything that exists or can be thought about." We now use *thing* as a highly generalized word-of-all-work to apply to whatever we cannot label with a more specific term. Or it may even be used, compounded with an indefinite pronoun, as a term of contempt, to describe something CHARACTERLESS—as Blake called the eighteenth-century parsons' God "Old Anything." Thus the word *thing* has been stretched until it covers an immense area of meaning. This is generalization with a vengeance.

**THING**

**A political or judicial assembly**

**A case before a judicial assembly**

**Any matter, whether before a court or not**

**Anything that is done or whatever is to be done**

**Anything that exists — or that can be thought about**

**Now, a generalized word-of-all-work to apply to anything that cannot be given a specific name.**

In its review of the all-time Hollywood superspectacle, *Time* wrote: ". . . *Cleopatra* was bound to be one of those colossal *Things* that periodically come charging out of the ACETATE jungle and gobble up millions of dollars." Did *Time* "stretch" or "shrink" the meaning of *thing?*

The word *gear* has undergone the opposite treatment: SHRINKAGE. Around 1200 it meant "habits" or "manners." Then it shifted to mean "equipment": apparel, armor, harness, or any kind of tool or apparatus. From "apparatus" it was narrowed to mean "an arrangement of fixed and moving parts in a machine for any special purpose"; and finally still further specialized to signify "a wheel having teeth that fit into another wheel of the same kind, usually of a different size, to make the second wheel turn at a different speed from the first." While we still occasionally speak of "household gear," the word alone would now call up one of the last two meanings given, and we'd think first of automobile gears, or steering gear. The specialized, restricted meaning has won out, although the second more general sense has also remained for occasional use.

The shuttle is always at work in our language, now constricting, now flaring out the threads of meaning. *Angle, line,* and *proposition* are now far gone toward generalization, following in the wake of *thing, business, concern, regard, account, circumstance, fact, matter, condition,* and *state.* These words have become the counters and markers in the game of speech; they are often called *counter* words, because they have lost specific meaning, and have no more individual character than POKER chips or billiard markers.

*Contact* has gone the same route. The dictionaries at one time gave it as a verb which applies only to the establishment of a JUNCTURE of an electrical circuit. Now it has finally widened out to include any kind of communication, whether a physical touching of objects or a phone conversation. The inability of people to "communicate" with one another in an age of INHIBITIONS may account for the popularity of *contact* in its generalized sense.[2] In a SYMBOLIC sense the "juncture of an electrical circuit" may be said to occur when the mind of one person *contacts* the mind of another. Or, to put it LEGALISTICALLY, there is a "meeting of the minds."

Tending in the other direction are such words as FISSION, which if standing alone, would probably be taken by most readers to refer not to any kind of "splitting," but to nuclear fission. *Nucleus* would simi-

[2] *Webster's Third Unabridged* has admitted the former slang sense of *contact* —"to get in touch with"—to the standard class. *Funk & Wagnalls Standard College Dictionary* labels it "Informal."

177

larly be taken as the nucleus of an atom, though before Hiroshima it was specialized for most readers as a "cell nucleus." RADIATION is now likely to make us think not of the "general process of spreading out of light or heat rays, wheel-like, from a center," but of "the diffusion of radioactive particles of EMANATIONS following an A-bomb explosion."

In like manner, *mutation* since De Vries has become specialized to mean a "sudden change in biological characteristics that becomes TRANSMISSIBLE." *Briefing* no longer suggests to most of us "preparing a written summary of legal arguments," nor its British sense of "the hiring of a BARRISTER to take into court a case a solicitor has prepared." In its most familiar use, it means to give final instructions, generally in capsule form, to anyone with a task, job, or mission to undertake.

So, too, *dialectics* is becoming specialized to mean not any kind of ARGUMENTATIVE reasoning by question and answer, but the Marxian variety used by Messrs. Khrushchev, Gromyko, Mao Tse-tung, and their SATELLITES. This word calls for a LEXICON of its own, of terms used in the long-winded argument between Moscow and Peking over which country is the more faithful guardian of COMMUNIST ideology.

Specialization is constantly taking place. So the "blues" (from which we got the "blue" notes in jazz) have reinforced the meaning of "melancholy" which Irving wrote about in 1807: "a fit of the blues," —short for "blue devils." And from the Red Flag, the Red Square, and the red ties of ANARCHISTS, we got the adjective and the noun *red* as the newspaper headline word for radicals, PARTICULARIZED now to Communists (or "Commies") of Russia and China and their followers throughout the world. Since the anarchists who were first labeled Reds believed in no government at all, the word has traveled to the opposite pole in meaning.

When the process of specialization has happened centuries—or even decades—before our time, we are not conscious of it. So MYTH, which at first in English meant any kind of story, now usually refers to one dealing with a god or semidivine being in one of the mythologies of the world. There is also a further special sense of the word, used by students of comparative religion, to mean the "story" which is the central feature of a particular CULT, as the myth of Buddha or the myth of Quetzal. When the word is so used, the primary emphasis is not on the truth or FALSITY of the story, but on its role in the religion

178

involved. Sometimes in this sense the full Greek spelling is used, *mythos,* and MODERNIST THEOLOGIANS speak of the central "mythos" of the Christian religion.

In our time *myth* is beginning to take the shuttle back to an APPROXIMATION of its original meaning. A false belief of any kind, of a religious nature or not, is called a myth, particularly when it is accepted by a group.[3] A political conservative might speak of the myth of Big Business domination of government. One who favors equal rights for Negroes would refer to the myth of racial inferiority. The movement of *myth* toward specialization and back to generalization shows how the history of a word also gives us a history of past and present times.

The word *fable* used to mean any "tale." Dryden used it to cover what we call "fiction," sometimes also in the narrower sense of "plot." But the word, while it still has its general sense of "fiction" in phrase combinations such as "fact and fable," is now more likely to suggest to us its specialized sense, of "a story made up to teach a lesson, especially one in which animals speak and act like human beings"—George Orwell's *Animal Farm,* for example. *Aesop's Fables* no doubt helped to give the word this special sense.

Another word which has been specialized is *run.* If we speak of "a run," Americans will think of baseball and Englishmen of cricket. A sheepman would mean a "sheep run," a salmon fisherman a "run" of fish upstream. When a horse-racer says "he gave him a run for it" he means that the runner-up pressed the winner in a race. To a ROULETTE player, a "run" would mean a continuing RECURRENCE of the red or the black, or of some one number. It is thus that every man is his own specializer, when it comes to ringing the changes on the meaning of common words.

## A Special Kind of Quiz

How have the following words become specialized in meaning during the last few years? Which of them can still be used in their earlier senses as well, without causing misunderstanding?

[3] *The American College Dictionary* defines *myth* in this sense: "5. *Sociol.* a collective belief that is built up in response to the wishes of the group rather than an analysis of the basis of the wishes."

| 1. JAMMING | 4. JET | 8. FADE |
|------------|--------|---------|
| 2. BOOSTER | 5. IMAGE | 9. SEGREGATION |
| 3. HARDWARE | 6. CLASSIFIED | 10. MISSILE |
| | 7. APPLIANCE | |

The above words give clues to what is happening in politics, sociology, business, radio and television, international relations, and other areas of contemporary life.

*Jamming* is what Moscow says it doesn't do to our radio broadcasts beamed overseas. *Newsweek* (July 1, 1963) reported that "The Reds [of East Germany] are bringing in dozens of mobile radio-jamming stations to blot out broadcasts from West Germany."

We associate *booster* now with rockets and television sets, but at one time it brought to mind a Babbitt. We still think of a *hardware* store as a place where we can buy nails and electric light bulbs, but the word is increasingly used to describe the "major items of military equipment or their components." [4] *Business Week* (March 30, 1963) wrote: "Surprisingly, California's aerospace industry itself reflects some feelings that more money than necessary is being spent on defense hardware." [5]

*Jet* is a shortened form of jet-propelled. It has a meaning in its own right: "a forceful rush of liquid, gas, or vapor through a narrow opening or a nozzle." [6] But its most common association today is with a jet airplane.

In an era when the package seems more important than the product, the term *image* has acquired a new connotation. Even the South Texas onion, says *Business Week* (March 30, 1963), is being glorified. " 'It's sweeter and milder,' say the growers, who are busy creating an image, laced with glamor." The word will continue to be used in its photographic sense, of course; and it is widely used in many other senses.

[4] *Webster's Seventh New Collegiate Dictionary.*

[5] *Hardware* is acquiring another meaning described in *The American College Dictionary* (Random House, Inc.) as "2. *Colloq.* the mechanical equipment necessary for conducting an activity, usually distinguished from the theory and design which make the activity possible." An example is its use in astronautics. Frank Gaynor in his *Aerospace Dictionary* (Philosophical Library, Inc., 1960) calls it "A colloquial term for guided missiles, rockets, and weapons in general, their components and machinery. In a missile, the hardware covers the airframe, the metallic or ceramic parts of the motor, and the instruments. It does not include the fuel."

[6] *Webster's Seventh New Collegiate Dictionary.*

*Classified* illustrates how a word can acquire a split personality in its grammatical forms. To *classify* has this general meaning as a verb: "to arrange or distribute in classes; place according to a class." [7] One meaning of classified, as in classified ads, is close to this definition. But *classified* in government lingo means "withheld for reasons of security"; thus it has acquired a specialized meaning, one associated with hot and cold wars.

In recent years *appliance* has been specialized to mean a refrigerator, range, electric iron, or anything else of like nature purchased for home use. A *fade* or *fadeout* describes what happens when the picture on your television screen gradually disappears. *Segregation* is very much in the news and has the special meaning of separation of racial groups.

The Space Age has brought many terms into specialized use. A *missile* in its general sense is something capable of being thrown at a target. Now it is used mostly in its specialized "guided missile" sense. We read daily about the ICBM, the interceptor missile, and the anti-missile missile.


## WORDS IN WIDER USE

*Missile* is an example of how uncommon and less common words appear more frequently in print. Listed as 13 at the time of Thorndike's word count, it is probably well under the 10 mark today. Words are a key to the culture that uses them. At a time when man-made vehicles are orbiting the Earth, when powerful nations such as Russia and China cast their shadow over their weaker neighbors, the frequency in print of the word *satellite* (12 in Thorndike's count) reflects what is happening in science and politics.

Today, when everybody wants to be liked (including corporation presidents and proud parents) the word PERMISSIVE (over 20 in the original Thorndike count) is frequently in print and on the air. Teachers have had to be permissive in classrooms since the DIRECTIVE went around that post-Freudian children were not to be inhibited from doing whatever they felt like doing. Fathers and mothers, afraid of destroying their "image" in the eyes of their children, are permissive toward them, and their offspring are having a field day at their ex-

[7] *The American College Dictionary.*

pense. Bosses are permissive with their secretaries; society women are permissive with their maids. Even *Webster's Third Unabridged* has been called permissive in its tolerance of questionable speech.

In *The Domesday Dictionary* (a word spoof by Donald M. Kaplan and Armand Schwerner) *permissiveness* is defined as "A recent doctrine of child-rearing informed by a special interpretation of psychoanalytic scripture and the myth of the Noble Savage. The interpretation is that man is PERFECTIBLE; the myth has it that human nature is basically good."

Sometimes an esoteric word formerly confined to literary and academic circles becomes a journalistic word-pet. It is now a mark of SOPHISTICATION to use ENCLAVE, a word that was too infrequent in print even for Thorndike. The older meaning of *enclave* was "a tract or territory enclosed within foreign territory." [8] Cultural changes have added a new meaning: "a district or region (as in a city) inhabited by a particular race or set apart for a special purpose." [9] In the interests of sophistication—and, indeed, sociological accuracy— *Fortune* (July, 1963) describes the new glamour buildings in Manhattan as "clusters of these enclaves . . . in the geographically narrow financial district at the southern tip of Manhattan Island and in the 40's and 50's. . . ." In the same issue: ". . . a private park that is an enclave of solitude. . . ."; "And there is Lincoln Center for the Performing Arts, which in one $160.7-million integrated enclave will eventually be the greatest artistic center in the world." Arthur Cantor in *Theater Arts* (July, 1963) calls Broadway a "hyperthyroid enclave where commercial theater lives and dies a little day after day. . . ."

The use of a word such as *enclave* becomes a social commentary when we consider its two meanings. The second meaning—"a distict or region . . . inhabited by a particular race or set apart for a special purpose"—has grown historically out of the first meaning—"a tract or territory enclosed within foreign territory." The IMPLICATIONS are subtle, but they do point to the state of mind of the people described in the *Fortune* article. In a city where expressways are considered more important than trees, a park becomes a place where the citizen may escape for a moment of solitude. The concert-goers at Lincoln

[8] *Webster's New Collegiate Dictionary*, which was based on *Webster's Second Unabridged*.
[9] This meaning appears with the older meaning in *Webster's Third Unabridged*.

Center may think that they have found temporary sanctuary from the harsh noises and pressures of the surrounding metropolis. Corporation executives and their management teams may well feel that they are a "particular race" for whom their sleek buildings have been "set apart for a special purpose." And Broadway may be an isolated area as it "dies a little day after day."

Arthur Cantor is direct in his use of the word to describe the financial ills and the "hyperthyroid" temperament of the theater district. *Fortune*, in its frank appeal to the business elite, uses the same word with a rather SUPERCILIOUS air.

Perhaps *The Domesday Dictionary* should have the last word. Its tongue-in-cheek definition of the Pentagon reads: "A very large five-sided enclave in Washington, D.C., concerned with Defense, Contracts, and Pressure . . . a CRYPTOSTATE within a State."


## RADIATION

Besides the shuttlelike RECIPROCAL action of generalization and specialization (with its CONCOMITANT wider use of certain words) there is a third important process by which words extend their meaning. This is the method of radiation. Take the word *action*, for example. Its primary or central meaning is "doing." It may refer (1) to actual and simple doing ("a prompt action"); (2) to a state of activity ("Sonny Liston in action"); (3) to INITIATING court procedure ("starting an action to recover"); (4) to enterprise ("a man of action"); (5) to the succession of events in a play ("there must be unity of action"); (6) to attitude or position expressing a certain passion ("the action denoting extreme agony in *Laocöon*"); (7) to a military or naval battle ("the action at Midway"); (8) to the natural or intended motion of anything ("the action of the cardiac muscle"); (9) to the force exerted upon something ("the action of the wind upon the sails"); and finally (10) to a mechanism acting ("the valve action in an engine"). In all of these many and varied senses of *action*, there remains the primary notion of "doing." By the necessities of printing, the different meanings are given in sequence. Actually the meanings really radiate out from the central sense of "doing," like the spokes of a wheel. This is what is meant by radiation.

## WHEELS OF MEANING

*Order, power, force, head, foot, class, rank, range,* and *turn* have had their meaning extended by radiation. Jot down all the meanings you can think of for each, and arrange them like the spokes of a wheel. *Power,* for example, will require a large wheel showing its five main divisions: Power in General; Authority, Control, and Influence; Personal Attributes; Source of Energy; and Magnitude. Under each main heading will be subheadings, where the particular sense has radiated again; under the subheadings, such as Authority Granted by Law, there are further radiated senses (A Right, Power of Attor-

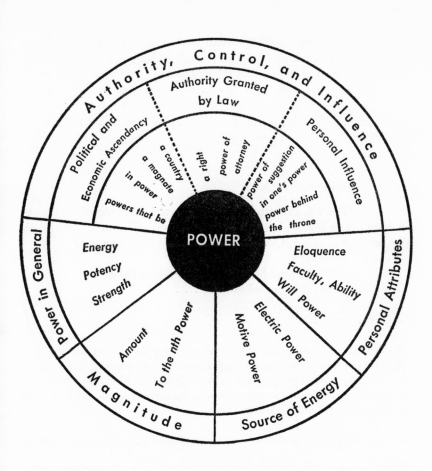

The diagram contains the following text:

Authority, Control, and Influence

Authority Granted by Law

Political and Economic Ascendancy

Personal Influence

a country in power
a magnate
powers that be
a right
power of attorney
power of suggestion
in one's power
power behind the throne

POWER

Power in General

Energy
Potency
Strength

Eloquence
Faculty, Ability
Will Power

Personal Attributes

Amount
To the nth Power

Electric Power
Motive Power

Magnitude

Source of Energy

This diagram is based upon the classifications of power given in *Roget's International Thesaurus*. There is, of course, a certain amount of overlapping. *Energy, potency,* and *strength* (power in general) may apply to personal attributes or to those that give rise to or result from the authority and influence of a national power or institution. *Authority, control,* and *influence* suggest both personal qualities and those that derive from political, economic, legal, and physical power.

ney). *Turn* also will require several subheadings within its circle of meaning. Make each sector large enough so that you have room for a phrase or short sentence illustrating the use of the word in its various radiated senses (see examples for *action* on page 183). After you have finished, check your work with reference to an unabridged dictionary; preferably, if you have access to it in a library, consult the OED.

### TRANSFERENCE

There is a fourth way in which words shift meaning: TRANS-FERENCE. Ruskin complained about it, in the well-known passage on the *pathetic* FALLACY. Quoting from Kingsley's *Alton Locke,*

> They rowed her in across the rolling foam—
> The cruel, crawling foam . . .

he continues

The foam is not cruel, neither does it crawl. The state of mind which attributes to it these characters of a living creature is one in which the reason is UNHINGED by grief. They produce in us a falseness in all our impressions of external things, which I would generally characterize as the "pathetic fallacy."—*Modern Painters,* Vol. 3, chap. 12.

Yet this projection of feeling upon inanimate objects or forces is as common as the illusion by which, when we touch the table with a pencil, we feel the contact at the far end of the pencil, though a moment's reflection will tell us that there can be no SENTIENCE in the pencil. But the pathetic fallacy and the projection of feeling to the end of the pencil are analogous to a general method of changing word-meanings, which comes about through transference. At its lowest level, this transfer occurs in "a cold day." It is we who are cold, not the day.

What is true of words describing sensations, holds with the whole range of terms which deal with mental conceptions. Such words face either toward the person who entertains the notion, or toward the person or thing affected by it; or they may—and here arises the transference—shift back and forth from one to the other.

The word *character* is an ideal illustration, particularly since you have already sorted out its meanings. Here you can trace further how these meaning-changes have occurred. In the good old days when servants received "characters" when they were leaving someone's employ, these were in effect certificates of good "reputation." The term *character* was long employed in this objective sense. In the 17th century, it meant a GENERIC portrait of a certain type: the miser, the CHOLERIC man, the social climber, and the like. On the other hand, when we speak of the development of Hamlet's character, as revealed in his successive SOLILOQUIES and actions, we now think of something happening within him. The character of a man, as he himself conceives and reveals it, is SUBJECTIVE. The term really faces both ways, and by transference shifts from the OBJECTIVE to the subjective sense very easily.

In fact, the JANUS-FACED nature of the word accounts for a good deal of confusion in the discussion of problems of character. It is not always clear how far the LOCUS of character is in the person, and how far in the mind of the BEHOLDER. The moral aspect of character, in particular, has often been disputed bitterly, because of uncertainty as to whether the moral qualities and standards are in the man himself, or in the minds of his judges.

The Greeks, of course, did not bother about this difference between the subjective and objective. They used the word ETHOS to mean both the inward and outward aspects of character. We prefer the word *personality* for the impression which a man makes on other persons, but the Greeks, since they did not make the distinction, had no word for it. Nor did the Romans, for they used MORES ("manners," "habits," hence "character") to include both phases of character. What a man appeared to be, he was, and that was the end of it. (The word *persona* to them meant a mask assumed by an actor, so everybody in the huge AMPHITHEATER could tell what character in the play he was representing.) But we distinguish between the inward and outward aspects of experience, without always being too sure which is which. Hence the numerous terms in English which face both ways, and can be transferred from subject to object, and vice versa.

## DEGRADATION

Still a fifth method by which words shift meaning is degradation. Words with respectable associations slide down in the world, acquiring a DEROGATORY sense; some of them are brought still lower, becoming VULGARISMS. *Swell, lousy, hot, tight,* and *lit* have been overtaken by this fate. There are, however, two schools of thought about whether a word is a vulgarism and therefore degraded. The newer dictionaries do not use this label; *Webster's Third Unabridged* prefers "substandard" and "nonstandard." *Swell, lousy,* and *tight* (in the sense of being drunk) are listed as standard, over the bitter protests of the language purists. *Funk & Wagnalls Standard College Dictionary* lists *swell* as "Informal," *lousy* and *tight* as "Slang."

Even *Webster,* however, gives the slang label to *lit* (drunk) and *hot.* In doing so, *Webster's* editors do not set themselves up as critics; they merely record what is happening in the culture. Regardless of dictionary labels, however, if you have a nice ear for words, you can sort out what kind of society they belong in. In our time we know what has happened to the word *hot* at the hands of the jazz ADDICTS. Yet when Robert Burton wrote in 1626, "I would not grow hot in a cold cause," it was not slang then, though the process of degradation makes it sound that way today.


## VERBAL SOFT-PEDALING

Degradation of meaning leads to one amusing consequence: verbal soft-pedaling, commonly called euphemism. An *undertaker* becomes a "mortician," a *barbershop* a "tonsorial parlor." Canned goods are graded "extra fancy," "fancy," and "standard," and in the process the word *standard* is downgraded to mean, in trade language, the minimum quality that meets government or trade association requirements. It's a euphemism for the "lowest grade that will pass muster."

In an article about the proposed Truth in Packaging Bill in *Harper's* August, 1963, issue William Zabel writes: "Packagers are masterful NEOLOGISTS. Their currently popular terms include the 'giant half-quart' (a pint) and the 'jumbo' quart, which is a quart adorned only with an adjective and not an extra measure." This kind of euphemism in the marketing field makes one wonder if words have become ends in themselves rather than symbols for the objects and ideas they represent.

Harry Golden gives a graphic example of the way we respond to euphemisms (*New York Post,* June 28, 1963): "If the janitor is about

188

to quit and you decide to avoid the problem of explaining all the complexities of those mechanical things about which you understand nothing to a new man, you have one easy alternative. You give the janitor a separate office and promote him to 'maintenance engineer.' "

The term *engineer* has a special connotation in this technological age. The man who writes the orders is no longer a salesman but a "sales engineer." The high-school counselor is a "guidance engineer." And there have been theatrical agents (according to Harry Golden) who called themselves "talent engineers."

## STEAM-HEATED ADJECTIVES

At the opposite pole from euphemism is another process by which words decay in force: HYPERBOLE. Instead of the timid cough of the soft-pedaler, we have, in this type of exaggeration, the loud trumpet-bray of the press agent. He looks for heroically strong expressions that will convey the extremes of approval. *Delightful, magnificent, splendid, superb, wonderful, overpowering, enchanting, tremendous,* and COLOSSAL are used as EXCLAMATORY SUPERLATIVES. Hollywood has even coined *supercolossal,* which teen-agers have shortened to "super."

The shortening process, the increased use of clipped forms (see *Variety's* "exec," "prez," "b.o.") are typical of a jet-propelled, get-there-first-to-the-moon age. Sometimes the short forms have a logic of their own; but the tendency to blow up words like *sensational, terrific,* and *marvelous,* then shorten them to *sensaysh, terrif,* and *marvy* is to send the language downhill in a hurry.

There is a fast-diminishing return from the use of these steam-heated adjectives. Each hyperbole of this kind soon loses, like discharged lightning, all its real potential; then another and still stronger expression is devised and perhaps shortened, and it in turn degenerates. This holds also for overstrong words used to express DISAPPROBATION. If some petty annoyance is labeled *outrageous,* BESTIAL, ATROCIOUS, horrible, or NAUSEATING, the strong language often defeats its purpose. We feel that the words have little more meaning than loud-mouthed BRAGGADOCIO.

## FIGURATIVE EXTENSION

Any one of these five processes—generalization, specialization, radiation, transference, or degradation—may be involved in a FIGURATIVE *extension* of meaning. *Micawber* becomes a general term for all PROCRASTINATORS who "wait for something to turn up." *Servant* is specialized into one of the proudest titles of the Pope: "the Servant of the Servants of God." A businessman will speak of "the *line* he proposes to take on the financial *angle* of a *proposition*," thus generalizing two terms from mathematics and one from logic. Psychology, once "the science of the soul—or mind," is transferred to designate the study of how rats behave in a maze, or to measurement of nerve-muscle response. At the same time the word retains, for old-fashioned persons, its original sense, thus illustrating also radiation. *Idea* is degraded for a philosopher when it is attached to an "idea man" in an advertising agency. With all these processes of change at work, the meanings of words are indeed more fluid than we realize.


## ADULTERATION

Besides these orthodox, traditional ways in which words change meaning, there is also the technique of hijacking legitimate words and pouring new meanings into them. It's easy to do in the case of OMNIBUS words, those that already carry such a heavy load of meaning that you can never be sure which one will get off when the bus stops. Such terms as *Americanism, communism* (two of the overworked -*ism* words) *democracy, loyalty,* and *peace* are omnibus words often appropriated by the political bootleggers.

In the last decade or so, the adulteration of *democracy* and *Americanism* has gone beyond the point of political differences to the region of HYSTERIA. The groups who have hijacked these words can get away with it because they have become emotionally charged, loaded terms. In the minds of fearful citizens they carry CONNOTATIONS far beyond the specific (DENOTATIVE) meanings that stem from ideological preference. When a word is loaded, it stirs up feeling rather than thought. Rather than read constructive, positive values into *democracy* and *Americanism,* the weak-minded see these terms as symbols for an

190

uncertain defense against *communism,* which becomes stronger in their minds as *democracy* grows weaker. The two opposing terms move those of little faith and small vocabulary to fear of invasion, rape, and all the other horrors conjured up by XENOPHOBES.

Senator Kuchel of California wrote an article in the *New York Times* (July 21, 1963) describing the extremes of hysteria to which people can be driven by this kind of word hypnosis. He revealed the contents of the "fright mail" he received from the "patriots" who were so aroused by the connotations poured into the meaning of *communism* that they saw Reds under their beds:

Some of the more memorable "plots" that come to mind include these: 35,000 Communist Chinese troops, bearing arms and wearing deceptively dyed powder-blue uniforms, are poised on the Mexican border, about to invade San Diego; the United States has turned over—or will at any moment—its Army, Navy, and Air Force to the command of a Russian colonel in the United Nations; almost every well-known American or free-world leader is, in reality, a top Communist agent; a United States Army guerilla-warfare exercise in Georgia, called Water Moccasin III, is in actuality a United Nations operation preparatory to taking over our country.

The "fright-peddlers" can get away with this because their victims have been carefully nurtured to believe that such words as *Americanism, loyalty, democracy, peace,* and *communism* have meanings far removed from any rational evaluation of them. Senator Kuchel concluded: ". . . The fright peddler is the self-appointed saviour of our land who finds conspiracy, treason, and sell-out in almost every act or pronouncement of government or government officials here, there, and everywhere, and puts forth his findings with astonishing FECUNDITY."

Fear, hatred, anger—all the negative emotions are stirred up by such misuse of words. And the end result is violence—an act such as the assassination of President Kennedy. It is well to reflect on the power of words for good and for evil.

The same process takes place behind the Iron Curtain. Communist dictators have been brainwashing their followers with loaded terms like "imperialism" and "capitalism." Khrushchev must have been bewildered on his visit here when he was received politely and in some cases enthusiastically by American tycoons and given the cold shoulder by "working class" trade unionists. He might have wondered about the black-and-white labels of both the American and Russian word-hijackers if he noticed that many union leaders were on friendly and even intimate terms with corporation executives. Had he stayed to see the massive Civil Rights March on Washington he might have been impressed by the dignity and faith of the marchers and by the cordial reception given them.

Omnibus terms like *democracy* and *communism* do not remain fixed at one point. That is why it is necessary to review the meanings they have acquired or discarded from time to time. Such terms are dynamic; they EVOLVE from an historical and cultural background, and they are based on principles rather than narrow definitions. The men who fought against tyranny and for democracy—men like the Roosevelts, Carl Schurz, Mazzini—knew in their bones what it means: government of, by, and for the people, whose representatives are elected by a majority vote in free elections; operating with their consent and in accord with public opinion; conducting their affairs according to laws and a constitution, written or unwritten, that includes a bill of rights which safeguards the liberty of the citizen against arbitrary action by officials. The property system can be whatever the people decide: private ownership with a broad base of social security, as in Sweden; private ownership, with some government-sponsored programs such as health insurance, as in England; private ownership with government projects that bolster the economy and provide basic needs in some areas, as in the United States with the TVA and rural electrification.

Even in Russia there are signs of restlessness among those who find that the oft-repeated Marxian DOGMA is beginning to ring hollow in their ears. Lewis S. Feuer writes in the *New York Times* (August 18, 1963) on the "Dilemma of the Soviet Intellectual":

The Soviet ideologists have worn into SHIBBOLETHS and false guides the notions of "class," "masses," "people," "crisis," "system." They tend to stop thinking each time they hear these words. . . .

The ideologists are in conflict, however, with the new breed of Soviet thinker.

. . . they stand an uneasy guard against the restless searching for freedom which moves their younger colleagues. . . . The younger Soviet thinker is painfully aware that he cannot come to terms with the problems central to his society.

Both the American and the Russian word-hijackers follow the practice of Humpty-Dumpty in *Alice in Wonderland:* "When I use a word, it means just what I choose it to mean." But the purpose of the word-wrenching fright peddlers is not so innocent. They steal the word for its SLOGAN value, and use it to prettify the label on adulterated political NOSTRUMS.

Obviously, the highly charged words that figure in political, economic, religious, and social controversy are the most likely to suffer from this trick. The moral: be sure you know what you mean when you use these "omnibus words." That often means reexamining with care words that have long seemed commonplace and familiar.

## THE MEANING OF MEANING

What emerges from this inquiry into meaning-changes is the fact that you can greatly enlarge your vocabulary by going deeper into meanings of words you only half-know. It's not only that you can trace the steps by which a word acquires a *figurative* extension of meaning. If you have gone intensively into the full meaning of a complicated word like *democracy*, you won't be fooled by sloganeers. When people talk about *religion, capitalism, Americanism,* you'll recognize at once that these are broad terms covering a complex of ideas and a background of historical and cultural events; you won't jump to conclusions about what the terms mean, but you'll do some DISPASSIONATE investigating on your own. You'll consult UNABRIDGED and etymological dictionaries to get the most comprehensive meaning of these terms. You'll read about the people, the personalities, and the times which helped shape, add to, and perhaps change the form and meaning of these words.

And if you don't have time to be a word and idea detective, you'll simply hold your fire until you know more. You won't be stampeded by the connotations other persons give these words. You can safeguard yourself by using the SOCRATIC method. If somebody challenges you with an omnibus word, answer with, "But what do you mean by *religion, democracy, Americanism, communism, patriotism, imperialism, classes, masses?*" Send them packing in the direction of the library.

Equipped with real awareness—and WARINESS—about meanings, you will not be easily fooled by words.

# Word Derivation Quiz

This type of quiz is as much a test of your reading ability and ability to concentrate as it is a test of your word knowledge. Most of the questions directly quote or PARAPHRASE passages in Chapter 8. After doing the test, reread the chapter (and previous chapters) and take careful note of the words you missed.

1. A new word or phrase, or a word or phrase given a new meaning is a _____.
2. An _____ word is one used to carry a heavy load of meanings.
3. Words become specialized and generalized in a constant shuttling back and forth, or a _____ action.
4. Give five meanings of "action" that radiate out of "doing."
5. Verbal soft-pedaling is called _____.
6. An exaggerated mode of expression is _____.
7. What is the Marxian variety of argumentative reasoning called?
8. Where is the "acetate jungle"?
9. What word is humorously defined as "a recent doctrine of child-rearing informed by a special interpretation of psychoanalytic scripture and the myth of the Noble Savage"?
10. What is the method of debate that consists of asking questions?
11. What is the word for a "sudden change in biological characteristics that become transmissible"?
12. The moon is a _____ of the earth.
13. Poland is a _____ of Russia.
14. What is a "story" that is the central feature of a particular cult?
15. Fear and hatred of foreigners is called _____.
16. What does "noisome" mean?
17. When a person uses "illiterate" for "obliterate" or "lechery" for "lethargy," he is guilty of a _____.
18. What word means to "jeer," "agree," and "flip a sail"?
19. A word that refers to legal debate is _____.
20. _____ believe in no government at all.
21. What is a word that means "a tract or territory enclosed within a foreign territory"?
22. "In order," "out of order" are _____ combinations.
23. "Delightful," "magnificent," "splendid," "terrific" are s_____.
24. "Bestial," "atrocious," "horrible" are words used to express _____.
25. What is another word for a Micawber, a person who is always "waiting for something to turn up"?
26. A _____ is a catchword that tends to keep people from thinking.
27. Implied meanings of words are _____.

28. A word from Anglo-Saxon that refers to a fragment of pottery.
29. Shrinking of meaning is called _____.
30. Something that digresses goes off at a _____.

## WORD LIST

| | | | |
|---|---|---|---|
| euphemism | dialectics | euphony | asteroid |
| Africa | reciprocal | tangent | specialization |
| smelly | omnibus | onomatopoeia | hyperbole |
| permissiveness | neologism | delinquency | New York |
| xenophobia | neophyte | clamorous | ceramics |
| spoonerism | Hollywood | Socrates | exurbs |
| enclave | patriotism | mutation | hypercritical |
| superlatives | forensic | satellite | agoraphobia |
| disapprobation | nihilists | malapropism | sententious |
| oratorical | gambler | anarchists | jibe |
| denotations | Socratic | informal | bastion |
| transference | phrasal | connotations | periphery |
| fragmentation | myth | shard | schizophrenia |
| generalization | shibboleth | constricted | disenchantment |
| procrastinator | joust | Dr. Spock | radiation |

## ANSWERS

| | | |
|---|---|---|
| 1. neologism | 11. mutation | 21. enclave |
| 2. omnibus | 12. satellite | 22. phrasal |
| 3. reciprocal | 13. satellite | 23. superlatives |
| 4. see page 184 | 14. myth | 24. disapprobation |
| 5. euphemism | 15. xenophobia | 25. procrastinator |
| 6. hyperbole | 16. smelly | 26. shibboleth |
| 7. dialectics | 17. malapropism | 27. connotations |
| 8. Hollywood | 18. jibe | 28. shard |
| 9. permissiveness | 19. forensic | 29. specialization |
| 10. Socratic | 20. anarchists | 30. tangent |

## SCORING KEY

30 right—You've earned your doctorate
27–29 right—Master's degree (you're getting there)
23–26 right—College graduate (ready for your M.A.)
18–22 right—Above average in word knowledge
12–17 right—Average (mediocre)
Under 12 right—Substandard

SCORE: _____

# 9

## How to Learn 1000 New Words Through Word Relatives and Word Opposites

A word, like a note in music, does not function in isolation. We can understand it more clearly and define it with greater precision in relation to words that are close to it in meaning (synonyms) and to words that have an opposite meaning (antonyms). Just as a musical tone may be part of a scale or chord, a word may be one of a cluster of word relatives or word opposites. By studying the fine shades of meaning that separate it from its near relations, you can learn a whole new batch of words at one time.

Knowing the fine shades of meaning is necessary if you want to increase your vocabulary of talking and writing. Suppose you found this letter in the morning mail:

> I got on horseback within ten minutes after I got your letter. When I got to Canterbury, I got a chaise for town; but I got wet through, and have got such a cold that I shall not get rid of it in a hurry. I got to the Treasury about noon, but first of all got shaved and dressed. I soon got into the secret of getting a memorial before the Board, but I could not get an answer then; however I got intelligence from a messenger that I should get one next morning. As soon as I got to my inn, I got my supper, and breakfast, and, having got dressed, I got out in time to get an answer to my memorial. As soon as I got it, I got into a chaise, and got back to Canterbury by three, and got home for tea. I have got nothing for you, and so adieu.

You might think Rose Macaulay made it up, as a "spoof" on Basic English. Perhaps Gertrude Stein decided to give the verb *get* a work-out. Or the writer was a MONOTONE. Actually, this is a patch out of Brewer's *Dictionary of Phrase and Fable.* Logan Pearsall Smith quotes it in his tract on English IDIOMS, while exhibiting the idiomatic uses of *get,* in the same breath that he cautions against thus employing it as a verb-of-all-work. If you'll just start rephrasing the story, from the point where the record "got" stuck, you'll realize how many other

196

verbs *get* can pinch-hit for. It is a prize specimen of a word with multiple meanings, and at the same time, in this case, a warning, heightened to absurdity, of the need for a ready command of synonyms to avoid monotony, REPETITIOUSNESS, and WOOLLINESS of expression.

There is all the less excuse for thus working a word to death, because English is as rich in synonyms as in words with plural meanings. In fact, it has a greater wealth of synonyms than any other known language, ancient or modern.

Because of the COMPOSITE nature of English, there are for many of the commonest meanings in the language two words, one of Anglo-Saxon, the other of Latin origin. Sometimes the Anglo-Saxon (more precisely, Old English) word is the commoner, and for ordinary purposes it is to be preferred. No one but a PEDANT—or Earl Wilson, if he happened to learn the word—would speak of a LUPINE appetite, when he meant *wolfish;* or describe a wrestler as having a TAURINE instead of a *bull-like* neck. A politician is *foxy,* not VULPINE; and *horse-faced* conveys the idea better than EQUINE-VISAGED—unless you're afraid the children will overhear you.

But in many cases the word of Latin origin has become more familiar than the Saxon. *Doctor* or *physician* is usual, not LEECH, which is now obsolete. *Deny* and *contradict* have displaced GAINSAY except in Biblical English. *Pity* has won out over RUTH, though *harmful* has stayed on a par with *injurious.*

## Match Game

Give a synonym of classical origin for each of the following Saxon words (e.g., clothing—raiment):

| | | | | |
|---|---|---|---|---|
| 1. chew | 5. earnest | 9. mislead | 13. loathsome | 17. lighten |
| 2. drink | 6. feed | 10. outside | 14. manly | 18. shorten |
| 3. dwindle | 7. give | 11. BURDENSOME | 15. glee | 19. healthful |
| 4. draft | 8. mad | 12. healing | 16. lore | 20. balk |

### ANSWERS

| | | | |
|---|---|---|---|
| 1. masticate | 6. nourish | 11. onerous | 16. erudition |
| 2. imbibe | 7. donate | 12. curing | 17. alleviate |
| 3. diminish | 8. insane | 13. offensive | 18. abbreviate |
| 4. delineation | 9. deceive | 14. virile | 19. salubrious |
| 5. serious | 10. external | 15. hilarity | 20. circumvent |

There are usually wide differences in overtones (connotations) between the Saxon word and its classical ANALOGUE. It is hard to lay down any general rule, since in the past, the only academy that has determined the right usage for an English word is the accumulated practice of the best authors (although *Webster's Third Unabridged* has put politicians, movie stars, and the man in the street on an equal footing with literary figures and SAVANTS as authorities). We speak naturally of an *ardent* interest, but of *hot* soup; of *navigating* an ocean liner, but of *sailing* a small boat; of the INCULCATION of doctrine, but of *teaching* arithmetic. The cashier of a bank EMBEZZLES, but a common yegg *steals*. We talk of the ABATEMENT of a nuisance, but of the *lessening* of TENSION on a cable; of the *intelligence* of a great scholar, but of the animal *cunning* of an athlete in a tight spot. We dignify a BENEFACTION to a cathedral, but hand out a *dole* to the unemployed. Some of these pairs are not synonyms; others once were; and a few are still synonyms, though rarely interchangeable in all contexts.

Accumulate several thousand contrasts on this order, and it would be possible at least to gamble on the company the classical words usually keep. They seem to be used in formal and dignified circumstances. They are often employed if a FIGURATIVE rather than a plain blunt meaning is to be conveyed (as in the language of diplomacy). If the occasion is a full dress speech from the rostrum, or a prepared lecture read from the LECTERN, expect a heavy intermixture of LATINITY. If it is just a plain talking match, where everybody can join in, the Saxon words are far more likely to fit.

Shakespeare, who wrote more memorable dialogue and more quotable tags than anybody else who has used the language, ran to about 21 percent classical words; even if he had small Latin and less Greek, he had a superb ear for the Romance additions to our tongue. And he was writing, remember, for a popular audience, and his lines were meant to be spoken. It is of interest to the student of vocabulary-range to know that he used 17,677 different words, exclusive of proper and place names, in his plays; 14,652 of these are given as main word entries in the OED, and of this number around 1460 were first used by Shakespeare; while three-fifths of the 3025 compounds he put into circulation were of his own invention. And more than half of his word-novelties came from the Romance element in English. (A. Hart, *Review of English Studies*, 19:128–140.)

Do not be taken in by the common nonsense which Herbert Spencer helped spread, always to prefer the Saxon word. You can't help using a preponderance of them, for the bones, muscles, and sinews of the language come from Old English. But many who make a FETISH of SAXONISM are talking MUMBO-JUMBO. Try this puzzler on them.

### Trap for the Unwary Saxonizer

Which of the following are "good old Anglo-Saxon words"?

age, art, case, cost, fact, form, ink, mile, pain, pair, part, piece, price, rule, sound, ton, tone, and vail; apt, clear, cross, crude, firm, grand, large, mere, nice, pale, plain, poor, pure, rare, real, round, safe, scarce, sure, and vain; add, aid, boil, close, cook, cure, fail, fix, fry, mix, move, pay, save, serve, try, turn, and use; JILT, inch, date

(Not one of these words is of Old English origin: all are part of the classical layer in our language.)

Even in popular narrative there are occasions calling for a high percentage of classical words. The most skillful rewrite artist could not Saxonize the following passage from a detective story, without ruining its effectiveness and tone.

Hyer went on, *inventing* an *elaborate* and *pointless anecdote,* interlarding it with *parentheses,* drifting off now in this bypath now that, taking up and dropping *random biographies,* MEANDERING, GARRULOUS, *genial.* It was a *magnificent* FILIBUSTER.—Kurt Steel, *Ambush House,* p. 66.

(The words of classical origin are in italics or SMALL CAPITALS.)

## DOUBLETS ARE TRICKY

A lot of near-synonyms in the language turn up in the form of doublets, words that have come in from the same classical stem, but which entered at different stages in the development of the language. The usual pair of doublets comprises one word from the Latin direct, and another from the Latin through the French. Sometimes they have diverged widely in meaning; but in other cases the general significance is the same, only the words are used for different occasions.

We *abbreviate* a word, and we *abridge* a book. A *canal* is an artificial *channel.* An employer can be in a *devilish* bad humor without having DIABOLICAL intentions. A *crevice* in a rock is not usually dangerous; a CREVASSE in a glacier is. A university may be *endowed* with money without being *endued* with the virtues of learning. An *example* may—or may not—be a fair *sample* of a mass of data. A mushroom may be of an *edible* variety but not *eatable* after a bad cook has ruined it. The WARDEN of a PENITENTIARY may also be, as Thomas Mott Osborne was, an admirable *guardian* of the interests of society. An Australian bushman *hurls* a BOOMERANG, but after it is launched, it HURTLES through the air. *Palsy* now suggests the quivering that follows partial PARALYSIS.

All these doublets had originally much the same area of meaning, and even yet, in the instances chosen, there is a similarity of meaning, but not an IDENTITY. Many are no longer synonyms. Perhaps *eatable* and *edible* are most nearly INTERCHANGEABLE. But try translating Wilde's EPIGRAMMATIC description of the English country squire chasing the fox, "the unspeakable in full pursuit of the uneatable." Using the classical words, it becomes "the INEFFABLE in full pursuit of the inedible." Even Dr. Johnson at his most SESQUIPEDALIAN would not have said this.

Here's an instance of doublets that started out as identical twins.

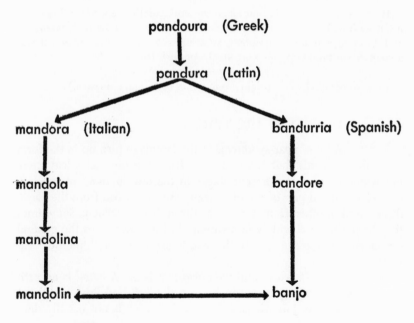

## A Precarious Test for Synonymity

Of the following doublets, which are interchangeable throughout all their uses and shades of meaning?

1. zero, CIPHER
2. pry, peer
3. REPRIEVE, reprove
4. mode, mood
5. naked, NUDE
6. guarantee, WARRANTY

7. entire, INTEGRAL
8. ENWRAP, envelope
9. evil, ill
10. plum, prune
11. shuffle, scuffle
12. SNIVEL, SNUFFLE
13. tight, TAUT
14. squall, SQUEAL

15. NAÏVE, native
16. fiddle, VIOL
17. complacent, COMPLAISANT
18. church, KIRK
19. guile, vile
20. fancy, PHANTASY

ANSWER—None

## DOWN ON THE FARM

There are also closely allied words from the same root, which, while not doublets, are particularly tricky. An URBAN person may or may not be URBANE, though the original IMPLICATIONS of the latter adjective held that a city man was AUTOMATICALLY polished in his manner; while a *rural* dweller was supposed to have a certain RUSTICITY. The adjective *rustic* is now applied mostly to pastoral scenery, or furniture which looks as if it was not long out of the woods. The noun *rustic* has that flavor, at once DEROGATORY and condescending, that all words associated with farm life seem finally to acquire in literary language determined by the CITIFIED. The word *villain*, originally a serf (*villanus*) attached to a country estate (*villa*), came to mean, in the Middle Ages, anyone not of noble birth, hence unacquainted with courtesy and CHIVALRIC manners; so *villain* was applied to a BASEBORN or low person, and finally *villainy* came to mean any low conduct. Eventually it took on its present meaning of SCOUNDRELISM. The words *churl* and *boor* have come down in the world in much the same way.

The word *farmer* shows some signs of a similar descent, but its decay was arrested in this country as farmers began to get more political power, and as autos and mail-order houses increased their

201

MOBILITY and access to urban styles. A retired major general turned governor in a northwestern state, unaware that the trend had been reversed, was defeated for renomination largely because he used the word in a contemptuous sense. He told a DELEGATION of GRANGERS, "You farmers should go home and tend to your spring plowing, listen to the birdies sing, and leave politics to your betters." Politicos since the ex-governor's time have been more CIRCUMSPECT in dealing with men of the soil.

## WATCH FOR THE HAZARDS

Interesting as the approach to synonyms through etymology may be, it is not a direct FRONTAL mode of attack for a writer who is worried over the right word. As we noted, the headline writer or rewrite man CUDGELS his wits for a synonym, when he has to refer several times, in the same sentence, or in successive sentences, to a term or an idea. Pronouns of reference will go only so far to meet this need. Here is where plenty of practice is needed in conjuring up, on short notice, synonyms for the commonest words and ideas.

Notice, however, the difficulties encountered. The original word may have a number of meanings. *Balance* may mean either *scales*, or EQUILIBRIUM, but equilibrium will not serve as a synonym for *scales*. *Business* may mean (1) *occupation,* as "She was in the business of baby-farming." Or it may mean (2) *affair* or *matter,* as "What was the business before the meeting?" Again, in its commonest sense in our *business* culture, it means (3) *trade* or *commerce,* including all the activities connected with purchase, barter, sale, and exchange of commodities, plus financial transactions involved in these, as distinct from the production of goods in agriculture and industry; though *business* is also used loosely to include industry, but not farming. The word may also mean (4) a "going concern," as "He sold his business." And it has a minor, specialized sense of (5) stage tricks—gestures and actions put into a play while it is in production, as "Moss Hart put in a lot of smart business when he directed *My Fair Lady.*" The obsolete literal sense of (6) mere activity, or "keeping busy," has been replaced by a modern coinage, BUSYNESS, as "the bright, brisk busyness of the squirrel," still observed in such forms of *business* as radio, television, advertising, public relations, and other EMPORIA peddling META-PHYSICAL goods. Clearly, the various synonyms for *business* are not INTERCHANGEABLE, and it takes some careful analysis to spot the particular meaning for which an equivalent is wanted.

202

Another difficulty often arises. *There may be no exact* synonym *for a given word,* not even one close enough to serve without doing violence to the sense intended. Gertrude Stein had the right answer for this DILEMMA. She told Ernest Hemingway to use the same word over, and he did, and see what it did for him. It almost did for her, too, when she overdid it. But she was not out of her mind, just outside of everybody else's. However, she was very lucid about refusing to strain for a synonym when none exists. Repeat the word, and while EUPHONY may suffer, what is lost in variety is gained in precision and emphasis. Not many of us can worry an idea as long as Miss Stein could, nor does it come home to us with the poetic vividness that forced her to an ECHOIC use of one word. But the fact that some words have no synonyms does not free those of us who are non-Steins from the obligation to search for synonyms, or the duty to find the best one to express a given shade of meaning. There is no excuse for impoverished language.

## Is There a Real Synonym for It?

For any of the following words that have only one meaning, supply a synonym if there is a real one. For those that have multiple meanings, furnish a synonym, if possible, for each of these meanings, as was done for *business.*

| | | | |
|---|---|---|---|
| 1. account | 20. company | 39. increase | 58. pain |
| 2. act | 21. control | 40. insurance | 59. pleasure |
| 3. adjustment | 22. cover | 41. interest | 60. point |
| 4. amount | 23. current | 42. join | 61. power |
| 5. amusement | 24. damage | 43. learn (ing) | 62. price |
| 6. approval | 25. death | 44. level | 63. produce |
| 7. argument | 26. degree | 45. limit | 64. profit |
| 8. attention | 27. earth | 46. liquid | 65. protest |
| 9. attraction | 28. edge | 47. loss | 66. punishment |
| 10. balance | 29. effect | 48. mass | 67. push |
| 11. base | 30. error | 49. measure | 68. question |
| 12. birth | 31. exchange | 50. middle | 69. range |
| 13. breath | 32. feeling | 51. move | 70. rate |
| 14. burn | 33. fiction | 52. music | 71. reaction |
| 15. burst | 34. government | 53. nation | 72. reward |
| 16. cause | 35. harmony | 54. need | 73. rule |
| 17. chance | 36. hate | 55. offer | 74. scale |
| 18. change | 37. history | 56. opinion | 75. self |
| 19. comfort | 38. humor | 57. order | 76. sense |

| | | | |
|---|---|---|---|
| 77. sex | 83. slope | 89. surprise | 95. twist |
| 78. shade | 84. sort | 90. system | 96. way |
| 79. shock | 85. statement | 91. thing | 97. writ(ing) |
| 80. side | 86. stretch | 92. time | 98. word |
| 81. size | 87. suggestion | 93. trade | 99. work |
| 82. sleep | 88. support | 94. trouble | 100. wound |

ANSWERS

| | | | |
|---|---|---|---|
| 1. report | 26. no synonym | 50. center | 77. gender |
| 2. deed | 27. world | 51. impel | 78. shadow |
| 3. adaptation | 28. border, | 52. no synonym | 79. concussion |
| 4. aggregate | margin | 53. race, people | 80. angle, aspect |
| 5. entertainment | 29. consequence | 54. want | 81. extent, |
| 6. approbation | 30. mistake | 55. tender | volume |
| 7. reason, | 31. swap | 56. sentiment | 82. slumber |
| reasoning | 32. sensibility | 57. systematize, | 83. slant |
| 8. concentration | 33. fabrication, | command | 84. kind |
| 9. affinity | fable | 58. ache | 85. account, bill |
| 10. equilibrium | 34. administra- | 59. delight | 86. expanse |
| 11. low | tion | 60. direct, aim | 87. intimation |
| 12. no synonym | 35. consonance | 61. force, | 88. advocate, |
| 13. no synonym | 36. loathing | authority | mainte- |
| 14. char | 37. chronicle | 62. charge | nance |
| 15. no synonym | 38. wit | 63. yield | 89. astonish |
| 16. reason | 39. augment | 64. avail, benefit | 90. method, |
| 17. hazard | 40. assurance | 65. object | plan |
| 18. alter | 41. no synonym | 66. discipline | 91. object |
| 19. ease | 42. unite | 67. shove | 92. occasion |
| 20. party | 43. erudition | 68. inquiry | 93. profession |
| 21. authority, | 44. even, flat | 69. scope | 94. distress |
| check | 45. confine | 70. upbraid, value | 95. turn, curve |
| 22. shelter | 46. fluid | 71. function | 96. manner |
| 23. stream, | 47. no synonym | 72. bonus | 97. no synonym |
| prevalent | 48. bulk, | 73. law, govern | 98. term |
| 24. injury | volume | 74. ascend | 99. toil, labor |
| 25. decease | 49. no synonym | 75. no synonym | 100. no synonym |
| | | 76. sensibility | |

The 100 words above are all from the Basic English list of 400 names of "general things" which C. K. Ogden, the inventor of Basic, regards as the most essential ideas for which terms must be maintained in the severely restricted vocabulary of Basic, numbering only 850 words in all. These ideas will recur often in ordinary discourse, and since most of us will not be writing Basic, it is particularly necessary to build up a stock of synonyms for these terms.

## WHAT IS BASIC ENGLISH?

This is not meant as a reflection on Basic English. That admirable invention is not a plot to impoverish vocabulary. It is a practical form of English for international use, simplified so that an intelligent foreigner who knows his own language well can learn to read Basic in a month, and to talk and write it after six months' work. It reads like ordinary English, except that there are a good many roundabout phrases. Also, it's likely to seem rather bare, abstract, and colorless. But it serves very well for ordinary purposes of business, social, and scientific communication, for which it was devised.

For a number of reasons Basic is of interest to any INQUIRER into vocabulary. Ogden, who has made a very careful philosophical analysis of our language, is of the opinion that a 20,000-word vocabulary is adequate for reading most ordinary English and American material. Note that his view sustains the premise on which this book is based. Ogden maintains that nearly all the necessary 20,000 words can be provided with equivalents and definitions in the 850 words of Basic. *The Dictionary of Basic English* makes this claim good. In this connection, an independent study shows that the Basic English words yield a total of 12,425 meanings (if limited to the senses accepted in Basic), an average of 14.6 meanings per word; or 18,418 meanings if the additional senses given for them in the OED are included—an average of 21 meanings per word (Fries—*Word Lists*, p. 81). Evidently the bright foreigner does well to master that many meanings in a short time.

## BASIC THROWS LIGHT ON SYNONYMS

One of the neat tricks that makes Basic possible is of especial interest in the study of synonyms. Because of a peculiarity of our language which permits the formation of PHRASAL verbs by adding to a simple verb a preposition indicating direction, Ogden in this SUPPLEMENTAL form of English replaces 4000 common verbs by 18 simple verbs plus tagged-on prepositions. Instead of saying *circumnavigate, circle*, DETOUR, or *skirt*, you say in Basic "go round," or "go around." To be sure, there is a little legitimate FUDGING. Two hundred of the Basic names of "general things" are terms denoting action, but you do not use them as verbs. Instead of *walking*, you "take a walk."

So you don't have to learn to conjugate these verbs, or master their principal parts. But the point is that about 4000 verbs can be reduced to *come, get, give, go, keep, let, make, put, seem, take, do, have, say, see, send, may, will, can,* plus the directive prepositions such as *about, round, around, down, in, with, from, to, through, for, against, out, over, of, up,* etc. These verbs and prepositions alike are called "operators" in Basic, because they all indicate action, direction, motion—something doing, so to speak.

The Basic method of providing phrasal equivalents for a flock of specific verbs throws a good deal of light on the requirements for a true synonym. "Go round" gives a fairly precise substitute for *circle,* and you can put it in the place of *circumnavigate,* in "Magellan's expedition was the first to circumnavigate the world." But "go round" doesn't convey all the meaning in "circumnavigate," which is to "sail round." "Go round" is more general. You can also "go round" the world by flying, though there is no verb *circumfly.* And you'd be more likely to say that the plane *circled* the field than that it "went round" it. Evidently a word acquires a certain "feel" as well as OVERTONES of meaning, which call for the use of a particular word in a given CONTEXT. *Such connotations call for careful* DISCRIMINATION *between* synonyms. But Basic is particularly stimulating in forcing us to focus on the exact *denotation,* which DELIMITS essential meaning.

Starting with one of the Basic verbs, we can also build up a whole collection of related and analogous words, some of which are synonyms for each other, and some not, though they overlap in some respects, and all of them share the essential, broad, general sense of the original Basic "operator." Take *go,* for instance. When Shakespeare wrote, "Stand not on the order of your going" (*Macbeth,* III, iv), a polite way of saying "Scram," the advice was good for his character, but not apt for anybody who is choosy about synonyms.

For the order of going is important. The various ways of going are: *to walk, to run, to ride, to fly, to crawl, to swim, to jump.* Each of these expands to describe the various manners and modes of walking, running, etc.:

*Walk,* plod, trudge, HOBBLE, limp, stalk, strut, tramp, march, schuffle, toddle, WADDLE, mince, stroll, SAUNTER, ramble, amble, CAREEN, slouch along, lumber, promenade, pace, tread, prowl, MEANDER, loiter, linger, lag, stride.
(Cf. the slang, "mosey along.") (Cf. "barge," as "barge into a room.")
*Run,* scamper, scurry, scuttle, SCUD, scour, pace, gallop, trot, lope, sprint, sweep.

206

*Ride,* gallop, trot, LOPE, canter, jog, amble, motor, cycle.
*Fly,* flit, hover, wing, glide, soar, dart, float.
*Crawl,* creep, "inch along," GROVEL, drag.
*Swim,* dive.
*Jump,* dive, hop, leap, skip, vault, HURDLE.

In addition, there are many slang inventions and phrases to express the sense of "go" as "get out." One of Shakespeare's contemporaries, Richard Carew, obligingly collected in 1595 the Elizabethan LOCUTIONS for conveying this *denigratory* sense:

. . . neither can any tongue . . . deliver a matter with more variety than ours, both plainly and by proverbs and metaphors; for example, when we would be rid of one, we use to say *be going, trudge, pack, be faring, hence, away, shift,* and by CIRCUMLOCUTION, *rather your room than your company, let's see your back, come again when I bid you, when you are called for, sent for,* INTREATED, *willed, desired, invited, spare us your place, another in your stead, a ship of salt for you, save your credit, you are next the door, the door is open for you, there's nobody holding you, nobody tears your sleeve, etc.* (spelling MODERNIZED).

Joyce adds the Dublin insult: "Who's keeping you?" In American slang, to meet this need, we have had successively (according to the date of first appearance in print),

ABSQUATULATE! (1833)
   Vamoose! (1848)
      Skedaddle! (1861)
         Scat! (1880)
            Cheese it! (1900)
               Skiddoo! (1907)
                  Fade away . . . (1911)
                     Rous! (from the German *heraus*) (1919)
                        Scram! (1920)
                           Blow! (1921)
                              Beat it! (1926)
                                Get lost! (Current) [1]

[1] The late Dr. Louise Pound, noted authority on substandard language, points out the increased use of short words as slang synonyms, as contrasted with the "mouthfilling" terms of the nineteenth century (from the Foreword to *The American Thesaurus of Slang,* Thomas Y. Crowell Company, 1953):

The older love of sonorous mouthfilling words, replaced by our present preference for the TERSE and vigorous, may be illustrated by such an evolution as that from early nineteenth-century "absquatulate" replaced in the Civil War period by "skedaddle" and in the twentieth century by "skiddoo," to our present-day forceful and MONOSYLLABIC "scram" or "beat it."

## WORD PACKAGING

By taking a few afternoons off, you could probably work out a similar ELABORATION of the modes of saying, making, keeping, etc. Luckily, it has all been done, not only for verbs, but for the whole range of language—in *Roget's International Thesaurus,* which groups words according to their idea relationships, from general to specific categories. The eight most inclusive categories cover all areas of knowledge and experience:

| | |
|---|---|
| *Class One:* | Abstract Relations |
| *Class Two:* | Space |
| *Class Three:* | Physics |
| *Class Four:* | Matter |
| *Class Five:* | Sensation |
| *Class Six:* | Intellect |
| *Class Seven:* | Volition |
| *Class Eight:* | Affections |

There are subclasses under each category that narrow down the general concept. Intellect, for example, divides into Intellectual Faculties and Processes, States of Mind, and Communication of Ideas. Under each of these are several subgroups, which are related because they come within the scope of the main heading. The groups under the subgroups are more and more specific until there are only fine shades of meaning that separate related words in a group.

Under the heading of Intellectual Faculties and Processes you'll see Theory, which splits off into "Theory, Supposition," and "Philosophy."

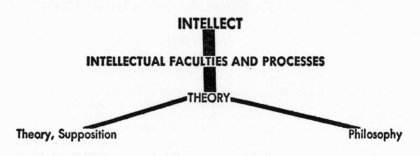

**INTELLECT**

**INTELLECTUAL FACULTIES AND PROCESSES**

THEORY

Theory, Supposition                                                        Philosophy

Under "Theory, Supposition" you'll find the word cluster described in Chapter 6—"hypothesis," "theory," "conjecture," etc. This method of word packaging enables you to see words grouped not only with their near relatives (synonyms) but also with other words (analogous words, associated words) that function in the same area.

## 498. THEORY, SUPPOSITION

NOUNS 1. **theory, theorization; theoretics,** theorics; **speculation,** contemplation; analysis, explanation; abstraction; Einstein theory, theory of relativity, continuum theory, quantum theory, Einstein's photon theory, Einstein's field theory, unified field theory, theory of exchanges, atomic theory, theory of evolution.

2. **supposition, supposal, supposing,** putation; **assumption, presumption, conjecture, inference, surmise, guesswork; presupposition,** presupposal; **hypothesis,** working hypothesis; **postulate, postulation,** postulatum; **proposition, proposal,** position, thesis, theorem.

3. **guess, conjecture, inference, surmise;** shot, stab [both coll.]; **rough guess, wild guess,** blind guess, shot in the dark [coll.].

4. (vague supposition) **suggestion, bare suggestion, suspicion, inkling, hint, intimation, impression, idea, notion,** sneaking idea [coll.]; vague idea, hazy idea.

5. **supposititiousness, presumptiveness,** presumableness, theoreticalness, conjecturableness, speculativeness.

6. **theorist, theorizer, theoretic, theoretician;** speculator, notionalist; **hypothesist,** hypothesizer; doctrinaire.

7. **supposer, assumer, surmiser, conjecturer, guesser,** guessworker.

*Roget's International Thesaurus* copyright © 1962 by Thomas Y. Crowell Company

## MANY WORDS AT A GLANCE

Each grouping from 1 to 7 is subdivided by semicolons into small word packages, with their own fine shades of meaning. Such discrimination of meanings may be compared to the separation of musical tones by whole steps, half steps, quarter steps, and so on to the most minute differences in pitch. The arrangement of words on the page tells you that "theory" and "speculation" are close relatives, but that "theory" and "theorization" are even closer. "Theory" and "speculation" in group 1 have the same closeness of relationship as do "supposition," "assumption," "hypothesis," "postulate," and "proposition" in group 2. "Assumption" and "conjecture," however, are more intimately related to each other than to the other three.

We see that "conjecture" appears in group 3 as well as in group 2 in another word cluster with "guess." Thus, words have two or three, sometimes four connotative senses which link them to different word clusters, each with a special aura of its own. Word packaging of this kind is vital for short-story, magazine, and television script writers, and for others who want to tie words more closely to the ideas they represent. For the student of vocabulary *Roget's International Thesaurus* provides many new words at a glance, grouped into packages by a common idea and separated from one another by fine distinctions of meaning.

We have followed the Roget groupings from the general to the specific. In actual practice, however, a writer or a speaker will be groping for a word and not be able to think of it; he will then use a key word such as "hypothesis" or "dialect" (see chart on p. 5) to help him find the exact word he needs. He will look up the key word in *Roget's* 600-page alphabetized index, which will take him directly to a whole battery of associated words from which he can make his choice. Thus, *Roget's International Thesaurus* is valuable as a *word-finder;* and, for anyone already well-versed in synonyms, it is the quickest and most efficient tool.

However, since Roget runs to over 240,000 word entries and 1258 pages, it cannot allow space for detailed discussion of synonyms. A companion book to *Roget, Webster's Dictionary of Synonyms,* performs this valuable function.

## WHAT IS A SYNONYM?

Anyone using *Roget's* who looks at a whole page of words relating to some subject will quickly realize that a HAZY-minded person may easily go wrong on synonyms. A word is not synonymous with another because of:

1. onetime identical meaning,
2. a mere likeness in meaning, or
3. some OVERLAP in the two areas of meaning.

A definition which rules out all BORDERLINE cases is found in *Webster's Dictionary of Synonyms.*[2]

A synonym in this Dictionary will always mean one of two or more words in the English language which have the same or very nearly the same *essential* meaning.

This definition, exemplified fully in the 900 pages of synonymies which follow, should stop all arguments on what a synonym is—and isn't. The same Dictionary's definition of antonym, while equally satisfactory, calls for a little preliminary warming-up exercise, to prepare for the ORDEAL.

## WHAT AN ANTONYM IS NOT

The French claim you prove that you know the meaning of a word if you can supply its precise antonym. The catch is in the word *precise.* If the French are right, whoever wrote the following CREDO for a new Monterey commercial art gallery had quite hazy notions:

When given to choose we shall prefer the incessant to the temporal, the magic to the MUNDANE, the DYNAMIC to both the STATIC and the nervous, the FULGENT to the SEDATE, and the organic to the contrived.

In these pairs, in only one case, *static* and *dynamic,* does one word come within miles of being an antonym of the other, and that ANTITHESIS is blurred because the writer apparently thinks *nervous* is a kind of middle term between them, which it is not. By mind-reading, you can make out that he means the gallery would follow a middle-of-the-road policy, but what kind of art lies on either side of the road, nobody could guess. If the painters supplying the gallery are as hazy-minded

[2] By permission. From *Webster's Dictionary of Synonyms,* copyright 1951 by G. & C. Merriam Co., Publishers of the Merriam-Webster Dictionaries.

as the writer who "plugs" their wares, the exhibit must be something to behold. The *New Yorker*, which picked up this specimen of word-torture, added the comment: "Any of these pictures for sale, by the way?"

With this awful example in mind, try your hand at the craft of antonymy.

### Word Game of Opposites

Give an antonym for each of the following:

| | | | |
|---|---|---|---|
| 1. PESSIMISM | 8. AMELIORATE | 14. BENIGNANT | 20. CIRCUMSTANTIAL |
| 2. ORNATE | 9. AMITY | 15. INTOLERANT | 21. CLANDESTINE |
| 3. HETERODOXY | 10. AMORPHOUS | 16. carnal | 22. PLIABLE |
| 4. ideal | 11. ANALYTIC | 17. URBANE | 23. VERBOSE |
| 5. ACCELERATE | 12. ASCETIC | 18. anterior | 24. rigid |
| 6. zenith | 13. ANODYNE | 19. CHAOTIC | 25. PROVISIONAL |
| 7. ALLEVIATE | | | |

ANSWERS

| | | | |
|---|---|---|---|
| 1. optimism | 8. worsen; | 13. stimulant; | 20. direct, |
| 2. austere | deteriorate | irritant | abridged; |
| 3. orthodoxy | 9. enmity | 14. malignant | summary |
| 4. actual | 10. morphous | 15. tolerant | 21. open |
| 5. retard; | 11. synthetic | 16. spiritual | 22. obstinate |
| decelerate | 12. voluptuary | 17. rude; clown- | 23. laconic |
| 6. nadir | (Webster | ish; bucolic | 24. elastic |
| 7. aggravate | gives *bon* | 18. posterior | 25. definitive |
| | *vivant!*) | 19. orderly | |

## WHAT AN ANTONYM IS

You're probably now ready to take Webster's definition of antonym on trust. It sounds a little as if the editors had sent up a rocket with instruments attached, to take a reading of the Van Allen radiation belts: [3]

An antonym is a word so opposed in meaning to another word, its equal in breadth and range of application, that it NEGATES or NULLIFIES every single one of its IMPLICATIONS.

[3] Ibid.

As Damon Runyon might have translated this: "It's a word says nix to another word all along the line, Mac."

## ANALOGOUS AND CONTRASTED WORDS

While the editors do not recognize Mr. Runyon's gifted recordings of spoken American, they do make a few concessions to human frailty. Under each synonym entry, they add, after the synonym and the antonym, groups of analogous and contrasted words. The analogous words are those closely related in meaning but not having the same or nearly the same *essential* meaning as the key word; sometimes, say the editors, they merit the name of "near-synonyms." The contrasted words are those which are sometimes very near synonyms of the antonym; others are opposed to the key word in only part of its meaning. The editors recognize that these analogous and contrasted words will be useful to anyone who wants to use *Webster's Dictionary of Synonyms* as a vocabulary builder.

## WORD CLUSTERS AS MEMORY JOGGERS

For this last purpose the work is an admirable tool. Here are whole clusters of words, grouped according to essential likeness of meaning, carefully discriminated one from another. Nearly always one word in each group will be familiar and will serve as a memory jogger for the others. For each group, the essential meaning which they have in common is stated in the first sentence. Then come the discriminations: the true glory of the work. Through these, the reader can deepen his word sense at the same time that he extends his word range.

Let's get back to "hypothesis." Four excellent desk dictionaries gave you a detailed picture of this word through their definitions and through their discriminations of the word's synonyms—"theory," "assumption," "supposition," "law," "conjecture." In this respect the new dictionaries are approaching but have not yet reached the completeness of discriminations that have put *Webster's Dictionary of Synonyms* in a class by itself. This book has more to tell you about "hypothesis" and its synonyms—and it adds more word relatives for your consideration. Here is the complete entry (with our annotations):

**Common Meaning** {

**hypothesis.** **Hypothesis, theory, law** are often interchangeable in general use. In the technical senses in which they are here considered, however, they are rigidly discriminated by the scientists and philosophers who employ them precisely. In general, the terms denote an inference from data gathered by observation and experiment that is offered as a formula to explain the abstract and general principle that lies behind them as their cause, their method of operation, their relation to other phenomena, or the like. In such usage, **hypothesis** implies tentativeness in the inference because of insufficient evidence or of the impossibility of obtaining further evidence. In such cases, *hypothesis* applies to a well-founded conjecture that serves as a point of departure for scientific discussion or as a tentative guide for further investigation or as the most reasonable explanation of certain phenomena now available. "A scientist says in effect—'Observation shews that the following facts are true; I find that a certain *hypothesis* as to their origin is consistent with them all' " (*Jeans*). "The resemblance to electric polarization is very close; it is in fact so close that it would not be foolish at all to make the *hypothesis* that the iron contains not only electrons but also tiny corpuscles of some subtle magnetic fluid" (*Karl K. Darrow*). "In the last chapter I proposed the *hypothesis* that a pure poetry exists, employing the term 'lyric' to describe poems which 'consist of poetry and nothing else' " (*Day Lewis*). **Theory,** in general use, often means little more than *hypothesis* or *conjecture* (as, " 'let us sit quiet, and hear the echoes about which you have your *theory*.' 'Not a *theory*; it was a fancy' "—*Dickens;* "In the course of my work in Egypt, I had formulated certain *theories* of my own about plague, and could not reconcile them to the findings of the Commission"—*V. Heiser*), but in the precise technical sense in which it is here considered, it presupposes much more supporting evidence than *hypothesis* does, a much wider range of application, and greater likelihood of truth. It is not always obvious when *hypothesis* and when *theory* should be used, the former being preferred by some scientists as the more modest in its claims, the latter being preferred by others as suggesting such confidence in the reliability of the inference and its supporting evidence as to imply that it deserves acceptance; thus, the Darwinian explanation of the origin of species is regarded by some as a *hypothesis*, but is more often designated as the "*theory* of evolution." "That exact verbal expression of as much as we know of the facts, and no more, which constitutes a perfect scientific *theory*" (*T. H. Huxley*). "In 1905 Einstein crystallised these concepts and *hypotheses* in his *theory* of light-quanta, according to which all radiation consisted of discrete bullet-like units, which he called 'light-quanta' at the time, although we now call them 'photons' " (*Jeans*). "There was also a nascent *theory* of sound waves; and out of it there grew...a tremendous mathematical doctrine of waves which nowadays has almost come to dominate the physics of these times" (*Karl K. Darrow*). **Law** (as here considered: for fuller

hypothesis ➡

theory ➡

**Discrimination of Meanings**

law ➡

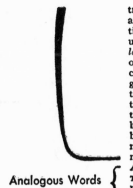

**Analogous Words**

treatment see PRINCIPLE) emphasizes certainty and proof and therefore applies to a statement of an order or relation in phenomena that has been found to be invariable under the same conditions; as, in philology, Grimm's *law* is a statement of the regular changes which the stops, or mute consonants, of the primitive Indo-European consonant system have undergone in the Teutonic languages. However, since even so-called "laws" are open to disproof or alteration by the discovery of contradictory or additional evidence, the term is often changed in the course of time to *theory;* for example, what has long been known as Newton's *law* of gravitation is currently being revised as a result of Einstein's discoveries and is now designated by careful scientists as Newton's mathematical *theory* of universal gravitation.

**Ana.** Conjecture, surmise, guess (see under CONJECTURE, *v.*): inference, deduction, conclusion (see under INFER).

Under the entry for "conjecture" we find the discrimination of the analogous word cluster of "conjecture," "surmise," and "guess." "Theory" and "law" are also entered separately with their analogous words and word clusters.

Look at the diagram on page 216. The white space within the large circle is the area of common meaning for "hypothesis," "law," and "theory." Each word has an additional area of meaning represented by the shaded portions of the smaller circles, which it shares with other words. "Theory," for example, has an area of common meaning with "assumption," "presupposition," "postulate," and "premise." These analogous, or nearly synonymous, words in turn extend into new circles and new word clusters.

The study of word clusters will add many new words to your vocabulary, often at a glance. When you first come across an unfamiliar or a half-familiar word, look for the key word in the cluster to which it belongs; next, explore the fine shades of meaning in all their RAMIFICATIONS, as described above. Use a good desk dictionary and back it up with *Roget's International Thesaurus* and *Webster's Dictionary of Synonyms.* These will help you to master words in groups and accelerate the rate at which you add new words to your vocabulary.

## REFINEMENTS OF RANCOR

One of the first things that strikes a systematic explorer in the treasure house of synonyms is the extraordinary richness of our vocabulary in terms of abuse. Joseph Conrad always thought it possible to convey in English the effect of PROFANITY without using it. This is a speculation worth testing.

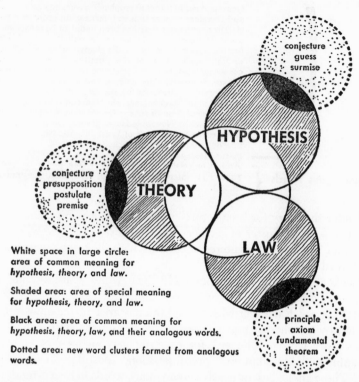

White space in large circle: area of common meaning for *hypothesis, theory,* and *law.*

Shaded area: area of special meaning for *hypothesis, theory,* and *law.*

Black area: area of common meaning for *hypothesis, theory, law,* and their analogous words.

Dotted area: new word clusters formed from analogous words.

If a writer wants to describe a man venting his spleen on an enemy, he can have his character *abuse, accuse, criticize, curse,* BULLDOZE, CASTIGATE, DISPARAGE, *frighten, malign, scoff at, scold,* or *threaten,* without ever repeating himself. For no one of these words is a synonym for any other on the list. They are just the main, simple, direct, UNREFINED ways of going after somebody. All permit of refinement, however, to express the exact degree of rancor felt. Many of the synonyms are longer than the parent word, and more satisfying, like polysyllabic profanity with a long rolling cadence. For simple abuse,

VITUPERATION, INVECTIVE, OBLOQUY, SCURRILITY, BILLINGSGATE,

can be delivered with ACRIMONY, or, if you wish, one of its two finer shadings,

ACERBITY or ASPERITY

but if mere DETRACTION is not enough, one can indulge in

BACKBITING, CALUMNY, *scandal,* or *slander.*

If the aim is to achieve that "measured MALIGNITY of slander" with which Lecky credited the later Junius, the offender will soon realize that *malign* may be refined by a VERSATILE opponent to

TRADUCE, ASPERSE, VILIFY, CALUMNIATE, DEFAME, *slander*, or *libel*.

And the *libel* (as a noun) may be in the form of a

SKIT, SQUIB, LAMPOON, or PASQUINADE

This last sounds like a formidable insult, and it can be. It was originally an ANONYMOUS lampoon, usually in verse, posted up on a mutilated statue of Pasquino, in Rome, as GRATUITOUS publicity for the writer's enemy. Some anonymous wag writing in the old *Bookman* provided George Moore with a pasquinade for his tombstone in the form of a premature epitaph:

> Women he loved, and after women art;
> Good friends he had, and used them all for copy.
> Had but his head been matchéd by his heart,
> Time had not mixed his laurels with the poppy.

When it comes to a more serious and sustained attack, however, the language still has many UNEXHAUSTED resources. When the object is to *curse* someone out roundly, you can choose whether to

EXECRATE, OBJURGATE, damn, or ANATHEMATIZE

him, though the last implies ECCLESIASTICAL language, and in view of the blasphemy laws, should perhaps be done with discretion. If long words seem inadequate to explode compressed rancor, consider the merits of *scoff*. Trailing it as synonyms are

jeer, GIBE, LEER, GIRD, *sneer*, and FLOUT,

expressive MONOSYLLABLES all.

If the occasion is a battle of the books between rival scholars where unduly strong language is barred, one can *disparage* the other or, with deliberate DISCRIMINATIONS in the form of DISPARAGEMENT, can

DEPRECIATE, DECRY, DEROGATE FROM, DETRACT FROM, BELITTLE, or MINIMIZE

the other's reputation. In a high-word level exchange of this kind, the derogator can be sure of an appreciative audience with a nice feeling for the gradations of meaning involved. As for the professor on the receiving end, he will understand all too well. No danger of his being in the predicament of one of Earl Wilson's friends:

Izzy Grove, the amazingly successful dance promoter, was at a meeting of the Anti-DEFAMATION League when somebody used some long words. "Wait a minute," said Grove. "What do them words mean? Ya know, once I was nominated for oblivion, and I accepted, with thanks, and it wasn't till two years later I found out what it meant."

To do the intellectuals justice, however, their wrangles conducted in public print are seldom as mild as mere depreciation. When *Webster's Third Unabridged* was unveiled in 1961, a War Over Words was declared and fought as bitterly as any on the battlefield or in the prize-fighting ring. Professors of English, magazine writers, EDITORIALISTS, lexicographers, and others in the word business dipped their quills in vitriol and peppered their opponents with word barbs. They *sneered*, they *jeered*, they *jibed*, they *scoffed*, they *depreciated*, they *disparaged*, they *belittled*.

The militant leader of the anti-Webster forces was Wilson Follett, to whom Webster's permissive approach to slang and careless speech was a call to arms. Follett *upbraided* Webster with this DIATRIBE: "Webster III has thrust upon us a dismaying assortment of the questionable, the perverse, the unworthy, and the downright outrageous." In an outburst of *vituperation*, he called the book "a scandal and a disaster." He hurled this *invective*: "The enemy it is out to destroy is every obstinate vestige of linguistic PUNCTILIO." He EXCORIATED Webster's editors as "the patient and dedicated SABOTEURS in Springfield." He continued in this mock-McCarthy mood with "To what is the definer contributing if not to subversion and decay?" And in a final burst of acerbity: ". . . you begin to apprehend the scope of the really enormous disaster . . ."

Dr. Philip Gove, under whose patient direction 10,000,000 "citation" slips and a host of scholar years were spent in research, sought to submerge his detractors with this tidal word wave: "The English language is not a system of logic. What we start with is an INCHOATE HETEROGENEOUS AGGLOMERATE that retains the INDESTRUCTIBLE bones of innumerable tries at orderly communication." But the opposition forces were not to be word-washed. The word-men are a hardy lot. They may reel from verbal blows, but they come right back and pile up points with polysyllabic punches. Their word weaponry is seem-

218

íngly inexhaustible. It repays a student of vocabulary to follow the battle script by script.

Bergen Evans, who usually has a genial and jolly way with a word, took to his typewriter in defense of Webster's policy. Replying in the same magazine that had printed Wilson Follett's article, *The Atlantic,* he belittled Follett with wordplay, coining the term "folletizing" to which he added, "—his mental processes demand some special designation." He *chided* the anti-Webster forces for emitting "wild wails"; he DEFLATED them by labeling their criticisms "BOMBINATIONS" (buzzing, empty words, "hot air"); he *dismissed* their arguments as mere "sound and fury."

Writer Dwight Macdonald, after what must have been an ASTRONOMICAL number of reader-hours devoted to studying Webster's fine print, wrote a derogatory CRITIQUE in the *New Yorker* (March 10, 1962).[4] His tone was more restrained but just as CENSORIOUS as Follett's. No brief commenter himself (his article ran twenty-six pages) he *disparages* Webster with: "Its sheer bulk is impressive—until one begins to investigate." He *depreciates Webster's Third Unabridged* in comparison with *Webster's Second Unabridged.* He REBUKES Webster's editors for "sometimes lacking common sense." He GIBES at them for including all the more important four- and five-letter obscene words but prudently leaving out "perhaps the most important one." Mr. Macdonald has too much dignity to *backbite* or TONGUELASH, *bawl out* or *rail at*—but the pen is twisted in the wound with remarkable effect.

Dr. James Sledd, of Northwestern University, who helped compile *Dictionaries and THAT Dictionary*[5] as a record of the controversy, joined the defenders of Webster by employing SARCASM and IRONY in his JOUSTS at Macdonald's armor. "I am struck by his [Macdonald's] confidence in his own learning, cultivation, intelligence, taste, and common sense." The scholars are not above becoming personal in these word wars. Dr. Sledd called Macdonald's *New Yorker* review of Webster "portentously bad . . . disgraced by ignorance and unfairness. . . ."

Another scholastic *sneer* came from Dr. Patrick Kilburn of Union College. "Wilson Follett erupted in one long splutter in the pages of *The Atlantic* . . . Out of the same well of LINGUISTIC arrogance comes

[4] "The String Untuned."
[5] In collaboration with Wilma R. Ebbitt (University of Chicago). Published by Scott, Foresman and Company (1962).

the article by Dwight Macdonald. . . ." He follows this with the clincher, the last word *leer*, a reference to the language purists as "generations of old maids of both sexes."

What was the battle all about that moved normally mild and cloistered men to such passionate utterance? Those who are concerned with language divide into two camps on the question of how dictionaries should screen, define, and label words. The PRESCRIPTIVISTS believe that dictionaries should set the standards of good taste in writing and speaking, that words or phrases that are vulgar, illiterate, or ungrammatical according to these standards should be omitted or clearly labeled as such.

The DESCRIPTIVISTS hold the view that good taste is a matter of usage, that the job of dictionaries is merely to record what is being said or written, not to make value judgments. The editors of *Webster's Third Unabridged* are descriptivists; so are Bergen Evans and Dr. Sledd. According to their view, when President Eisenhower said "Somebody made a *goof*," and when both Eisenhower and Kennedy used *finalize* in a sentence, these words graduated from the slang class into the standard category. A comparison of the latest dictionaries shows a difference of opinion on this matter. *The American College Dictionary* labels *goof* as "Slang" and *finalize* as "Colloq."

What is interesting about this controversy is that university professors such as Dr. Sledd, Dr. Kilburn, and Bergen Evans defend Webster's approach, while many journalists and professional writers such as Dwight Macdonald and Sydney J. Harris (columnist for the *Chicago Daily News*) tend to be purists and TRADITIONALISTS in matters of language usage.

The battle between the prescriptivists and the descriptivists is valuable in many ways to students of vocabulary. It is instructive to follow the skillful verbal fencing practiced by these ERUDITE gentlemen, the parries and thrusts of a wily word or phrase, the euphemistic, often pedantic substitutes for "You're another!" A study of the fine shades of meaning, the connotations, the auras of less common and uncommon words (and even of common words cleverly manipulated) used as refinements of rancor will help raise your vocabulary level to the "educated" category. And the next time you are tempted to punch someone in the eye, follow the lead of Sledd, Macdonald, Evans, et al.—try words instead.

## LADIES, TOO, FIGHT WITH WORDS

When the scolding shifts over to the distaff side, there is just as rich a synonymy of invective. In this respect the female is often deadlier than the male. Ladies who know the shattering effect of nasty words needn't resort to hair-pulling. A woman may label her BÊTE NOIR a VIRAGO; this expands into

AMAZON, TERMAGANT, *scold, shrew,* VIXEN, or *barge,*

all words which call for utterance in a

CAUSTIC, MORDANT, SCATHING, or MORDACIOUS

tone. Suppose, however, that the target, rather than being a bull-dozing virago, is a somewhat clinging creature, who prefers lying in bed and eating chocolates to honest employment; she can be put in her place as a *parasite,* or

SYCOPHANT, *favorite,* LICKSPITTLE, *bootlicker, hanger-on, leech,* or *sponge.*

Or if her cat-talk got down to the verbal clawing of an Albee or Lillian Hellman character, it could be called not merely *poisonous* but

*venomous,* VIRULENT, TOXIC, MEPHITIC, PESTILENTIAL, or MIASMIC,

depending on the particular poison exuded. But all these methods are probably too crude. To express a really telling insult in elegant and IMPECCABLE English, reflection on the other woman's taste in clothes is probably indicated. Here the INTIMATION that her taste runs to the

*gaudy,* TAWDRY, GARISH, or FLASHY

is too blunt. The one remaining synonym in the list is the one wanted for the very ACME of polite insult: "Isn't her taste in clothes a little MERETRICIOUS?" Admittedly, this is not the term now in use in the world of fashion, but it should be. It's really an ideal solution to the problem a reviewer once skirted so delicately by calling a movie a "DE-CANINED AMERICANIZATION of its original French title, *La Chienne,* a term which one doesn't sling around in free translation for family audiences." Beaumont and Fletcher would have solved that instantly, retaining even the canine connotations: they'd have rendered the title *Merrytricks.* (Latin *meretrix,* "harlot.")

Surely this exhibit shows Conrad was right. PROFANITY is a crude expedient in comparison with the far richer resources of denigratory and PEJORATIVE terms available in English. Conrad demonstrates his point pretty well when one of his NARRATORS tells how he was cursed out:

... began by calling me Pig, and from that went CRESCENDO into UN-MENTIONABLE adjectives.

Runyon, Lardner, and other writers have also shown great RESOURCE-FULNESS in conveying the effects of profanity and RIBALDRY through the use of slang equivalents—and in this department the PENCHANT of our language for developing synonyms is very much in evidence.

On the sober and serious side, there is infinite variety in synonyms, too. And it is one of the great pleasures of reading to be able to appreciate the fine shades of meaning which a master of synonyms can convey. The best of all tests for vocabulary depth—as well as width—is an ability to distinguish between synonyms, by supplying from a list the *one* which is most apt, and most in accord with the tone and color of the thought expressed.

### Pick the Right Synonym

The synonym lists which follow are picked from *Webster's Dictionary of Synonyms*, to allow for the addition of the maximum number of words to vocabulary. Most of the key words and equivalents belong to the learned part of the language. The ILLUSTRATIVE sentences, in which you are to fill in each blank with the best synonym, are not from Webster's examples, which are almost without exception on the sober side. Unless a source is cited, the sentences are by the author of this book; but they are devised to keep as close as possible to the DISCRIMINATIONS in Webster. To get the best results, do only one or two entries at a time, and try to fix each group of new words in your memory, at the same time mastering the NUANCES of meaning for each.

*Abjure:* renounce, FORSWEAR, RECANT, RETRACT

1. He was unwilling to take the pledge, because he knew he would soon _____ himself.
2. Galileo was forced publicly to _____ his belief that the earth revolved around the sun.
3. Gandhi required his followers to _____ force.

4. The columnist refused to _____ his statement that the politician had accepted a bribe.
5. George II of Greece was unwilling to _____ his claim to the throne.

Ant.: pledge, elect

*Abridgement:* abstract, brief, SYNOPSIS, CONSPECTUS, EPITOME

1. The secretary asked him for an _____ of his paper to include in the published program.
2. When Eutropius called his short history of Rome an _____, he stretched the meaning of the word.
3. The professor asked each RESEARCHER to submit a _____ of his thesis.
4. In his presentation to the publisher, he featured a _____ of the whole book in a form that would be taken in at a glance.
5. They sold an _____ of the book in a quarter edition.

Ant.: expansion

*Activate:* ENERGIZE, VITALIZE

1. Pure proteins are found to have the maximum _____ effect in aiding CONVALESCENCE from MALNUTRITION.
2. An artist in residence at a university is found to _____ the creative work of students.

Ant.: arrest

*Adjacent:* adjoining, CONTIGUOUS, ABUTTING, TANGENT, COTERMINOUS, JUX-
TAPOSED

1. The airline route to Moscow was _____ to the great circle course followed by ships, only at _____ (a naval secret!).
2. Their estates were _____ for three miles back from the point where they joined on the Potomac to the old mill which lay half on one property, half on the other; beyond that, they diverged.
3. The nearest ranch house _____ to the headquarters of the great King Ranch is distant a long day's ride.
4. The Hay and Adams mansions in Washington were _____, and doors opened between them.
5. He bought land _____ on the river.
6. The City of Seattle and King County in which it lies are _____.
7. A passage from North's translation of Plutarch _____ to Shakespeare's lines covering the same ground, shows what a fast and slick REWRITE job he could do.

Ant.: NONADJACENT

*Accidental:* casual, FORTUITOUS, CONTINGENT, incidental, ADVENTITIOUS (all are synonyms of *accidental,* but not always of one another)

1. The question of an immediate tax cut was _____ to the long-range necessity for tax reform.
2. Lucretius spoke of the _____ CONCOURSE of the atoms, but NUCLEAR PHYSICISTS would not agree with him.
3. Rhine claims that the results obtained in his SUPRASENSORY experiments cannot be merely _____, since the hits exceed the misses to a degree not to be accounted for by the laws of PROBABILITY. Other STATISTICIANS dispute his claim.
4. His research methods were seemingly _____, but he got living offspring from a cross between a sea-urchin and a sand-dollar, which was as if, said the Director of the laboratory, he had successfully crossbred a lion with a jackass.
5. The very high CORRELATION (.98) between the rate of melting of a certain Greenland glacier and the birth rate of the Bantus in equatorial Africa is purely _____.
6. Pay raises in this concern were _____ on the state of the business as shown in the balance sheet at the close of the fiscal year.

Ant.: planned, essential

*Cumulative:* ACCUMULATIVE, ADDITIVE, SUMMATIVE

1. A carefully planned educational program is in its truest sense _____, since the influence of each course upon the one that follows is noted, until a closely RETICULATED and integrated whole is attained.
2. The _____ effect of repeated DOSAGES finally weakened his heart, though curing his GLANDULAR deficiency.
3. INTEGRATION is a shortcut to replace the CUMBERSOME _____ methods which yield in any case only an APPROXIMATION.
4. The _____ whole which results from the efforts of the mound-building ants is very impressive.

*Addict:* VOTARY, DEVOTEE, HABITUÉ, fiend, fan (I add *aficionado,* because you often need a synonym for "fan.")

1. He came to the club, he said, expecting to see some of the old _____s, but it was such a stormy night that all he saw at the table were the sons of _____s.
2. Had Casanova been born in ancient Rome, he would have been a _____ in the temple of Venus.
3. Coleridge was a LAUDANUM _____, but in no sense a drug _____.

4. Anybody living in New York who is not a Met _____ is anathema to the rest of the baseball _____.
5. One who is a _____ of pure science often believes that an inventor is not a scientist in any real sense, if he adds nothing to theory.

*Allegory:* (I) SYMBOLISM

1. Proust's _____ often depends on memory-ENCRUSTED sensations of taste or smell.
2. Diego Rivera's great MURAL pageant of Mexican history above the grand staircase of the National Palace is a superb _____ of his country's long struggle against oppression.

(II) parable, MYTH, fable, APOLOGUE

1. It is no DISPARAGEMENT to speak of the Christian religion as having the most moving and effective _____ of any world faith; and the fact that Paul and St. Augustine turned it into an _____ for their own doctrines in no sense weakens the overwhelming impression made by the words of Christ, taken by themselves. The notion that Jesus is an invented character argues the existence of an epic-poet-dramatist greater than Homer, Shakespeare, and Cervantes rolled into one. Who was he? History is even more silent on this score and the silence argues that it was Jesus who existed, not some unknown literary creator.
2. Christ often taught by _____s.
3. *Animal Farm* is a true _____ though there are those who think that George Orwell draws an immoral moral.

*Apparition:* PHANTASM, phantom, WRAITH, fetch, ghost, spirit, specter, shade, REVENANT, spook, haunt, hant (to which I add *zombie* and *Poltergeist*)

1. Hamlet, I am thy father's _____.
2. Saul asked the Witch of Endor to summon up the _____ of Samuel.
3. The _____ of buried Denmark.—*Hamlet.*
4. The figure of the old Earl, appearing suddenly by the PARAPET in the twilight, looked too substantial to be an _____; yet the record showed that he had gone down at sea last year.
5. Looking on the ruins of Nurnberg, where he had spent so many happy days during his *Lehrjahren,* he knew how that illustrious Prince of India must have felt in revisiting Tyre, where three thousand years earlier he had known King Hiram when the city was in its high glory.
6. As he came out of the COMA, his fever was still high, and persistent _____ kept recurring—one, a group of Dutch travelers, carrying

tulip bulbs and leading horses. Five months later he saw these people in life, getting on a river steamer—an authentic instance of PREVISION.

7. A _____ is a lively _____, but the records show that the only one seen of man was the one which John Wesley saw at the Epworth Rectory.

8. The _____s which worried Hawthorne were really _____s from the Puritan past.

9. "It's no common _____," old Silas said; "for it comes in different shapes, but always whispers at him the same way. Maybe it's Old Nick himself, trying to collect on a bet for Jabez' soul, but Jabez' idear of gettin' Daniel Webster to defend him is a crazy notion. Daniel would uphold the contract, even if it was made with the devil himself."

10. Ichabod Crane saw the grisly _____ of the headless horseman.

11. The last time he saw her in the sanitarium, she was a mere _____.

12. It's hard to tell if a _____ is dead or alive; the Communist party is a perfect instance.

13. Judging by his story "The Horla," Guy de Maupassant must have been one of the few persons to see his own _____. Soon after he went mad and died.

14. Halfway between sleeping and waking, as he napped one drowsy afternoon, he thought he saw through the French window his old collie LOPING through the garden; and it proved to be no _____; the old dog had found his way across three states to rejoin his master.

*Aesthete:* DILETTANTE, VIRTUOSO, CONNOISSEUR

1. Horace Walpole was a mere _____ of the Gothic, but has to be taken seriously as a letter-writer.

2. Iris Barry of the Museum of Modern Art is not only a great collector of films, but one of the best _____s of CINEMATIC art alive.

3. Most _____s are _____s of several arts.

*Amateur:* dilettante, dabbler, TYRO (or TIRO). (Note that DILETTANTE also overlaps in meaning with AESTHETE.)

1. Adlai Stevenson is no _____ in the field of international relations.

2. A _____ usually tries to arrive at results as did George Eliot's Mr. Tulliver, by his own unaided intellect.

3. An _____ in all the arts may still become master of one.

4. Margaret Webster may seem to scholars a mere _____ of Shakespeare, but that is not how she strikes old stagehands—of whom Shakespeare was one.

Ant.: professional, expert

226

*Ambiguity:* EQUIVOCATION, TERGIVERSATION, AMPHIBOLOGY, AMPHIBOLO-
GISM. DOUBLE ENTENDRE (or DOUBLE ENTENTE). I add *double-talk.*)

1. Danny Kaye's famous songs in _____ are written by his wife, Sylvia Fine.
2. No one has ever found an _____ or _____ in Bertrand Russell's writing, for he always uses words to DELIMIT meaning—nor does he go in for _____s in his writings on love and marriage.
3. What he called an _____ in the wording of the contract seemed to me an INTENTIONAL _____, so I called the deal off.
4. There has been downright _____ in the Russian use of the terms democracy and freedom, though it is evident that they use *peace* in the same sense we do—to mean the temporary absence of war.

Ant.: LUCIDITY, EXPLICITNESS

*Appendage:* APPURTENANCE, adjunct, accessory

1. In *Oklahoma* the ballet was no longer a mere _____ to musical comedy, but an INTEGRAL part of the plot action.
2. They worked out a scheme for beating the OPA ceiling price on new cars by providing virtually built-in _____s.
3. St. Paul had no intention of becoming a mere _____ to Minneapolis.
4. He sold the manor and all its _____, except the gatehouse which he gave as a FREEHOLD to the old porter.

*Changeable:* changeful, variable, MUTABLE, PROTEAN

1. It is hard to devise tests that really measure vocabulary range, because the difficulty of words, even in groups of like frequency and range of occurrence is _____ within wide limits for different persons, depending on their experience and reading choices.
2. Alec Guinness has a _____ genius for assuming many different characters.
3. The _____ temper of the skies.—Dryden.
4. They put the CHAMELEON on _____ silk, but it did not burst.
5. The INFINITESIMAL universe within the atom is revealed as infinitely _____.

Ant.: stable, UNCHANGEABLE

*Celerity:* ALACRITY, LEGERITY

1. The motto of a good restaurant is "Service with _____," not with slow motion.

2. Voltaire's style always kept that certain _____, even when he was eighty; and Shaw's style kept it, too.
3. She reached for her gun with the _____ of a crocodile snapping at a stick.

*Change*, n.: (I) alteration, variation, MODIFICATION

1. Shops dealing in men's suits usually undertake _____ free.
2. The Senator suggested a slight _____ in the wording, which effectively EVISCERATED the bill.
3. Human nature may be always the same; but there are tremendous _____ in the methods of reading it; from humors to COMPLEXES is a long jump.
4. There were a good many _____s between the books he presented to the Internal Revenue and the set of accounts which he kept for use in negotiations with the union.

(II) MUTATION, PERMUTATION, VICISSITUDE, ALTERNATION

1. The total of possible moves in a game of chess is a number so great that a hundred billion years would not suffice to try out all the _____s.
2. There proved to be very rapid _____s of phase in the CIRCUIT.
3. The _____s of the twenty-one civilizations that have so far existed are interpreted by Toynbee in his *Study of History*.
4. General PHYSIOLOGISTS are now trying to find the PHYSICOCHEMICAL processes which account for the sudden _____s which DeVries discovered.

*Clear*, adj.: (I) transparent, translucent, lucid, PELLUCID, DIAPHANOUS, LIMPID

1. Glass bricks are _____ but not _____.
2. Her spoken words had a _____ quality, and her "voice delicately divided the silence" (Elinor Wylie).
3. In British drapery shops, *muslin* means a _____ fabric, not suitable for men's pajamas.
4. It is a myth that all French styles have in common the quality of being _____. Proust often is not; and the SYMBOLISTS were often obscure, as were the TROUBADOUR poets who favored the *trobar clus*.
5. Ellis' style was both _____ and _____.

(II) PERSPICUOUS, lucid

1. Neither Veblen nor Dewey had a _____ style in the lecture room, yet they were two of the most influential teachers America has produced.

2. Bertrand Russell commands a style as _____ as his thought.

Ant.: (I) TURBID (of air, days, water), confused (as to minds, thoughts, etc.);
(II) UNINTELLIGIBLE, ABSTRUSE

*Inconsonant:* inconsistent, INCOMPATIBLE, INCONGRUOUS, UNCONGENIAL,
UNSYMPATHETIC, DISCORDANT, DISCREPANT

1. The Secretary of State gave the Cuban representative a decidedly
_____ hearing.
2. Salisbury found Disraeli a rather _____ colleague; and the feeling
was reciprocal.
3. Santa Ana's and Zack Taylor's accounts of the battle were not merely
_____; they were _____ in details beyond the point where
the DISPARITY could be explained as due to different standpoints for observation. Actually, Santa Ana and Taylor both lied.
4. Elizabeth's court orchestra was called The Queen's Noise, but not because there was anything _____ about their playing.
5. That they were mentally and morally _____ was apparent.
6. There was nothing _____ between Jefferson's taste and his
powers of assimilation, even on the level of food and wine. As he put
it, "I am blessed with a digestion that can accept and CONCOCT whatever
my palate chooses to consign to it."
7. The toastmaster's humor was decidedly _____ with the occasion.

Ant.: consonant

*Appetizer:* HORS D'OEUVRE, ANTIPASTO, SMÖRGÅSBORD, APÉRITIF

1. The Italian restaurant had very good _____.
2. If you offer most Americans an _____ in solid form instead of
liquid, they won't come to your parties again.
3. During wartime the quality of _____ falls off, even at the best
French restaurants.
4. The beatniks made the rounds of the Village cocktail parties and ate
up all the _____s.
5. We had _____ at the Swedish Restaurant.

*Dictatorial:* MAGISTERIAL, MAGISTRAL, authoritative, AUTHORITARIAN, DOG-
MATIC, DOCTRINAIRE, ORACULAR (Webster, at the entry for
authoritarian, gives TOTALITARIAN.)

1. The _____ tone of the Pope's ENCYCLICALS is to be expected, since
he is the chief lawgiver of the Church when he speaks *ex cathedra.*
2. To judge by Stalin's pictures, he did not have a _____ manner;
but his utterance in answering questions was _____.

229

3. So long as it leaves to Caesar the things that are Caesar's, the Church is not a _____ REGIME, though it may be called _____.
4. Mr. Justice Holmes did not indulge in _____ language, preferring a dry, ironic style; and while he spoke with finality he was never _____, being a disciple of Hume's skepticism.
5. The dogma that human nature is always the same has _____ finality with generals and cheapjack politicians.
6. A petty classroom tyrant usually assumes a _____ manner; whereas a great teacher, as a rule, keeps to a simple natural style.

*Enormous:* immense, huge, vast, giant, gigantean, gigantic, colossal, mammoth, ELEPHANTINE, TITANIC, HERCULEAN, CYCLOPEAN, ANTEAN, GARGANTUAN, BROBDINGNAGIAN

1. The road-building machine, moving slowly down the island at night, with its single searchlight high on the forty-foot mast from which the boom swung, seemed like some _____ monster.
2. Hamsun's novel, *Growth of the Soil*, has an _____ power to remind us how closeness to elemental things is a source of strength.
3. He had _____ strength and no sense of how to use it.
4. The famous GOURMAND of Monterey had a _____ appetite, which required five pounds of steak and eleven chickens at a meal.
5. The HULLABALOO over *Cleopatra* can be described by Hollywood's favorite adjective, _____, with "success" or "bore" added, depending on the reviewer.
6. The CYCLOTRONS involve ever more _____ VOLTAGES.
7. Beyond the cliff lay only the _____ reaches of the ocean.
8. Many of the HIDALGOS' HACIENDAS covered an _____ expanse.
9. Some theories about PREHISTORIC man hold that he attained _____ proportions.
10. Ringling's circus is no longer a _____ spectacle.
11. Dr. Johnson had an _____ gait.
12. Hitler cast a _____ and horrifying shadow upon world history, quite in contrast to his actual insignificance of body and soul. He was the worst of the half-witted geniuses who have scourged mankind.
13. The ORCHID attained _____ size.
14. e. e. cummings' _____ room was the best novel of prison life to come out of World War I.
15. Even among the prehistoric animals, the DINOSAUR loomed up as _____.

*Impostor:* FAKER, EMPIRIC, quack, MOUNTEBANK, CHARLATAN

1. Was Nostradamus a _____ and a _____, or was he an inspired prophet?

2. Huey Long had a good deal of the _____ about him, perhaps a carryover from his peddling days; but he also had great, though misused, powers, as Robert Penn Warren shows in his *roman à clef* about the first American *Führer*, and, one hopes, the last.
3. Many UNDISCERNING Americans are hoodwinked by cheap political _____s.
4. NATUROPATHS and CHIROPRACTORS are considered _____ by organized medicine, and are labeled _____s who have not taken advantage of the experimental discoveries and of the PHARMACOPEIA on which orthodox doctors rely.
5. The Indian RAJAH who escaped from his own funeral PYRE was considered an _____ by all his relatives for twenty-five years, until a week before his death he was VINDICATED by the Privy Council.

*Compendium:* SYLLABUS, digest, PANDECT, survey, sketch, PRÉCIS, APERÇU

1. A _____ course often involves little firsthand contact with the SALIENT works of the periods covered; at its worst, it is a comic _____.
2. Protagoras' summer course was a _____ of his winter lectures.
3. Peale's Popular Educator was an old-fashioned _____ of knowledge on all subjects, much of it inaccurate and none of it the result of original research.
4. Jefferson asked Freneau to put a _____ on the back of each document filed.
5. The _____ for the course gave its mere bare bones.
6. Coleridge excelled at giving _____s which provided for his listeners sudden flashes of insight.
7. The _____s of Justinian as transmitted to Western Europe had curious results on local law.

*Discernment:* DISCRIMINATION, perception, PENETRATION, insight, ACUMEN, DIVINATION, CLAIRVOYANCE

1. Very few news commentators have his blend of logical _____ and INTUITIVE _____. And he brings to bear also natural _____ in deciding on a course of action.
2. Secretary McNamara runs the Defense Department by intellect, not by _____.
3. Dr. Rhine believes that his experiments in ESP prove the existence of _____.
4. Caesar had particular _____ in picking men.
5. _____ between *mystical* and *mysterious* is no problem for anyone with acute _____ as to the basic distinction in meaning. The two words come close to being antonyms.

*Inconstant:* fickle, capricious, MERCURIAL, UNSTABLE

1. An _____ policy in government REGULATORY activity is less easily endured by business than CALCULABLE severity. Under the latter, business at least feels that the government knows its own mind and will stay put.
2. For anyone who likes variety, a _____ temper in a spouse is more endurable than a stolid one.
3. An _____ woman used to be more of a shock to society than a man of the same breed.
4. A _____ woman may or may not be _____ as well. She may take out all her VAGARIES on one man.

Ant.: constant

*Controversial:* POLEMIC, POLEMICAL, ERISTIC, APOLOGETIC

1. What is valid in art has always been _____; many artists with a flair for CAPTIOUS criticism could be called skilled in the _____ art.
2. Dean Inge's series of sermons in St. Mary's Church at Oxford on "What Is Christianity" were rather _____ than _____. He chiefly indulged in _____ blasts against the schools of religion which he disliked: MODERNISM, the social gospel, etc.

*Insubordinate:* rebellious, mutinous, SEDITIOUS, FACTIOUS, CONTUMACIOUS

1. The Copperheads during the Civil War engaged in activities that were downright _____.
2. The _____ spirit in the Democratic Party is always LATENT, and loud squabbling in its ranks is no sure HARBINGER of a pending split of the type which led to the formation of the Republican Party in 1854.
3. Savonarola persisted in his _____ conduct, and finally got himself burned at the stake.
4. The _____ sailors at Kronstadt became heroes in the annals of the Russian Revolution.
5. An _____ attitude in the staff usually argues a failure to lead in a way that gains consent.
6. The openly _____ MANEUVERS of the troops were not allowed to get into the news.

*Integration:* ARTICULATION, CONCATENATION

1. The _____ of events that led up to the Korean War can be given a variety of explanations.

232

2. There can only be _____ between subjects in a college curriculum where there is a complete _____ of the materials.
Ant.: DISINTEGRATE

*Neurologist:* PSYCHIATRIST, ALIENIST, PSYCHOPATHOLOGIST, PSYCHOTHERA-
PIST, PSYCHOANALYST

1. Although he has no M.D. degree, he is one of the best _____s now in the country, with rare skill in DIAGNOSING personality disorders.
2. William A. White, although he edited the *Psychoanalytic Review*, was recognized as one of the best all-around _____ in the country, since he used ordinary medical THERAPY and HYDROTHERAPY to supplement the techniques of the _____.
3. The _____ whom George Gershwin was consulting had no suspicion that the real difficulty was a brain tumor, which decidedly called for the services of a _____ skilled also in brain surgery.
4. The _____ declared that the accused man was sane.

*Ornate:* ROCOCO, BAROQUE, FLAMBOYANT, FLORID

1. There is more that's _____ about most opera than the style of decoration of the opera houses where it is given; but Wagner suggests rather a relapse into _____, with German-PSEUDO-Gothic trimmings.
2. The FOYER of the typical movie palace is worse than _____. Its _____ statues of overripe cupids and nymphs, and occasional fountains surrounded by the best bathing-beauty art of the _____ period, prepare the discerning patron for tasteless CINEMATIC EXTRAVAGANZAS.
3. Some college campuses have buildings that, far from being _____, are in the best warehouse tradition: strictly UTILITARIAN and ATROCIOUSLY ugly.
Ant.: chaste, austere

*Pacify:* appease, PLACATE, MOLLIFY, PROPITIATE, CONCILIATE

1. The Aztecs believed that human sacrifices would _____ the wrath of Huitzilopocholi.
2. The Democrats have found it hard to _____ the hostility of some businessmen.
3. Even Aaron could not _____ Moses' wrath at the Jews for setting up the Golden Calf.
4. The Chinese have accused Khrushchev of _____ing the United States.
5. As our Ambassador to the UN, Stevenson has done a good job in

233

_____ing representatives of nations that are suspicious of American foreign policy.

6. Troops sent by the United Nations have not been able to _____ the excitable Africans.

*Pseudonym:* ALIAS, NOM DE GUERRE, pen name, NOM DE PLUME, INCOGNITO, ALLONYM

1. Some authors have come to be known almost exclusively by their _____s, Mark Twain, George Sand, and George Eliot, for instance.
2. We should like to know what _____ Haroun Al Raschid used when he went slumming in Bagdad.
3. That second-story man had a curious sense of humor: he used as his _____ the name Jay Gould. Strictly, this was an _____.
4. Henry Adams chose to write his SATIRIC novel *Democracy* under a _____; after all he was a historian by trade.
5. Stalin was the _____, so to speak, of Josef Djugashvili; but when he was sticking up silver trains in the hills above Tiflis to fill the Party Treasury, he had another _____.

*Realize:* (I) ACTUALIZE, EMBODY, INCARNATE, MATERIALIZE, EXTERNALIZE, OBJECTIFY, SUBSTANTIATE, SUBSTANTIALIZE, HYPOSTATIZE, REIFY

1. Da Vinci spent fifteen years trying to _____ in the face of Christ, in the Last Supper, all the complex and many-sided character which he felt lay behind Jesus' seeming simplicity.
2. James was able to _____ his own thoughts to analyze them.
3. Laymen, accustomed to _____ time and space, find Einstein's theories very hard going.
4. Some SPIRITUALISTS hold that soul stuff is _____ in ECTOPLASM.
5. A great actor is ADEPT at _____ing the emotion which the character is supposed to feel; but the actor cannot without grave risk to his acting, indulge in the luxury of feeling the emotion he is projecting.
6. The Athanasians held that in Christ was _____d the actual substance and essence of God; that Jesus was not merely of like nature, but of the same nature as the Father.
7. He was able to _____ his project of starting a modest publishing business when one of his friends made him a character loan.
8. The energy LATENT within the nucleus of the plutonium atom was _____ as explosive power at Los Alamos.
9. Some THEOLOGIANS _____ the factors involved in the sacraments, in order to symbolize for the layman the doctrine conveyed.

234

10. The COMMUNICANT is supposed to accept the bread and wine as _____, or strictly, TRANSUBSTANTIATED into the body and blood of the Saviour.
11. To make the inward workings of the atom clear to laymen, popular EXPOSITORS of science often _____ the energy bundles concerned, to a degree that does violence to strict scientific views.

(II) Think, conceive, imagine, fancy, ENVISAGE, ENVISION

1. It is hard for the nonmathematician to _____ INFINITY, though he _____ he understands zero, because he can readily _____ its symbol: O. If he knew the symbol for infinity, a figure eight on its side, would that help him _____ what infinity is? It would not.
2. I _____, therefore I am.—Descartes.
3. Southey's poetry, said Coleridge, was based on _____, not imagination.

*Vociferous:* clamorous, BLATANT, STRIDENT, boisterous, OBSTREPEROUS (to which I add STENTORIAN)

1. Sarah was a decidedly _____ girl, and her play for attention was quite _____, but her methods worked.
2. A hog caller needs a _____ voice.
3. He was so _____ in protesting his innocence, that I concluded he was guilty.
4. Castro's demands are even more _____ than those of other dictators; and his _____ tones grate on American ears.

*Jest:* joke, JAPE, QUIP, WITTICISM, wisecrack, crack, gag (to which I add *witcrack* [Shakespeare, *Much Ado About Nothing*, V, iv, 102])

1. He was as full of merry _____s as Bob Hope.
2. True _____s are as rare as _____s are plentiful.
3. There is many a salty _____ spoken by Falstaff in Shakespeare's *Henry IV*.
4. Many a _____ contrived by Benny's _____ men deserves the ARCHAIC term _____, already OBSOLETE in Shakespeare's time.
5. "You take that _____ back, or I'll get your mother to paddle you," the director told the pert child actor.
6. The Devil's _____ Book is truly a DIABOLICALLY funny work.
7. Fred Allen was known for his wit, but he once tickled his audience with an action _____ by grabbing his neck with his hand, elbow extended—the trick of the old comedian who was apparently being held in the wings by somebody, but who, when he appeared, was just holding his own neck.

*Saying:* saw, maxim, ADAGE, proverb, motto, EPIGRAM, APHORISM, APO-
THEGM

1. "There's no arguing over questions of taste" is an _____ more
   honored in the breach than in the observance.
2. A prospector must always bear in mind the old _____, "All is not
   gold that glitters."
3. Our _____, "Penny-wise and pound foolish" is put more con-
   cretely by the Chinese: "What profiteth it a man if he retire early to
   bed to save candlelight, and beget twins?"
4. Erasmus liked to collect _____s from the Greek and Roman
   MORALISTS, and he invented some of his own, such as, "It's no fun discussing prohibition when your GULLET's dry."
5. Motley adopted as a firm _____, "Clothes make the woman."
6. Polonius was full of wise _____s.
7. "You can't get blood from a turnip" is a popular American _____.
8. "Those who marry for money always earn it" comes pretty close to
   being an _____.

*Suave:* URBANE, diplomatic, bland, smooth, politic

1. LaGuardia could not be called _____, but he was actually
   _____ in his bluntness, and he DISCOMFITED _____ and oily
   hypocrites to good purpose.
2. Chesterfield's manners were both _____ and polished, but they
   had at core the essence of good breeding: consideration for others.
3. A career man in the State Department should have a _____
   manner, in the best _____ tradition.
Ant.: bluff

*Sensuous:* sensual, luxurious, VOLUPTUOUS, SYBARITIC, EPICUREAN

1. A good restaurant caters to _____ tastes in food, but is no friend
   of gluttons.
2. Milton's IMAGERY in English is often strongly _____; but he confined strongly _____ moments to his Latin verse.
3. Before 1700 the word _____ meant either LASCIVIOUS or pas-
   sionately desirous after something.
4. That Tiberius retired to Capri to indulge in _____ pleasures was
   widely believed; but the notion that the only Puritan among the Roman
   emperors would take to VENERY at the age of 66, and still maintain his
   vigor and powers until he was 78, is fantastic, according to Beasley.
5. Beaumont and Fletcher wrote plays full of _____ INTERLUDES.

236

*Substitute,* n.: (I) surrogate, resource, resort, expedient, shift, makeshift, stopgap

1. Often his _____ appointments proved to be permanent, for he was notoriously reluctant to fire anybody.
2. When he could not get Congress to accept a long-range solution, Roosevelt was a master hand at devising _____s and _____ measures.
3. The OED is the court of last _____ on English usage.
4. Queen Elizabeth liked _____s and STRATAGEMS; particularly she delighted in fooling her Council.
5. Bridge is a welcome _____ when the guests have little gift for conversation.
6. In logic, there is no easy _____ for RIGOROUS thinking.
7. Instead of adopting the learned word, _____, in connection with foodstuffs, we imported *Ersatz* from the German.

(II) supply, LOCUM TENENS, alternate, UNDERSTUDY, double, stand-in, pinch hitter

1. A _____ in Hollywood leads a dog's life.
2. He was sent in as a _____ for the pitcher, but he struck out.
3. In his prime, Shaw came close to being a perfect _____ for Pope Innocent X, not only in looks, but in PONTIFICAL tone and manner.
4. Each member country sends an _____ as well as a regular representative to the Security Council.
5. Well-to-do DRAFTEES could hire _____s during the Civil War.
6. The doctor got a _____ to come down from London to handle his practice while he went on vacation.
7. The Huguenot clergyman who came over to London as a _____ during the summer was supposed to have adequate English. His first text he gave as "Cahn de layopar shanzh his spoe, or the Aytiope hees skā? ("Can the leopard change his spots, or the Ethiope his skin?")

*Transient:* TRANSITORY, passing, EPHEMERAL, momentary, fugitive, fleeting, EVANESCENT, short-lived

1. The AMETHYSTINE glow in the West was _____, and quickly gave way to heavy purple as the storm clouds closed in.
2. Virgilia's PREVISIONS were hardly more than _____ and _____ glimpses into the future, but _____ as they were, they shook her to the core of her being, for she soon learned that they would be borne out by the event.

3. Heyst knew that his joy would be _____, but it was nevertheless a fulfillment of his deepest hopes.
4. What started as a _____ fancy, developed into a permanent LIAISON.
5. Pleasures of the senses are _____; study, says Gibbon, is the only passion that is not destroyed by its satisfaction.
6. Hotels generally have accommodations for both permanent and _____ guests.
7. A dragonfly enjoys only an _____ life.

Ant.: perpetual

*Universal:* (I) ECUMENICAL (or OECUMENICAL), cosmopolitan, COSMIC

1. Caesar became a true _____ without ceasing to be a Roman.
2. The _____ order is now more extensive than it was in Newton's time; yet we are informed by Kasner that it is still FINITE, and that the universe will hold PROTONS and ELECTRONS to the number of $10^{110}$, assuming no blank spaces.
3. One of Pope Paul VI's first moves was to reconvene the _____ Council.
4. The _____ truths affirmed by medieval science have been knocked, if not into a cocked hat, at least into cocked-hat curves by modern mathematics.

(II) general, GENERIC, common

1. These traits were clearly _____, not specific.
2. The English language is _____ to the United States, Great Britain, and the Dominions, but slang used in these different areas is by no means _____ to all.
3. The _____ reading of human nature which a novelist accepts or invents in part determines his chances of being _____ in his appeal, while his skill in INTERLACING the _____ with the particular is the measure of his power as a thinker—as witness Tolstoi, Stendhal, and Proust.

Ant.: (II) particular

*Presuppose:* presume, assume, POSTULATE, PREMISE, POSIT

1. If we _____ for the sake of argument that TELEPATHY occurs, many PARAPSYCHOLOGICAL PHENOMENA can then be explained in QUASI-scientific terms.
2. In urging that we are not forced to choose between two such polar opposites as FASCISM and COMMUNISM, Korzybski _____s that

238

Aristotle's principle of the excluded middle is wrong and that the logic of classes is of limited application.

3. No writer can succeed as a POPULARIZER who _____s on the possession by his reading audience of too wide a vocabulary.
4. The French wit _____ed his syllogism thus: "All general propositions are more than half wrong (including this one)."
5. He next _____, as his minor PREMISE, "That human nature is always the same is INCONTESTABLY a general proposition"; therefore, he concluded, it is more than half wrong.
6. According to Paley, just as the existence of a watch argued that there must have been a watchmaker, so the creation _____s a creator.

*Secret:* COVERT, stealthy, FURTIVE, CLANDESTINE, SURREPTITIOUS, UNDERHAND, underhanded, privy, backstairs (or backstair)

1. Secret police have to employ some _____ scheming.
2. The Cardinal's *Eminence grise* was available for his _____ intrigues, political and AMOROUS.
3. The President has at his disposal some _____ funds, but nobody could think of it as his _____ purse.
4. A _____ visit to his bride was the only kind permitted to a young Sparton husband. Such a _____ approach was thought to develop greater ardor.
5. A _____ RENDEZVOUS is usually carried out in _____ fashion, and invariably has about it a suggestion of _____ intrigue.
6. Richelieu preferred to use _____ methods, even to achieve good purposes.

*Unruly:* UNGOVERNABLE, INTRACTABLE, REFRACTORY, RECALCITRANT, willful (or wilful), headstrong

1. The Old Bolsheviks were _____ and _____ men, and since they threatened the ruling dynasty, they were LIQUIDATED.
2. _____ peasants, especially the Kulaks, were finally shipped off to Siberia, or to the work camps in the Arctic area.
3. The General had an _____ tongue and an _____ temper, but in battle he was cool and LACONIC.
4. Shaw was quite _____ to all efforts to form his mind by bullying; but he was never _____ merely out of WAYWARDNESS, rather from conviction.

Ant.: TRACTABLE, DOCILE

*Vagabond:* vagrant, truant, tramp, tramper, hobo, bum, stiff, swagman (or swagsman), sundowner (I add bindle stiff or bundle stiff.)

1. The _____ *News* has quite swank offices in Newark (New Jersey).
2. _____s are so called because they usually try to arrive at a station in the bush in time for dinner.
3. A _____ in Australia corresponds quite closely to a _____ in the Northwestern U.S., only the former carries food as well as blanket roll; the latter usually carries only his bedding.
4. A boy who starts out as a _____ may turn into a _____.
5. The yard police rounded up all _____s and _____s they caught riding the rods, and took them into police court, where they were entered in the record as _____.
6. George Borrow loved a _____ life, but he was not himself a _____.
7. HALLELUJAH, I'm a _____.

*Winding:* SINUOUS, SERPENTINE, TORTUOUS, FLEXUOUS, ANFRACTUOUS (I add MEANDERING.)

1. We followed the _____ paths through the Carlsbad Caverns.
2. The channels of the middle ear are very _____.
3. A HAREM dancer needs a more _____ body than a tap dancer.
4. At one point Route 101 is so _____ that it doubles back under itself.
5. The Meander had a _____ course.
6. If there was any place else to carry _____ curves, that baby star would have brought art to the aid of nature; but she didn't need to.

ANSWERS

*Abjure:* 1. forswear   2. recant   3. abjure   4. retract   5. renounce

*Abridgement:* 1. abstract   2. epitome   3. synopsis   4. conspectus
5. abridgement

*Activate:* 1. energizing   2. vitalize

*Adjacent:* 1. tangent   2. contiguous   3. adjacent   4. adjoining
5. abutting   6. coterminous   7. juxtaposed

*Accidental:* 1. incidental   2. fortuitous   3. accidental   4. casual   5. adventitious   6. contingent

*Cumulative:* 1. accumulative   2. cumulative   3. summative   4. additive

*Addict:* 1. habitué, habitués   2. votary   3. addict, fiend   4. fan, aficionados   5. devotee

*Allegory:* (I) 1. symbolism   2. allegory

   (II) 1. myth, apologue   2. parables   3. fable

*Apparition:* 1. spirit   2. shade   3. ghost   4. apparition   5. revenant   6. phantasm   7. *Poltergeist,* spook   8. haunts, revenants   9. hant   10. specter   11. wraith   12. zombie   13. fetch   14. phantom

*Aesthete:* 1. virtuoso   2. connoisseur   3. aesthetes, dilettantes

*Amateur:* 1. tyro   2. dabbler   3. amateur   4. dilettante

*Ambiguity:* 1. doubletalk   2. amphibology, amphibologism, double entendre   3. ambiguity, equivocation   4. tergiversation

*Appendage:* 1. adjunct   2. accessories   3. appendage   4. appurtenances

*Changeable:* 1. variable   2. protean   3. changeful   4. changeable   5. mutable

*Celerity:* 1. alacrity   2. legerity   3. celerity

*Change:* (I) 1. alteration   2. modification   3. changes   4. variations

   (II) 1. permutations   2. alternations   3. vicissitudes   4. mutations

*Clear:* (I) 1. translucent, transparent   2. pellucid   3. diaphanous   4. clear   5. lucid, limpid

   (II) 1. lucid   2. perspicuous

*Inconsonant:* 1. unsympathetic   2. uncongenial   3. inconsistent, discrepant   4. discordant   5. incompatible   6. inconsonant   7. incongruous

*Appetizer:* 1. antipasto   2. apéritif   3. hors d'oeuvre   4. appetizers   5. smörgåsbord

241

*Dictatorial:* 1. authoritative   2. dictatorial, oracular   3. totalitarian, authoritarian   4. dogmatic, doctrinaire   5. magisterial   6. magistral

*Enormous:*
| | | | |
|---|---|---|---|
| 1. Cyclopean | 5. colossal | 9. Brobdingnagian | 13. giant |
| 2. Antaean | 6. titanic | 10. mammoth | 14. enormous |
| 3. herculean | 7. vast | 11. elephantine | 15. huge |
| 4. Gargantuan | 8. immense | 12. gigantic | |

*Impostor:* 1. quack, charlatan   2. mountebank   3. fakers   4. quacks, empirics   5. impostor

*Compendium:* 1. survey, sketch   2. digest   3. compendium   4. précis   5. syllabus   6. aperçu   7. pandects

*Discernment:* 1. penetration, insight, acumen   2. divination   3. clairvoyance   4. discernment   5. discrimination, perception

*Inconstant:* 1. unstable   2. mercurial   3. inconstant   4. capricious, fickle

*Controversial:* 1. controversial, eristic   2. polemical, apologetic, polemic

*Insubordinate:* 1. seditious   2. factious   3. contumacious   4. mutinous   5. insubordinate   6. rebellious

*Integration:* 1. concatenation   2. integration, articulation

*Neurologist:* 1. psychotherapist   2. psychiatrists, psychoanalysts   3. psychoanalyst, neurologist   4. alienist

*Ornate:* 1. flamboyant, baroque   2. flossy, florid, rococo   3. ornate

*Pacify:* 1. propitiate   2. mollify   3. placate   4. appeasing   5. conciliating   6. pacify

*Pseudonym:* 1. pseudonyms   2. incognito   3. nom de guerre, alias   4. nom de plume   5. pen name, allonym

*Realize:* (I) 1. embody   2. objectify   3. hypostatizing   4. substantialized   5. externalizing   6. incarnated   7. realize   8. actualized   9. substantialize   10. substantiated   11. reify

(II) 1. conceive, imagine, envisage, envision   2. think   3. fancy

242

*Vociferous:* 1. boisterous, vociferous  2. stentorian  3. blatant  4. clamorous, strident

*Jest:* 1. quips  2. witticism, wisecracks  3. witcrack  4. joke, gag, jape  5. crack  6. jest  7. gag

*Saying:* 1. aphorism  2. adage  3. proverb  4. apothegm, maxim  5. motto  6. saws  7. saying  8. epigram

*Suave:* 1. smooth, politic, bland  2. urbane  3. suave, diplomatic

*Sensuous:* 1. epicurean  2. sensuous, sensual  3. luxurious  4. sybaritic  5. voluptuous

*Substitute:* (I) 1. makeshift  2. expedients, stopgap  3. resort  4. shifts  5. resource  6. substitute  7. surrogate

(II) 1. stand-in  2. pinch hitter  3. double  4. alternate  5. substitutes  6. locum tenens  7. supply

*Transient:* 1. evanescent  2. fleeting, momentary, fugitive  3. short-lived  4. passing  5. transitory  6. transient  7. ephemeral

*Universal:* (I) 1. cosmopolitan  2. cosmic  3. ecumenical  4. universal

(II) 1. generic  2. common  3. general, universal

*Presuppose:* 1. assume  2. postulate  3. presumes  4. premised  5. posited  6. presupposes

*Secret:* 1. covert  2. backstairs  3. secret  4. surreptitious, stealthy  5. clandestine, furtive  6. underhanded

*Unruly:* 1. headstrong, willful  2. recalcitrant  3. unruly, ungovernable  4. intractable, refractory

*Vagabond:* 1. hobo  2. sundowners  3. swagman, bindle stiff  4. truant, tramp  5. bums, stiffs, vagrants  6. vagabond, tramper  7. bum

*Winding:* 1. winding  2. anfractuous  3. flexuous  4. serpentine  5. meandering  6. sinuous

It may have struck you that in this list of synonyms, very few technical or scientific words are found. Even in the complete Webster collection of synonyms, technical jargon has very little place. The reason is a simple one: most technical and scientific terms are names of specific objects or processes, for which there are no synonyms, nor are any desired. What the writer wants is to have the meaning DELIMITED. He wants a word that will mean a particular thing or process and nothing else.

Yet these technical words are often such convenient verbal shorthand that many of them make their way into common use in a figurative sense derived from their narrower technical denotation. There is a kind of shuttle service which carries these words across the gap that separates technical and scientific jargon from the common stock of usable words. (See diagram on page 84.) So we speak of learning by *osmosis:* letting facts seep into the mind; not, it must be admitted, the most fully alert type of learning.

PSYCHOLOGICAL terms have in the last fifty years been the most numerous MIGRANTS, invading the standard language as the Goths and the Vandals overran the Roman Empire. PURISTS usually think these terms barbarous, but the barbarians seem to have settled down to stay.

In any case, this shuttle service for technical terms is of commanding interest to the explorer of the English vocabulary—all the more because the methods by which these jargon terms become NATURALIZED in the common stock have been too little examined by the literary persons who in the main COMPILE our dictionaries. This technical element is treated fully in Chapter 11.


## WHO WERE THEY?

When you were making your choice of synonyms to fill in the blank spaces in the previous pages, did it help if you understood the context of each incomplete sentence? Did you know who Veblen and Dewey were? Casanova? Coleridge? Galileo? Did you know that Justice Holmes was the greatest JURIST of his time? That Gandhi was the apostle of passive resistance, and that peaceful protests in the form of sit-ins, freedom marches, and the like probably stemmed from his example?

Coming closer to the present day, you should know who the baseball Mets are; you may be aware that *Oklahoma!* is considered a landmark in the history of musical comedy; you may have heard of J. B.

Rhine and his experiments in ESP. There is a close INTERACTION between the words you read and hear and the events and personalities that activate these words. Words are keys to the culture of the past and the present. Whether it's a word that comes into popular usage from the pages of literature (Don Juan, Micawber, Babbitt, etc.); a name that suggests an era in history or a system of philosophy (Bergsonian, Spenglerian, Trotskyite); or a slang term that is part of everyday speech in any era—such words not only enrich your vocabulary but tell you the story of times past, and of your own time.

Some of the questions from the word games *within* each chapter are repeated in the quiz at the end of the chapter. If you miss such questions, do the word games again.

1. Pick out the one Anglo-Saxon word from the following: mix, real, scarce, art, forth, sure, firm, pay. (Not in Word List)
2. Give ten verbs that describe various modes of walking. (Not in Word List)
3. Which pair of words is closer in meaning: theory-hypothesis or law-conjecture?
4. Give three more words that form a word cluster with "theory," "law," and "hypothesis." They may be synonymous or analogous words. (Not in Word List)
5. Give five more words from the word cluster that includes "dialect" and "argot." (Not in Word List)
6. An_____ words may be called "near-synonyms."
7. "Look for the key word in the cluster to which it belongs. . . . Next, explore the fine shades of meaning in all their _____ations."
8. What word does not belong in this cluster: pacify, appease, mollify, castigate, propitiate, conciliate? (Not in Word List)
9. Supply the missing word in this cluster: controversial, polemic, polemical, e_____.
10. Fill in the blank space: accidental, contingent, fortuitous, ad_____.
11. Something that is adjacent may also be "adjoining," "contiguous," "tangent," "coterminous," or "j_____."
12. Words that are analogous with "amateur" are "dilettante," "dabbler," and "_____."
13. Words related in meaning to "ambiguity" are "tergiversation," "amphibology," "doubletalk," and "equi_____."
14. A synonym for "variable" or "mutable" is "p_____."
15. Something that is diaphanous is _____.
16. *Webster's Dictionary of Synonyms* lists these words in a word cluster with "ornate": "rococo," "florid," and "fl_____."
17. A "saying" may also be a "saw," "maxim," "proverb," "epigram," "apothegm," or "_____."
18. Something that is secret may also be, depending on the fine shade of meaning that you need, "covert," "stealthy," "furtive," "clandestine," or "s_____."
19. What is a word of classical origin that is a synonym for "burdensome"?
20. What is a Saxon word for "salubrious"?

246

21. What is the antonym of "zenith"?
22. What is the antonym of "alleviate"?
23. What are two words closely related to "acrimony"?
24. A word that means "to curse" is _____.
25. What is a synonym for "scoff" that is also a homonym with two other words?
26. What highfalutin word did Bergen Evans use that means "buzz-buzz"?
27. Lexicographers who believe that dictionaries should set the standards of good taste in word usage are called _____.
28. A fawning follower is a s_____.
29. "Harmony" is "_____ance."
30. Someone like Samuel Johnson who uses many polysyllabic words may be described as _____alian.

## WORD LIST

| | | | |
|---|---|---|---|
| sesquipedalian | tyro | surrogate | aphorism |
| flagrant | sycophant | sage | anathematize |
| adventitious | jamming | prescriptivists | anonymous |
| fluorescent | eristic | adventuresome | ruminations |
| asperity | protean | jeer | egregious |
| jibe | prodigious | acerbity | bombinations |
| dissonance | eccentric | egotistical | juggled |
| exile | opaque | juxtaposed | surreptitious |
| anomalous | obscure | equivalence | heavy |
| peregrinations | chin music | consonance | descriptivists |
| etymologists | sidekick | aesthete | aggravate |
| ease | latitudinarian | grateful | healthful |
| flamboyant | nadir | ramifications | equanimity |
| bungler | translucent | antediluvian | equivocation |
| onerous | analogous | apogee | adverse |

### ANSWERS

1. forth
2. see page 206
3. theory-hypothesis
4. conjecture, assumption, postulate, pre-supposition, surmise
5. see page 5
6. analogous
7. ramifications
8. castigate
9. eristic
10. adventitious
11. juxtaposed
12. tyro
13. equivocation
14. protean
15. translucent
16. flamboyant
17. aphorism
18. surreptitious
19. onerous
20. healthful
21. nadir
22. aggravate
23. asperity, acerbity
24. anathematize
25. jibe

247

26. bombinations     27. prescriptivists
28. sycophant     29. consonance
30. sesquipedalian

## SCORING KEY

30 right—Ph.D. (Star pupil)
27–29 right—Master's degree (Near the top)
23–26 right—Bachelor's degree in word discrimination
18–22 right—Above average (Keep plugging)
12–17 right—Average (Get out of your rut)
Under 12 right—Substandard (Read more carefully)

SCORE: _____

# 10 ~

## How to Use Words as Keys to the Past and Present

~~~ If you could combine H. G. Wells's time machine with an
Oriental magic carpet, and follow some English words back through
space and time, you'd do some tall traveling. You could go with
ODYSSEUS on the original ODYSSEY; find out about QUIXOTIC conduct
by following Don Quixote on his adventures; hear DEMOSTHENES give
a PHILIPPIC against Philip of MACEDON; learn true EPICUREAN doctrine
by walking with Epicurus in his garden; and acquire the SOCRATIC
method by listening to the IRONIC old soldier and stonemason himself.

Words of this ALLUSIVE type are the literary COUNTERPARTS of scientific symbols. Each condenses a fund of meanings into a shorthand
term. The difference lies in the greater richness of associations—or
AURA—in the case of the literary and historical allusions. "Quixotic"
is an EPITOME of a great book. The Romans had no name for the high,
generous, and fantastic gallantry which the word describes. Nor
would most Romans have been able to understand what is meant by
the FAUSTIAN spirit: that heaven-storming, adventurous thirst for the
infinite which led Faust to sell his soul to the devil in return for universal knowledge and experience.

The spiritual history not merely of a decade, but of a whole epoch,
is summed up in such a word. There is a certain substance in Field-
ing's claim that the great novelist is a better historian than most
professional CHRONICLERS. Certainly the great poets and dramatists
have often given a "local habitation and a name" to the spirit of an
age, "in little room confining mighty men,"—as GOETHE did with
Faust and Shakespeare with Hamlet. Or a poet's own name may come
to express a quality and temper for which we have no other single
word. So we speak of VERGILIAN pity: that sense of POIGNANT, sensitive sadness over the tragedy IMPLICIT in most human life, and the
feeling of regret over vanished beauty and the doom visited on great-
hearted courage in the face of a malign destiny—all rendered through
the golden autumnal haze of memory. Again, "Socratic"—to expand

249

on the reference a little—epitomizes the apparently artless and innocent technique used by Socrates to help his hearers realize what they
did not know, at the same time bringing home to them the limitations
on knowledge and the knowable.

It may have occurred to you by this time that we actually have an
invention which comes pretty close to the time machine–magic carpet
combination: the book. The allusions which great books have left in
the language constitute a guide to good reading, if you want to take
them that way.

Here, however, we are concerned with acquiring the meaning of
these allusions in summary form. Since a literary or historical reference
often telescopes an incredible wealth of meaning into one word, it is
a hard task to boil it down into a short CUE phrase, and still convey
anything like its full import. But if you can identify many of these
allusions from significant CLUES that suggest even a part of their rich
content, it is pretty good PRESUMPTIVE proof that you know your way
around in CULTURAL history—which includes many characters who
lived only in their creators' imaginations, and numerous incidents
which never happened. Yet they are as real as, if not more real than,
actual historical personages and events.

There is a lot of satisfaction to be had from knowing how some
character, real or imagined, came to have his name become the symbol of something universal in common experience. If you have delved
deeply and thoughtfully into the literature and history of past eras,
you already know the meaning of many of these proper names that
have become common nouns—and you're that much further ahead in
the game of words. But if your reading has been sketchy and DESUL-
TORY, these words may awaken in you a desire to trace them back to
their source, to the literature or historical events that gave them birth.

### Fifty Key Words to the Past

In each group of ten one-time proper names that have become common words, put in column 1 the letter of the equivalent term in
column 2. For example:

|  |  |
|---|---|
| I. [ ] MICAWBER | [a] self-righteous man |
| II. [ ] BABBITT | [b] PROCRASTINATOR |
| III. [ ] PHILISTINE | [c] booster |
| IV. [ ] PHARISEE | [d] person of smug tastes |

The letters in column 1 above should run: [b], [c], [d], [a].

1. [   ] AMPERE
2. [   ] ANGORA
3. [   ] ARABESQUE
4. [   ] ARGOSY
5. [   ] ARMADA
6. [   ] BARABBAS
7. [   ] BEDLAM
8. [   ] BENEDICK
9. [   ] BOLOGNA
10. [   ] BOURBON

[a] REACTIONARY
[b] merchant fleet
[c] thief
[d] mad confusion
[e] ex-bachelor
[f] sausage
[g] battle fleet
[h] lacy FRETWORK
[i] goathair
[j] unit of current

11. [   ] BOYCOTT
12. [   ] BROUGHAM
13. [   ] BUNSEN
14. [   ] CABAL
15. [   ] CANUTE
16. [   ] CASSANDRA
17. [   ] CAYENNE
18. [   ] CENTAUR
19. [   ] CHINOOK
20. [   ] EGERIA

[a] gas jet
[b] would-be tide-stopper
[c] hot pepper
[d] half-horse, half-man
[e] CONFIDANTE
[f] political plot or plotters
[g] carriage
[h] not having any
[i] prophetess of doom
[j] gentle, warm wind

21. [   ] FABIAN
22. [   ] GALVANIC
23. [   ] HELOT
24. [   ] JEHU
25. [   ] KNICKERBOCKER
26. [   ] QUISLING
27. [   ] LUCIFER
28. [   ] LYNCH
29. [   ] MACADAM
30. [   ] MADRAS

[a] knee pants
[b] match
[c] traitor
[d] slave
[e] fast driver
[f] execution without court action
[g] delayer
[h] paving process
[i] responding to electrical stimulus
[j] fabric

31. [   ] MAUSOLEUM
32. [   ] MECCA
33. [   ] MOGUL
34. [   ] MUNICH
35. [   ] NARCISSUS
36. [   ] NEMESIS
37. [   ] OHM
38. [   ] PANTHEON
39. [   ] PARTHIAN
40. [   ] PASQUINADE

[a] supreme personage
[b] supreme goal
[c] APPEASEMENT
[d] SATIRIC SQUIB
[e] doom
[f] large tomb-edifice
[g] catchall for all gods
[h] parting shot
[i] unit of electrical resistance
[j] self-admirer

| 41. [ ] PHOENIX | [a] palace guard |
|---|---|
| 42. [ ] PLATONIC | [b] tough customer |
| 43. [ ] PRAETORIAN | [c] carriage |
| 44. [ ] RUBICON | [d] king-maker |
| 45. [ ] STOIC | [e] kind of boot |
| 46. [ ] TARTAR | [f] noncarnal, idealistic |
| 47. [ ] TITIAN | [g] resurrected itself from ashes |
| 48. [ ] VICTORIA | [h] CRUCIAL, IRREVOCABLE step |
| 49. [ ] WARWICK | [i] UNFLINCHING |
| 50. [ ] WELLINGTON | [j] reddish-brown |

ANSWERS

| | | | | |
|---|---|---|---|---|
| 1. [ j] | 11. [h] | 21. [g] | 31. [f] | 41. [g] |
| 2. [ i] | 12. [g] | 22. [ i] | 32. [b] | 42. [f] |
| 3. [h] | 13. [a] | 23. [d] | 33. [a] | 43. [a] |
| 4. [b] | 14. [f] | 24. [e] | 34. [c] | 44. [h] |
| 5. [g] | 15. [b] | 25. [a] | 35. [ j] | 45. [ i] |
| 6. [c] | 16. [ i] | 26. [c] | 36. [e] | 46. [b] |
| 7. [d] | 17. [c] | 27. [b] | 37. [ i] | 47. [ j] |
| 8. [e] | 18. [d] | 28. [f] | 38. [g] | 48. [c] |
| 9. [f] | 19. [ j] | 29. [h] | 39. [h] | 49. [d] |
| 10. [a] | 20. [e] | 30. [ j] | 40. [d] | 50. [e] |

## AN -*ISM* WORD FROM HISTORY

Suppose you want a word to express the following:

The theory and practice of power politics: how to seize and hold power by guile, fraud, force, or frightfulness (used in that order). How to combine the traits of the lion and the fox in ruling a city or a country. The UTILIZATION of common enemies as political cement to tighten an alliance; and the techniques of deceiving and discarding such allies when the common enemy is defeated. How to trick your enemies into a trap where you can massacre them with impunity. Using SCAPEGOATS to escape the consequences of harsh actions by a ruler: in situations requiring frightfulness, dirty undercover espionage, and the killing of some victims to scare the rest, the ruler should use as his tools and EXECUTORS persons whom he can put an end to, when their dirty work is done. By these means he can avoid the stigma of public crime, and put the blame on his subordinates. Reasons of state justify any degree of departure from private morality; a ruler cannot take account of Christian or any other ETHICS except the rule of expediency and the aim of preserving and extending his power; to those ends everything must give way. The ruler needs to control and manipulate all propaganda media. He should never forget that in politics it is not the facts that are decisive, but men's opinions and feelings about them; therefore propaganda should address itself to spreading whatever version of the facts will suit the convenience of the government. Particularly the ruler should remember the Roman maxim for empire: divide and conquer.

The word for all that is MACHIAVELLIANISM. Once when he was out of a job, and needed one badly, Machiavelli wrote *The Prince,* telling how the CONDOTTIERI or bandit-rulers of Italian city-states turned the trick of acquiring and holding power. Machiavelli was himself no believer in the INIQUITOUS doctrines that go by his name. He was a stout republican (as you'll find by looking into his *Florentine Histories* and *Discourses on Livy*) and he was socially democratic to a degree that made his womenfolk complain when he sat around with the local woodcutters and charcoalmen in the local pub near his small farm. But like any politician who wanted to make a comeback, Machiavelli was willing to do a bit of pamphleteering (campaign speaking was not yet in vogue) to attract attention to himself—and it happened that his pamphlet was just what the princes and tyrants were looking for. So from Catherine de' Medici to Khrushchev and Castro, Machiavelli's pamphlet trying to promote himself a job has been an invaluable handbook on how to fool the people and keep a throne.

The "ism" from Machiavelli's name is therefore a SHORTHAND synonym for a very big package of meaning. It saves a half page or so of writing every time we want to refer to the concept. In view of the evil implications of the power-politics doctrine, it is not surprising that the name of the hardworking Florentine secretary of state was twisted into Make-evil, and Match-a-villain; but these left-handed compliments should not distract us from seeing that he gave the classic description of SKULLDUGGERY in high places. And when we want a single word to express all this complex of theories and activities that make up Big-Power maneuvering, even today, Machiavellianism is the word. And there are many more such words, which are ALLUSIVE (they should not be ELUSIVE) and difficult going at first encounter; but they open up a PANORAMA of persons, places, and ideas, once you get acquainted with them. They are in very truth epitomes, or condensed versions, of cultural history.

# Proper Adjectives Packed with Meaning

Match each adjective from a famous name with the right clue.

1. [　] HEGELIAN     [a] Music-drama at Bayreuth
2. [　] MARXIAN     [b] *Decline of the West*
3. [　] NIETZSCHEAN     [c] Syllogistic logic
4. [　] WAGNERIAN     [d] Relativity
5. [　] SPENGLERIAN     [e] *Creative Evolution*
6. [　] ARISTOTELIAN     [f] *Beyond Good and Evil*
7. [　] NEWTONIAN     [g] Dictatorship of the proletariat
8. [　] EINSTEINIAN     [h] Pragmatism
9. [　] BERGSONIAN     [i] The Absolute
10. [　] JAMESIAN     [j] Laws of gravitation and of motion

11. [　] CARTESIAN     [a] Conflict between production engineers and financiers bent on profit through scarcity
12. [　] BACONIAN     [b] Pressure of population on food supply
13. [　] VEBLENITE     [c] Christian nonresistance
14. [　] MALTHUSIAN     [d] Believer in continuous world revolution
15. [　] TOLSTOYAN     [e] New Dealer
16. [　] KROPOTKINITE     [f] Empiricist, believer in applied science and induction
17. [　] LENINIST     [g] Socialism first in one country
18. [　] TROTSKYITE     [h] Socialize through hydroelectric development and collectivizing agriculture
19. [　] STALINIST     [i] "I think, therefore I am."
20. [　] ROOSEVELTIAN     [j] Substitution of voluntary cooperation and mutual aid for coercive power of the state

## ANSWERS

| | | | | |
|---|---|---|---|---|
| 1. [i] | 5. [b] | 9. [e] | 13. [a] | 17. [h] |
| 2. [g] | 6. [c] | 10. [h] | 14. [b] | 18. [d] |
| 3. [f] | 7. [j] | 11. [i] | 15. [c] | 19. [g] |
| 4. [a] | 8. [d] | 12. [f] | 16. [j] | 20. [e] |

Now you may be able to see the gaps in your knowledge of science, philosophy, music, political history, and literature. In this respect you are not alone; but if you give some thought to the words you missed, you'll not only add some new words to your vocabulary, but you'll

254

open the door to a whole new world teeming with colorful personalities, real and imaginary—and with ideas that have figuratively moved mountains. (And literally, too, if you include engineering know-how that has won wars and blasted paths through seemingly IMPENETRABLE barriers.) Words such as *Trotskyite* (believer in continual world revolution) will whet your desire to find out more about the Russian Revolution and about the way its leading figures—Lenin, Trotsky, and Stalin—influenced world history and brought many new words into the language. Adjectives such as *Baconian* will lead you to the meaning of EMPIRICISM and to a knowledge of the principles upon which science is based. Thus, words from cultural history radiate outward to form new word clusters and idea clusters.

## WORDS AND IDEAS: RECIPROCAL ACTION

We hope this game becomes more fascinating as you go along. The object is to set up a reciprocal action between words and ideas. Knowledge of the larger canvas of literature and history leads to knowledge of the allusive word; CONVERSELY, the word is the key that opens the door to the real or imaginary background that gave it to the language. If you've read *Hamlet*, you'll know that Polonius is a "long-winded and self-appointed NESTOR, full of wise saws." (We gave that one away, but now you'll have to figure out who Nestor was.) If you've managed to escape seeing *Hamlet* or if your high school teacher ruined your interest in Shakespeare, you may want to know more about Polonius and what he represents in literature. Do you connect him with this DICTUM?

> This above all: to thine own self be true,
> And it must follow, as the night the day,
> Thou canst not then be false to any man.

Shakespeare was full of "wise saws" and quotable quotes, which are as expressive today as they were in the Elizabethan era. Do you know from which plays the following proverbs are taken? Can you give the exact wording of the original passage?

1. A woman conceals what she knows not.
2. A word spoken is past recalling.

3. Familiarity breeds contempt.
4. Things done cannot be undone.
5. Love is blind.
6. It is an ill wind that blows nobody good.
7. Strike while the iron is hot.
8. Discretion is the better part of valor.
9. There is a tide in the affairs of men, which, taken at the flood, leads on to fortune.
10. Brevity is the soul of wit.

## ANSWERS

1. *Henry IV*
   "Constant you are, But yet a woman . . . for I well believe Thou wilt not utter what thou dost not know"
2. *The Comedy of Errors*
   "Passed sentence may not be recall'd."
3. *Sonnet 102*
   "Sweets grown common lose their dear delight."
   *Merry Wives of Windsor*
   "I hope upon familiarity will grow more contempt."
4. *Macbeth*
   "What's done cannot be undone."
5. *Romeo and Juliet*
   "If love be blind, love cannot hit the mark."
   *The Merchant of Venice*
   "But love is blind, and lovers cannot see
   The pretty follies that they themselves commit."
6. *Henry VI*
   "Ill blows the wind that profits nobody."
7. *Henry VI*
   "Strike now, or else the iron cools."
8. *Henry IV*
   "The better part of valour is discretion."
9. *Julius Caesar* (as is)
10. *Hamlet* (as is)

Knowing that VOLPONE is the "foxy schemer who outfoxes himself; the biter who gets bit" should lead you to a reading of Ben Jonson's very amusing play of the same name. Jonson was a contemporary of Shakespeare and one of his greatest admirers; it was he who EULOGIZED the Bard by saying that in an era when all educated men were grounded in the classics, Shakespeare could write the greatest of all plays and be the most lyrical of poets, though he "knew little Latin and less Greek."

## A Potpourri of Words from Cultural History

Now try eighty more words (you already have been told two of the answers) from the literature and history of the remote and recent past. Match the scrambled clues with the names or terms given in the left-hand column. They are grouped by tens. For example:

I. [   ] Ishmael      [d] he prophesied Christ's coming
                                  [e] Jacob's new name after he wrestled with the angel
                                  [f] outcast driven into the wilderness

Here the right clue is "outcast driven into the wilderness," so you put *f* in the brackets following I. Now for the list:

1. [   ] Circe      [a] champion grumbler and SEDITIONIST in the Greek camp before Troy
2. [   ] Adonis      [b] wanted his pound of flesh as penalty interest on loan
3. [   ] Don Juan      [c] worldly PSEUDO-pious hypocrite, supposedly SATIRIZING JESUITS
4. [   ] Mrs. Grundy      [d] long-winded self-appointed Nestor, full of wise saws
5. [   ] Munchausen      [e] fussy, pompous, self-important small-time DIGNITARY
6. [   ] Thersites      [f] enchantress who turned Odysseus' men into swine
7. [   ] Tartuffe      [g] No. 1 wolf in literature
8. [   ] Bumble      [h] fertile, RESOURCEFUL, and ingenious liar on the grand scale
9. [   ] Shylock      [i] the beau ideal of masculine beauty (yes, beauty)
10. [   ] Polonius      [j] self-appointed female POLICER of conventional proprieties; what Will Hays was to Hollywood

11. [   ] Bobadil      [a] the wisest old Greek COUNCILLOR at Troy; silver-tongued
12. [   ] rodomontade      [b] Doctor of that name who brought his ROBOT monster to life (not the monster)

13. [  ] BRAGGADOCIO      [c] buddy of the forty thieves

14. [  ] BABBITT      [d] the most famous sailor before Popeye

15. [  ] FRANKENSTEIN      [e] No. 2 wolf in literature

16. [  ] PECKSNIFF      [f] THRASONICAL soldier, captain or better

17. [  ] NESTOR      [g] loud-mouthed RANTING, from the speech habits of an ARIOSTO character

18. [  ] SINBAD      [h] jovial ROTARIAN, apostle of business culture

19. [  ] ALI BABA      [i] fancy boasting, named from a character in the Faerie Queene

20. [  ] LOTHARIO      [j] unctuous hypocrite, prating of benevolence; won't give more than a quarter

21. [  ] FALSTAFF      [a] alley cat who liked variety; her motto: TOUJOURS GAI

22. [  ] EUPHUISM      [b] female REVELER, given to wild abandon in liquor and love

23. [  ] PETER PAN      [c] flossy, elaborate VERBIAGE, full of FAR-FETCHED images

24. [  ] VOLPONE      [d] a witty young woman who knows the ways of the world; object: MATRIMONY

25. [  ] MEHITABEL      [e] the boy who never grew up; the ultimate in WHIMSY

26. [  ] BACCHANAL      [f] a married, adventurous MINX, looking for a SUPPLEMENTARY *sugar daddy*

27. [  ] MILLAMANT      [g] Charlemagne's PALADIN as a mad RENAISSANCE epic hero

28. [  ] BECKY SHARP      [h] foxy schemer who outfoxes himself; the biter who gets bit

29. [  ] OLD NOBADADDY      [i] Blake's label for the 18th-century parson's God

30. [  ] ORLANDO      [j] Shakespeare's greatest COMIC character: the fat knight who loved sack and wit

31. [  ] JOB      [a] he built the hanging gardens of Babylon and ate grass in them.

32. [  ] GOLIATH      [b] Queen Esther got him hanged, with his own cooperation

33. [  ] SAPPHIRA      [c] wife of King AHAB, wickeder and more IMMORAL than her husband

34. [  ] BELSHAZZAR      [d] backed up her husband's lies to help him best the church tithe on land which he had sold

35. [　] SENNACHERIB     [e] saved her home town BETHULIA by seducing and beheading HOLOFERNES

36. [　] NEBUCHADNEZZAR     [f] had the head of John the Baptist served on a platter for scorning her

37. [　] HAMAN     [g] had more troubles and afflictions than anybody else in the Bible

38. [　] JEZEBEL     [h] giant who was felled by stone from David's SLINGSHOT

39. [　] JUDITH     [ i] the Assyrian (who) came down like a wolf on the fold

40. [　] HERODIAS     [ j] saw the handwriting of doom on the wall at a banquet; "pillar of the Babylon-Jerusalem axis"—(H. Rome)

41. [　] GOLGOTHA     [a] LUKEWARM ADHERENT looking for a third side of the fence

42. [　] ARIAN     [b] believer in perpetual struggle between forces of Light and Darkness

43. [　] ATHANASIAN     [c] church chant style; calendar system from a later Pope of same name

44. [　] NICENE     [d] describing "Crosstianity" spread by the Apostle to the Gentiles

45. [　] LAODICEAN     [e] describing OUTLOOK and doctrines of the African Bishop of HIPPO

46. [　] MANICHEAN     [f] describing doctrine that Jesus was one of the sons of God, of like nature but not the same

47. [　] GREGORIAN     [g] Creed adopted at Church Council which NIXED the above heresy

48. [　] PAULINE     [h] same as [g]

49. [　] AUGUSTINIAN     [ i] hill in Jerusalem on which the Cross was erected

50. [　] THOMIST     [ j] describing the doctrines and philosophy of the Angelic Doctor, still dominant in Catholic and ADLERIAN philosophy

51. [　] BOWDLERIZE     [a] SHODDY FAKE; phony

52. [　] COMSTOCKERY     [b] SNOBBISH talking or writing about small points of ETIQUETTE

53. [　] EMILYPOSTING     [c] given the works in a savage, INTEMPERATE but polished style

54. [　] VICTORIAN     [d] to EXPURGATE a classic for use in a young ladies' SEMINARY

55. [   ] PEGLERIZED     [e] SNOOPING and hounding of writers and artists for violating Puritan TABOOS

56. [   ] PINCHBECK     [f] ham actor; any actor

57. [   ] SYBARITE     [g] stuffily moral

58. [   ] THESPIAN     [h] "My country, right or wrong"

59. [   ] CHAUVINISTIC     [i] STEREOTYPED in the movie tradition

60. [   ] HOLLYWOODEN     [j] elegant VOLUPTUARY and BON VIVANT

61. [   ] ARISTOPHANIC     [a] characterized by noble restraint, supreme mastery of dramatic construction, and controlled intensity

62. [   ] EURIPIDEAN     [b] characterized by ARCHAIC grandeur, awe at the SUPERHUMAN fearlessness of great rebels, and Miltonic phrasing

63. [   ] HOMERIC     [c] combining immense COMIC VIRTUOSITY, lyric grace, a mastery of SYNCOPATED verse, and COLLOQUIAL elegance

64. [   ] SOPHOCLEAN     [d] moving even more to pity than to fear, intensely human, SKEPTICALLY IRONIC about political and religious traditions

65. [   ] AESCHYLEAN     [e] polished, SOPHISTICATED, and given to higher naughtiness in elegant and beautiful phrasing

66. [   ] HORATIAN     [f] SATIRIC in a hard, iron-biting style; CENSORING evil and corruption with REMORSELESS wit

67. [   ] JUVENALIAN     [g] expressing philosophical and scientific ideas in lofty and majestic verse, giving the poetry of science

68. [   ] CICERONIAN     [h] characterized by superb FELICITY of phrase, expressing sentiments with Pope's precision, LIN YU TANG's COMPLACENCY

69. [   ] LUCRETIAN     [i] ORATORICAL, in the grand manner, sometimes FULSOME, sometimes ATTIC in phrasing

70. [   ] OVIDIAN     [j] characterized by greatness of accent, MAGNANIMITY, open-air ROBUSTNESS, superb sweep, and fast action; heroic

71. [   ] PETRARCHAN     [a] COMIC in the broadest and most ROBUST style, dealing with heroic feats of eating, drinking, jesting, and begetting

260

72. [　] BOCCACCIAN      [b] gifted in telling of AMOROUS intrigue in frank but polished narrative

73. [　] RABELAISIAN      [c] CONFESSIONAL lyric style marked by Romantic SENSITIVITY and classical feeling for form

74. [　] BALZACIAN      [d] characterized by HYPERSENSITIVITY in describing sensations as the key to memory, and immense skill in social high comedy

75. [　] PROUSTIAN      [e] revealing the human comedy throughout its range

76. [　] SWIFTIAN      [f] a crushing, pile-driver style full of POLY-SYLLABIC LATINITY, but immensely convincing and memorable

77. [　] JOHNSONIAN      [g] characterized by lyrical wit, great skill in nonsense patter, a respectful treatment of the ludicrous

78. [　] GILBERTIAN      [h] characterized by genial humor, fine touch in character PORTRAYAL, and strong social sympathies

79. [　] DICKENSIAN      [i] characterized by MORDANT wit, CONCISION of phrase, and savage indignation quietly expressed

80. [　] SHAVIAN      [j] expressed with exasperating levity, and profound conviction of having ultimate truth by the tail; also with breath-bereaving insolence; but deeply concerned about human welfare

## ANSWERS

| | | | | | | | |
|---|---|---|---|---|---|---|---|
| 1. [f] | 11. [f] | 21. [j] | 31. [g] | 41. [i] | 51. [d] | 61. [c] | 71. [c] |
| 2. [i] | 12. [g] | 22. [c] | 32. [h] | 42. [f] | 52. [e] | 62. [d] | 72. [b] |
| 3. [g] | 13. [i] | 23. [e] | 33. [d] | 43. [g] | 53. [b] | 63. [j] | 73. [a] |
| 4. [j] | 14. [h] | 24. [h] | 34. [j] | 44. [h] | 54. [g] | 64. [a] | 74. [e] |
| 5. [h] | 15. [b] | 25. [a] | 35. [i] | 45. [a] | 55. [c] | 65. [b] | 75. [d] |
| 6. [a] | 16. [j] | 26. [b] | 36. [a] | 46. [b] | 56. [a] | 66. [h] | 76. [i] |
| 7. [c] | 17. [a] | 27. [d] | 37. [b] | 47. [c] | 57. [j] | 67. [f] | 77. [f] |
| 8. [e] | 18. [d] | 28. [f] | 38. [c] | 48. [d] | 58. [f] | 68. [i] | 78. [g] |
| 9. [b] | 19. [c] | 29. [i] | 39. [e] | 49. [e] | 59. [h] | 69. [g] | 79. [h] |
| 10. [d] | 20. [e] | 30. [g] | 40. [f] | 50. [j] | 60. [i] | 70. [e] | 80. [j] |

The two- or three-line clues for these richly allusive terms merely skim the surface of their meaning. It would take a wide and varied course of reading to gather the full sense of many of these terms. They are deposited in the language like valuable old coins that have acquired a rich PATINA with age.

Readers quite rightly object if a writer plasters his text thick with these allusive words. But their occasional use is quite justifiable, to save spelling out at great length the qualities that are intended.

Once an Oxford tutor, well known as a kindly man, was irked by a student's reply upon being asked to read Bossuet's sermons:

"But, Doctor, I don't read French."

"Don't boast of your ignorance, my boy. Go to France and remedy it," the tutor answered.

Luckily, to remedy a lack of knowledge of cultural history, we need not go to France: only to the nearest library.

## Now—Go to College

The matching test you just took is similar to one you might get in a freshman or sophomore college survey course. On a quiz of this kind, you might encounter additional questions about the list:

1. Which groups of ten refer to imaginary characters?
2. In the group of BIBLICAL references, for which characters named do we have independent historical evidence, apart from the Bible?
3. Which group consists of theological terms, except for one?
4. Which group consists of terms derived from proper names used in a derisive sense? How many of these are of American origin?
5. Which group refers to classical authors?
6. How many British authors' names are the basis for the entries in the group in which they appear? Why, do you suppose, is SHAKESPEAREAN omitted?
7. Can you suggest five other invented literary characters (e.g., Cyrano)?

ANSWERS

1. First, second, and third groups.
2. 34, 35, 36, 40.
3. 41–50, except Golgotha

4. 51–60.
5. 61–70.
6. Five. Try to characterize Shakespeare in three lines!

## Odds and Ends

Quite a different—and in some ways a homelier—phase of cultural history is represented in the proper or place names which have come to be used to designate inventions, fabrics, CULINARY discoveries, and innovations in fashion. Here's a job lot of them. What are they, and from what person or place was each named? Can you place each one in the right century?

1. LILLIAN RUSSELL
2. BAZOOKA
3. bloomers
4. DEMIJOHN
5. MORPHINE
6. NICOTINE
7. PRUSSIC acid
8. muslin
9. CAMBRIC
10. bovril

### ANSWERS

1. A bustle. So named in the late nineteenth century from the popularizing of this adjunct to fashion by the American actress whom King Edward VII so greatly admired.
2. First, a rudimentary musical instrument, named from the slang word for mouth, "bazoo"; by figurative extension, because of a resemblance in shape, also applied to a crude rocket gun invented by an American in World War II.
3. Ample gymnasium knickers for girls and women. First devised by the American feminist, Dr. Amelia Bloomer, about 1850.
4. Corruption of French *dame-jeanne*, "Lady Jane." OED gives instances with the French spelling as of 1769, but cites the 1828 Webster for the spelling *demijohn* and gives a quotation from Dickens' American Notes of 1842.
5. Named from the Roman god of sleep, Morpheus. First quotation in OED is dated 1828.
6. The chief drug in tobacco. Named by a Frenchman, Jean Nicot, 1560.
7. Named from Prussian blue. First in print, according to OED quotation, in 1790.
8. A diminutive Italian form of Mosul, in Mesopotamia, is *mussolina*, from which we get muslin.
9. From Cambray, in France. The more recent *chambray* is from the same source.
10. A trade name for a kind of concentrated meat extract for making beef tea by pouring on boiling water. A manufactured word, presumably from *bos, bovis*, "a cow," plus *v(i)rilis*, "manly" or "powerful."

Of all the proper names which have become common nouns, perhaps the richest in historical associations is the word BEDLAM, now used to mean a tumultuous confusion, or mad jumble of noises. Late in the era of the Crusades, there was a religious house in the Holy Land dedicated to St. Mary of Bethlehem, that is, the Virgin. A branch of this in London was at first a HOSTEL for visiting members of the order traveling in England. Eventually this London branch devoted itself to caring for a certain type of afflicted, namely lunatics. When Henry VIII DISESTABLISHED the monasteries, this HOSPICE was turned over to the City of London, which continued it as an insane asylum, under the name of Bethlehem Hospital, or Bedlam, as it was called for short, with that turn for telescoping proper names so marked in England—as witness the pronunciation "Chumley" for CHOLMON-DELEY, and "Marchbanks" for MARJORIBANKS. Bedlam came next to be applied to any insane asylum. From the continual din heard in bedlams, it was not long until the word became a general term for any noisy confusion.

It is interesting to observe that in the history of this word we have involved the FOUNDING of the Christian religion, the passing of the Holy Land into the control of the Saracens, the Crusades, which restored it to CHRISTIANITY, the continued relations between the Latin Orient and Western Europe, the whole theory and practice of monastic institutions and fraternities, with their labors in behalf of the poor and sick, the Reformation in general, and, in particular, the Reformation in England under Henry VIII, with its confusion of religious and secular motives.—Greenough and Kittredge, *Words and Their Ways in English Speech.* (The Macmillan Company.)

The title *Chancellor* has a curious history. It comes ultimately from cancer, "a crab." This had a plural diminutive CANCELLI, which meant "a grating," from the resemblance of cross-hatched bars or lattice-work to a crab's TENTACLES. Cancelli was thus the name given to the gratings which separated from the rest of the chamber the part of a large hall used as a court. The usher of the court, who stood just inside the gratings was *ad cancellos*, "at the cross-bars"; he was called *cancellarius*, which became "chancellor" in Law French. As his office grew in dignity, the title came to be one of great honor; and it is now applied to a high legal official or the head of a great educational system. The original connection with crabs and gratings is usually quite forgotten.

CABAL, for a political intrigue or a group of conspirators, has an interesting history. It comes from the Hebrew word for a hidden or mysterious interpretation of the Scriptures: *kabbala*, which we have borrowed in this more proper form to refer to the mystical writings of MEDIEVAL Jewish schoolmen. But *cabal* was reinforced in its present sense by the accident that Charles II had a clever and intriguing cabinet council for foreign affairs whose initials spelled CABAL: Clifford, Arlington, Buckingham, Ashley, and Lauderdale. And so it goes. There are countless words whose records are INTERWOVEN with the movements and events of history.

## WORDPLAY: FROM "HUMOURS" TO "HUMOR"

There is no better index to the course of CULTURAL history than the changes in meaning which occur in words having to do with the feelings, the will, the instincts, or the mind—in short, all terms which relate to human nature and its interpretation, whether individual or social PSYCHOLOGY is concerned. For while the old saying of the HUMANISTS, that human nature is always the same, may be partly true, so soon as one raises the question, wherein does the sameness consist, a great variety of answers will be offered. And there is no simpler way to study the many readings of human nature than by tracing the changes of meaning in a single PSYCHOLOGICAL term. We have already noted this fact, in examining the word *character*. But there are terms which yield just as much.

The word *humor*, for example, means literally, in Latin, "liquid." It early came to be specialized in English to the four bodily *humours*, which according to ARISTOTLE and GALEN, and ancient PHYSIOLOGISTS generally, determined, by their balance, the temperament of a man. If the blood was dominant, a man had a sanguine temperament; if the CHOLER was in excess, he was CHOLERIC; if the BILE ruled over his body, he was melancholy; and if the PHLEGM was in the ASCENDANCY, he was PHLEGMATIC. These terms remain in the language, though the science from which they come is OUTMODED.

By an easy transfer, the word *humour* was also applied to the mood or EMOTIONAL set resulting from a PREDOMINANCE of one humour over the others. As Ben Jonson puts it, speaking of the use of the term to which he was to give a wide currency,

265

It may, by metaphor, apply itself
Unto the general disposition;
As when some one peculiar quality
Doth so possess a man, that it doth draw
All his affects, his spirits, or his powers
In his CONFLUCTIONS, all to run one way,
This may be truly said to be a humour.
　　　　—Ben Jonson, INDUCTION to *Every Man out of His
　　　　Humour.*

*Humour* in this sense meant more than a QUIRK or queer VAGARY; it
implied a single dominant passion or PREOCCUPATION; and Shadwell
in the late seventeenth, and Dickens in the early nineteenth, century
employed this conception of a humour as the basis for character construction, just as Ben Jonson had done. Uriah Heep is an animated
*humour* walking around, a bundle of sneaking, crafty submission.

From the fact that *humours* characters were employed on the stage
as COMIC creatures, the word *humor* acquired the further extension of
meaning which it now has. It came finally to mean a gay, good-
tempered variety of the comic. In *humor* proper in the modern sense,
one is inclined to laugh both with and at the person, or in some cases,
only with him.

Humor still retains its associations with the emotions, although
they are only lightly involved; traditionally humor has been distinguished from *wit* on the grounds that the latter involves the intellect.
*Wit* may be chiefly intellectual, but if it's at somebody's expense, it
also calls into play the unkinder feelings, both in the sender and in
the receiver. That is another story, however, which would take as
long as humor to unfold. Luckily, when we start prying into the
derisive use of language as a key to cultural history, we have at hand
a rich storehouse of material.


## SLANG AS A CULTURAL KEY

At first glance, it might seem INCONGRUOUS to bracket slang
with words such as TARTUFFE, MICAWBER, and SENNACHERIB—or with
the "humours" of Shakespeare's contemporary, Ben Jonson. Slang
seems so vividly "here and now," everyday talk that apparently
springs full-blown out of the air around us. But slang has its history,
too; and slang words are keys to both the past and the present. There
is an incredible wealth of slang terms that give us clues to current

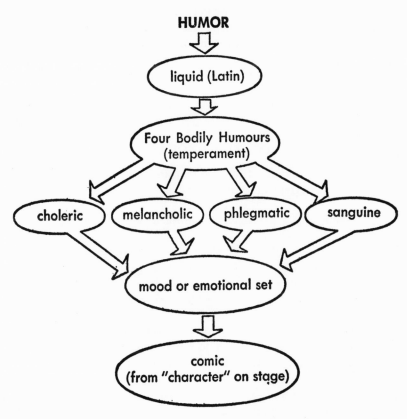

**HUMOR**

liquid (Latin)

Four Bodily Humours
(temperament)

choleric    melancholic    phlegmatic    sanguine

mood or emotional set

comic
(from "character" on stage)

events and past history in the same way that adjectives such as STOICAL, EPICUREAN, and PLATONIC are clues to the mental and emotional life of the Greeks.

## SLANG OF THE PAST

Slang is an epitome of our history. At its best and most inventive, it is marked by picturesque and PROVOCATIVE similes:

(A) go *like a bat out of hell*
(B) crazy *as a loon*
(C) lit up *like a cathedral* (or *Christmas tree*)

These expressions are not current slang, but they're still alive and no one would look askance at you if you used them in a conversation.

Do you know how far back they go? The earliest date for A is 1908; B goes back to 1905; C is the most enduring with a birth date around 1848. There is evidently something in the American temperament that likes colorful similes in its slanguage. How about "Crazy like a fox"? "Nutty as a fruitcake?" "Busy as a beaver?" (This last one goes back to Revolutionary days—1775.)


## SLANG FROM THE UNDERWORLD

Slang deriving from underworld cant or argot is often full of metaphors as grim as they are funny:

chill, give a permanent, take for a slay ride, scrag

They all mean "to kill" and they remind us uncomfortably of the Prohibition era when Al Capone and other gangsters were fighting over the ILLICIT liquor trade. Other tidbits from the glossary of gangsterdom are "Chicago piano" (six-barreled pompoms or antiaircraft guns) and "Chicago mowing machine" (machine gun or Tommy gun).

Underworld terminology does not belong exclusively to the bygone days of the 20's and 30's or to a particular city, as the hearings before the Kefauver, McClellan, and other Congressional committees of the 60's have so clearly demonstrated. The underworld has been with us a long time, and the mixture of slang, cant, and argot in which the testimony was given are a key to the culture. Gangland structure described by the sociological term "families"; gangland procedures revealed by the business and legal term "contract"; gangland symbolism expressed in the "kiss of death" gesture; and gangland revenge tactics of "rubbing out" an enemy—these terms tell the story of a big business operation on a nationwide scale that should give pause to the COMPLACENT.

Bergen Evans writes in *The Atlantic* (May, 1962): ". . . a rudimentary knowledge of the development of any language [indicates] that the underworld has been a far more active force in shaping and enriching speech than all the SYNODS that have ever convened." Since the underworld IMPINGES upon activities such as sports, racing, the amusement world, and other seemingly innocuous American occupations and pastimes, its terminology follows the course of its operations and becomes a vital force in shaping the language.

268

## SLANG AS A KEY TO HUMOR

Fortunately, slang also has its relaxed side. The America of Mark Twain, Will Rogers, and Artemus Ward had to find a kind of humor in everything, and humorous words and phrases have been constantly coined for this purpose. The slang terms for certain trades are apt:

baggage-smasher (for a porter)
gold-mining (plumbing)
ten-percenter (an actor's agent)
Maud (an engine in oil workers' jargon)
schneiders ⎫
kluppers ⎬ (garment worker's terms for a slow, inefficient operator)
noodle-twister (cigar maker)

Slang often has had the COMPRESSION that helps out wit:

cat-chat (malicious female gossip)
yawner (a flat or boring joke)
duck a date (to fail to keep an appointment)
shoot Niagara (take a desperate chance)
bum steer (bad advice, often given deliberately)
on ice (all settled and arranged)

Brevity is, of course, the soul of today's slang, but another characteristic of offbeat vocabulary past and present, is the "nonce" or nonsense word that comes and goes in a hurry. Here are some current slang terms with their nonce-word equivalents.

bugged (botherated)
shook-up (discombobulated)
rhubarb (conbobberation)
yakker (monowongler)
cronked (stifflicated)

Current slang reveals interests and attitudes. Americans are PRE-OCCUPIED with sex and they associate it with food in such expressions as:

cheesecake (a provocative pose)
poundcake (a beautiful girl)
cookie (a girl)
quail (young, desirable girl)
pigeon (same as quail; also means "victim of a confidence game")
chicken, or chick (young girl)
tart (prostitute)
dish (a girl)


One-syllable words that describe a drunkard are plentiful. In addition to "cronked" we have "squiffed," "blind," "fried," "gassed," "stewed," "juiced," "lit," "looped," "oiled," "lush," "soused," "stiff," and "tight." It would be difficult to discriminate the fine shades of meaning; the proper term may depend upon the degree of intoxication or the social standing of the bar one staggers out of. A diligent researcher could compile an interesting dictionary of such terms analogous to *Webster's Dictionary of Synonyms*.

Our AMBIVALENT attitude toward intellectuals comes out in slang terms describing them. On the one hand, we use wordplay to bring them down to earth; on the other hand, we admire their expanse of forehead. We call them "highbrows," "eggheads," "brain trusters," or "double-domes."

## SLANG IS OFF THE BEAT

In the main, slang is derisive, or at least derogatory. While it includes many invented or scrambled words, it also calls into service a job lot of standard words. In doing so, it gives their RESPECTABILITY the "old heave-ho." Ruling out the actual coinages and the nonce words, take apart any of the slang phrases above and you'll find that the elements which compose it can be used as legitimate words. But in combination they form a decidedly "blue" jazz chord.

Slang is in fact to language what jazz is to music. Slang is off the beat. It SYNCOPATES and BLURS standard words. Just as jazz employs many regular CHORDAL combinations in UNORTHODOX style, so slang fuses words, makes PUNNING blends, and generally plays monkey tricks all along the verbal scale. And slang is often IMPROMPTU; it gives the effect of IMPROVISATION, just as jazz today is often improvised from a set of chords.

270

Slang is best when it is used for humorous effect, by a speaker or writer who knows what he is doing. Slang tells what people laugh at; it reveals the whole ROBUST side of folk life—eating, drinking, love-making, merrymaking. Movie, radio and television, theatrical cant, labor jargon, teen talk are often side-splitting; and the comedy is sometimes a cover-up for the tragedy and heartbreak that lie beneath the surface.

## HOW OLD IS SLANG?

In using slang as an INDICATOR of cultural history—and of the social patterns and habits of mind which gave it birth—the first necessity is to date it. The one FEASIBLE way to do so is to find out when the term first appeared in print. By the time it gets into print, a slang phrase has presumably been knocking around in oral use for some time.

The regular dictionaries are not much help in dating slang, except that the OED records vintage slang. Writers who plan to use a slang phrase as supposedly current in a certain past period—as *Time* often does—have to be very careful not to get slang of different decades mixed up. That's where dating becomes a necessity. Fortunately, there are a few books in which slang terms and Americanisms have been compiled and dated. Eric Partridge's *A Dictionary of Slang and Unconventional English* and his *Slang Today and Yesterday* give full coverage of American and English slang terms dating back many centuries.

The next most likely work to consult for American slang of an older period is Henry L. Mencken's massive *The American Language* or its *Supplement One* and *Supplement Two*. Richard H. Thornton's *An American Glossary* yields many Americanisms and their dates from the early part of this century and before. For recent American slang, however, the DEFINITIVE work is Harold Wentworth's and Stuart Berg Flexner's *Dictionary of American Slang*. Another good source is *The American Thesaurus of Slang*, which groups slang terms according to subject ("fried," "looped," "boiled," etc., for "drunk") in the manner of *Roget's International Thesaurus*.

A delightful and AUTHORITATIVE publication that records language as it keeps changing is *American Speech*, available in most libraries. By combing the back issues of this magazine, which spots new words from every source as they come into the language, you can piece together the running story of American slang since 1925.

## Can You Tell Recent from Vintage Slang?

In the following FABRICATED passage, check slang you think of recent American vintage—say not older than ten years.

### PETE LEADS WITH HIS CHIN

I am having me a fit of the *blues*, so I go over to Buckshot Dull's joint and get into a small dice game. When the *bones* come round to me, I feel they are *fishy*, and it is gefillte fish. Second time round, I am getting ready to blow my top and I say to Buckshot, "Since when are you running a *chiseling* game?" I am *cuckoo* to broadcast it, for Buckshot socks me and I go down for the count. Then he wants to know how would I like to get rubbed out, and I am all shook up, but he starts laughing and says, "Pete, for a minute I think you are blue around the gills." I tell him it's a great *gag*, but that's not what my chin tells me. I drift out and get me a *lift* home with Peewee Jones in his jalopy. We stop for a big *feed* at McGinty's place, and Peewee tells me I'm a kook to tangle with Buckshot. I am too low to come back at him with "*You're another!*" for telling me. But next week I hear Buckshot is doing a stretch in the *jug* and I really dig that.

In this patch of narrative, written in the Damon Runyon historical present (though evidently not by Runyan) none of the words in ITALICS is original American slang in the sense used here. In CHRONO-LOGICAL order, here are the first known instances of the use of each word in the sense occurring above, the date it appeared in print, and the author or source:

| | | |
|---|---|---|
| bones (dice) | c. 1386 | Chaucer |
| You're another | 1534 | Udall |
| cuckoo | c. 1600 | |
| lift (a ride) | 1711 | Swift |
| blues (melancholy) (from "blue devils") | 1807 | Washington Irving |
| chisel (to cheat) | 1808 | Jamieson |
| gag (an actor's interpolation) | 1823 | |
| feed (a meal) | 1830 | Lytton |
| jug (prison) | 1834 | |
| fishy (dubious) | 1858 | Brooks |

272

The fact that the best authors have used the words in the same slang sense that Pete does, does not make them any less slang today. As a matter of fact, many of them are not very apt because of the mixture of several STRATA of slang. The real Pete of 1963 would use more terms like *cat, cool, pad, man.* He might use an in-word from jazz circles and call Buckshot a "badface" (surly cat). Instead of arriving at Buckshot's or at the restaurant, he might "fall" there. He would use words in their reverse 1963 sense: "crazy" would mean exciting or different, "in" rather than "out." "Square" would mean not a square-shooter but an outsider. Instead of going to a restaurant, Pete might use the popular *-eria* ending and call it an "eateria."

If Pete spent any time in White House circles he would learn the special jargon of that environment. Reporters would be "newsies"; "the Flap House" would be the Special Operations Center in the State Department. At the Pentagon getting down to work would be "get cracking"; "rug rank" would describe an official with "a position so lofty he would rate a rug on the floor of his office."

Informal or slang speech of today is a hodgepodge of terms from all areas of American life. Some of the in-words, or jargon, known only to those in a given trade, profession, or special group, sift through into general slang use, and there is a blurring of the terms "slang," "jargon," "informal," "colloquial." The slang that sounds fresh-minted is often dated but still very much alive. Even though Pete's slang style is mixed (Runyonese, old slang, older slang, new slang) a little inquiry of this kind is revealing. Here are some slang terms that have endured for almost six hundred years!

All this rather effectively confounds the schoolmarm view of slang. Actually, since it is language in the making, hot off the forge, slang is of extraordinary interest to professional—and amateur—students of linguistics. Slang, like technical words, is at the growing edge of the great coral reef which makes up English vocabulary, and the choicer bits of it eventually turn into colorful, if not elegant, ornaments of the language. (This is not meant as any defense of slang vulgarisms, or of those tiresome and REPETITIOUS slang CLICHÉS which teen-agers use—the modern analogues of *sweetie, all rightie,* such as *natch* [for *naturally*] and similar BANAL ATROCITIES).

## Translate this Passage

You didn't have any trouble understanding "Pete Leads with His Chin," even though several of the slang terms are HOARY with age. Read the following passage and guess what century it was written in. Are the words in it now considered "slang," "rare," "archaic," "obsolete"?

When the dummy was grogging with that jumbo rumpscuttle, they decided to run a rig with some gringo; but this old squawker blabbed to the Dogberry that the hot donna was a horse, and the stirk threw them out of the snuggery.[1]

No, not the seventeenth, the eighteenth, even the nineteenth century. The above is made up of standard words that appear in *Webster's Second Unabridged*, until recently considered the final authority on matters of word labels and usage. It is still considered so by many writers and others concerned with words, who have not accepted *Webster's Third Unabridged* (see Chapter 9). The point here is that many slang words endure through the centuries and many standard words sicken and die.

## TWO AMERICAN SLANG STYLISTS

One way to trace the history of American slang is to study writers who used it as an integral part of their style. Two such writers, forty years apart, were O. Henry and Damon Runyon. Around the turn of the century O. Henry was one of the first to make extensive use of slang, not only in dialogue but in the narrative proper. His collection of slang locutions is fearful and wonderful.

He sometimes uses slang as an important plot device. In one of his stories in *Cabbages and Kings*, the president of a banana republic has eloped with all the money in the treasury and the opera singer of whom he is ENAMORED. American FILIBUSTERERS helping the REVOLUTIONISTS in the capitol went to wire their U.S. assistants in the port town to warn them that the president is making for the coast, and to head him off before he embarks. They baffle the Spanish TELEGRAPHERS,

[1] *Dictionaries and THAT Dictionary.*

274

who are in the president's secret service, by sending this message over the wires:

*His Nibs skedaddled* yesterday per *jackrabbit* line with all the coin in the *kitty* and the *bundle of muslin* he's *spoony* about. The *boodle* is six figures short. Our crowd in good shape, but we need *spondulicks*. The *main* guy and the *dry goods* are headed for the *briny*. You know what to do.

This smacks of 1904. But a lot of the contrived slang here is even older. *His Nibs* dates from around 1860; *skedaddled* (colloquial since c. 1900, slang until then) is a Civil War coinage, with a probably fanciful ETYMOLOGY from the Greek *skedunamai*, to scatter; *jackrabbit* is a mule, from the long ears the two animals have in common; *bundle of muslin* (from 1823) is one of the innumerable derogatory terms for a woman; *spoony*, now almost obsolete, was current from 1836; *kitty*, for the "jackpot," dates from 1892; *spondulicks* from 1857—it was ANGLICIZED around 1885. *Briny*, says Eric Partridge in his *Dictionary of Slang* (from which the above dates are taken) has been colloquial since 1856.

One can never be sure whether or not O. Henry's slang was really current at the time he wrote, since he depended as much on books as on his ear. He was himself a wordsmith of RABELAISIAN or JOYCEAN PROCLIVITIES, except that he had to keep within narrower limits of DECORUM. Within these limits he FABRICATED to his heart's content.

Not so Damon Runyon. There is nothing bookish about his MANIPU-LATION of the VERNACULAR. He collected it along Broadway and Third Avenue. He does not, like O. Henry, come on the stage himself and put fancy VERBIAGE into his characters' mouths. He keeps the language always within the compass of his first person narrator, who is usually a small-time hanger-on of the Broadway mob or amusement outfit which figures in the story.

Actually, Runyon's American is much more a matter of sentence pitch and rhythm than it is of slang. He does not, like O. Henry, use orthodox SYNTAX, but keeps to the historical present. His narrators run on and on, but always keep in the clear. They have an argot of their own, and the words in it are slang or the wreckage of legitimate words. A man is a "guy," a nasty one a "wrong gee"; a girl is a "doll," and the "guy" telling the story does not approve of calling her a "tomato" or a "broad," though he knows the terms, and now and then quotes some "wrong gee" as using them. A killer "cools off" somebody

275

to order, while a kidnapper is "on the snatch." ADULTERATED liquor is "cut goods." A "doll" takes a "run-out powder" on her husband. There is a code for sums of money: a "grand" is $1000; a "c" or "century" $100; $10 is a "sawbuck"; $5 "a finif," or "a pound note"; $2 is "a deuce" or a "two-spot"; and a dollar is a "buck" or "bob." These are all the terms which E. F. Bentley, writing a most appreciative introduction for *The Best of Damon Runyon*, thinks the British reader needs by way of GLOSSARY. The rest he should be able to guess at from the CONTEXT. How many can an American of the 60's sight-read out of context?

## Do You Know Runyonese?

To keep the game honest, cover up the right-hand column of equivalents in the following glossary, and check each of Runyon's *bons bouches* that you can translate.

| | | |
|---|---|---|
| 1. | sneezer | prison |
| 2. | mouser | mustache |
| 3. | what is eating him | what's bothering him? |
| 4. | the main drag | Main Street |
| 5. | burg | town (usually small) |
| 6. | noggin | head |
| 7. | gendarmes | police (euphemism for) |
| 8. | once in a coon's age (colloq.) | rarely |
| 9. | from A to Izzard | from alpha to omega is the Biblical equivalent |
| 10. | sored up at | enraged at |
| 11. | sucker | he who gets trimmed |
| 12. | old equalizer | a revolver |
| 13. | John Roscoe | a revolver |
| 14. | blows his topper | flies off the handle |
| 15. | off his nut | crazy |
| 16. | scrag | kill |
| 17. | loogan | insignificant person |
| 18. | corned | drunk |
| 19. | bang | excitement, "lift" |
| 20. | old do-re-mi | money |
| 21. | moola, mazuma | money |
| 22. | potatoes | money |
| 23. | a rock | a diamond |

276

| | |
|---|---|
| 24. old warm squativoo | the electric chair |
| 25. churned up | angered |
| 26. to gum up | to mess up |
| 27. to holler copper | to call in the police |
| 28. a beef | a complaint (also a verb) |
| 29. hoofer | a dancer (usually tap or buck and wing, etc.) |
| 30. heave into the can | put in jail |
| 31. deal off the arm | wait table ("sling hash" is equally common in the West) |
| 32. pitching | making a play for, making love to |
| 33. give a tumble | pay addresses to; or encourage such addresses |
| 34. dodge | business or occupation, equivalent to "racket" in the innocuous sense —the same meaning it had in 1812—simply a "line of business" |
| 35. heel | a bounder plus, e.g., Pal Joey |
| 36. bending in an ear | listening |
| 37. shivved | killed (literally, "knifed") |
| 38. moxie | courage |
| 39. ticker | courage (literally, "heart") |
| 40. artichoke | old-fashioned gold watch, and by extension "pickpocketing" |
| 41. had a piece of the joint | owned a share of the place—of some enterprise |
| 42. sawed-off | clipped form of "sawed-off shotgun" |
| 43. rodded up | armed (with one or more revolvers) |
| 44. hotter than a stove | illicit: police are on the lookout for it—whether it's a joint or stolen goods |
| 45. haybag | old, large, and shapeless (generally of a woman) |
| 46. guzzled | killed |
| 47. put the old sleeve on | arrest |
| 48. kisser | mouth |
| 49. half-portion | very small (usually of a person) |
| 50. scratch | money |
| 51. put the blast on | excoriate; kill |
| 52. convincer | a gun |
| 53. marker | I.O.U. |

277

| | |
|---|---|
| 54. high grade merchandise | good though illicit liquor |
| 55. lammister | fugitive, one on the run |
| 56. croaker | a doctor |
| 57. promote | persuade someone to give something —a loan—"for free" tickets— whatever it is. The verb takes a personal object. |
| 58. duckets | tickets |
| 59. chinee | an Annie Oakley (see p. 283) or free ticket ("chinee," from Chinese cash with a hole in the center— like complimentary tickets which are punched full of holes) |
| 60. beezer, schnozzle | nose |
| 61. monicker | name |
| 62. put the lug on | "hit up for," impose on |
| 63. boff | sock or hit, usually with a blunt weapon |
| 64. bladders | newspapers (from German *Blatt*, newspaper) |
| 65. scribe | a newpaperman |
| 66. boat race | a "fixed" horse race |
| 67. poke | (woman's) purse |
| 68. flea bag | hotel one notch above flop house |
| 69. cutting up old touches | recounting old exploits |
| 70. jerry | aware of ("hep to") |
| 71. slum | trashy (jewelry) |
| 72. jug | bank |
| 73. ka-zip | head |
| 74. flogger | overcoat |
| 75. cocoanuts | money |
| 76. tongue | lawyer |
| 77. mouthpiece | lawyer |

Adding the slang locutions listed by Bentley, Runyon's slang ration runs to about 96 words—or perhaps 100, if BORDERLINE phrases are included—in the 200 pages of *The Best of Damon Runyon*, roughly 75,000 words. There are many repetitions, but even allowing for these, the percentage of slang to standard words is under one-half of one percent. He gets his effects with a relatively slight infusion of slang, which flavors the whole mixture. Taken in CONJUNCTION with the use of the historical present, it gives the impression of an argot very remote from the standard language. Actually, it is not, except in carefully chosen spots.

The late Dr. Louise Pound observed that a good deal of the dialogue and narrative in such work as Runyon's would before many years require a glossary, just as Chaucer does. The Runyon stories in the collection referred to were written between 1928 and 1935, a period which includes the great days of bootlegging and rum-running. When this test was first given, in 1946, the average reader knew all but thirteen of the slang locutions listed above. In the 60's about 36 of them are in LIMBO. Can you pick the 36 specimens of slang already obsolete, among the 77 above?


## A SLANG MISHMASH

Here is a PASTICHE which uses Runyon's historical present and in part draws on his reservoir of slang. It brings a Broadway character in contact with some of our leading lexicographers and reports his version of a discussion of slang as a key to American cultural history.

The Broadway character Pete is a hanger-on in many areas of city life. He is on the fringe of the gangster crowd; he is a familiar figure in a gambling joint or at the racetrack; he does a little dabbling in politics; and he has a few beatnik friends in Greenwich Village. Most of the time he is out of work. Mixed in with the Runyon style is the idiom of the 60's.

SUBSTANDER LANGUAGE

Doc Gove Takes Pete to a TV Panel
Show Featuring the Scholars vs.
the Scribes. Pete Reports:

The unemployment office is on my back, so I get me a job for three days and it turns out to be a breeze. All this cat wants me to do is yak, so I make with the chin music while he scribbles on pieces of paper, although I cannot figure out what is his racket and I keep waiting for the gimmick. He has a real crazy pad, which looks like a library, with a bunch of guys and gals pushing pencils, and when I ask one of the dolls what cooks with Phil, she shakes her finger at me and says his name is Doc

Gove and that he makes book, so now I know what the deal is. It seems he is queer for a hot pony which has the handle of Webster, and I hear them talking about what Webster is going to do in the Third, which I figure is the third race, so I make up my mind I will get a wad and place it on this nag.

Anyway, after two days Phil takes me in his jalopy to meet a couple of pals which has the name of Bergie Evans and Jimmy Sledd, and they are both making their headquarters in Chi. I ask them who is their mob, and they tell me they operate north of Chi on a piece of turf called Evanston, where is the Northwestern gang. Another joker is joining us and the boys call him Pat the Killer and they ask him how are things at the union. Now this makes me very uneasy and I begin to worry about Washington and maybe the Feds snooping around. Later I find out I have made a mistake, it seems his name is Kilburn and he is from Union College, and I am very surprised there should be a school for kluppers and schneiders.

We stop in front of a building and Phil says we are going to be on a panel, but I think he means somebody is on the pan, and I wonder who is the sucker. I ask him where is his Annie Oakley, but he says we do not need tickets, as they are waiting for us, so we go inside and the first thing I see is a flatfoot which is giving me a dirty look. Now this makes me very nervous, and I begin to perspire and wonder if I am their pigeon, in fact they sit me down at a table and shove a mike in front of me, so now I figure the heat is on and I am all shook up. Over at the other side of the table is three guys and a guy in the middle which are giving me the double-O, I think maybe Bobbie sent them down, and I want out of there. The guy in the middle calls the other guys Mac and Willie and Syd Harris, who is also from Chi, but I think he is from another mob and there is going to be a rumble.

Mac is short for Macdonald and I find out he is called Dwight, which sounds very suspicious to me, and besides he is hiding behind a beaver like he does not want anyone to know who he is. But it is this other character, Willie Follett, who is giving me butterflies, he acts like he is real burned about something and it is my fault. Anyway, they push a camera in front of me, and the lights is beating down on my noggin, so I figure I am being mugged and maybe fingerprinted and here I have not been in on any fixes lately except when I need bread. The guy in the middle is flapping his lip about what kind of a job Webster pulls off, and I wonder how a hayburner is getting in the act. Then Phil turns to me and says, "All right, start talking," and now I know it is the squeeze, and I yell into the mike, "You can't put the finger on me—I ain't done nothin'!"

Well, I am amazed when Phil pumps my hand and says, "That's great —that's terrif! The real McCoy! Genuine Americana!" And Jimmy is smiling and Pat is slapping me on the back. Then Phil writes something on a piece of paper (this oddball is always writing on pieces of paper) and I get worried and look at it and I see "ain't" with my name written under it. He explains that it is a citation slip and I start to perspire again because I do not want the coppers on my neck, but Phil nixes me and says it is not that kind of slip, it is for Webster, and I am wondering if this horse is a paper-eater.

Well, I am not out of the woods by any means, because Willie Follett is trying to stare me down, and I look him right back in the eyeball, and he reaches for his rod and I go real quick for mine, only he comes up with a pencil and he starts to doodle on a piece of paper. I never see such a crowd of doodlers and I wonder what kind of kooks I am mixed up with. Then this guy in the middle says we now have a battle between the scribes, which is the guys on the other side of the table, and the scholars, which he calls them doctors—Doc Gove, Doc Evans, Doc Sledd, and Doc Kilburn —and suddenly it comes over me—I am on TV! I think maybe it is a hospital or headshrinker show, but then, what am I doing here—I do not need tranquilizing.

So now the name-dropping begins, all about some cutie which is called "Pat Waugh" and her boyfriend "Vern Acular." Willie Follett and Bergie Evans are beating their gums at each other, and Bergie says Willie is full of "buzz-buzz," which I think he means "hot air," and Willie is coming right back at him about dirty work in Springfield, which he is calling "sabotage." Now this gets me very upset, I think maybe I am being tagged for a Commie and I do not care to have J. Edgar and his boys on my tail. Pat and Mac are chewing each other out and Pat calls Mac an "old maid," to which Mac replies, "Why, pal, I have an ever-loving better half and we are hitting it off like crazy for a lot of years"—well, he does not say that exactly, but that is what I think he means.

The guy in the middle says now we will have a word from our sponsor, and it is a pleasure to see on the screen a stacked chick with gorgeous gams, she dives into the water and comes up smoking a cigarette. A voice says something about it tasting good like a cigarette should, and Bergie likes this but Willie blows his top, and they start a donnybrook about Winston, but I do not understand if it is the cigarette or a dictionary. It is getting to be a real rhubarb with a lot of yak about "vinyl eyes" or "final eyes," which sounds absolutely nutty to me, and about how Phil Silvers is saying "nauseous" when he means "nauseated" and Doc Gove says why not, which makes Willie run a very high temperature, in fact he is about to pop a cork.

Then Mac is making a dirty crack about substander words, and Doc Gove says, why we have always had substander words, which I am thinking is about guys like me which has to stand in the subway. Doc says, take for instance a hundred years ago when they want some jerk to amscray, they tell him to *absquatulate*,[2] and when the Yankees are mixing it up with the Dixies, they each say the other is doing a *skedaddle* when they take a powder. Everybody smiles at this because we do not use such sixty-four-dollar words anymore, instead we are saying *beat it* or *get lost*. This shows we are jazzing up the old lingo with the old razzmatazz so we have plenty of the old bazazz.

Jimmy Sledd says that substander words tell us just as much about the people that use them as egghead words and he says, remember, fellows, back in the days when the boys are getting crocked and they shoot off their mouths about how they are *ring-tailed roarers?* Now everybody thinks this is very funny, and Syd Harris says how about the time this bunch of dandies start themselves a club and call themselves *macaronis*,[3] which is about fifteen years before we are giving King George the bum's rush, and they will not eat limey chow but instead are filling up on spaghetti and ravioli. In fact, the tunesmith who writes "Yankee Doodle" sticks it in his jingle about the pony:

"He puts a feather in his cap
And calls it macaroni."

The scholars and scribes are laughing very hard at this, even Willie is grinning and he says what about flappers, which is what they call fillies who make you flip back in the days of hooch, raccoon coats, and bubble baths spiked with gin. Everybody is in stitches at this, and they are haw-hawing and punching each other in the ribs, but now Pat tops them all with a spiel about substander words which come in and skedaddle right out again, like *boyology* for the way hip chicks put the bite on lover boys, and *bumpologist* for a con artist who plays a tune on your noodle and tells you what kind of a character you are like.

Well, the whole crowd is howling now and wiping the tears out of their eyes, including the guy in the middle, and we are really a swinging crew. Bergie says, after all, why be a party pooper, and Doc Gove says that is the way the cookie crumbles, and even Willie admits you cannot make an omelet without first cracking open the egg, and everybody is shaking hands and calling everybody else by their first name, which is like the politicos who give each other the business in public, then they are buddy-buddy when they go out and get stinko together.

Syd Harris has got to get back to his column, and Doc Gove says the book is waiting for him, so I ask him if Webster won the third race, and everybody laughs and writes it down on a piece of paper. Then the Doc slips me an extra finif, which I blow pronto at Barney's Bistro and Jerry's Juice-Joint, where I have me a couple of short ones, after which I fall into the unemployment office and file a new claim. The clerk starts bugging me

[2] First in print in 1837.  [3] First in print in 1764.

282

about going out and getting a steady job and not getting in their hair, but now I am puffed up by what I am learning about substander words, so I tell this creep to

ABSQUATULATE!

Supply standard equivalents for the slang locutions in the preceding pastiche. Where Pete's dates are a bit sketchy, specify the decade meant. Were there any other proper names besides Annie Oakley that have become slang terms?

## PROPER NAME INTO SLANG

When slang terms can be traced back to proper names, you know there's a story behind them, a story that made news against the background of a particular day and age. Often the dictionary record on such a word doesn't tell the juicier part of the narrative. Take this entry in *Funk & Wagnalls Standard College Dictionary:*

> **Mc·Coy** (mə·koi/), **the (real)** *U.S. Slang* The authentic person or thing. [Appar. from an episode, existing in many versions, in which a celebrated American boxer, Kid McCoy, spectacularly established his identity]

"Spectacularly established his identity" has the dry, succinct quality of a dictionary definition that must tell a colorful tale in a few words. Norman Selby, the MIDDLEWEIGHT boxer of the twenties, who fought under the *nom de guerre*, Kid McCoy, was an amiable, quiet sort of man who outside the ring didn't look like a tough fighter. One night, wearing evening dress, he went into a restaurant bar with friends. A quarrelsome drunk addressed offensive remarks to McCoy, and started to paw him. McCoy warned him, saying quietly that his name was McCoy, and it would be better to lay off him. The drunk said, "Aw, you're not McCoy." The fighter let him have a right to the jaw. When the drunk came to, several hours later, he found McCoy's card on his chest. "It was the real McCoy," he muttered.

An "Annie Oakley" is a COMPLIMENTARY ticket punched full of holes. Annie Oakley was Buffalo Bill's star EXHIBITIONIST with a pistol; the playing cards were thrown into the air as her targets. It took the dictionaries quite awhile to recognize her, but she's very much in the air today—and she gives you a complimentary ticket to the period when O. Henry was writing—the period of Buffalo Bill, Jesse James, and other "ripsnorters."

Did you know that "bunk" came from a proper noun? It was presented to the language with the compliments of a North Carolina Congressman when he admitted that his speech on the House floor was intended mainly for the benefit of the folks back home in Buncombe County. His name is forgotten, but buncombe is still with us, though it's been shortened, first to *bunkum*, then to *bunk*.


## WORDS ACROSS THE SEA

The story of Buncombe → bunkum → bunk is told in H. L. Mencken's *The American Language*. Mencken tells another fascinating story—how our forefathers brought the mother tongue over from England and began to add words INDIGENOUS to their new soil. There is the word *squat*, for example, which originally meant to "strike down, crush" but added the meaning "to occupy land without the owner's permission." Such words have the aura of pioneer days.

Not only did early American settlers add new words to the original stock (*logroll, bullfrog, backwoods,* etc.), but succeeding generations began to export our home-grown terms to British soil. During the first part of this century there was a heavy INFLUX into English of words such as *hobo, graft, cinch,* and *dive*. Movies gave them the first big push, and radio and television followed.

The British, however, are quite capable of holding their own in these exchanges, and there will continue to be a wide difference between the language as it is spoken over there and the American version. A British businessman, for example, calls bonds DEBENTURES. He gives his employees not a raise in salary but a "rise." A soft snap (or a "breeze") is a cushy job. In advertising a billboard becomes a HOARDING.

There are novel words for items of ordinary living. The American in London must not look for an apartment but for a "flat" or for a "service flat" if he wants maid service. He goes up, not in an elevator, but in a "lift." If he forgets the key to his "flat," it would do him no good to try to climb in through the TRANSOM, for in British NOMENCLATURE that means the horizontal bars across a door—or window—top; what we call a transom is a "fanlight." An American porch-climber or second-story man is a "cat burglar." For dinner you have a "sweet"—the MASQUERADE for dessert; the "biscuits" served at tea-time are neither hot nor are they biscuits in our sense; they are what we call cookies.

There are also terms for common objects that differ in British and American. A British bride, joining her American husband in New York, starts out on a shopping tour. She has on her list: a dustbin, a scent-spray, a tin-opener, a washing-up bowl, a spanner, and minerals. She first draws a blank when she asks for these items from a clerk in a chainstore (she thinks of it as a "multiple shop"). After explaining her needs, she finally piles into the baby carriage ("pram" to her) a garbage can, an ATOMIZER, a can opener, a dishpan, a monkey wrench, and some ginger ale and bottled soda—these last-named items are the "minerals."

If she goes into a garage, she learns that "PETROL" is "gas" in American; a "gear lever" is a "gearshift"; an ACCUMULATOR is a "storage battery." If she buys something on credit, she learns to say, "Charge it, please," rather than to have it "put down." "Porridge" is "oatmeal"; "tart" is "pie"; a "BARROW" is a "pushcart."

Here are a few more more Briticisms alongside their American equivalents:

| | |
|---|---|
| booking-hall | ticket office |
| breakdown lorry | tow car |
| dust-up | row (argument) |
| disallowed | forbidden |
| matey | friendly |
| lead one up the garden path | deceive him |
| nosey-parker | snoop |
| hire-purchase system | installment-plan buying |
| underground | subway |
| subway | underground pass |
| freight car | goods wagon |
| conductor | guard |
| ticket agent | booking clerk |

To realize how far American slang differs from British, you need only imagine a Britisher (of the type of Wodehouse's Bertie Wooster) describing the American scene:

American night clubs are extraordinary places. I dropped into one where they had an outsized girl as "chucker-out." The place was full of young ladies "dressed up to the nines"—I should hazard a guess they were models. When a bloke at the next table began a bit of "badinage," I couldn't think of any "retorts," and I'm afraid they thought I was a bit of a "duffer." I really felt a perfect "mug." One of the girls held out a little WHIRLIGIG device, and said, "Don't fool around with the thingamajig, Daddy-O." My American escort told me that meant, "Don't mess up the works, fella," but I don't know what he meant, either. Dashed odd, what?

His American escort should have told him that a "chucker-out" is a "bouncer"; "dressed up to the nines" is "all dolled up"; "retorts" are "comebacks"; a "duffer" is one who "flubs the dub"; a "mug" is a "square."

## SLANG INTO CANT AND ARGOT

Whether it's a "chucker-out" or a "bouncer," a "mug" or a "square," a "dust-up" or a "row," informal language (slang, colloquialisms, substandard words, etc.) illustrates how ordinary standard words in American or English furnish new and colorful synonyms for all areas of living. A *cowboy*, in police terms, becomes a reckless driver; in underworld argot a *cowboy* is the leader of a mob. A *flap* means a "rumble" or fight between rival street gangs; or it may mean a "noisy party" to teen-agers. Slang phrases formed from standard words give us vivid equivalents for criminal activities; for teen and beatnik talk; and for the whole range of the amusement world— circuses, carnivals, gambling joints, racetracks, movies, theaters, radio and television studios, music publishing and recording. Politics also adds to the slang lexicon. Various crafts, trades, and professions contribute, and that catchall occupation, business, has its own word lore. At this point, slang often verges on jargon: the "trade lingo" or shoptalk of a particular occupational group.

## SLANG INTO SHOPTALK

Such shoptalk needs to be explained for the layman. The terms employed are often legitimate words, but most dictionaries label them "technical" or "scientific," or break them down into specific fields. If used in speaking or writing intended for the general public, such words call for UNOBTRUSIVE translation in the text. But they are constantly shuttling over into standard use, and they are so important a factor in adding to the growing English vocabulary that they call for special treatment. It is the *technical terms* in TRANSIT that concern us in our own vocabulary-building.

# Literary Words Quiz

Most of the missing words are keys to cultural history. Many of them appear in classical quotations in that most literary of dictionaries, the *Oxford English Dictionary* (OED). You'll find the names of several writers and fictitious characters in the Word List.

1. Demosthenes delivered many a _____ (bitter speech) against Philip of Macedon.
2. The ironic old Greek who was Plato's mentor used the method of debate which is named after him. This word is quoted in the OED: "But there are three sorts of disputation, . . . which are distinguished by these three names, namely, _____, forensic, and academic."
3. Again from the OED: "To _____ with him! Is the man growne mad?" The word now means "mad confusion" but at one time it referred to a lunatic asylum.
4. A prophetess of doom in Greek tragedy was _____. Now any female given to PROGNOSTICATION may be called one.
5. _____ was a self-adulator who gazed admiringly at his own reflection in the pool.
6. "All these receive their Birth from other Things; But from himself the _____ only springs: Self-born, begotten by the Parent Flame In which he burn'd, Another and the Same." (OED)
7. Here is a quotation from the OED that uses the adjectival form of a name that belonged to a wily political manipulator: "*Divide et regna* [divide and rule] is an old _____ maxim and trick."
8. Who was the METAPHYSICIAN who believed in the doctrine of Creative Evolution?
9. Who is the "foxy schemer who outfoxes himself; the biter who gets bit"? A quotation in the OED mentions ". . . windings, intrigues and nimble diversions."
10. A _____ian character is one who is fat, jolly, and given to hearty self-enjoyment.
11. The OED describes the kind of person who is possessed of this one of the four bodily humours: "Cold and _____ must he be who is not warmed into admiration by the surrounding scenery."
12. An American humorist of the 19th century was _____ _____.
13. "Slang is often impromptu; it gives the effect of _____."
14. The "bones" is a word that goes back to 1386, when it was used in the writings of Geoffrey _____.
15. "His collection of slang locutions is fearful and wonderful." (An

288

American short story writer in his prime at the turn of the century.)
16. He wrote about Broadway characters and used the historical present.
17. Damon Runyon's characters, who are on the fringe of the gangster world, have a style of speech, or _____, all their own.
18. A piece of writing that combines different styles may be called a _____.
19. What was a substandard word in use around 1837 that means "get lost"?
20. What is an Annie Oakley?
21. "Bunk" comes from the missing word in the following quotation from the OED: "The philosopher is tempted to talk a good deal of what we may call scientific '_____.'"
22. An attitude that is impractically romantic could be called _____, after the name of Cervantes' hero.
23. A _____ is a person of materialistic bent, insensitive to art and literature.
24. A _____ was a Spartan serf.
25. An unflinching attitude is described as _____, a word taken from the Greek philosophy that preached indifference to pain.
26. When Caesar crossed the _____ (a river between Italy and Gaul), he took an irrevocable step. From the OED: "Giving her to understand . . . that she had passed the _____; that she had taken such a step of her own accord."
27. Another quotation in the OED refers to a German composer of operas: "Richter's great superiority to Herr Levi as a _____ian conductor."
28. "The plain, or _____ian chant, is where the choir and people sing in unison, or all together in the same manner." (OED)
29. Who was the Assyrian Byron wrote about who "came down like the wolf on the fold"?
30. What ardent feminist had the head of John the Baptist cut off because he scorned her?

WORD LIST

| | | | |
|---|---|---|---|
| Herod | the real McCoy | Sennacherib | Machiavellian |
| Milton | O. Henry | Falstaffian | phaeton |
| Bergson | gypsy | egotist | philippic |
| Wagnerian | philatelic | Socratic | Gregory |
| choleric | helot | improvisation | paraphrase |
| Rubicon | Phoenix | bunco | argot |
| skiddoo | bastille | sanguine | quixotic |
| beldam | Mark Hellinger | Artemus Ward | hellion |
| quisling | Meyerbeer | phlegmatic | Tiber |

argumentative    quizzical    Nebuchadnezzar    complimentary
absquatulate    Herodias    buncombe    ticket
George M. Cohan    ingenuousness    stoic    Cassandra
Bedlam    argosy    Adonis    Gregorian
Narcissus    Damon Runyon    philistine    Volpone
Darwin    epicurean    pastiche    Chaucer
   gigantean

## ANSWERS

| | | |
|---|---|---|
| 1. philippic | 11. phlegmatic | 21. buncombe |
| 2. Socratic | 12. Artemus Ward | 22. quixotic |
| 3. Bedlam | 13. improvisation | 23. philistine |
| 4. Cassandra | 14. Chaucer | 24. helot |
| 5. Narcissus | 15. O. Henry | 25. stoic |
| 6. Phoenix | 16. Damon Runyon | 26. Rubicon |
| 7. Machiavellian | 17. argot | 27. Wagnerian |
| 8. Bergson | 18. pastiche | 28. Gregorian |
| 9. Volpone | 19. absquatulate | 29. Sennacherib |
| 10. Falstaffian | 20. complimentary ticket | 30. Herodias |

## SCORING KEY

30 right—Ph.D. in literature and cultural history
27–29 right—Master's degree
23–26 right—B.A. degree
18–22 right—College-freshman level
12–17 right—Average American (Read more widely)
Under 12 right—Substandard (uneducated)

SCORE: _____

# II ~

## How to Enrich Your Vocabulary with Technical Terms from Business, Politics, Labor, and Science

~ The shuttle service which carries some technical terms into standard use is not a one-way train. It takes a return load of common words back to the shop, office, factory, or laboratory. There, like ISOTOPES exposed to ATOMIC pile EMANATIONS, these words radiate new meanings—though they still look just the same.

Take *sport*, for example. How did it come to mean, in biology, a "freak" or "MUTATION"—a sudden departure from type, such as a white or pink elephant? The Latin phrase *lusus naturae* was translated "sport of nature," nature supposedly having its fun by creating such freaks. BIOLOGISTS found the term handy. It gradually lost its humorous connotations; and now "sport," in the sense of a sudden DEVIANT from type, is a proper and sober technical term—and what a stumbling block it is to readers UNVERSED in its scientific sense.

It is these everyday words that have acquired by RADIATION a special technical meaning, that really make trouble. How do translators find an equivalent for KNOW-HOW in French or German? At the International Business Conference at Rye, the problem was solved by going the long way round. *Know-how* was spelled out in the English text in a form that would go into the other fifty languages represented:

Technical knowledge of the tricks of the trade which make it possible to put into mass production new machines, processes, or chemicals by utilizing patents and/or formulas, at the same time eliminating IMPERFECTIONS ("bugs") in the end-product.

That's the technical sense of *know-how* in thirty-nine words. The term, though first in print as a noun in 1935, really came into wide vogue only during World War II. It is now standard in *Webster's*

291

*Third Unabridged* and will probably be with us for a long time. It has made its way, not only in the technical sense, but as a word-of-all-work. A *New York Times* editorial (Nov. 30, 1961) gibing at President Kennedy for using *finalized*, says: ". . . please be careful where you walk, because there may be some loose syntax lying about. Meanwhile, let's invite the cleaners in. They'll have the know-how to get the job finishized."

## MORE VERBAL SHORTHAND: ACRONYMS

There is already a familiar ring to the other verbal shorthand that came out of World War II and is common in all areas today, technical and otherwise. Words such as RADAR and TELERAN are called ACRONYMS: words formed from the first letter or letters of a combination of words.

> loran—LOong-RAnge Navigation
> radar—RAdio Detecting And Ranging
> teleran—TELEvision RAdar Navigation
> sonar—SOund NAvigation Ranging

Acronyms function as time and space savers, as they telescope very long and complex phrases describing even more complex apparatus and processes into short usable words.

Time was that technical lingo ran to long and mouthfilling terms, to impress the layman, and keep amateurs from muscling in. Sixty-four dollar words in high-priced books led to correspondingly high fees. Latinized language was a part of the craft mystery. But modern American TECHNOLOGISTS prefer to use contractions when they can. And it's not only in technology and science that verbal shorthand develops.

## THE VOCABULARY OF ECONOMICS

A. VERBAL SHORTHAND IN BUSINESS

Ours is a business culture, and magazines and books dealing in a professional way with business activities have developed a specialized vocabulary. Many of the terms come from statistics, accounting, or ECONOMICS. Others are ordinary words used in a specialized sense —and these are the tricky ones for the layman.

Of the business terms needed to read *Fortune* and *Business Week* with full understanding, here are twenty-one that are employed in nonbusiness writing in other senses. These are the specialized meanings they have acquired in business usage:

Margin. (a) In accounting, the difference between cost price and selling price, at any level of production or distribution. It is usually expressed as a percentage of the cost price or selling price, depending on the line of trade.

(b) In Wall Street, collateral security, as a percentage of the price paid in money, deposited with a broker to protect him from loss on contracts entered into by him on behalf of his principal. Margin trading is regulated by the Securities and Exchange Commission and the Federal Reserve Board, which may change the percentages required from time to time, raising it to discourage speculation or lowering it when stock prices slump.

Edge. A competitive advantage.

Capacity. Amount a plant can turn out if operated at maximum.

Merger. The absorbing of one business by another. When two equally large or strong businesses merge, this is, strictly speaking, a consolidation.

Potential. The possible as distinct from the actual current production or sales; the theoretical size of a market.

Output. Production—actual amounts of goods turned out.

Liquidation. Settling of accounts and distributing the assets of a corporation or partnership when it is dissolved.

Facilities. Factories or any other plants and productive establishments that produce goods or render services.

Equipment. The machines, furniture, vehicles, etc., that enable a business concern to operate.

Tools. Short for machine tools, and for the ANCILLARY devices such as powered screwdrivers, drills, cutting edges, etc., which do the actual work. (This does not mean a workman's kit of small tools, when used in the business sense.)

Subsidy. Payment to a manufacturer, exporter, mine or ship operator, to enable him to compete with more favored ENTERPRISERS, at home or abroad, or payment to an agricultural producer to enable him to keep prices down.

Inventory. Amount and value of goods or parts on hand: to take INVENTORY is to make an exact check on the above.

Index. Ratio between the level of prices, wages, output, or any other MEASURABLE factor at any time or period, and the same factor or factors at a fixed and agreed-upon date or period in the past (see PARITY, page 296). The level during the base period is customarily taken as 100 percent. If you take, as the Bureau of Labor Statistics does, the base period 1957–1959 average for the Consumer Price Index as 100 per cent, and find out how far the figure is above that on a given date, say May, 1963, that percentage increase is the readng of the BLS index. If it stands at 106, then the level of consumer prices, or the "cost of living," is up 6 per cent above the base rate.

Monopoly. Loosely, a degree of control of the market either for buying or selling a given commodity or service, which enables the possessor either to raise the price above that which would exist under free competition, or to exclude others from the market, etc. Legally the degree of control that constitutes monopoly is whatever the courts say it is under the Sherman Antitrust Act and the Clayton Act. When Wilson Mizner used to ask, if anybody made him a business proposition, "Where's the monopoly in it?" he meant what is the inside track or exclusive feature that will give a half-Nelson on the market. The law rightly grants an inventor, author, or composer a monopoly on his intellectual property for a certain number of years. Even in the case of patents, which are a LEGALIZED monopoly, or pooled copyrights, the courts will not tolerate the use of these monopoly rights to a point where competition is precluded. The holder of a patent, for example, can not require a customer to buy unpatented supplies from him in a "tie-in" sale, when he buys the patented machine.

Absorption. The process by which a seller bears some of the expenses that would ordinarily be passed on to the customer. The seller may pay the freight charges, for example, or absorb a price increase by his suppliers.

Discrimination. Granting an advantage, favored treatment, or concession to one buyer that is not given to another. When this injures competition, it is a violation of the antitrust laws.

Stabilization. Keeping price levels steady (stable), particularly during war and its aftermath.

Depreciation. Percentage of initial capital outlay which a business writes off (or is allowed by the Internal Revenue Service to write off) in a given FISCAL year of operation.

Specifications. Bill of particulars fixing the standards that must be met for a given type of industrial or commercial goods; the engineering shorthand which expresses these standard requirements is usually in figures, formulas, or measurements.

Inflation. A relatively rapid increase in prices, brought about by an increase in the supply of money, an artificial shortage of goods (as in wartime), or an increase in costs, such as wages, when demand is high. Without controls, the resulting wage-price spiral may lead to a disastrous drop in the value of money.

294

Float. (a) To arrange for financing for a business operation. For instance, a new corporation might float a stock issue to raise funds, or a businessman might float a loan to meet his money needs.

(b) In banking, the total value of all the checks that have been presented at the receiver's bank, but not yet charged against the payer's account on which they are drawn. At today's volume of business, this amounts to millions of dollars of "free" deposits, and is one of the main reasons for the introduction of magnetic printing and electronic sorting of checks for faster handling.

In addition to these ordinary words used with specialized meanings, the business page has a sizable QUOTA of trade jargon—i.e., words peculiar to business, some of them requiring unobtrusive translation when used in prose addressed to the general reader. (This illustrates the transit service whereby technical terms gradually become common.)

End-product. What finally comes off the assembly line, out of the chemical plant or any other manufacturing setup in a form ready for the buyer.

Set-aside. A part of the total supply earmarked for a special purpose or group, usually by government order. A percentage of government contracts is reserved for small businesses as a set-aside, for example, and producers of critical materials may be required to set aside a share of output for the military services.

Low-end. An adjective describing goods at the bottom of the price range. A maker who specializes in such goods is a *low-end manufacturer*.

Cartel. A combination of two or more business firms or trusts which agree to limit their output, fix prices, and divide the available market between or among them. Loosely, it usually means an international combine to do this kind of market-rigging. This is a European word, and derives originally from the small card or note containing the terms of the agreement.

Royalties. A share of the product, cash income, or profit (as from a mine, forest, etc.) paid to the owner as a form of rent by a user of the property; or a compensation paid to the owner of a patent or copyright for the use of it or the right to act under it.

Cross-licensing (patents). The agreement by patent owners to permit each other to use their patented machines or processes, usually without any payment of royalties.

Weighted Average. In statistics, an average in which the various items are rated according to their relative importance—i.e., before you add you multiply each item first by whatever factor is necessary to give the right weight to each, and then add up the column as thus modified, and divide by the sum of the weights to get the weighted average.

Bottleneck. A place or point where a log-jam or block forms in the even flow of materials, parts, paper work, or finished goods, thus holding up production or distribution.

Allocation. Assignment of shares to each user of materials or facilities; the enforcement of sharing according to some recognized principle of division, such as past usage, during a period of scarcity.

Reconversion. Transformation back to peacetime production of plants and facilities converted for war purposes. Also used, inexactly, to denote transformation of new war facilities for peacetime use.

Tie-in (sales). An enforced arrangement under which the customer has to take an item he doesn't need or want, or can get cheaper elsewhere, in order to get another he does want.

Parity. A calculated ratio between the prices paid by farmers for the things they buy, and the prices received by farmers for the crops and livestock they sell. Various farmer subsidies depend on the parity ratio, which is based on an index of farm prices and a special price index of goods and services, both with the same base.

Basing point. The geographic location on which shipping costs are determined for certain commodities, no matter what the actual point of origin, and hence on which the price quotation is based. Detroit is the basing point for most automakers' prices, so that whether the car you buy is made in Detroit or is assembled somewhere else, the price is figured as if it had been shipped from Detroit. When a single manufacturer uses one basing point for his several plants, what he does is merely logical, but when several competing manufacturers agree to use a single basing point regardless of where they are located, their action is illegal.

Durable goods. Stuff that will last—usually applied to such producer goods as tools and machinery; and to such consumer items as autos, refrigerators, and the like, which take some time to wear out.

Nondurable goods (soft goods). Things that are consumed in use, or wear out rapidly. These include such consumer items as food, soap, etc., and such industrial items as fuel, lubricants, chemicals, and so forth. Between hard goods and soft goods there is a "gray area" category of semidurable goods, such as clothing, light bulbs, etc., which are classed with nondurables in the statistics.

Write-off. The act of removing an item, such as a bad debt or an obsolete machine, from the asset accounts by reducing its value to zero and making a balancing entry in a loss account.

Stockpile. A reserve supply of goods or materials against future emergencies, such as the inability to import during a war period. The federal government maintains stockpiles of critical materials, particularly defense materials, against such emergency possibilities.

296

Marginal. Term descriptive of an enterprise so near the line of UNECO-
NOMIC operation that it would be the first to fold if times got any
tougher; small farmers with poor land and meager equipment are "marginal" farmers; mines profitable to operate only with a public subsidy,
below a certain world or controlled market price for their metal, are
marginal mines.

Bullish. Optimistic; looking toward a rising stock market and a bigger take.

Bearish. Antonym of bullish. Bears cash in on a downward trend by selling
short.

AMORTIZATION. Gradual reduction of debt, such as a mortgage, for the
purpose of extinguishing it; the annual rate of reduction is usually stated
in percentage.

B. FROM BUSINESS TO ECONOMICS

For the following list of terms, which include some of those defined
above, and in addition terms from economics proper, write out your
own definitions, and check them with the desk dictionary you have at
hand. Then see how far you can sight-read the connected passage
below the list, noting down any blackouts of meaning which you experience in the case of the italicized words.

| | | | |
|---|---|---|---|
| annuity | cost of production | internal revenue | production |
| automation | credit | labor | profit |
| amortization | currency | land nationaliza- | profiteering |
| balance of pay- | customs duties | tion | purchasing power |
| ments | direct taxation | Malthusian | *rentier* |
| bank | distribution of | margin | sales tax |
| bimetallism | wealth | market | single tax |
| boycott | division of labor | Marxism | socialism |
| business | economics | medium of ex- | speculation |
| capital | excess-profits tax | change | supply |
| capital gains | Federal Reserve | money | syndicalism |
| clearing house | system | monopoly | tariff |
| collateral | finance | option | taxation |
| commerce | gold standard | paper money | tontine |
| communism | indemnity | personal property | trades unions |
| consumption | input-output | tax | trusts |
| cooperation | interest | private property | vested interests |
| corporations | | | wealth |

Karl Marx calls his brand of *socialism* "scientific," to distinguish
it from the so-called "rationalistic" socialism of Saint-Simon, Robert
Owen, and others. The *Utopian,* or rationalistic socialism, draws a pic-

ture of an ideal society whose members behave "reasonably," so that unhappiness and injustice are banished. This, of course, presupposes a radical change in human nature, and belongs, therefore, to the realms of fancy. *Marxism*, on the contrary, is devoid of idealistic coloring; it merely states that the *private capitalistic system* is breaking down, and that the next step in *social evolution* must inevitably be a *collective ownership* of the means of *production* by the *proletariat*. *Socialists* say that *labor* creates all values. As values, goods are nothing but crystallized work, and are worth the number of hours of work that has gone into their production. The cost of work is determined by the wages of labor. Under capitalistic systems, wages are minimal, hence the value of what a worker produces is in excess of what he gets for it. This is *surplus value* and constitutes the profit of the employer. The fact that part of this surplus value goes to pay *ground-rent, middleman's cost*, etc., does not bother Marx, for, he says, it makes no difference how many members of the *bourgeoisie* split the profit—the worker is cheated of what is due him. The antagonism between the *bourgeois* and the *proletarian*, arising from the former's self-interest and injustice, Marx calls the *class struggle*, and regards it as the basis for his *economic* interpretation of history. As the gulf between the employer and the worker increases, and as the latter comes to the realization of his desperate position, a violent upheaval becomes inevitable, the proletarian revolts, dispossesses and destroys the bourgeois, and gathering all property into his hands, creates a *communistic* state. Under *communism*, the means of production are common property, and production and *distribution* of goods is in the hands of the government consisting of workers. How far has this theory been borne out in practice in Russia?

C. MANAGEMENT SPEAKING

Besides these general terms of business and economics, there are several areas of business activity which have developed specialized vocabularies of their own. Management-labor relations figure largely in the business picture. So do owner-management-executive relations. Vance Packard in *The Pyramid Climbers* describes how the depersonalizing of the corporation man is reflected in such terms as "managerial lag" (where can we find the ideal executive?); "age-position relationship" (does his CHRONOLOGICAL age match his position-level?); "geographical FLEXIBILITY" (can he sell his home and relocate at a moment's notice without losing his equilibrium?); "executive front" (is he the tall, slim Anglo-Saxon type who is physically the ideal executive?); "personal inventory" and "cultural-values" tests (can he periodically pass psychological tests that show if he has deviated from the executive norm?). Does he score high (but not uncomfortably high) in "togetherness" and "motivation"? Does he have the ideal "corporate wife"? Are his children "corporate brats"? Is he, in Packard's words, a "well-packaged executive"? Does he belong at top-level, middle-level, or low-level management?

This terminology tells us a good deal about our corporate culture. The new office buildings in Manhattan are an enclave of modern castles that house the lords and ladies of our business ELITE. But membership in this nobility is not easily won or kept; it demands a rigid kind of initiation and a constant loyalty check. The picture emerges of a tall, slim, blond, and bland type who allows himself to be moved about as a pawn on a chessboard. He has the intelligence of a college graduate and a degree to match from the proper university; he is more than just a well-oiled cog in a machine because he knows what the functions of the other cogs are and he approves of the total operation; and his emotions are just vital enough for him to care about the operation but not strong enough for him to be more than casually involved in anything else.

A psychological tester's EVALUATION of one executive is a good example of corporate gobbledygook:

> [He has] the capacity to utilize his high
> level of intelligence without interference
> from internal or external emotional factors.

In brief (to quote Packard), he can be objective.

### D. LABOR LINGO

The lingo of labor unions goes back a long way in our history and tells us something about the struggles of immigrants who came to a land of opportunity to find dignity and security. There's a good deal of humor in this story, revealed in the jargon terms of special trades. The aura of the "old country" surrounds words such as *schneiders* and *kluppers* or the German word for beer-time in the brewery trade —*beer-schiessen*. Bricklayers gibe at a poor craftsman by giving him the label of "barber," "boot," or "cobbler." Mortar and cement are called "mud." A carpenter who is inefficient at his trade is a "bull-staller." When he's working up high he's "riding the air."

299

The other side of the coin is not a pretty one; it shows a picture of violence and bloodshed. Terms such as "goons," "rats," "nobles," and "finks" describe the strong-armed plug-uglies hired in the past for "strikebreaking" and "union-busting." The fact that words and phrases used in labor-management relations today suggest conference tables and not guns and knives is an indication of how times change. More in evidence today are the sweeter-sounding *escalation clause, incentive bonus plan, arbitration, Wagner Act.*

All is not sweetness and light, however. There are still *slowdowns* —i.e., the workers, while they stay on the job and exhibit the appearance of busyness, are really *soldiering.* And employers often accuse workers engaged in a slowdown of "stretching out the work" to make it last longer. As unionists use the term STRETCH-OUT, however, it has almost exactly the opposite sense. The *stretch-out* on an assembly line implies a *speed-up,* to get more unit production per man without any corresponding pay increase. This is an excellent illustration of shift of meaning by transference (see page 186). It all depends on the point of view from which you look at a given piece of work, whether it's "stretching it out" or a *stretch-out.*

Despite the occasional strained relations between employer and union, working conditions in general have improved IMMEASURABLY since the days of the sweatshop and child labor. Now, however, AUTOMATION (the process of making completely automatic certain mechanical and clerical operations that once involved human labor and judgment) casts a shadow over the future of workers in many areas of the economy.

E. THE CASE OF FEATHERBEDDING

An ironic commentary on our business culture is the existence of FEATHERBEDDING: spreading jobs by limiting the amount of work a man may do in a shift, or requiring the employer to pad the payroll with extra jobholders. This practice has arisen in most cases because of what economists call *technological unemployment,* which is the result of automation.

The origin of a word, the background of its usage, and the way it is defined and labeled in a dictionary are SIGNPOSTS in the direction of cultural history. The story of featherbedding as described in a paragraph in the *Dictionary of American Slang* is a capsule record of labor, economics, science, warfare, and SEMANTICS in the last hundred years.

*featherbed v.i. 1* To loaf; to work halfheartedly; to seek easy tasks. *Some c 1850 use.* → 2 To create extra and unnecessary work in order to earn more money; to demand work for unnecessary employees. 1956: "Featherbedding clauses in labor agreements call for such things as the extra man in a diesel locomotive and standby musicians at a recorded program. This word goes back to the American frontier army in the 1850's. A soldier who had a soft touch was called a featherbed soldier. Hence, a job with little or no work is a featherbed job." *Labor's Special Language from Many Sources.*

This definition is, of course, a loaded one, not because the writers of the *Dictionary of American Slang* have any bias for or against labor (their job is merely to report what is being said), but because a dictionary of slang must record the connotations implied by slang terms, which are mostly derisive and derogatory. The writers of the *Dictionary of American Slang* are merely giving us the history of the word and the attitude of those who use it in its slang sense.

The dictionaries that are not confined to special kinds of vocabularies such as slang and jargon do not label featherbedding as slang anymore. But they are still faced with the problem of definitions and the semantic overtones of language. *The American College Dictionary,* for example, calls featherbedding "a type of coercion . . . by a labor union. . . ." *Webster's Seventh New Collegiate Dictionary* skillfully avoids EDITORIALIZING by defining it as "the requiring of an employer usually under a union rule or safety statute to pay more employees than are needed or to limit production." Thus do words semantically sting or soothe.

The classic example of featherbedding is the situation of the railroads, which are now fighting for survival in their competition with the trucking industry and the airlines. With the gradual introduction of diesel engines, featherbedding came to be an accepted practice and spread to other industries. The musicians union, alarmed by the advent of canned music, demanded featherbedding. In most cases automation was the culprit. In some areas, such as the legitimate theater, featherbedding became a convenient device for creating jobs that an enterprise might not be able to afford.

Featherbedding is a word that has left the closed area of labor-management relations to become a term that impinges upon many aspects of the culture. So much can be packed in a word: the fight for survival of men who must support themselves and their families, regardless of the RELENTLESS logic of science and automation; the plea

301

of ENTREPRENEURS such as railroad executives and theatrical producers that costs must not go beyond the point of successful business operation; the IMPARTIALITY, indeed the IMPASSIVITY of engineers whose job it is to advance technology; the indifference of the average person who is too busy about his own concerns to take a stand until his comfort and convenience are threatened by an emergency such as a railroad strike.

And, of course, a word such as featherbedding eventually must have its IMPACT on politicians in an era when labor disputes are peacefully negotiated and ARBITRATED rather than settled by guns and knives, "rats" and "goons."

## THE VOCABULARY OF PUBLIC LIFE

### A. THE LINGO OF POLITICS

Politics, too, has its own lingo. Some of these terms remain within the confines of smoke-filled rooms, some break away and become part of the common vocabulary. Our old-line political vocabulary is too well known to call for much embroidery, except in a few instances. GERRYMANDERING, for example, is REJIGGERING the boundary lines of voting districts to give the party making the shift a majority in the newly outlined area. The process was so labeled by telescoping the surname of Governor Elbridge Gerry of Massachusetts (who in 1812 did the first job of this kind) and the last half of SALAMANDER.

The controversy over our ELECTORAL college system, which has been under public scrutiny in our recent elections, has brought the word more frequently into print. *Time* in its June 21, 1963, issue, writes that one of the objections to the proposal to divide each state into an electoral district is that "state legislatures would be tempted to *gerrymander* electoral districts." *Time* also coined an antonym for the word by calling the rezoning of an area in San Francisco for the purpose of desegregating schools *ungerrymandering*.

Most of us are familiar enough with political cant to recognize:

ward-heeler, graft, pork-barrel legislation, political fence-mending, lobbying, pressure groups, farm bloc, labor block, oil lobby, majority (minority) whip, Gallup Poll, nepotism.

And in recent years we have been hearing a great deal of discussion about the "right wing" of the Democratic party and the "left wing" of the Republicans. We have had the "New Deal" of Roosevelt, the "Fair Deal" of Truman, and the "New Frontier" of Kennedy. Eisenhower brought in "Modern Republicanism." There is the "radical right" composed of those cheerleaders for the nineteenth-century pioneer spirit, whose very literate and persuasive spokesman is William F. Buckley, Jr., of the *National Review*.

Some of these terms have boarded the shuttle and gone into general use. *Graft* is an example. Another is NEPOTISM (giving political jobs to relatives). Meanwhile the shuttle has brought words from other specialized areas into both politics and common use. MAVERICK was originally an unbranded calf; now it means a nonconformist in a political or other group. "Grass roots" was an agricultural term that became a popular political expression. "Brass hats" started with the military, was modified to "brass" and became a fixture in politics and the Pentagon. Now we hear about "top brass" in any organization.

## B. PENTAGONIA

Pentagonia is not a mythical kingdom. It is another name for that "very large five-sided enclave in Washington, D.C." called the Pentagon. Here the brass hats speak a language all their own which can be labeled "jargon" (esoteric language of a class, profession, or cult from the point of view of one unfamiliar with it and confused and baffled by it).

Some of these terms have an INEXORABLE logic. Every husband, henpecked or otherwise, will understand why an officer's wife is called the "chief of staff." The word "flap," which has many meanings in specialized vocabularies, refers in Pentagonese to a problem that must be solved. The Pentagon itself is variously called a "Yogi Palace," a "Puzzle Palace," or other kinds of wordplayful names coined by inhabitants of an enclave.

Other jargon terms have already ventured out into the field. A "bind" as a state of tension is now in the general vocabulary. "Poop sheet" (set of instructions) has made the rounds. A "wheel" is now a "big wheel." Most of these terms have humorous connotations and are part of the private vocabulary of the in-group. When we come to what is known as CHANCELLERY style, however, we are in another area of word usage that is common to all departments in Washington and is a form of "officialese."

Many of the terms referred to as chancellery style, the official jargon of the nation's capitol, came out of the military jargon of World War II, i.e., *deploy, activate, brief*. Madison Avenue's contribution has been to add the now-despised suffixes—*ize, ise*—and thus turn respectable adjectives into not-so-respectable verbs and nouns (depending upon what side of the fence you're on). The classic "finalize" (which has shortened the life of many a lexicographer) is an example.

Here are some of the terms of "officialese" and their colloquial equivalents:

finalize—wind it up
expertise—know-how
classified—off limits
directive—the word
activate—get going
team—the boys
recession—sag in the economy
bipartisanship—political truce between rounds
globalize—think big

brinkmanship—diplomatic cliff-hanging (another of the many *-ship* words)
process—put through the [bureaucratic] wringer
deploy—spread out
implement—carry out
facilitate—cut the red tape
expedite—push through
brief—clue in

# INTERNATIONAL VOCABULARIES

A new kind of vocabulary comes into being when nations talk to each other. The polite euphemistic words of many syllables and classical origin are taken from the files and sent on their mission, with the brass knuckles carefully hidden. One such vocabulary, formerly based on economic theory (see page 298) has become a strange kind of weapon in an ideological war.

## A. COMMIE TALKS TO COMMIE

The lexicon of communism was conceived by Karl Marx to give what he thought was a true picture of politics and economics. Unfortunately for his theory, splinter groups rose, each claiming in the manner of religious DISPUTANTS that it had the key to Marxian gospel. For Americans this interfaith squabbling was of little or no concern. A Commie was a Commie whether he was a Socialist, a Socialist Worker, a Trotskyite, or a member of the American Communist party. Since good times have raided the ranks of these groups and reduced them to skeleton organizations, we haven't had to bother too much about making fine distinctions of doctrine on the domestic scene.

But the battle arena has now shifted. If we were confused by the backbiting of our home-grown radicals, we thought at least we had a clear-cut view of the Communist international conspiracy. According to Marxian dogma, the workers of the world, no matter what their country, form a solid brotherhood, ready to take over when the capitalistic system finally collapses of its own weight. But the conspirators have fallen out among themselves. Nationalism has a way of rearing its ugly head and blurring idealistic TENETS. The conflict between Russia and China has pointed up the fallacy of the Marxian theory. All that is left (not a pun) of brotherly ties between the two countries is the DIALECTIC of MARXISM.

It is grimly amusing to watch these two COLOSSI of communism turn their dialectic upon each other. The tired words and phrases that have been emptied of meaning have become weapons in a word war. Dialectics, if you recall, is a word APPROPRIATED by the Communists for their own use, but it may someday (if not already) be a synonym for ideological gobbledygook.

The *New York Times* of July 15, 1963, gave us a verbal blow-by-blow description of the RECRIMINATIONS that the two Big Brothers of the Communist movement hurled at each other. Here are some EXCERPTS from this INTERNECINE (though bloodless) warfare. The words in italics in the paragraphs under "Racism," "Yugoslavia," and "Communist Parties" belong to the common cant mouthed by the leaders of the two countries:

### RACISM

Chinese: The Soviet leaders are really supporting *colonialism* . . . by refusing to give top priority in *world revolutionary activity* to the national *liberation* struggle in Asia, Africa, and Latin America.

Soviet: The Chinese are actually following a . . . policy having nothing in common with *Marxism-Leninism,* and they are harming the national liberation movement by seeking to divorce it from the *working-class revolutionary movement.*

305

### YUGOSLAVIA

Chinese: Yugoslavia is not a *Socialist* country and the Yugoslav leaders are *capitalist agents.*

Soviet: Yugoslavia is a *socialist* country though its leaders do have some *incorrect ideas.* . . . The Chinese effort to excommunicate the Yugoslavs . . . is precisely what the *imperialists* want.

### COMMUNIST PARTIES

Chinese: The Soviet leaders are trying to rule the *world Communist movement.* . . .

Soviet: The Chinese Communists are deliberately trying to split the world Communists . . .

To help their readers understand what the phrase-making was all about, the *Times* printed a glossary of Communist terms culled from the Soviet party's letter to the Chinese party:

### IDEOLOGICAL TERMS IN RIFT

*Marxism-Leninism*—The doctrines of Marx and Lenin that are differently understood and expounded today by the Soviet and Chinese Communist parties.

*Proletarian internationalism*—Loyalty to the international Communist movement. This was originally the term used for unswerving allegiance to the Soviet Union when it was the only significant Communist-ruled country in the world.

*Moscow declaration of 1957*—An over-all statement of policy agreed to by the 12 Communist parties, excluding Yugoslavia, then holding national political power.

*Moscow statement of 1960*—An over-all statement of policy agreed to by all 81 Communist parties attending a Moscow meeting in November, 1960. (The 1957 and 1960 formulations were compromises between Soviet and Chinese views.)

*Presidium of the Communist party of the Soviet Union*—The top Soviet Communist party policymaking group.

*National liberation movement*—The effort of peoples in a colonial country to gain sovereignty; also the efforts of Communists in formerly colonial countries to overthrow new non-Communist governments.

*Stalin Personality Cult*—The near-worship of Stalin, which occupied the Soviet Union and the world Communist movement at the height of the dictator's reign from the early nineteen-thirties to his death in 1953.

306

*Dictatorship of the Proletariat*—According to Karl Marx, the interval between the overthrow of capitalism and the institution of utopian communism; working-class control over all other classes.

*Program of the Communist party of the Soviet Union*—The blueprint for building an "ideal" Communist society during this generation. It was adopted at the 22d Soviet party Congress in October, 1961.

*Opportunism*—Abandonment of principle to take advantage of any opportunity that may arise.

*Reformism*—Emphasis upon making immediate changes in capitalism rather than upon overthrowing it.

*Revisionism*—The illegitimate alteration of the doctrines of Marx and Lenin. The Chinese accuse the Russians and the Yugoslavs of being "modern revisionists" who have altered, abandoned and betrayed true Marxism-Leninism.

*New York Times,* July 15, 1963

A postcript to the *Times* article was added by Joseph Barry in his *New York Post* column (Aug. 1, 1963):

He [Lenin] is as dead, one might say, as George Washington. His MESSIANISM, his dream—or menace—of a single Communist movement, of a *working class revolution,* is part of the myth but as outmoded as Washington's warning about foreign entanglements . . . Moreover, as Khrushchev cuts loose from foreign Communist entanglements, foreign Communists are cutting loose from the Kremlin. Swedish Communist leader, Hagberg, for instance, told the Moscow conference . . . that the old *Marxist-Leninist* notion of the *dictatorship of the proletariat* belongs to the distant past. . . .

We hope you understand the terms in italics. Both Khrushchev and Mao Tse-tung seem confused by them.

### B. HOW THE UNITED NATIONS TALK TO ONE ANOTHER

The United Nations has no part in the Russia-China controversy, of course, since Red China is not a member. But the UN has its own kind of language which derives from the nature of disputes that arise between its member countries. These terms are mostly self-explanatory, but some of them overlap with those used in the area of diplomacy and with the kind of dialectical jargon exchanged by communist countries—terms such as "racism," "aggressor," "colonialism," etc. UN language, has, however, its own subtle overtones that reflect the essentially diplomatic function of this DELIBERATIVE body. Here is a list of such oft-repeated terms heard in the halls of the UN. They have been taken from several issues of the *U.N. Review:*

| | | |
|---|---|---|
| airspace | self-determination | unilateral |
| summit | aggression | bilateral |
| peaceful coexistence | mediators | multilateral |
| self-containment | sovereignty | draft resolution |
| confrontations | territorial integrity | regrettable incident |
| violation of territory | overflight | relaxation of tension |
| corrigendem | frontier incident | spate of allegations |
| solemn commitments | allegation | categorically denied |

You will recognize some of the terms as Latinized euphemisms intended to ASSUAGE hurt feelings and PACIFY sword-wavers. Among these are "regrettable incident," "overflight," and "frontier incident." Many of the words and phrases such as "allegation," "solemn commitments," and "categorically denied" are overworked and verge on cant. "Self-determination," "territorial integrity," and "sovereignty," for example, are terms that might be used to describe the legitimate aspirations of small nations seeking their places in the sun, but they might also be used by aggressive nations to lend an aura of legitimacy to their unlawful acts. (Some synonyms for *cant* are *hypocrisy* and *sanctimony.*)

C. TRADITIONAL DIPLOMATIC LANGUAGE

Earlier diplomacy used to talk a more elaborate language, though Americans of Theodore Roosevelt's day were perhaps not much concerned with it, confining their verbal inventiveness in this sphere mostly to such varieties as shirt-sleeve, big-stick, black-jack, kid-glove, silk-stocking, petticoat, or dollar diplomacy. And they knew when Teddy Roosevelt was "flying a diplomatic kite," or engineering the filibustering that split Panama off from Colombia. But the top-hat-and-spats school who succeeded the frock coats of the Palmerston era and the knee-breeches-and-ruffles practitioners of Metternich's day had a fairly elaborate code, which still turns up now and then in the history books, or among the attention-getters in *Time's* lexicon.

Diplomatic language is the language of the soft answer carried to its ultimate degree. It is no accident that so many of the traditional exchanges (and even the recent ones) are wrapped in a mantle of

Latin or French. English diplomats, who are masters of their trade, prefer to borrow from classical and romance language sources rather than from the blunt words of their Saxon ancestors. Practiced diplomats must be artists at concealing the true feelings and objectives of the nations they represent.

## Can You Define the Flossier Terms of Diplomacy?

Some of the diplomatic terms below are of the historical variety, others are of more recent vintage. Can you define them?

| | | |
|---|---|---|
| 1. balance of power | 11. mutatis mutandis | 21. force majeure |
| 2. chargé d'affaires | 12. ceteris paribus | 22. rapprochement |
| 3. precedence | 13. de novo | 23. détente |
| 4. the Kremlin | 14. plebiscite | 24. de facto |
| 5. Quai d'Orsay | 15. en rapport | 25. de jure |
| 6. Downing Street | 16. en règle | 26. aide-mémoire |
| 7. persona non grata | 17. quid pro quo | 27. consulate |
| 8. nuncio | 18. ad hoc (reasoning) | 28. embassy |
| 9. sine qua non | 19. sub rosa | 29. ad interim |
| 10. coup d'état | 20. sui generis | 30. entente |

ANSWERS

1. prevention of war by equality of military strength
2. diplomat lower in rank than an ambassador
3. priority in rank; the order observed in rank on state occasions
4. Russian Communist hierarchy
5. French Foreign Office
6. British government or cabinet
7. unacceptable person
8. envoy of the Pope to a civil government
9. absolute prerequisite
10. seizure of power by surprise show of military force
11. allowing for the necessary changes
12. other things being equal
13. anew; once more; again
14. popular vote to choose sovereignty
15. in accord
16. according to rule
17. one thing in return for another
18. for this situation only

19. quietly and confidentially
20. individual; unique
21. overpowering force
22. establishment of a state of cordial relations
23. easing of tensions between nations
24. existing in fact as opposed to what is assumed
25. by right
26. written memorandum of important items of diplomatic communication
27. premises or residence of a consul
28. residence and offices of an ambassador
29. in the meantime; temporary
30. an understanding between nations for a common course of action

The above definitions are for the most part on the discreet, gloves-and-spats side. Here are eight translated into straight-from-the-shoulder, colloquial terms:

3. official pecking order
7. someone who is kicked out of a country and told not to return
9. a necessity
10. military take-over
17. give and take

19. under the table
22. friendship or truce between two countries (often inspired by a desire to get even with a third country)
23. a cooling-off period

If you read the newspapers and popular magazines, you'll recognize several of the terms as being very much alive: *détente, entente, de facto, rapprochement, consulate, embassy,* the *Kremlin, balance of power.* Others have used the shuttle: *sub rosa, en rapport, ad hoc, sine qua non.*

### *FORTUNE* COVERS THE FIELD

Any or all of the technical terms so far covered in the fields of business, politics, and diplomacy, might turn up sooner or later in *Fortune.* There would not be too many in a single issue. Fortune makes a sparing but strikingly effective use of technical terms, drawing on the stock of learned language in just the right measure for emphasis. Its editors and staff writers pride themselves on interweaving economic theory with business practice. For the most part they make the theory serve OPERATIONAL needs; that is,

310

it's put so that businessmen who have the wit can act upon it. To achieve this result, the editors need some technical jargon, which they usually explain unobtrusively in the course of the story; or else they make it come alive by charts, PICTOGRAPHS, or animated diagrams. But the traditional and currently fashionable terms used in economic wrangles, they take for granted as COMPREHENSIBLE to their readers.

*Fortune* believes it appeals to a special type of reader—members of the "elite" class who also are the business leaders. The July, 1963, issue makes this comment under the heading "Some Thoughts About the Readers of *Fortune*": "*Fortune* is talking to the men who manage American business; of their principal advisors, mainly engineers, economists, advertising men, scientists, lawyers, financial specialists. . . . They [people] are accusing *Fortune* of encouraging the *Fortune* reader to think of himself as somebody special. . . . To this opinion *Fortune* cheerfully pleads guilty."

And so we read about an enclave of buildings where the managers of our corporations can insulate themselves from the ugliness of the surrounding landscape. *Fortune* writes about "sophisticated reactors," "sophisticated transmissions," "sophisticated technology," "technological subtlety," "esoteric basic research." Language like this does appeal to the "elite," men with upper-bracket incomes (based on a *Fortune* survey) who pull the strings of our economy but who are not mere hard-driving businessmen. They are, or like to believe that they are, sophisticates; they know what is going on in the world, even though they view events from the standpoint of corporate welfare; and they are widely read. They recognize words from cultural history that appear frequently in *Fortune*—APOCALYPTIC, EBULLIENCE, PERIPATETICS. The last is a happy choice of word to describe Henry Kaiser's companies—they move around a lot—which is a far stretch from Aristotle's students who walked around while listening to the master discourse. Other allusive words and phrases in *Fortune* are "utopian dream" and "ORWELLIAN nightmare." A wild economic "hayride" is described as a WALPURGISNACHT (a witches' Sabbath orgy with the devil presiding, on the eve of May 1).

Sometimes the language is prosaic, other times it is colorful, depending on the subject matter or the contributing writer. Articles on business and technology tend to be on the dry and matter-of-fact side. A description of the changing face of Manhattan sometimes verges on the LYRICAL: ". . . the grid grows like a magic crystal. The power structure for MEGALOPOLIS is mapped and plotted . . .

last architectural testament . . . pink terrazzo plaza . . ." Occasionally the writer goes overboard with ". . . a Japanese employee's
heart belongs to his corporate daddy"; "extra-territorial executive
AMENITY"; "GUSTATORY business hideout"; "bucking antlers like elk
in heat"; "hot breath of the atom."

But these are minor and infrequent lapses. *Fortune's* articles reveal a depth of background in all aspects of our business and technological culture and make it a valuable source for anyone who wishes
to enrich his vocabulary.

### Can You Sight-Read *Fortune*?

Jot down rough definitions of the following thirty terms from *Fortune*
and add labels to indicate to which field each belongs—business, economics, labor, physics, plastics, etc.

| | | |
|---|---|---|
| 1. transistor | 10. motivation research | 19. electroluminescence |
| 2. satellite | 11. discretionary income | 20. polystyrene |
| 3. chlorophyll | 12. stockpiling | 21. space probes |
| 4. stereophonic | 13. guidelines | 22. Project Mercury |
| 5. disposable income | 14. escalation | 23. exurbs |
| 6. polymer | 15. fiberglass | 24. liquidity |
| 7. bevatron | 16. thermoelectricity | 25. diversification |
| 8. ultrasonics | 17. payload | 26. kitsch |
| 9. paperbacks | 18. G.N.P. | 27. haute cuisine |

### ANSWERS

1. See page 315. *Electronics.*
2. a) A heavenly body that revolves around a planet. *Astronomy.*
   b) A country dominated by another. *International relations.*
3. Green colored material in plants essential to photosynthesis. *Biology.*
4. See page 317. *Electronics.*
5. Total income of an individual available for savings and consumer
   goods. *Economics.*
6. A synthetic chemical compound composed of long chains of identical
   molecules. *Chemistry, plastics.*
7. A type of atom smasher capable of accelerating protons to extremely
   high energy levels. *Physics.*
8. Science dealing with the properties of sound above the audible range.
   *Physics.*
9. Paper-covered books. *Publishing.*

312

10. A branch of psychological investigation concerned, among other things, with consumer behavior. *Psychology, business.*
11. Income available for luxury items. *Economics.*
12. Building up of a reserve supply of something. *Business, government.*
13. An indication or outline of future policy or conduct. *Business, government.*
14. An adjustment of prices or wages to compensate for a rise in cost of materials or cost of living, etc. *Labor, economics.*
15. Glass in fibrous form. *Chemistry.*
16. Electricity produced by direct action of heat. *Electronics.*
17. Cargo of a rocket; the explosive charge in the warhead of a missile. *Astronautics.*
18. Gross national product: the total value of goods and services produced in a country during a given period (usually a year). *Economics.*
19. Light resulting from a discharge of high-frequency current through a gas or a layer of phosphor. *Electronics.*
20. Rigid, transparent plastic molded into products of all sorts. *Plastics.*
21. See page 336. *Astronautics.*
22. Manned orbital flight training program. *Astronautics.*
23. See footnote on page 153. *Sociology.*
24. The degree to which an individual or a business can meet its liabilities without selling off fixed assets. *Business, economics.*
25. The process of spreading out and placing personal or corporate interests and assets in several areas. *Business, economics.*
26. Tawdry literary or artistic efforts. *Literary.*
27. Fancy food. *French.*

## SHOPTALK IN TECHNOLOGY AND SCIENCE

There are two kinds of technical and scientific words that shuttle over into general use. First: names for objects, processes, or phenomena for which there are no other terms available, so the scientists have had to invent labels. Many of these are familiar.

Nobody would be surprised by the word CAFFEINE, or by NICOTINE; *thein* and *theobromine,* ALKALOIDS in tea, are not so familiar. GLUCOSE has made its way into general use, in more ways than one; but *fructose* and *galactose,* other special forms of sugar, are not so commonly known; nor do we all realize that the familiar CELLULOSE, from which RAYON and a host of other products are made, is composed of sugar MOLECULES.

It's not surprising that when a technical term shuttles over into general use, most of us have only a very hazy notion of its exact scientific meaning. Hence the case for some systematic work on vocabulary in this field. We can't hope to learn all the new technical terms: what we want are those that are on their way into the common stock. These names of concrete objects, processes or phenomena we can always look up, just as we do the names of spare parts or new items of hardware, or new birds or flowers or insects.

But the second kind of scientific label that makes its way into the general vocabulary is CHARACTERISTICALLY a technical term that lends itself to FIGURATIVE use, in a PICTURESQUE extension of meaning based on its original scientific sense, but not identical with it. *Allergic* is an example. Psychoanalysis has given us such terms as PHOBIA, for an habitual fixed fear, and *complex,* for a deep-set cluster of emotional associations; REPRESSION and TRANSFERENCE; PROJECTION and SUBLIMATION (though this term was already known in connection with ASCETIC self-denial and the search for ways to transform LIBIDO into art, music, poetry, or mystical ECSTASY). And since the shuttle is always making a return trip, it has brought REINFORCEMENT from general into specialized use in psychology.

When it's a problem of acquainting ourselves with the full meaning of some fundamental term of pure science, often we need to associate it with a picture, or a memory of some crucial experiment. What does the term ELECTROMAGNETISM mean to you? You will think straight off of motors, dynamos, and other devices that depend on electromagnetic action. But it will help to recall the simple basic experiment that underlay all of Edison's and Steinmetz's inventions in this field. When Michael Faraday moved one pole of a magnet through a looped coil of wire with its ends attached to a sensitive device (a GALVANOMETER) that registered ELECTROMOTIVE force, he found that where the wire loop thus cut a magnetic field, electric current was induced in the wire. This discovery laid the way for the whole development of electromagnetism.

## ELECTRONICS

ELECTRONICS, too, is a word to conjure with; along with ATOMIC energy, PLASTICS, SILICONES, the light metals, ASTRONAUTICS, and jet propulsion, it has ushered in a new age that is beginning to transform TERRESTRIAL life and that promises exciting adventures in outer space.

314

The term *electronics* derives from the behavior of a SUBATOMIC particle called the electron. By directing the energy of the electron through the vacuum tube and the TRANSISTOR, it has been possible to send rockets to Venus, to send and receive visual images through the atmosphere, to reproduce sound throughout its range, and to construct devices that can perform mathematical feats of which the mind is not capable. Electronics has been responsible for the MUSH- ROOMING [1] of industries such as television, radio, sound recording, for devices such as electronic computers (known also as "electronic brains" or "thinking machines") and for revolutionary advances in other commercial fields. It has also been the basis of new techniques in medicine, particularly surgery.

Recent technological progress, especially in astronautics, has been characterized by a trend toward MINIATURIZATION: reduction of components to the smallest possible size. This process has implications for every scientific venture, governmental or commercial. Smaller components mean more efficient rockets and missiles capable of lifting greater payloads both for military purposes and in our attempt to reach other planets. Small components are a boon to the radio and television equipment manufacturers, who are always concerned with reducing the size of their products, whether they are to be used in a studio or in an apartment. And if tinier and more sophisticated parts are available in machines, industry as a whole can function more efficiently and economically.

The key component in the trend toward miniaturization is the transistor, a blend word formed from two words, *transfer* and *resistor*. The transistor's function is to *trans*fer a signal across a re*sistor*. Transistors can replace vacuum tubes in most circuits. Some computers now in operation are entirely TRANSISTORIZED and are much smaller and cooler in operation than earlier vacuum tube models.

The transistor is one of several *solid-state* devices designed not only to be smaller than the components it replaces but to increase the reliability and sensitivity of the electronic equipment in which it is used. Other solid-state devices are *crystal diodes, masers, magnetic amplifiers, magnetic memory units,* and *parametric amplifiers.*

---

[1] *Mushrooming* is an example of a word that is common in its original sense but less common in its extended meaning. As a food, it is well within the under-10,000 range. As a verb meaning "to grow rapidly," it is less often in print.

## ELECTRONIC COMPUTERS

New terminology has come out of the field of electronic computers. There are two kinds of "thinking machines": *analogue computers* and *digital computers*. Digital computers use numbers to perform their COMPUTATIONS; this type of computer is the INTEGRAL unit in *electronic data processing* (EDP)—the storage of records and mathematical calculations necessary in business transactions. Analogue computers work out specific problems. For instance, when it is not practical to carry out a physical experiment, an analogue computer can be built to simulate electronically the mechanical system. Information required by computers is usually charted by a *programmer*, who also interprets computer language. Sometimes data is in such form that it cannot be read directly by the computer; a *transducer* changes it into a form that a computer understands. In aircraft and missile design, for example, physical data obtained from testing stresses and strains is converted by the transducer into digital form.

Many words in general use have become part of computer terminology—"digit," "character," "bit," "number." Technical phrases are "binary code," "alphanumberic characters," and "memory units" (devices for storing information magnetically in "tapes," "discs," "cores," and "drums").

Associated with the field of electronic computers is that of CYBERNETICS, a science that makes comparisons in structure and function between living organisms and complicated machines such as computers. "Thinking machines" have electrical circuits similar to the NEUROLOGICAL connections in human beings; they are capable of far more complex operations in some areas than a living brain can perform. They will still be machines, however, under the control of human minds and hands, until the day that the cyberneticists discover how the machines can be wired for feeling and reflection as well as calculation.

## GUIDED MISSILES

Electronic computers also figure largely in the terminology of guided missiles. An *inertial guidance system* keeps long-range missiles on their flight course. The *electronic brain* in the missile follows PREDETERMINED instructions stored within it and interprets instructions sent from the *launching site*. The guidance system may be *preset*, so that an *automatic pilot* merely steers the missile to its target. In *command guidance*, a human pilot on the ground sends out instructions with the aid of ground radar and an electronic computer.

Although many guided missiles have been designed for use in war, many have been and will continue to be used for peaceful purposes. The successful Mariner II flight to Venus (to be described later) was a triumph for the electronic age, a giant step forward in our plan to unravel the mysteries of outer space.


## THE JARGON OF HI-FI

The latest development in the field of high-fidelity sound is *stereo* (short for *stereophonic*), a Greek word meaning "solid." The sound that is recorded and reproduced gives the feeling of depth; it is transmitted through two microphones and heard through two speakers. *Super-stereo* will involve sound images recorded from several angles and picked up by several speakers STRATEGICALLY placed.

The specialized vocabulary of *hi-fi* includes the *enclosure* that houses the speaker or speakers; the *woofer* and *tweeter* (onomato-poetic names), two types of speakers that reproduce the "lows" and "highs" respectively of the sound range; the *coaxial* and *triaxial* speakers that combine woofer and tweeter; the *wow* and *flutter* (more onomatopoeia) of distorted sounds; the *pre-amp* (preamplifier) and *amp* (amplifier) that build up the sound signal before it goes into the speaker; the *cartridge*, a transducer that converts the mechanical energy of a record into electrical signals; and the *turntable, tone arm, tuner, tape recorder.*


## PLASTICS GLOSSARY

*The American College Dictionary* defines *plastics* as "any of a group of synthetic or natural organic materials which may be shaped when soft and then hardened, including many types of resins, renoids, polymers, cellulose derivatives, casein materials, and proteins." There are two main types of plastics: *thermoplastics,* which will soften when heated and harden when cooled; and *thermosetting* plastics, which set into final and IRREVOCABLE form on the application of heat and pressure.

Plastics are molded by EXTRUSION: forcing molten thermoplastic material through a shaping die to form continuous sheets, rods, and special shapes. Another way of shaping is by LAMINATION (from Latin *lamina,* a thin plate, scale, or layer of metal). PLIES of material are alternated with layers of plastic RESINS, stacked between highly polished steel plates, and subjected to high heat and pressure until cured, i.e., made strong and durable.

One group of plastics is the *synthetic fibers,* which have revolutionized the apparel industry. The first synthetic fiber was prepared from CELLULOSE, the purest base for textile materials such as cotton and linen. Through the process of *polymerization* (artificial linking of molecules) plastic fabrics such as NYLON have been produced in the laboratory. Nylon, made out of *polyamides,* is actually the family name for a whole series of thermoplastics having great strength and toughness. Other synthetic fibers are the *acrylics* (orlon, acrilan, dynel) and the *polyesters* (Dacron, Kodel, and Teron).

Other plastics produced from *high polymers* (heavy molecules) are the *polyethylenes* and *polypropylenes,* which are taking over the functions of metals. Insulating materials have been made available such as FIBERGLASS. Linoleum and asphalt tiles have been replaced in part by VINYL plastics. *Polystyrene* is used to make synthetic rubber. There is literally no limit to the kinds of plastics coming into the market and to their uses in industry.


## SILICONE TERMINOLOGY

One of the oldest known families of plastics, the SILICONES (rhymes with "chilly bones"), developed in their fundamentals almost sixty years ago, were abandoned as of little practical utility by the boys looking for an honest dollar. World War II, however, brought them back into the picture, and they represented an important technological advance.

Silicones are designed as water-REPELLENT and heat-resistant lubricants. They are semiorganic compounds, half-brothers to the organic materials for which they can do more than pinch-hit. They are not devised by atom-splitting. Rather, some slick chemist figures out a way to CAJOLE one of the *hydrocarbon-ring* molecules into rearranging its internal housekeeping so that it throws out one of its carbon atoms and lets a silicon atom move in. Actually, the chemist backs some organic compound into a silicon *oxide* or *halide,* and effects the swap. The carbon atom is not left an orphan—it gets a new home, too. But once the little silicon stranger is taken into *his* new family, he sticks as tight as a leech.

The silicon atom is a tough and durable customer. And it is no such rare bird as U-235 or PLUTONIUM. In the form of SILICA (SILICON DIOXIDE, $SO_2$) it forms about three-quarters of the earth's crust—as quartz or sand or rock. No wonder it gives a strong backbone to the new combination into which it enters, making it more stable.

The basic materials from which silicones are made—brine, sand, coal, and air—are cheap and plentiful, and in the long run the price should be competitive. Already several thousand silicones have been SYNTHESIZED. Since almost any organic compound may be reshuffled into a silicone form, the number that can be synthesized depends only on the number of organic compounds available for starters—and their number is legion. Since any organic chemist can play around on paper at discovering a new silicone, and since the properties can be predicted to some degree on a THEORETICAL basis, the possibilities are almost limitless.

### Do You Know the Commonest Technical and Scientific Terms?

Try your hand at the following quiz, devised to test the knowledge of high school and college students who have had only one year's work in general science. If you have read *Popular Science* or *Popular Mechanics,* or have had ABC work in the sciences, you should score 95 out of a hundred. Which of the key words are in current *literary* use?

Instructions: Can you supply the right word for each blank? Use the first letter and the suggestions in PARENTHESES to help you find the ONE word you need. None of the words in parentheses is the one you want. When you have thought of the right word, write it on a sheet of paper numbered to correspond to the blanks in the test.

Example: Scientists prefer to use the m_____ (pertaining to a system of measurement commonly used in the natural sciences) system in physics. Answer: metric.

1. We felt the v_____ (quick motion to and fro) of the engine.
2. The airplane has a greater v_____ (speed) than the automobile.
3. The t_____ (act of sending from one person or place to another) of sound without even the aid of a wire was a great discovery.
4. We have a t_____ (an instrument to measure heat) in the school room to aid us in keeping the room at an even temperature.
5. Brine is a s_____ (preparation made by dissolving a solid in a liquid) of salt and water.
6. The air was s_____ (full of) with the perfume of flowers.
7. The violin string is r_____ (able to return sound).
8. Wool and fur have a r_____ (quality of not yielding to force) against wind and cold.
9. The mirror causes a r_____ (change in the direction of rays of light).
10. We feel the r_____ (emission of rays of light or heat from a center) of heat from the stove.
11. That is a n_____ (medium) tint of blue.
12. The n_____ (unfinished photographic picture) was shown to us before we ordered the pictures finished.
13. A man comes to read the m_____ (an instrument to measure gas) each month.
14. The m_____ (power of attraction) of the lodestone draws many things to it.
15. They used a l_____ (a bar used to sustain a weight at one point of its length) to pry up the board.
16. I_____ (illustrating the distribution of heat) lines connect points on the earth's surface having the same annual temperature.
17. We shall i_____ (separate from other bodies by means of nonconductors) the electric wires.
18. Sand is i_____ (incapable of being dissolved).
19. We did not have i_____ (white or glowing with heat) lights in Benjamin Franklin's time.
20. Water is composed of h_____ (a chemical element) and one other gas.
21. A h_____ (pertaining to fluids in motion) pump was placed in the well.
22. Oregon has much h_____ (moisture) in the air.
23. They will f_____ (use a device for straining liquid) the water at the camp before drinking it.
24. The f_____ (that change of organic substances by which their

starch, sugar, gluten, are broken up and recombined in new compounds) of the grape juice caused it to become wine.

25. Rust causes the e_____ (eating away) of iron.
26. One of the e_____ (an essential ingredient) of the air is argon.
27. There is much e_____ (peculiar condition of the molecules of a body or of the surrounding ether developed by friction, chemical action, heat, or magnetism) in the air tonight.
28. We saw the big d_____ (a machine that converts mechanical into electric energy by rotation of copper wire coils in a magnetic field) that furnishes us with electric power.
29. The d_____ (operation of extracting spirit from a substance) of whiskey from corn and other grains has been legalized.
30. The d_____ (compactness) of iron is greater than air.
31. We will wait for the leaf mold to d_____ (decay).
32. The c_____ (shrinking) of rails on the railroad is caused by the cold.
33. Air is held in a liquid state by c_____ (to bring within narrower limits of space).
34. An automobile has an internal c_____ (development of light and heat accompanying chemical combination) engine.
35. The b_____ (quality of floating) of the balloon enabled it to go a long way.
36. The b_____ (apparatus that is essential to ignition) in an automobile is a new one.
37. The b_____ (an instrument for determining the weight or pressure of the atmosphere) shows there is going to be a storm.
38. Along the coast of Florida, there are many a_____ (wells formed by boring into the earth till the instrument reaches water, which, from internal pressure flows spontaneously like a fountain) wells.
39. We find much a_____ (one of a class of caustic chemical bases, soda, potash, ammonia, and lithia) in eastern Oregon.
40. Vinegar is an a_____ (chemical that is sour, sharp, or biting to the taste) derived from apples.
41. Spring is the time for the g_____ (sprouting) of seeds.
42. The e_____ (undeveloped) plant is in the seed that is put in the ground.
43. Alfalfa is a p_____ (that which comes up year after year).
44. The c_____ (green coloring matter) is the thing that makes the leaves green.
45. B_____ (the science which treats of plants) should be interesting to a farmer.
46. We should s_____ (make pure) the jars before canning.

47. We found the s_____ (bony framework) of a bear in the woods.
48. The liver s_____ (to separate, elaborate, and emit by natural process) bile.
49. S_____ (liquid poured into the mouth) helps in the digestion of our food.
50. His r_____ (act of breathing) was natural.
51. We shall p_____ (sterilize by exposure to high temperature) the milk before using.
52. We need plenty of o_____ (colorless, tasteless gas) to breathe.
53. Some things we eat do not have much n_____ (food value) in them.
54. Do not i_____ (draw into the lungs) the poisonous gas.
55. The i_____ (that which poisons or corrupts) caused blood poisoning in his arm.
56. One of the vital organs of the body is the h_____ (organ that serves to keep up the movement of the blood).
57. There are many g_____ (tissue in animals or plants, producing some peculiar substances) in the body.
58. A bud is a g_____ (portion of organism capable of becoming a new one) of a fruit or a leaf.
59. The g_____ (fluid produced in the mucous membrane of the stomach) juice helps to digest food.
60. We shall f_____ (to expose to smoke or gas as in cleaning clothing) all our old clothes.
61. People e_____ (give off from the lungs) waste products in the form of gas.
62. We shall d_____ (cleanse from disease) the house.
63. The d_____ (breaking up and absorption of foods) is the work of the alimentary canal.
64. We have red and white c_____ (minute discs) in the blood stream.
65. He has poor c_____ (movement of blood through the body).
66. Each c_____ (a small closed cavity) in the body is a living organism.
67. The end of bone was covered with c_____ (a smooth, whitish, elastic substance).
68. When we breathe we take in air and throw off c_____ (a gas that contains impurities).
69. The water rose through the soil by c_____ (attraction by which liquid is drawn up) action.
70. The b_____ (microscopic rod-shaped vegetable organism) are found in decomposing liquids.
71. The a_____ (act of taking a substance through the tissues) by the plant is a wonderful process.

322

72. Wheat grown anywhere without attention to the selection of pure seed is likely to show many v_____ (deviations from a standard type).

73. The t_____ (a small mass of the roots of leguminous plants) on the roots of the clover are of the highest value to the farmer.

74. People now know that t_____ (cultivation of the soil) is of greatest importance during times of drouth.

75. The farmer tries to enrich the s_____ (the bed of earth which lies immediately below the surface soil) when it is plowed.

76. G_____ (insertion of a small shoot of a tree into another tree) has improved our apples in the Northwest.

77. The farmer has a large s_____ (pit or airtight chamber for ensilage) near his barn.

78. Spring is the time for p_____ (lopping off, as superfluous branches of trees) of apple trees.

79. The p_____ (spreading or extension of anything) of plants from seeds is a form of agriculture.

80. The honey bee is a great help in the p_____ (conveyance of pollen to the pistil of the plant) of plants.

81. N_____ (an atmospheric gas) is necessary for plant life.

82. A mass of growing bread m_____ (woolly fungus growth formed on moist surfaces) is composed of many white threads.

83. We sometimes find m_____ (growth of minute fungi on plants) on the under side of grape leaves.

84. The youngberry is a h_____ (cross between two varieties of plants) between the loganberry and the blackberry.

85. Flowering plants are unable to flourish unless there is considerable h_____ (vegetable mold) in the soil.

86. H_____ (gardening) is a fundamental industry.

87. The fruit tree had fire b_____ (a kind of plant disease).

88. Plants that have food stored up in their roots during the first summer's growth and grow seeds in the second season are called b_____ (two year long).

89. Sugar cane is a s_____ (juicy) plant.

90. The mud was made by the s_____ (matter which subsides to the bottom) in the pond.

91. There is more n_____ (nourishing) value in cereals than in fruits.

92. We worked out the experiment in the l_____ (place for scientific experiments).

93. There is much e_____ (changing of water into vapor) on a warm day.

94. The c_____ (to cause to change into a curdlike state) of the food in the stomach is caused by the action of the juices on the food.

95. A part of the sugar is converted into c_____ (substance forming framework of plants).
96. C_____ (many heat-giving food stuffs—sugar, starch) form a large part of all plants.
97. Copper is a good c_____ (that which transmits) of electricity.
98. We can use this stone as a f_____ (point of support for a pry) when we pry open the manhole.
99. Do you know of any s_____ (liquid in which a substance will dissolve) for rubber?
100. The p_____ (living substance, that of which all living things are made) of each living thing, from the daisy to the elephant, varies a trifle from any other in its chemical composition.

## ANSWERS

| | | | |
|---|---|---|---|
| 1. vibration | 26. elements | 51. pasteurize | 76. Grafting |
| 2. velocity | 27. electricity | 52. oxygen | 77. silo |
| 3. transmission | 28. dynamo | 53. nutrition | 78. pruning |
| 4. thermometer | 29. distillation | 54. inhale | 79. propagation |
| 5. solution | 30. density | 55. infection | 80. pollination |
| 6. saturated | 31. decompose | 56. heart | 81. Nitrogen |
| 7. resonant | 32. contraction | 57. glands | 82. mold |
| 8. resistance | 33. compression | 58. germ | 83. mildew |
| 9. reflection | 34. combustion | 59. gastric | 84. hybrid |
| 10. radiation | 35. buoyancy | 60. fumigate | 85. humus |
| 11. neutral | 36. battery | 61. exhale | 86. Horticulture |
| 12. negative | 37. barometer | 62. disinfect | 87. blight |
| 13. meter | 38. artesian | 63. digestion | 88. biennials |
| 14. magnetism | 39. alkali | 64. corpuscles | 89. succulent |
| 15. lever | 40. acid | 65. circulation | 90. sediment |
| 16. Isothermic | 41. germination | 66. cell | 91. nutritive |
| 17. insulate | 42. embryonic | 67. cartilage | 92. laboratory |
| 18. indissoluble | 43. perennial | 68. carbon dioxide | 93. evaporation |
| 19. incandescent | 44. chlorophyll | 69. capillary | 94. coagulation |
| 20. hydrogen | 45. Botany | 70. bacteria | 95. cellulose |
| 21. hydraulic | 46. sterilize | 71. absorption | 96. Carbohydrates |
| 22. humidity | 47. skeleton | 72. variations | 97. conductor |
| 23. filter | 48. secretes | 73. tubercles | 98. fulcrum |
| 24. fermentation | 49. Saliva | 74. tilth | 99. solvent |
| 25. erosion | 50. respiration | 75. subsoil | 100. protoplasm |

All but ten are in general literary use, though not always in the scientific sense.

## SCIENCE FOR THE LAYMAN

How can you spot the scientific terms most likely to make their way into the common stock of words? One of the best ways is to note the terms regarded as usable without explanations by the leading science writers for newspapers and magazines. Consistent reading of *Time, Newsweek, Fortune, Business Week,* and other magazines will put you on a familiar speaking and writing basis with the technical words in current use. Turn to the science section in the Sunday edition of your favorite newspaper; it will supplement your other reading.

The shelves of your neighborhood library are filled with popular works on every branch of science. Reading such books is perhaps a better and certainly a more systematic way to FAMILIARIZE yourself with the background of science that gives rise to its terminology. A very versatile, sound operator in this field is Lancelot Hogben, author of *Science for the Citizen.* Hogben's book, which was written in 1938 and revised in 1956, puts science in its SOCIOHISTORICAL setting; it also shows what science means for human life and thought: that at its best it appeals to the deepest and strongest drives which make us human. This philosophy, of the social and human significance of the scientific approach, Hogben calls scientific HUMANISM.

A more recent work that explains all branches of science for the benefit of the intelligent layman is a two-volume work by Isaac Asimov, called, appropriately, *The Intelligent Man's Guide to Science.* Asimov covers the whole area of the physical sciences in Volume One, taking the reader step by step from the origin of and theories about the universe, down to an explanation of the Earth, its atmosphere and composition, and then into a discussion of matter. Volume Two treats of the biological sciences and provides a background of knowledge which will help the reader understand what is happening today in the field of plastics, silicones, medicine, psychology, etc.

### Do You Know the Basic Terms in the Life Sciences?

If most of the following terms are not familiar to you, this should be an incentive to peruse Hogben's *Science for the Citizen* or Volume Two of Asimov's work. The following list of words was compiled from these two books.

# Familiar Terms from Biological Science

## A

1. [ ] METAMORPHOSIS
2. [ ] MUTATION
3. [ ] NEURONES

4. [ ] NUCLEUS
5. [ ] ORIENTATION

6. [ ] PARASITES

7. [ ] PHOTOSYNTHESIS
8. [ ] PITUITARY
9. [ ] POLLINATION

10. [ ] STERILITY

[a] conducting nerve cells
[b] change of form
[c] carrying yellow powder from ANTHERS to PISTILS in plants
[d] condition of being unable to reproduce
[e] heritable new feature or change in plant or animal
[f] organisms living on or within another organism, from which they get food
[g] central core of cell
[h] gland at base of brain
[i] process of getting "located," to get directions straight
[j] plant manufacture of CARBOHYDRATES from CARBON DIOXIDE and water in presence of CHLOROPHYLL and light

## B

1. [ ] CRETINISM

2. [ ] CURARE
3. [ ] ECOLOGY
4. [ ] ELEPHANTIASIS

5. [ ] ENSILAGE

6. [ ] EPIDERMIS

7. [ ] STERILIZATION
8. [ ] STIMULUS
9. [ ] SYNAPSE
10. [ ] VIRUS

[a] juncture where impulse passes from one nerve to another
[b] filter-passing organisms
[c] top layer of skin
[d] idiocy and failure to mature, due to extreme THYROID deficiency
[e] branch of biology dealing with relation of living things to environment and each other
[f] disease marked by enlargement of limbs and skin-coarsening
[g] arrow poison
[h] fodder stored in SILO to keep it fresh
[i] something that stirs to action, or effort
[j] DEPRIVATION of power to reproduce

## C

1. [ ] CAROTIN

2. [ ] CARBOHYDRATES

[a] part of brain regulating INVOLUNTARY movement and lying below cerebrum
[b] layer of gray matter covering brain-surface

3. [　] CEREBELLUM     [c] blood relationship
4. [　] CEREBRUM     [d] compounds of carbon, hydrogen, and oxygen
5. [　] CHAMELEON     [e] plant pigment convertible by animal into VITAMIN A
6. [　] CHOREA     [f] lizard that can change its skin-color
7. [　] CHROMOSOMES     [g] part of brain that is seat of conscious thought and voluntary movement
8. [　] CILIA     [h] ST. VITUS' dance
9. [　] CONSANGUINITY     [i] heredity-carrying microscopic FILAMENTS
10. [　] CORTEX     [j] hairlike filaments

## D

1. [　] ALBINISM     [a] shelled animal that clings to ship bottoms, etc.
2. [　] ALGAE     [b] hairlike tubes
3. [　] ANEMIA     [c] unequal CURVATURE in eye lens causing blurring
4. [　] ANTHROPOMORPHISM     [d] water plants minus roots, stems, leaves; often scummy
5. [　] ANTISEPTICS     [e] lack of color PIGMENTATION
6. [　] ANTITOXINS     [f] deficiency of red blood corpuscles
7. [　] ASEPSIS     [g] attribution of human form
8. [　] ASTIGMATISM     [h] counter-poisons
9. [　] BARNACLES     [i] condition of surgical, germ-free cleanliness
10. [　] CAPILLARIES     [j] infection preventives

## E

1. [　] EUGENICS     [a] druglike substances produced in body, which elicit specific responses when distributed by bloodstream
2. [　] FUNGI     [b] masses or groups of nerve cells
3. [　] GANGLIA     [c] non-starch-making PARASITIC molds
4. [　] GENES     [d] cross-breeding
5. [　] HYBRIDIZATION     [e] trancelike state induced by a MESMERIZER, in which attention of subject is DIFFUSED and SUGGESTIBILITY heightened.
6. [　] HYPNOSIS     [f] medieval botanical treatises about medicinal plants

327

7. [    ] HERBALS

8. [    ] HOMUNCULUS

9. [    ] HORMONES

10. [    ] INHIBITION

[g] pre-formed EMBRYO ("little man") assumed by medieval thinkers to exist in SPERM or OVUM

[h] blocking or dampening down of response

[i] scientific improvement of stock by deliberate selection of mates

[j] material particle in CHROMOSOME which carries hereditary trait from parent to offspring

ANSWERS

| A | B | C | D | E |
|---|---|---|---|---|
| 1. [b] | 1. [d] | 1. [e] | 1. [e] | 1. [i] |
| 2. [e] | 2. [g] | 2. [d] | 2. [d] | 2. [c] |
| 3. [a] | 3. [e] | 3. [a] | 3. [f] | 3. [b] |
| 4. [g] | 4. [f] | 4. [g] | 4. [g] | 4. [j] |
| 5. [i] | 5. [h] | 5. [f] | 5. [j] | 5. [d] |
| 6. [f] | 6. [c] | 6. [h] | 6. [h] | 6. [e] |
| 7. [j] | 7. [j] | 7. [i] | 7. [i] | 7. [f] |
| 8. [h] | 8. [i] | 8. [j] | 8. [c] | 8. [g] |
| 9. [c] | 9. [a] | 9. [c] | 9. [a] | 9. [a] |
| 10. [d] | 10. [b] | 10. [b] | 10. [b] | 10. [h] |

### Try Words from the Physical Sciences

Now see how familiar you are with the following list from the physical sciences:

A

1. [    ] EQUINOX

2. [    ] EUCLID

3. [    ] FOOT-POUND

4. [    ] GALENA

5. [    ] GALVANOMETER

6. [    ] INDUCTION (ELECTRO-
MAGNETIC)

7. [    ] INERTIA

8. [    ] IONS

[a] equal-angled, as to compass variations

[b] instrument for reading voltage

[c] equal-pressure line on weather map

[d] production for electricity in wire by cutting a magnetic field

[e] electrically conducting submolecules

[f] when day and night are of equal length

[g] lead SULPHIDE

[h] tendency to remain in state of rest or motion

[i] first great GEOMETER, and the GEOMETRIC system he devised

9. [ ] ISOBARS       [ j] unit of work in British system of meas-
10. [ ] ISOGONAL      urement

## B

1. [ ] ANODE

[a] tube packed with loose metallic particles which stick together when a high
frequency alternating current is run
through them

2. [ ] BENZENE

[b] DEVIATION of compass needle from true
north

3. [ ] BUOYANCY

[c] coal tar DERIVATION, the molecule represented by six carbon atoms in ring,
with six hydrogen atoms hitched on

4. [ ] CALCULUS
5. [ ] CATAPULT
6. [ ] CATHODE

[d] power to float
[e] launching or throwing device
[f] branch of mathematics dealing with
variables and changing rates

7. [ ] CENTRIFUGE
8. [ ] COHERER

[g] positive ELECTRODE
[h] whirling machine acting on cream-sep-
arator principle

9. [ ] CONVECTION

[i] conveying of heat by movements of
particles in gas or liquid

10. [ ] DECLINATION

[j] negative electrode

## C

1. [ ] DIELECTRIC
2. [ ] DIFFRACTION

[a] magnetic rock
[b] device to detect presence of minute
charges of electricity, showing if
they're positive or negative

3. [ ] DISTILLATION
4. [ ] DOPPLER EFFECT

[c] negatively ELECTRIFIED particles
[d] branch of PHYSICS dealing with action
of force on bodies in motion

5. [ ] DYNAMICS
6. [ ] ELASTICITY
7. [ ] ELECTRONS

[e] breaking up of light or other ray
[f] INSULATOR
[g] heating a liquid and condensing the
vapor thus given off

8. [ ] ELECTROPLATING

[h] pitch of sound from a moving source
apparently growing higher or lower to
listener

9. [ ] ELECTROSCOPE

[i] resistance of matter to stretch or DIS-
TORTION

10. [ ] LODESTONE

[j] covering with a metal coating by ELEC-
TROLYSIS

329

# D

1. [　] ISOTHERMS
2. [　] ISOTOPES
3. [　] MICROTOME
4. [　] OSMOSIS
5. [　] OXIDATION

6. [　] OZONE

7. [　] PROTONS
8. [　] RADIATION

9. [　] SILICON

10. [　] TRINITROTOLUENE

[a] positively charged electric particles
[b] act or process of giving out rays,— light, heat, electronic, etc.
[c] element found most commonly as sand, which CRYSTALLIZES also into precious forms
[d] high explosive
[e] any of two or more FRACTIONALIZED forms of an element having similar chemical properties but slightly different atomic weights
[f] lines of weather map joining points of equal temperature
[g] device for cutting very thin sections
[h] combining with oxygen,—e.g., burning or rusting
[i] TURPENTINE—soluble oxygen that gives out stimulating odor
[j] mutual diffusion of gases or liquids at different pressures through POROUS membrane

# E

1. [　] VITRIOL

2. [　] ZENITH

3. [　] VOLTAGE

4. [　] ALCHEMY

5. [　] ASTROLABE
6. [　] CALORIE

7. [　] ELECTROLYSIS

8. [　] KINETIC (energy)

9. [　] MEGALITH
10. [　] METEOROLOGY

[a] work done to make a body at rest attain a given velocity if no heat is lost
[b] large stone pillars of CAIRNS used in measuring SOLAR SOLSTICE
[3] chemical DECOMPOSITION by electric current of substance in solution
[d] ancient QUADRANT for measuring angular altitudes above horizon
[e] SULPHURIC acid
[f] medieval PSEUDO-science which sought secret of turning base metals into gold
[g] electrical potential determining direction and distribution of ELECTRIFICATION
[h] amount of heat required to raise one gram of water one degree CENTIGRADE
[i] science of atmosphere and weather
[j] point in the heavens directly overhead

330

| A | B | C | D | E |
|---|---|---|---|---|
| 1. [ f] | 1. [g] | 1. [ f] | 1. [ f] | 1. [ e] |
| 2. [ i] | 2. [ c] | 2. [ e] | 2. [ e] | 2. [ j] |
| 3. [ j] | 3. [d] | 3. [g] | 3. [g] | 3. [g] |
| 4. [g] | 4. [ f] | 4. [h] | 4. [ j] | 4. [ f] |
| 5. [b] | 5. [ e] | 5. [d] | 5. [h] | 5. [d] |
| 6. [d] | 6. [ j] | 6. [ i] | 6. [ i] | 6. [h] |
| 7. [h] | 7. [h] | 7. [ c] | 7. [a] | 7. [ c] |
| 8. [ e} | 8. [a] | 8. [ j] | 8. [b] | 8. [a] |
| 9. [ c] | 9. [ i] | 9. [b] | 9. [ c] | 9. [b] |
| 10. [a] | 10. [b] | 10. [a] | 10. [d] | 10. [ i] |

Most of these terms are scientific shorthand: words which pack a lot of meaning into short compass. This drive for terms that can be taken in only one way finally winds up in the use of letters and formulas, whereby words are further reduced to arbitrary symbols. "The ratio of the circumference of a circle to its diameter" becomes $\pi$, which the mathematician describes further "an INCOMMENSURABLE" —not expressible in FINITE fractions. A computer could work $\pi$ out to GOOGOL places, googol being the name which Professor Edward Kasner's nine-year-old nephew obligingly supplied for 10 with 100 zeros after it (mathematicians write it $10^{100}$). But $\pi$ expressed NUMERICALLY even to googol places would still be only an APPROXIMATION.

Mathematicians have to use the concept INFINITY in some of their calculations, too, and they've adopted a handy symbol for it, a figure eight on its side: $\infty$, which looks as if it could work a lot of magic.

But no RUNIC character or magical ABRACADABRA ever worked such awe-inspiring results as Einstein's formula for energy-mass EQUIVALENCE; that energy equals mass multiplied by the square of the velocity of light. Lise Meitner's reflections about the bearings of this formula, $e = mc^2$, on the experiments in FISSION which she and Hahn performed in Berlin in 1938, made her realize as she was on her way out to Denmark as a refugee that they must have released 250 million electron volts of energy from each split nucleus—which is what makes an atom-splitting chain reaction so frighteningly powerful.

Not since PROMETHEUS stole fire from heaven and brought it down to earth has anybody so stormed the ultimate secrets of nature as has Einstein with his pencil. He not only upset NEWTONIAN physics and astronomy, but he challenged AXIOMS that since the Greeks had been taken as the foundations of geometry, and since Newton as the basis for the laws of motion and gravitation. The explosions at Hiroshima and Nagasaki were implicit in that harmless-looking equation, though he would never have willed any such use of his work. Now that physicists are puzzling over the behavior of subatomic matter, new theories and new formulas are being PROMULGATED. Someday another concept as revolutionary as Einstein's might shake the scientific world.

The symbols and formulas of science are not really words. But to a quickened imagination they may have some of the power of those COLLOCATIONS *of words* in a great poetic line that echo right up to the edge of Old Chaos and on into the Dark Night of Time of which Lucretius, the great Roman poet of science, wrote. These symbols interpreted enable us in an INTERMITTENT flash to see things under the aspect of eternity.

Newton's answer to the friend who congratulated him on having plumbed all knowledge expresses the scientist's humility in the face of the infinite: "I feel," he said, "like a child picking up pebbles on the shore of the unknown ocean of truth."

The symbols and formulas may look dry and abstract to those who cannot read them. But they convey a wealth of meaning and an AURA of history to anybody who can approach them with imagination. And surely the work of the atomic scientists (horrible as was its first FRUITION at Hiroshima) makes it possible for man to envision in their awful majesty Lucretius' "flaming walls of the world."


## SCIENCE FICTION AND FACT

Hiroshima was still eighteen months in the future when agitated Military Intelligence officers paid a business call on the editor of *Astounding Science-Fiction,* a few days after that magazine published a story with the title "Deadline" in its March, 1944, issue. This yarn told of a successful secret service mission to destroy an atomic bomb in the making. The spy, dropped by parachute, was captured and taken to the research headquarters of the physicist who had finally assembled a workable atomic bomb. To prove to the

332

scientist that he was himself a nuclear physicist, the spy, when shown the bomb in its stand, describes its mechanism:

Two cast-iron hemispheres, clamped over the orange segments of CAD-MIUM alloy. And the fuse—I see it is in—a tiny can of cadmium alloy containing a speck of radium in a BERYLLIUM holder and a small explosive powerful enough to shatter the cadmium walls. Then . . . the powdered URANIUM OXIDE runs together in the central cavity. The radium shoots NEUTRONS in this mass—and the U-235 takes over from there. Right? [Actually, says Editor Campbell, this bomb would not have worked.]

All this supposedly happened on an imaginary planet, Cathor. But the bomb pattern was so close to the blueprint for the one Oppenheimer and his aides were starting to put together at Los Alamos, New Mexico, that the G-2 men wanted to know who *on earth* in the Manhattan Project had been talking. No one, the editor told them. The technical data on which the story was based came out of articles published in the learned journals in 1940—including abstracts of German and Russian material.

Well then, said the G-2 CONTINGENT, would he for godsake quit carrying these stories about atomic energy. The dean of science-fiction editors, John W. Campbell, countered with the argument that total suppression of all such stories, which he'd been running since 1939, would arouse more suspicion than would their continuance. His argument carried the day.

Had the G-2 men done their homework on the back issues of science-fiction magazines, they would have found some stories even more prophetic. One, published in 1940, "Blowups Happen," by Robert Heinlein, Annapolis graduate and plastics engineer, dealt with the psychological hazards of SERVICING an atomic pile. After one young engineer cracks up, engineers are required to work in pairs, and a psychologist is always on duty in a control tower, checking on them. The minute an engineer shows any signs, either on duty or off, of a change in his behavior pattern, the psychologist yanks him off the job for a PSYCHOMETRICAL check. Needless to say, the psychologists (the engineers call them "witch doctors") are about as popular with the engineers as political COMMISSARS were with Red Army generals. Finally feeling gets so bad that the general superintendent calls in his head psychologist, to summon the best expert to solve the dilemma. Lenz, who was a pupil of Korzybski, is called in. He is an expert in SYMBOLIC logic and PSYCHIATRY who had

333

checked the "PANDEMIC NEUROSES of the Crazy Years of Atomic Warfare." Lenz proves able to handle the problem, and also gives an "assist" when it is found that a mistake in the equations on which the safety factor depends necessitates dumping the molten metal in the pile, and RELOCATING the prime energy source on a spaceship 15,000 miles out. The private company which owns the pile objects, but Lenz forces their hand, and the world is saved.

## VOCABULARY OF THE SPACE AGE

Attention in recent years has shifted from atom-splitting to rocket-propulsion. With manned and unmanned spacecraft setting up a traffic problem in the regions beyond our atmosphere, new words from the science of astronautics are taking the shuttle service into popular usage. Many of the older words—such as THRUST, BOOSTER, and MISSILE—are on the shuttle going the other way and now have specialized meanings.

Science fiction has for decades (and back in previous centuries) been CONCOCTING stories about the problems of overcoming terrestrial gravity in the attempt to penetrate outer space. Robert Heinlein's classic story, *The Man Who Sold the Moon*, was written in 1949, but Heinlein, an engineer, used technical words and phrases that anticipated the scientific terminology of today. Arthur C. Clarke, who has a thorough background in science, has written many imaginative accounts of our future adventures in space—*Islands in the Sky, Childhood's End, The Other Side of the Sky*. It was Clarke who, in 1946, suggested the principle of SYNCHRONOUS ORBIT, a concept that resulted in Syncom II, a communications satellite that can "relay messages by line-of-sight radio to more than one-third of the Earth's surface." (*Time*, August 2, 1963)

Paralleling his work in the science-fiction field, Clarke has written nonfiction books explaining the science of *missilery*. *The Exploration of Space*, published in 1952 and revised in 1959, uses many technical terms that are now a familiar part of our scientific LEXICON. Clarke draws attention also to Jules Verne and other writers of the nineteenth century and earlier, who made some remarkable EXTRAPOLATIONS about the time when space flight would be a reality. One of these writers was Cyrano de Bergerac (not the fictional hero of Rostand's play) whom Clarke calls "the most ingenious writer of the period [seventeenth century]." De Bergerac wrote *Voyage to the Moon* in 1656. Clarke continues: "To Cyrano must go the credit for first using *rocket propulsion* . . . . he anticipated the *ramjet*." Does *ramjet* carry any meaning for you? Here are some technical terms Clarke uses. Study them as you have the words in small capitals and try to figure out what they mean from their contexts.

The *payload* of a high-performance rocket is not likely to be more than a twentieth of its total weight. . . .

At the moment it still takes about a hundred tons of *rocket propellant* to place one ton of *payload* into a *satellite orbit*.

A whole technique of *micro-instrumentation* and *telemetering* is growing up. . . .

The rocket will be so accurately aimed [or steered later in its *trajectory*] that it hits the moon. . . .

Here are words and phrases from *The Exploration of Space* taken from their setting or context.

| | | |
|---|---|---|
| MULTISTAGE ROCKETS | THRUST AGAINST GRAV- | CIRCULAR VELOCITY |
| STEP-ROCKETS | ITY | DEEP-SPACE PROBE |

Do you know what they mean? How about:

| | | |
|---|---|---|
| CHEMICALLY-FUELED | WEIGHTLESSNESS | ROCKET-BRAKING |
| STEP-ROCKETS | ACCELERATION | RETRO-ROCKETS |
| ORBITAL REFUELING | FREE FALL | LUNAR GRAVITATIONAL |
| ESCAPE VELOCITY | PAYLOAD | FIELD |
| BOOSTERS | STEERING JETS | MAGNETIC OBSERVA- |
| ENTRY BY BRAKING | LOW-POWERED ROCKET | TIONS |
| ELLIPSES | THRUSTS | SPECTROSCOPIC MEAS- |
| SPACE-STATIONS | | UREMENTS |

You'll recognize many of the terms from your reading of the daily newspapers and weekly news magazines. Others may make you scratch your head, but if you COGITATE a moment, their meanings may come through to you. With the passage of time, much of the jargon of astronautics will be familiar to most laymen. And some of the terms which have used the shuttle service to the area of specialized meanings will be coming back into popular usage in new and extended senses.

Scientists such as Arthur Clarke are not confined to the terminology of their profession. They range broadly over many fields of knowledge. *The Exploration of Space* dips into cultural history for some of its terminology. Do you recognize the following? Can you give the approximate period of their origin?

1. *lebensraum*  3. Pope's aphorism   6. Darwin's Theory of Evolution
2. cosmos        4. Punic Wars        7. Freudian psychology
                 5. Copernican astronomy

ANSWERS

1. See page 351.
2. The universe as a harmonious whole. From the Greek *kosmos* ("order").
3. "The proper study of mankind is man."
4. Wars between Rome and Carthage in the third and second centuries B.C.
5. The astronomer *Copernicus* lived from 1473 to 1543. He PROMULGATED the theory that planets revolve in orbits around the sun.
6. Darwin lived in the nineteenth century.
7. Freud practiced psychoanalysis in the early part of this century.

The reason for this digression is to point up the necessity for an ECLECTIC approach to words. Although we have made arbitrary distinctions—labeling words as technical, business, etc.—language is fluid and words are constantly on the move from one category to another.


## A GLOSSARY OF SPACE TERMS

A breakthrough in our knowledge of other planets occurred in the successful Venus-probe of Mariner II, an unmanned spacecraft that passed within 22,000 miles of the planet Venus in 1962. J. N. James's excellent article in *Scientific American* (July, 1963) provides what is practically a glossary of terms covering the successive phases in the launching of this type of vehicle. *Countdown, launching trajectory, second-stage rocket* are followed by the new phrase PARKING ORBIT and words describing space environment: *Van Allen belts, Doppler shift.* Some items of spacecraft instrumentation are *cosmic-dust detector, microwave radiometer,* and *ion chamber.*

The technical words and phrases on the opposite page are from Heinlein's *The Man Who Sold the Moon* (1949) and J. N. James's

| From The Man Who Sold the Moon | From The Voyage of Mariner II |
|---|---|
| power satellite | microwave channel |
| power piles | magnetic fields |
| isotopic artificial fuels | cosmic rays |
| orbit ———————————— | orbital speed |
| synthetic radioactive fuel | solar wind |
| chemi-fuel motors | Van Allen belts |
| atomic-powered rocket | tracking |
| shuttle rocket | astronomical unit |
| mass ratio | solar energy |
| rocketry | launching vehicle |
| X-fuel | "altitude-stabilized" spacecraft |
| atmospheric braking | "spin-stabilized" spacecraft |
| blastoff | solar panel |
| reaction vector | trapped radiation |
| acceleration ——————— | acceleration |
| design stresses | ⌈ secondary radiation |
| cosmic radiation ————— | infrared radiation |
| pyrotechnics rocket | ⌊ solar radiation |
| line-of-sight transmission | solar cells |
| relay station | ion chamber |
| space station | spin stabilization |
| sonic | payload |
| first step-rocket stage⌉ | launching pad |
| fifth stage | ⌈ staging |
| booster stages ⌋ | ⌊ second-stage rocket |
| supersonic | sensing device |
| subsonic | gyroscope |
| Plexiglas | minimum-energy trajectory |
| trajectory ———————— | launching trajectory |
| ballistics computer | parabolic antenna |
| nuclear engineers | interplanetary dust |
| hydroponics | countdown |
| decelerate | gravitational field |
| guided missile | Doppler shift |
| terminal velocity ———— | radial velocity |
|  | cold-gas jets |
|  | scanning |
|  | magnetometer |
|  | solar plasma |
|  | macroscopic particles |
|  | Roentgens |
|  | ionosphere |
|  | disk of the planet |
|  | microns |
|  | Kepler's laws |
|  | solar satellite |

article on "The Voyage of Mariner II." Your trial run with the terms from *The Exploration of Space* should help you figure out some of them. Notice the similarity between some of the fictional terms used in Heinlein's story and the factual technical labels in the Mariner II list. While you're working out definitions for these words, guess how many may take the route from specialization to generalization. How many took the shuttle in the other direction?

Note the similar preoccupation with concepts such as *velocity, radiation, trajectory, stages, acceleration.* Many of the other terms from Heinlein's book are from science but are used imaginatively in the construction of his fictional rocket. A term such as "X-fuel" is purely fictitious, of course. "Line-of-sight transmission" is very much alive with the successful launching of Syncom II.

Did you try to pick out the technical terms from both examples that may one day shuttle over into general use? You could have some fun with *launching pad. Countdown* will probably come into general usage as the climactic moment of a big event. *Orbit* has taken the shuttle both ways. The successive stages of firing a rocket may be used to describe the progressive steps in other kinds of projects.

HYDROPONICS is a favorite word among science-fiction writers. It was coined by Dr. W. F. Gerike, co-inventor of the process of growing plants with NUTRIENT solutions rather than in the soil. Hardly a science-fiction story about space travel has been without its hydroponics expert, who lovingly watches over the growth of his vegetables during the journey in space.

Although science-fiction is commonly rated in the literary sub-cellar, don't downgrade it as a source for ideas and terminology that describe the present age and the one that will follow. The scientific assumptions on which the stories are based are usually plausible extrapolations of known science. (Extrapolation: finding by computation or curve-plotting, based on known terms of a series, other terms, whether preceding or following—more often the latter. This is a kind of legitimate scientific prophecy.)

You can have fun reading Heinlein, Clarke, Bradbury, Pohl, *et al.*, and can pick up a few new words at the same time. Thus our theme about enriching your vocabulary by making a game out of it comes full circle.

## Technical Words Quiz

This is the last test you will score yourself on before you take your Comprehensive Vocabulary-Level Test at the end of the next chapter. Before you go on to Chapter 12, add up your scores for Chapter 2 through Chapter 11.

1. Pick out three acronyms from your Word List.
2. What is the word applied to an international combine that fixes prices, limits output, and divides the available market?
3. "The antagonism between the *bourgeois* and the _____, arising from the former's self-interest and injustice, Marx calls the class struggle."
4. Changing the boundary lines of voting districts for the purpose of political advantage is called _____.
5. When a Senator gives political jobs to his relatives, he is guilty of _____.
6. What is the Latin phrase used in diplomacy that means "one thing in return for another"?
7. What is a word that suggests religious prophecy?
8. What is a "synthetic chemical compound composed of long chains of identical molecules"?
9. Transistors, magnetic memory units, and diodes are s_____ devices.
10. What is the transducer that converts the mechanical energy of a phonograph record into electrical signals?
11. In biological science, the "juncture where impulse passes from one nerve to another" is the _____.
12. What is the part of the brain that is the "seat of conscious thought and voluntary movement"?
13. "Positively charged electric particles" are _____.
14. "The point in the heavens directly overhead" is the _____.
15. Something that occurs only periodically could be called _____.
16. An _____ approach is one that draws material from several sources.
17. The scientist who first promulgated the theory that the earth revolves in an orbit around the sun was _____.
18. Bands of radiation around the earth are known as _____.
19. The rate of increase of a moving object is _____.
20. The process of growing plants in nutrient solutions rather than in the soil is known as _____.
21. Scientific prophecy, based on present knowledge, is called _____.

22. A close-linked chain of events is sometimes called a _____ of events.
23. What is another name for the "super-suburbs"?
24. What is the science that deals with the "properties of sound above the audible range"?
25. What is the German word applied to "tawdry literary or artistic efforts"?
26. An organism that is "biologically deficient" is _____.
27. What is a "gland-produced catalytic agent?"
28. What is another word for "beginner"?
29. When a hypothesis about a principle in nature is verified, it may be called a _____.
30. A person who is _____ is deprived of his chartered right.

## WORD LIST

| | | | |
|---|---|---|---|
| disenfranchised | territorial | divination | apocalyptic |
| desegregated | hydroponics | perigee | polymer |
| protons | law | concatenation | Copernicus |
| decibels | megalopolis | cerebrum | cartridge |
| interstitial | conflict of interest | acceleration | postulate |
| solid-state | zenith | ultrasonics | gerrymandering |
| radar | presupposition | tie-in sale | velocity |
| toxic | cerebellum | sonar | thyroid |
| dialectic | Doppler shift | extrapolation | television |
| eclectic | cartel | dysgenic | apocryphal |
| Newton | tyro | synthetics | nepotism |
| quid pro quo | enfranchised | enzyme | proletarian |
| teleran | coaxial | intermittent | deus ex machina |
| gemütlich | exurbs | neologism | synapse |
| Van Allen belts | kitsch | neutrons | mythology |

## ANSWERS

10. cartridge
9. solid-state
8. polymer
7. apocalyptic
6. quid pro quo
5. nepotism
4. gerrymandering
3. proletarian
2. cartel
1. sonar, teleran, radar

11. synapse
12. cerebrum
13. protons
14. zenith
15. intermittent
16. eclectic
17. Copernicus
18. Van Allen belts
19. acceleration
20. hydroponics

21. extrapolation
22. concatenation
23. exurbs
24. ultrasonics
25. kitsch
26. dysgenic
27. enzyme
28. tyro
29. law
30. disenfranchised

340

30 right—Ph.D. in special and technical vocabularies
27–29 right—Master's degree
23–26 right—Bachelor's degree
18–22 right—Above average (freshman level)
12–17 right—Average American (not good enough)
Under 12 right—Substandard

*Rating for Scoring Quizzes*

(Add your scores for Chapters 2 through 11)

295–300 right—Ph.D. (You won't have to take your final exam)
270–294 right—Master's degree (Get ready for your doctorate)
230–269 right—College graduate (Ready for postgraduate work)
180–229 right—Above average (Keep working for your degree)
120–179 right—Average American (Read this book again—carefully)
Under 120 right—Substandard (Start over on page 1)

Now you know your present vocabulary level. Read Chapter 12, then re-view the book and quizzes before taking your Comprehensive Vocabulary-Level Test.

# 12 ～

## How to Double Your Vocabulary by Keeping Your Eyes and Ears Open

～ This book started out with the THESIS that you can double your vocabulary by playing a game with words. This means keeping your eyes and ears open for the key word in a joke, the coined words in a Winchell or Wilson column, the clipped words you'll read in *Variety* or hear during a musician's jam session. You can make a game of learning the less common and uncommon words just beyond the range of your vocabulary by testing yourself in multiple-choice quizzes, figuring out what a word may mean in its context, studying the fine shades of meaning in a cluster of related words, taking note of the opposites of words and of other clues to word meanings. On your desk should be one of these dictionaries: *Webster's Seventh New Collegiate Dictionary, Funk & Wagnalls Standard College Dictionary, The American College Dictionary, Webster's New World Dictionary,* the *Thorndike-Barnhart Comprehensive Desk Dictionary,* or the *Winston Dictionary.* Next to your desk dictionary keep a copy of *Roget's International Thesaurus* and *Webster's Dictionary of Synonyms.*

You can make words work for you even while you're playing a game with them. You can take apart a long, hard word as you would a mechanical gadget and find out how it is glued together with Latin or Greek roots, suffixes, and prefixes. You can trace a word back to its source by looking it up in an etymological dictionary or by following its historical progression of meanings in *Webster's Third Unabridged.* If you want to know how the best writers used words in context, go to your nearest library and open up the *Oxford English Dictionary;* or buy a copy of the *Concise Oxford Dictionary* or the *Pocket Oxford Dictionary of Current English.*

You can learn to recognize the words of technical and specialized vocabularies—business jargon, space-age terminology, lawyer talk, labor lingo, the language of politics and diplomacy—and follow the shuttle service that carries these words over into general usage, or takes popular words and specializes their meanings. How did the word meaning "a thin piece split or rent off lengthwise: SLIVER" [1] come to be compounded in the political phrase *splinter groups?* How did *buff*, which originally referred to a leather garment, arrive at its current meaning of "a fan, an enthusiast"?

## WORDS KEEP MOVING

Words don't stand still. They are restless ENTITIES that hop around like the electrons in an atom. When *Webster's Third Unabridged* was unveiled in 1961, it had 100,000 new words and new word meanings among its 450,000 entries. The changing nature of words was at the root of the controversy over this dictionary. You don't have to take sides in the battle so long as you are aware of the processes by which words change meaning, acquire new meanings and special meanings, go up and down in social standing, team up with other words to form new blends and compounds, clip off their endings to save time and space. Webster's editors are right in saying that language is in a state of FLUX and that in their descriptivist approach to words they are interpreting the culture of the times. However, while they are patiently sorting out citation slips for the next thirty years or so for their new edition, many of the doubtful words may be discarded and much of the questionable usage that they regard as proper now may be RELEGATED to limbo. A dictionary may reflect the times, but times keep changing, and it takes many years and a world of patience to compile a dictionary.[2]

There is another aspect to this difference of opinion about *Webster's Third Unabridged* that reaches to the very heart of our cultural conflict. Permissiveness has been the keynote of INTERPERSONAL relations for the last generation; there has been a loosening of the reins of discipline in all areas—self-discipline and discipline imposed from without. Writers such as Dwight Macdonald have felt that language was the last BASTION of defense against the policy of "any-

[1] *Webster's Seventh New Collegiate Dictionary.*

[2] In reply to an inquiry about the noun *razz*, which is labeled "slang" in *Webster's Third Unabridged* and "standard" in *Webster's Seventh New Collegiate Dictionary,* Dr. Gove wrote: "The noun *razz* is a difficult borderline case. When the two books differ one should usually prefer the later-edited—that is, the *Collegiate.*"

thing goes" as long as you can get away with it. Artists who dab paints willy-nilly on canvases, poets who write only when the Muse moves them, actors who throw the script away and express their mood of the moment—all are children of the era of progressive education, of self-expression without self-discipline.

At least, said the defenders of tradition (and strangely enough, in this world of PARADOXES, it was the journalists who protested against the relaxation of standards while the educators were in favor of it)—at least let us preserve the niceties of language, the finely honed cutting-edge of the exact word that expresses a specific idea, the grammatical forms that logically separate one part of speech from another, the social distinction between words that suggest the gutter and those that express higher levels of thought and taste.

Sydney J. Harris, writing in the *Chicago Daily News* (October 20, 1961) summed up the point of view of the prescriptivists:

What's the point in any writer's trying to compose clear and graceful prose, to avoid SOLECISMS, to maintain a sense of DECORUM and CONTINUITY in that magnificent instrument, the English language, if that peerless authority, *Webster's Unabridged,* surrenders abjectly to the permissive school of speech?

RELATIVISM is the reigning philosophy of our day, in all fields. Not merely in language, but in ETHICS, in politics, in every field of human behavior. There is no right or wrong—it is all merely custom and superstition to believe so. If the majority behave a certain way, that is the way to behave. Popularity gives sanction to everything.

There are COGENT arguments on both sides, and you can take your pick, depending on your temperament and the way you view the society around you. However, Webster has not ABDICATED its authority. As Dr. Gove says, only a small percentage of the words in *Webster's Third Unabridged* were the target of its critics. The vast majority of the 450,000 entries are handled in noncontroversial fashion.

## LANGUAGE HAS CONTINUITY

What it comes down to is that you should keep your ears and eyes open to what is being said and written and recorded in dictionaries. Listen for the changes in language but don't lose sight of what is permanent. It is true that words change and add new meanings and that new words constantly come into the language while many old ones fade away. Yet there are innumerable entries in *Webster's Third Unabridged* that have retained the same meanings for hundreds of years. These are the words of Shakespeare, of Thoreau, of Milton, of many writers who have spanned the centuries with language and ideas that are still vital today.

This fact is of the greatest importance to anyone who wants to double his vocabulary. Although Thorndike's word count was made a generation or more ago, most of the words he checked in print are still in use and at about the same frequency of occurrence. These are the words you have been observing in context and testing yourself on in the word games. They are the solid core of the language, the less common and uncommon words you must learn if you want to raise your vocabulary level to a place well up in the "educated" category.

### STOP, LOOK, AND LISTEN

The words in SMALL CAPITALS and *italics* have been culled from reading matter of every level of difficulty: the popular newspapers and magazines, technical journals, textbooks, Shakespeare and other classics, the Bible, radio and television programs. If you are a faithful reader of the *New York Times*, the *St. Louis Post-Dispatch*, *Time* magazine, *Newsweek*, *The Reporter*, the *Saturday Review*, or other newspapers and magazines that appeal to a middlebrow and highbrow following; and if you listen to thought-provoking programs on radio and television, you'll meet many uncommon words and you can start your word-detection game with them.

Words from cultural history will have more meaning for you if you read Dickens, Proust, Rabelais, George Bernard Shaw. If you're familiar with Sinclair Lewis, no one will have to tell you what a Babbitt is. If you've studied political and social history, you'll know that a *Munich* means APPEASEMENT, that a HELOT was a Spartan slave, that a PHILIPPIC is a DENUNCIATORY speech.

What a vocabulary doctor would prescribe is a well-rounded diet of words from the present and past. If you can enjoy a novel by Faulkner or a poem by Frost, if you've read Shakespeare and seen

345

his plays performed (there are many opportunities these days), if your library includes books on a wide variety of subjects, you'll have a firm grip on many of the less common and uncommon words that make up the bulk of the entries in the big *Webster*. As for the 100,000 new words and new word meanings, they're in print and in the air around you, and they are the symbols of today's culture.


## THE LANGUAGE TWISTERS

You may be a bit bewildered by the way language is twisted and turned inside out by teen-agers, gunmen, angry young men, advertising copywriters, saxophone players, racing touts, and ground crews at missile-launching sites. But nothing reveals a culture more than the way it uses words. Clipping off the ends—*ad* for advertisement, *bach* for bachelor, *mick* for micrometer, *ridic* for ridiculous—tells us we're all in a hurry, that we are words, phrases, and sentences apart from the more leisurely nineteenth-century style of Emerson, George Eliot, the Brontës. Everything must move quickly. Automobiles must have speed and power and must be junked yearly for new models. Jets must get there faster. A Broadway musical must bounce along at a fast pace.

Beatnik talk is short, terse, punchy; it has a jazz rhythm. Hear the beat-beat-beat of "Man, there's a cool cat," "Dig a slick chick," "He blew the gig." Note what the *Dictionary of American Slang* calls reduplications: *buddy-buddy, buzz-buzz, chi-chi*. Rebellion against the law is expressed in the slang word *flatfoot*, contempt for the intellectual in *egghead* or *nob*. But there's always an unmistakable beat—the word *beat* itself, *kooks, fast buck, real gone*.

One way of showing rebellion is to reverse the intent of words as we have known them. *Crazy* is a word of approval; a *square* reverses the old connotation of "square shooter" or "square deal"; in musicians' jargon a girl who is *nuts* is a "doll." Something that is *terrible* or "mean" is actually "great." What is *tough* is "the best, the greatest."

Perhaps the clipped forms or the beat-beat words stem from unconscious fears of the A- and H-bomb. We use words that suggest sudden destruction and death: the increase of population becomes an *explosion;* there are *space shots, crash programs, breakthroughs*.

346

There is a *blitz*, a *blast-off*, a *gasser*. Teen-agers get *bombed* (drunk) at parties. There are *kicks* and *thrusts* and ominous words like *fall-out* and *ground swell*. Everywhere we are steering a *collision course*.

Ideas are expressed in compounds that save time and space and punch home the thought: *girl-chaser, doubletalk, double-think, crying jag*. Suffixes are added to replace whole words: *pay-ola, banana-head, quick-ie, litterbug*.

Ours is a complicated age. Part of the population is angry, stirred up, rebellious. Beatniks grow beards, forget to wash, and bed down in unkempt pads. Delinquents organize in gangs and carry knives. They give themselves and others animal characteristics: *cat, fox, wolf, dog, beast, pigeon, filly;* existence becomes a *rat race*. These forms of revolt are suspiciously conformist in the end, since the rebels do travel in packs.

### THE SOFT-SELL SIDE

Another part of the population is trying to forget the unpleasant side of our culture by putting gift wrapping around it. On Madison Avenue we encounter the polished words that put a gloss over the tough epidermis of the age. We pay the ad boys plenty to soothe us with word-syrup, and they design attractive packages with labels such as "image" and "status symbol." There is a line-of-sight transmission between Madison Avenue and Washington, with an exchange of soft-sell words and ideas. The *-ize*, *-ise*, and *-wise* words fly back and forth: expert-*ise*, concret-*ize*, global-*ize*, word-*wise*.

The *-ize* words take us into other areas where the techniques of manipulation are practiced. New words are coined with tacked-on endings to describe what happens when disagreements are resolved not by overt conflict but by wily maneuvering. A military man who disagrees with the administration is not dismissed but *Portugaled*—made ambassador to the country of that name. A senator who is persuaded by President Johnson to change his vote on an important bill complains that he has been *Lyndonized*. The act of teetering on the edge of war without loosing balance becomes *brinkmanship;* the art of getting the upper hand in personal relationships, *one-upmanship*.

*Credit-cardmanship*, coined by *Time* Magazine, is a one-word

347

description of our MORES. Ann Geracimos, in the *New York Herald-Tribune* of August 29, 1963, calls the charge card the "status symbol of our credit economy." She points up the fact that a person who wishes to be a NONCONFORMIST, if only in the sense that he pays cash for purchases, is often put to trouble and inconvenience for daring to buck the system:

> A woman makes out a personal check at a midtown airline office to pay for her ticket and she has to be interviewed by the office manager when she can't show a charge plate for identification. A driver's license won't satisfy them anymore. . . .
> A New York police sergeant always paid cash. The time he wanted to buy a house, he had a tough job getting a mortgage—despite the fact he has some five thousand dollars in savings. He never had established a credit rating which, in this age, is sometimes TANTAMOUNT to being a credit risk.

Still on the soft-sell side, there is the "sweetening" process in the form of commercials that urge us to consume large quantities of ice cream, gooey cakes, rich puddings. We surreptitiously read magazines featuring *cheesecake* photos of luscious girls. A beautiful girl is a *poundcake*. In musician's lingo a fat girl is a little too rich for consumption; she is *heavy cream*. But a *cookie* or a *cupcake* is just right.


## MICROCOSM AND MACROCOSM

Moving to other areas of the culture, we learn that technology has been a prime factor in the new-word, new-meaning category. As physicists study the atom more closely, they find that there may be a whole new universe of antimatter that differs in its behavior from matter as we have known it. The splitting of the atom has revealed minute particles such as the electron, neutron, neutrino, proton, and mesons. There is speculation now that these INFINITESIMAL particles are capable of being broken down into even smaller subdivisions. The MICROCOSM shrinks and the MACROCOSM expands: we have coined new *micro* and *macro* words to express our ability to think and create in ever larger units and to compress matter through *miniaturization* into smaller ones: *microfilm, micromodules, micrometers, microwaves, microns, macroeconomic, macroscopic.* We literally must "think big" these days. An item in *Newsweek* (August 12, 1963) says:

348

. . . Scientists have had to coin a new word to measure blast effect. It is *"teraton"* and stands for 1 *trillion* tons of TNT. The theoretical upper limits of the stockpiles has outgrown *megaton* (1 million tons) and *gigatron* (1 billion tons).

A new language is taking shape at Cape Kennedy. Much of the jargon spoken by ground crews follows the trend of slang and jargon in other areas. A missile is a *bird*. A *chicken switch* can stop the progress of a manned spacecraft. "Go-No-Go" is a beat-beat term which means the decision to launch or not to launch a spacecraft. *Eyeballs in* is the effect of gravitational pressure on an astronaut caused by *liftoff*. A *cherry-picker* is a device that allows the astronaut to escape from the *capsule*.

New scientific terms in the space field are *cryogenics* (science of extremely low temperatures); *spatiography* (geography of space); *astrophysics* (science combining physics and astronomy); *astrionics* (applying electronics to aerospace flight). The old word *probe* has now been specialized in such projects as *lunar-probe, Venus-probe,* and other *space-probes.* A guided missile is a form of *servomechanism,* a term which also applies to the electronic devices in a missile or machine that control its performance. *Programming* refers to the instructions in the missile's guidance unit. This term links missilery with electronic computers, which have human programmers who feed instructions to the machines.

There is also a new field of *space medicine. Dysbarism* is a general term that includes disorders within the body caused by changes in barometric pressure. Specific disorders are *aeroembolism* (formation of gas bubbles in the body), *barotitis* (inflammation of the ear), *barosinusitis* (congestion of the mucus membranes), and *barodontalgia* (dental discomfort). A *barotraumatic* injury can result from an improperly pressurized cabin or space suit.

## WORDS THAT OVERLAP

Moving over to the social sciences, we find many culturally-determined new words that overlap into many areas. Sociologists are disturbed by *distressed* and *depressed* areas; so are government officials, labor representatives, and some business leaders. Juveniles who indulge in *drag racing* and *hot-rodding* are an annoyance to law-enforcement agencies and often to their usually permissive parents who live in *split-level* homes in *suburbia*. Most Americans want *social security* in the form of *fringe benefits*, business offers labor *wage incentives, wage dividends, escalator clauses,* and *on-the-job* training. Civil service employees compare their salaries with that of their neighbors in private industry, and go off *moonlighting.*

For many persons, *adjustment* in the form of job security and marital bliss is not enough. They suffer from *occupational neurosis* at work and *combat fatigue* at home. In the science-fiction society of the future they would be thoroughly BRAINWASHED; our benevolent corporate culture packs them off to the *marriage counselors,* psychologists, or psychiatrists. Some of the MALCONTENTS have aches and pains that are without organic basis; they are sent to doctors who practice *psychosomatics.*

Two weeks out of each year are set aside to prevent workers from *blowing their tops.* At this time they practice *tourism,* a form of release from tension that consists in driving *compact* or *power-steering* automobiles over *superhighways, turnpikes,* and *interchanges.* In the few areas where there are no toll booths, they travel on *freeways.* Generally they visit resorts or state parks of great natural beauty. Or they may take a *quickie* trip to Europe, where they seek out other Americans and munch hot dogs while they observe old cathedrals.

Most Americans avoid areas where INTEGRATIONISTS and SEGREGATIONISTS are in conflict. They have only a vague notion about what are *separate-but-equal* facilities, *public accommodations, tokenism, gradualism, sit-ins, lie-ins, pray-ins.* If the world of reality becomes too painful for them, there are a host of new *tranquilizer* pills to keep them insulated from pain. If they should become seriously ill, however, they are quickly REVITALIZED with "wonder drugs" and vitamin pills and restored to their MEGALOPOLITAN enclaves.


## BORROWED WORDS

A leisurely examination of *Webster's Third Unabridged* will convince you that the language-makers (all of us) are consistently INVENTIVE. And you would think that the 450,000 words in the big Webster would be enough for most purposes. But we keep up the ten-centuries-old custom of importing alien terms into English, where they gradually become naturalized. Usually these foreign words make their way because English does not have exact equivalents. As a rule they encounter strong resistance, and many writers bar them. But a few such words get over the immigration barriers because they can do special jobs. Generally, they first appear in the daily newspapers and weekly magazines, so watch for them in the course of your reading.

Like slang, jargon, coined and blend words, etc., many of them stay and become an integral part of the language. Others quietly expire when they've outlived their usefulness. What was the fate of *Luftwaffe* and *lebensraum*, contributed by the late, unlamented Mr. Hitler? Since the Luftwaffe (German Air Force) was thoroughly liquidated by our armed forces, it is absent from *Webster's Third Unabridged*. But lebensraum (living space) is now a standard word. Currently, and for a long time to come, as Aldous Huxley points out in his book *Island*, overpopulated nations will be seeking more lebensraum. The *New York Post* (July 5, 1963) quotes Huxley:

Another 10 or 15 years of uninhibited breeding, and the whole world, from China to Peru via Africa and the Middle East, will be fairly crawling with Great Leaders, all dedicated to the suppression of freedom, all armed to the teeth by Russia or America or, better still, all waving flags, all screaming for Lebensraum.

Many Yiddish words crop up in newspaper columns because they have a special aura no English word can convey. Leonard Lyons and Earl Wilson have a field day with such words. In a recent column in the *New York Post*, Lyons wrote: "Alan Bennett, of 'Beyond the Fringe,' entered a discussion about a man, and said: 'To put it in plain English, he's *meshuga!*'" Or: "When the Micheners, who are in Israel, heard the news [that James Michener's *Caravans* was bought by MGM for $500,000] Mrs. Michener—who is of Japanese descent —cabled his agent, Helen Strauss: '*Mazel Tov!*'"

*Meshuga* and *mazel tov* are wordplay when used this way; they are somehow funnier than "crazy" or "congratulations" (English equivalents that are far wide of the mark). Other foreign terms are borrowed because they describe something in the culture of their origin for which we have no parallel. The growth of Israel as a nation has introduced the word *kibbutz*, which is a kind of collective farm. We have no word that corresponds to the French *aperitif*, though it's just as tasty without the French label. When we read about Japanese

351

businessmen, *kabuya* and *zaibatsu* are common terms. The Italian *squadristi* and *paparazzi* have been in the news lately. The diplomatic term *rapprochement* is a frequent visitor in print in an era of test-bans, cultural exchanges, and Common Markets.

Latin and French terms used in diplomatic circles have been overworked in print recently. *Détente, de facto, quid pro quo, entente* should be in the under-10 range according to their frequency in newspaper and magazine print. *Entente,* the only one of the four in Thorndike, is listed at 18, but it would probably be rated much lower today. If words are a gauge that measures the spirit of an age, we can be sure that there is greater communion between nations today than there was in Thorndike's time.

## HOW TO APPROACH FOREIGN WORDS

There is always a reason why a foreign word comes into the language as a visitor and often remains as a permanent resident. Next time you encounter such a word in print or on the air, try to break it apart as you would a word of classical origin. You may find out through this method why it has been allowed to take out first papers.

Two journalists in the country on a holiday came on the word *Poltergeist.*

"It's an athletic ghost," said one, "it throws furniture around, drops things over the stair BANISTER, bangs away at walls, and is generally a practical joker."

"I don't doubt it," said the other, "and I know that *Geist* means 'spirit' in German. But what's *Polter?*"

"This high school dictionary doesn't give the word *Poltergeist,* let alone tell what it comes from."

"Then the dictionary can't be much good."

"I don't see that that follows. How often would the word *Poltergeist* turn up in student reading?"

"Not often. —But look up the derivation in the big Webster."

"That gives us *Poltern*—to knock or rattle."

"Of course, it's a first cousin of our word 'pother.'"

"So a *Poltergeist* is just a noisy ghost?"

"That should settle it—even if it doesn't EXORCISE the ghost."

352

"A *Poltergeist* needs no exercise!"
"Sign off on that one—before it starts throwing things at you!"

## Foreign Words and Phrases Recently in Print

This test is going to be different; we'll give you the clues and you'll figure out the foreign terms that fit. All of the words described have been in print or on the air recently. The Latin phrases came into the language some time back but are now in constant use. Most of the others have filtered in during the last ten or fifteen years. A few are too new even for the dictionaries.

1. A Latin phrase meaning someone or something that makes a sudden appearance in a contrived manner to resolve a difficult problem. Literally, "the god from the machine."
2. A German word used in criticism of plays, books, etc. that means "trash."
3. A French word describing an unorthodox or experimental approach to the arts.
4. A Latin phrase that is a mark of distinction upon graduation from school or college.
5. A French word referring to an administrative district in France.
6. An Italian word meaning palace or palacelike residence.
7. A German word meaning "good-natured, jolly, comfortable."
8. A Russian word meaning "traveling companion."
9. A Latin phrase meaning a way to get around a difficulty.
10. A Japanese term that describes a group of businessmen who are associated by reason of their wealth.
11. A German word that means noisy and mischievous spirits.
12. An Israeli word meaning a collective farm.
13. A Spanish word that refers to a spirited dance or dancer.
14. A Latin term in law that refers to the basic facts of a crime.
15. A French phrase describing highborn ladies of easy virtue.
16. A South African word that is almost synonymous with "segregation."
17. A Japanese stockbroker.
18. A French phrase meaning the sudden overthrow by force of the existing government.
19. A Latin phrase meaning without end.
20. A French word referring to a fashionable shop for women.

353

ANSWERS

| | | |
|---|---|---|
| 1. deus ex machina | 8. sputnik | 14. corpus delicti |
| 2. kitsch | 9. modus vivendi | 15. grandes cocottes |
| 3. avant-garde | 10. zaibatsu | 16. apartheid |
| 4. magna cum laude | 11. poltergeist | 17. kabuya |
| 5. arrondissement | 12. kibbutz | 18. coup d'état |
| 6. palazzo | 13. flamenco | 19. ad infinitum |
| 7. gemütlich | | 20. boutique |

## THE "EDUCATED" VOCABULARY

Examples have been given of prose composed in Damon Runyonesque style, with a dash of slang of the past and present. Informal words can be RACY, ZESTY, and colorful, and it pays to tune in on them if only to know what is going on in the world around you. But slang and jargon come and go, with only a small percentage of such words staying in the language on a permanent basis. Even Runyonese, which caught the Broadway rhythm of its day, is dying out as you noticed when 36 of the 77 terms given were no longer INTELLIGIBLE. Still, you can place a small bet, as one of Runyon's characters would do, on the chances of a few of these terms becoming part of the cultural heritage bequeathed to the future.

Words come and go, but so many of them have endured through the centuries that they have become the base upon which the educated man builds his vocabulary; they are the keys to the best that has been thought and said. These are the words in SMALL CAPITALS that you will meet again in your Comprehensive Vocabulary-Level Test. They are the words that invariably appear in serious writing, the words that grace the pages of that last word in lexicons—the OED. And they are in the OED because great writers have used them in quotable contexts.

You will find many of these words in Time and Newsweek, in The Atlantic, New York Times, Fortune, and other current magazines and newspapers. But the best place to look for them is in the best literature. This takes an eye and an ear not only for the words themselves but for the MILIEU in which they move, for the company they keep. Even a commonplace word becomes something richer and more uncommon when it is spoken in a Shakespearean poem. And

354

the less common and uncommon words take on an even more MEAN-INGFUL aura in these surroundings.

Shakespeare and other great writers need not be approached in fear and trembling with your hand nervously clutching at the dictionary. The Bard was writing for a popular audience, which couldn't care less about the ratings of words in small capitals but which appreciated a word come alive in speech and action. To the Elizabethan audience words were not objects to be alphabetized in a dictionary-vacuum; they were vital and lusty; they had personalities.

Let's take a book that is thought to be the most widely read in the English language—the Bible. When was the last time you read it? Whether you are religious or not, the Bible, with its fine cadences and rhythms, is a work of literature, and a storehouse for words that will help you build your vocabulary. Here are a few:

| | |
|---|---|
| PROCURATOR (20-plus) | SCAPEGOAT (18) |
| BEATITUDE (20-plus) | SHEKEL (20-plus) |
| PSALMODY (20-plus) | SERAPHIM (20-plus) |
| PSALTER (20-plus) | SOOTHSAYER (12) |
| SACKBUT (20-plus) | SWADDLING (clothes) (20-plus) |

These words are all keys to cultural history because the language of the Bible does reveal the events, attitudes, and philosophies of the period in which it was written. And though this book has currency throughout the world, most of the above words are seen and heard only occasionally outside its pages. But in their IMPACT upon the language, in the aura they convey, they have undeniable power. To go back and read the Bible as a cultural document is a rewarding experience, and a boon to one's vocabulary.

The best writers shape words as instruments of thought and feeling, and this is perhaps the most significant reason for reading literature. The word in small capitals, any word for that matter, ceases to be an isolated unit and is incorporated into the framework of an idea. Whether it's an uncommon word above Thorndike's 20-plus level, a less common word in the minus-20 group, or an everyday word from the commonest 10,000, it loses its word-ness and becomes a building block in an AESTHETIC structure when molded by a master writer.

# UNCOMMON WORDS AND PHRASES
# IN CONTEXT

Ideally, it would be admirable to meet all new words IN
SITU—so you would first encounter them in the surrounding MATRIX
of which they are a part, just as the archaeologist studies the objects
which he digs up as belonging to the strata in which they lie, and
in relation to other ARTIFACTS with which they are found. But time
and space will not always permit of this leisurely procedure. When
Casanova asked Voltaire, "Why not read only in the book of life?"
Voltaire answered, "Because it's so unwieldy." To cover the ground,
we often have to deal with words in isolated units as they appear in
the dictionary.

But in winding up an inquiry, we can well afford to be leisurely in
taking another kind of word test to see how far new-found mastery
makes it possible to avoid blackouts of meaning. And that calls for
taking the words not singly, but in context.

Here you should make a free-wheeling approach. Don't worry
about dictionary definitions until you're hopelessly stumped. Try
to figure out, by all the devices at your command, what the meaning
is. For, as Frank Colby remarks, in his *Confessions of a Gallomaniac:*

. . . a word is not a definite thing susceptible of a dictionary explanation.
It is a cluster of associations, reminiscent of the sort of men that used it,
suggestive of social class, occupation, mood, dignity or the lack of it,
PRIMNESS, violences, PEDANTRIES or PLATITUDES.

Evidently, to sense words in this way, you must take them in place
—unless they are words so rich in historic, religious, or literary associations that even alone they convey the rich aura of meaning
Colby had in mind. Hold his statement in SUSPENSION in your consciousness, as you work through the following passages.

In this test there are several common words and phrases used in
special contexts. On the first run-through (1) check only any blackouts of meaning that you experience. Then (2) note how many of
the words that puzzled you are in small capitals or italics. They are
the key words in these examples.

356

## A. Nuclear Physics

The *bevatron* produced, on order and as predicted, the previously unobserved particles of *antimatter,* the *antiproton* and *antineutron.* And it provided a rich PROFUSION of puzzling *K-meson tracks* that led, in 1957, to the overthrow of the physicists' *sacred principle of parity.*—The Editors of *Fortune, America in the Sixties* (Harper & Row, Publishers)

## B. Astronomy

The great *Palomar* telescope, in less than ten years, has doubled and redoubled the estimated size and age of the *universe.* And in COLLABORATION with *radio telescopes,* it has produced the first evidence of *galaxies* meeting in TITANIC *collision.* Finally, the *pre-Sputnik rockets* carried measuring instruments to the edge of the earth's atmosphere for the first time. They provided brief TANTALIZING glimpses of a new frontier of discovery.—Ibid.

## C. Theater

In the *tragic drama* of our own time, the playwrights seem to be still consolidating the revolution of IBSEN, CHEKHOV, and the *Irish dramatists,* reshaping the *tragic vision* to fit a world of new *classes* and *values,* a world with neither villains nor heroes, a world that has lost much of its faith and most of its hope. Perhaps least typical of our time is T. S. ELIOT's *Murder in the Cathedral. . . .* Here, telling the story of the martyrdom of ST. THOMAS À BECKET in the twelfth century, Eliot finds tragedy in the vision of man as a *flawed agency of divine purpose.*—Stanley Hyman, "The Tragic Vision," *Adventures of the Mind* (Alfred A. Knopf, Inc., 1961)

## D. Communist Dialectic

As communist SEMANTICISTS attained VIRTUOSO skills, they discovered that, in many instances, communications can be made to serve a *dual purpose*—to say one thing to communists while simultaneously conveying quite a different message to noncommunists. . . . This *"double-think"* or *"double-talk"* mission is accomplished by applying a practice developed more than sixty years ago by LENIN, who

357

also coined the expression *"Aesopian language."* AESOP, the
sixth-century B.C. Greek FABULIST, invented the technique
of hiding moral and political points behind seemingly
INNOCUOUS stories and originated such *colloquialisms* as
"sour grapes," "the wolf in sheep's clothing," "the dog in
the manger," and "belling the cat." . . . By now most of
the original communist vocabulary has been given an *Aesopian equivalent.* "Dictatorship of the proletariat" grew into
"democracy"; "expropriation" was transformed into "planning"; "revolution" was CAMOUFLAGED as "liberation"; and
"communism" itself was disguised as *"anticolonialism,"* "anti-
imperialism," or "anti-fascism."—Stefan T. Possony, "Words
That Divide the World," *Adventures of the Mind* (Alfred
A. Knopf, Inc., 1961)

How many blackouts of meaning did you have? How many times
did a word or phrase interpret the flow of idea rather than clarify
it? As you deal with more complex subject matter, you will have
more blackouts of meaning unless you make an effort to understand
the context in which the words are used. It may not always be your
INTERPRETATIVE skill that is at fault; if an idea is not clearly expressed,
blame the writer. But first make a concentrated effort to understand
what is being said.

## WHAT IS YOUR VOCABULARY RATING?

You figured your vocabulary score at the conclusion of Chapter 11.
Is your rating average, above average, college graduate, master's degree? Did you achieve genius level—300 correct answers? Or did
you fall miserably into the substandard group? No matter how you
made out, don't be discouraged; you can REDEEM yourself on the
Comprehensive Vocabulary-Level Test. But first review the material
on the Word-Analyzer.

## THE WORD-ANALYZER

This Word-Analyzer is meant as a working tool, to be used when you feel the need for it. Regard it as a standby service, and consult it at leisure. It will not make you an ETYMOLOGIST overnight. But it should be useful in showing you how to break down classical words in English into their component parts. You can thus get at their literal meaning, which is a good start.

The Word-Analyzer includes

1. The 70 commonest Latin stems. Memorize them.
2. The 30 commonest Greek stems. Memorize them.
3. Latin prefixes and suffixes.
4. Greek prefixes and suffixes.

Suppose you want to analyze the word SUPERSCRIPTION: First break it down into its parts, then look them up in the tables—main stem first, then the suffix, finally, the prefix:

| *super* | *SCRIPT* | *ion* |
|---|---|---|
| "above" | "written" | "state of being," or "that which" |

Of the two meanings of the suffix, "that which" makes more sense. Superscription is "that which [is] written above"—such as a heading.

Here's the recipe in general terms:

First, break off the prefix and/or suffix. The main stem (or stems) should then be apparent.

Second, look up the meaning of the stem in the checklists. Put it under the stem in the breakdown.

Third, try to identify the prefix and/or suffix in the appropriate lists. Because their combining forms are tricky, and the Latin and English suffixes of identical spelling have different meanings, this may take a bit of trial-and-error procedure before you get a combination that seems to make sense.

Fourth, rearrange in English order the equivalents you have set down under the elements of the word. This should give the literal meaning.

# WORD-ANALYZER

**Latin Prefixes**

*ab-* away from
*ad-* to
*ambi-, an-,* around
*ante-* before
*bene-* well
*circum-* around
*con-, cum-* with
*contra-* against
*de-* away, down
*dis-* apart, not
*ex-* out of
*inter-* between
*in-* not
*in-* into, in
*male-* evil, badly
*non-* not
*ob-* against
*per-* through
*post-* after
*pre-* before
*pro-* for
*re-* again
*retro-* back
*se-* away from
*sub-* under
*super-* over
*trans-* across

The 100 commonest Latin and Greek stems figure in more than 5,000 English derivatives in the range just beyond the average American's vocabulary of 10,000 words. Learn to use the 100 classical stems to sight-read these 5,000 words and you have a shortcut that will put you a long way on the road toward doubling your vocabulary. Many of the 5,000 are terms used in business, medicine, chemistry, technology. If you know the 100 stems, and the most used Latin and Greek affixes (prefixes and suffixes), you can analyze many words new to you, when you run into them in your reading. A breakdown of the word will show you first the

| inter- | POSIT | -ion | |
|--------|-------|------|--|
| between | placing | act of | 'act of placing between' |

| LATIN STEM | MEANING | DERIVATIVES |
|------------|---------|-------------|
| AG, ACT | to do, to drive | transaction, exigency |
| AM, AMAT | to love | amative, amicability |
| APT | fit or fitted | adaptability, readaptation |
| ART | art, skill, method | artifact, artificer |
| AUD, AUDIT | to hear | inaudible, audition |
| CAD, CAS | to fall | casualty, decasualize |
| CAN, CANT | to sing | recantation, incantation |
| CAP, CAPT | to take, to seize | capacity, exceptionable |
| CAPIT | head | decapitation, precipitate |
| CED, CESS | to yield, to go | intercession, antecedent |
| CERN, CRET | to distinguish | discernible, indiscretion |
| CLAM, CLAMAT | to cry out | exclamatory, reclamation |
| CLUD, CLUS | to close | exclusivity, occlusion |
| COR, CORD | heart | discordant, concordance |
| CRED, CREDIT | to believe | incredibility, accredited |
| CUR, CURAT | to care for | insecurity, procurator |
| CURR, CURS | to run | precursor, recurrent |
| DAT | to give | extradition, antedate |
| DIC, DICT | to speak, to say | abdication, noncontradictory |
| DIGN | worthy | indignity, condign |
| DUC, DUCT | to lead | deduction, noninductive |
| EQU | equal | inequitable, inequivalent |
| FAC, FACT | to make, to do | benefactor, unification |
| FER, LAT | to bear, to carry | correlation, nontransferable |
| FORM | form | conformation, conformity |
| FRANG, FRACT | to break | irrefrangible, refraction |
| GER, GEST | to bear, perform | congestion, vicegerent |
| GRAT | pleasing | ingratitude, gratuity |
| HAB, HABIT | to have | rehabilitation, inhibition |
| JAC, JECT | to throw | trajectory, interjection |
| JUNG, JUNCT | to join, bind | disjunctive, conjuncture |
| LEG, LECT | to read, choose | predilection, lectern, dialectic |
| MAN | hand | manumission, manuscript |
| MITT, MISS | to send | intermittent, emissary |
| MOD | measure, manner | immoderate, accommodation |
| MOV, MOT | to move | motivation, demobilize |
| NOT | to know | connotation, denotation |
| PAND, PASS | to spread | expansive, surpassable |
| PAR, PARAT | to prepare | reparation, irreparable |
| PART | part | departmentalize, partisan |
| PET, PETIT | to seek | centripetal, repetitive |
| PLAC, PLACIT | to please | implacability, complacency |
| PLIC, PLICAT | to fold, bend | complicity, implication |
| PON, POSIT | to place | deposition, transposition |
| PORT, PORTAT | to carry | deportation, exportation |
| PREHEND | to seize | reprehensible, apprehension |
| QUER, QUISIT | to seek | inquisitorial, perquisite |
| RAP, RAPT | to seize, hurry away | surreptitious, rapturous |
| REG, RECT | to rule, direct | insurrection, rectitude |
| RUPT | to break, destroy | incorruptible, irruption |

**Greek Prefixes**

| a(an)- not | amphi- on both sides | ana- up | anti- against | apo- from | cata- down | di(a)- through | ex(ec)- from |
|-----------|---------------------|---------|--------------|-----------|------------|----------------|--------------|
| hyper- over | hypo- under | meta- beyond | para- beside | peri- around | pro- before | pseudo- false | syn- with |

stem, and by the method of remainders, the prefix and suffix that make it up. You can thus get at its literal meaning. Since you have seen it also in context, you can guess at its present meaning, once you know the literal sense. Below is the technique for sight-reading meanings: Pick out the stem involved, and locate it in the table. The prefix and/or suffix will stand out as separate. Locate them in the lists. Place the English equivalents under the prefix, stem, and suffix. Reshuffle the English equivalents to make sense. A word from the Latin is analyzed on the left-hand page; a Greek word just below.

| anti- | PATH | -y | means |
|---|---|---|---|
| against | feeling | state of | 'state of feeling against' |

| Stem | Meaning | Derivatives |
|---|---|---|
| SAL, SALT | to leap | salient, exultation |
| SCRIB, SCRIPT | to write | indescribable, scriptorium |
| SED, SESS | to sit | nonsedentary, residuary |
| SENT, SENS | to feel, perceive | insensibility, presentiment |
| SEQU, SECUT | to follow | obsequious, prosecutor |
| SERV, SERVAT | to save, protect | conservatory, preservative |
| SIGN | sign | assignation, designation |
| SPIC, SPECT | to look at | inauspicious, perspicuity |
| STA, STAT | to stand | transubstantiation, circumstantiality |
| SIST | to cause to stand | inconsistency, irresistible |
| STRING, STRICT | to bind | astringent, constriction |
| TANG, TACT | to touch | tangential, contingent |
| TEN, TENT | to hold | untenable, sustenance |
| TEND, TENS | to stretch | tensile, distension |
| TRAH, TRACT | to draw | retraction, contractile |
| UT, US | to use | usury, peruse |
| VEN, VENT | to come | provenience, contravene |
| VERT, VERS | to turn | irreversible, transverse |
| VID, VIS | to see | provisional, improvident |
| VOC | voice | provocation, vociferous |

| GREEK STEM | MEANING | DERIVATIVES |
|---|---|---|
| AGON | contest | protagonist, antagonize |
| ALLO | other | allotropic, allomorph |
| ARCH | chief, first, rule | anarchical, monarchical |
| BIBLIO, BIBLO | book | bibliography, bibliophile |
| DEMO | the people | antidemocratic, demotic |
| DRA | to do, act | dramaturgy, dramatize |
| DYNAMI | power | hydrodynamics, aerodynamic |
| ELECTRO | amber (electric) | electronics, dielectric |
| ERGO | work | allergy, ergometer |
| GEO | earth | geological, gemetrical |
| GRAPH | to write | epigraphy, graphology |
| HOMO | the same | homonym, homophone |
| HYDRO | water | hydrostatic, dehydrate |
| ISO | equal | isometric, isotope |
| K(C)LINO | to bend, slant | declination, isoclinal |
| K(C)RYPTO | hidden | cryptography, cryptic |
| LOGO | word, reason, study | neologism, physiological |
| METRO | measure | geometrical, photometer |
| NEO | new | neophyte, neologist |
| PATHO | feeling | psychopathology, empathy |
| PHILO | loving, fond of | philology, zoophile |
| PHOB | fear | zoophobia, photophobia |
| PHONO | sound | phonology, gramophone |
| PHOTO | light | photoelectric, photometric |
| PHYS | nature | monophysite, physiography |
| PROTO | first | protozoa, prototype |
| PSYCHE | mind, soul | psychometric, parapsychology |
| TECH· | art, craft | technological, electro-technology |
| THEO | god | theological, theocentric |
| ZOO | animal | zoophyte, zoography |

**Latin Suffixes**

-able, -ible, able to be
-acy, state or quality of being
al, pertaining to, act of
-an, -ant, -ent, one who or -ing
-ary belonging to
-ate having
-ency state of being
-er, -or one who
-ern belonging to
-ic pertaining to
-ice state or quality of being
-ive one who, that which is
-oon, -ion one who
-ory relating to, thing which, place where
-ose, -ous full of
-tion state of that which
-tude state of being
-ure state or act of
-y state of being

| -ac | -et | -ic, -ical | Greek Suffixes |
|---|---|---|---|
| pertaining to (adj.) | one who (noun) | pertaining to, made of, one who | |
| -ic, -ice | -ise, ize | -ist | -y |
| science of (noun) | to make, to give (verb) | one who (n) | state of being |

# WORD-MATCHING TESTS

If you've studied your stems thoroughly, take the following practice tests, which will prepare you for the Comprehensive Vocabulary-Level Test. See how readily you can slip words already identified as coming from a given stem into the right slots in a short fable. After you've made your best guess, look up in the dictionary all the words of which you have the least doubt. The more carefully you do these tests, the higher will be your score on the Comprehensive Vocabulary-Level Test that follows.

*Note carefully:* There are in each list more words than there are blanks to be filled in the sentences. Many have appeared elsewhere in SMALL CAPS.

AG, ACT (ig, g, actu), from *agere, actus:* to do, move, urge on, put in motion, drive.

| | | | | | |
|---|---|---|---|---|---|
| act | management | agent | navigate | AMBIGUITY | LITIGATION |
| exact | manager | prodigal | synagogue [1] | VARIEGATED | CASTIGATE |
| manage | agitation | transaction | PEDAGOGUE [1] | ACTUATE | COGITATE |
| agency | enact | mitigate | AMBIGUOUS | COGENT | MANAGEABLE |
| actor | | | | EXIGENCY | AGENDA |

## War on the Landlord

What the renting ____1____ called an ____2____ in the lease, I called downright SKULLDUGGERY. They had a lot of fancy and ____3____ legal VERBIAGE which just invited ____4____. Add to that the fact that the building ____5____ was a thoroughly bad ____6____, and you'll readily see why I ____7____ the ____8____ for the landlord when he called for the rent. The ____9____ was not exactly ____10____ with heat, either. I wrote them a few ____11____ reasons why I might have to go to court. They said they didn't want any of that kind of ____12____ starting and that so far as they were concerned, I could move into the ____13____ next door, or buy a houseboat or trailer. This didn't ____14____ my wrath, and ____15____d by the strongest public spirit, I wrote back a letter full of massive insults for all landlords.

APT (att, ept), from *aptus:* fit or fitted, the p.p. of obsolete verb *apere,* to fasten, join together.

| | | | | | |
|---|---|---|---|---|---|
| apt | adapt | adaptation | APTITUDE | ADAPTABILITY | INAPT |
| attitude | | | | ADAPTABLE | INEPT |

[1] Strictly, from the Greek through the Latin.

## Reporter's Arch-Enemy

The cluck on the copy desk was so ____1____ that he'd murder any ____2____ phrase that survived the rewrite man. Every time he uttered PLATITUDES in stained glass ____3____s, he broke the glass. His ____4____ was NIL, and his ____5____ to the work was minus zero.

CERT, CRET (cre), from *cernere, cretus:* to see, to sift, to distinguish, to separate.

| certain | secretary | certainly | discretion | certify | discernment |
|---|---|---|---|---|---|
| secret | decree | certificate | secrecy | EXCRETION | INDISCRETION |
| concern | discern | discreet | secretion | INDISCREET | DISCERNIBLE |
| | | | SECRETIVE | | |

## Little Flower

Mayor LaGuardia, while a man of ____1____, was famous for his calculated ____2____s. Though ____3____ by habit, he could on occasion be glaringly ____4____. His motives for exploding were not always immediately ____5____, but his secretary usually could make a pretty good guess as to what was in the wind. Sometimes the blast backfired, and the Mayor was accustomed to say, "When I make a mistake, it's a beaut."

ART (artis, ert), from *ars, artis:* skill, art, method.

| art | artistic | inert | ARTLESS | INERTIA | INERTLY |
|---|---|---|---|---|---|
| artist | artillery | artifice | ARTIFICER | ARTISTRY | ARTIFACT |
| artificial | artful | artisan | | | |

## You Can't Hurt an Elephant with Buckshot

It was always hard to say when the party maverick was just being ____1____, when ____2____, and when ____3____, so skillfully were his personal and political ____4____s INTERWOVEN. When he moved up the lighter ____5____ of his wit to shoot buckshot at the ____6____ and CHUCKLE-HEADED leaders of his party, he showed rare ____7____ in placing his shots. Not that he really jolted the massive ____8____ of the elephant, or reached its MAHOUTS with their still thicker hides; but for the moment the beast and its riders gave the illusion of moving less ____9____. But even he could not dislodge the PETRIFIED FOSSIL planks in the platform; these will last until they are dug up as ____10____ by the ARCHAEOLOGISTS of 4964, and pronounced the work of clumsy ____11____s.

AUD, AUDIT (audi, edi, ey, eis), from *audire, auditus:* to hear.

| obey | obedient | audible | disobedience | AUDITORY | INAUDIBLE |
|---|---|---|---|---|---|
| audience | disobey | auditor | OBEISANCE | AUDITORIUM | AUDIT |
| obedience | | | | | AUDITION |

363

## Too Bad It Can't Happen

The Committee Against Television Trivia, not content with writing nasty letters about soap operas, spot announcements, middle commercials and other abominations, decided to organize flying SQUADRONS to salt studio ____1____, and make their disapproval ____2____. When the cheerleader called for applause, they hissed or jeered, and kept it up until the succeeding lines were ____3____. Refusing to make ____4____ to the HUCKSTERS of the air, they were denied tickets to programs; but other members of the committee took their places. Pretty soon ____5____ for the advertising agencies and the sponsors reported that the jeering caused a drop in sales of the product advertised; and, even more deadly, the Nielsen ratings were falling fast. Soon these ____6____s had their effect. Programs improved, and there were a lot of ____7____s for new talent.

CAN, CANT (cent, chant), from *canere, cantus:* to sing.

| | | | | | |
|---|---|---|---|---|---|
| accent | enchant | CANT | CANTO | RECANT | CANTATA |
| chant | enchantment | ACCENTUATE | RECANTATION | CANTICLE | |

## Collegiate Conductor

The CHORAL conductor had a slangy ____1____, wore a sweater and unpressed slacks, but he could cast a kind of ____2____over his singers. Whether he was conducting a ____3____, a ____4____, or a stately ____5____, he got results. He was criticized for swearing, but far from being willing to ____6____, he violently ____7____d the negative. And he never talked musical ____8____.

CAP, CAPT, CAPTUS (cip, ceiv, cept, ceipt, ceit), from *capere, captus:* to take, seize, hold.

| | | | | | |
|---|---|---|---|---|---|
| except | capable | exception | exceptional | susceptible | RECIPIENT |
| accept | conceive | reception | precept | acceptable | PARTICIPLE |
| occupy | capture | captivity | participate | deception | INCIPIENT |
| deceive | occupation | conceit | anticipation | emancipation | PARTICIPANT |
| principal | capacity | deceit | incapable | municipal | |
| perceive | captive | capacious | principality | CAPABILITY | |

## The Politico

Politics is an odd trade, but make no mistake about it, it's a full-time ____1____. A politician must have a good ____2____ of himself, must be able on occasion to ____3____ without getting a reputation for ____4____. He has sold himself into ____5____ to his backers, and he is usually ____6____ to pressure. WILLY-NILLY he must be a ____7____ in community activities, must attend ____8____s and other ceremonial functions, and on occasion demonstrate his ____9____ to carry liquor. While in office, he cannot hope for ____10____ from these social duties, even if ____11____ affairs suffer. He must mouth conventional ____12____s at church gatherings, and have a fund of ____13____ jokes for service club luncheons. Yet he will be criticized if he gets tangled up in a dangling ____14____ when he orates, and accused of ____15____ SENILITY if he muffs his words in a radio or television talk.

COR, CORD, CORDI (cour), from *cor, cordis:* the heart.

| according | encourage | accord | core | RECORDER |
|---|---|---|---|---|
| record | accordingly | discourage | encouragement | CONCORDANCE |
| courage | cordial | courageous | concord | discord |

## Son of a Lexicographer Goes Astray

A Shakespeare ____1____ shows that he used just 17,677 different words in his works. It is hard to reconcile this figure with the findings by a son of a LEXICOGRAPHER that a good American vocabulary runs to 150,000 words—8½ times as many as Shakespeare used. There's a ____2____ here somewhere.

CRED, CREDIT (cre), from *credere, creditus:* to believe, trust to.

| credit | creed | discredit | CREDENTIAL | CREDIBLE | CREDENCE |
|---|---|---|---|---|---|
| creditor | credulous | CREDITABLE | MISCREANT | ACCREDIT | INCREDIBLE |
| credulity | incredulous | INCREDULITY | | | |

## The Mystery of Faith

Tertullian said that he believed the Christian ____1____ because it's ____2____. Cynics say that such ____3____ ____4____ is to the Church Father's ____5____. Themselves giving no ____6____ to faith, they do not ____7____ it with the efficacy which believers find in it.

CED, CESS (ceed, ceas), from *cedere, cessus:* to go, yield, give up.

| proceed | exceed | ancestor | precede | procedure | ANTECEDENT |
|---|---|---|---|---|---|
| success | process | procession | predecessor | accessory | CESSATION |
| succeed | successful | access | concede | cede: recede | PRECEDENT |
| recess | decease | intercession | ABSCESS | ACCESSIBLE | ACCESSION |

## A Legal Puzzle

The ____1____ server finally ____2____ed in catching up with him, and he was hauled into court for failure to pay the third month's rent. He ____3____d it was due, but said he couldn't pay because he hadn't recovered his government check for the hogs he had agreed not to raise under the Department of Agriculture program. His lawyer said that the young man's immediate paternal ___4___ of the same name had collected the check. The lawyer thought the court could well take a long ___5___ on the case while action was PENDING in an upstate court to recover the check. He did not ask for a ___6___ of the action, he said. However, he wished to say for the record that he felt the upstate judge would be hard put to it to find ___7___s on which to decide which of the two, father or son, had not raised the hogs.

CURR, CURS (curri, corri, cur, cor, couri, cours) from *currire, cursus:* to run, more quickly.

| course | incur | occurrence | COURIER | CONCUR | DISCURSIVE |
| current | excursion | succor | COURSER | CURSORY | PRECURSOR |
| occur | corridor | recur | | | |

## A Detective Story

The State Department ___1___ was traveling in a plane which just out of Denver ran into heavy weather that proved to be the ___2___ of a terrible storm. DOWNDRAFTS ___3___ again and again. The pilot told everybody to get ready to bail out, remarking this wasn't an ___4___ trip. The State Department man, with more than a ___5___ glance at the pouch he was carrying, said he ___6___ed in the pilot's view, and added he was under instructions to destroy the pouch rather than risk having it picked up from the wreck. "What is it, the hydrogen bomb formula?" the pilot asked.

CLAUS (clos), (clud, clus, in compounds), from *claudere, clausus:* to shut.

| close | closet | clause | cloister | SECLUSION | CLOSURE |
| include | exclusive | conclusion | exclusion | PRECLUDE | INCLUSION |
| conclude | inclose | exclude | SECLUDE | RECLUSE | |

## No More Lonely Hearts

The modern ___1___ need not lead a hermit life, even though his retreat is ___2___d. In his ___3___ed retreat, he is not ___4___ from enjoying television, and he may ___5___ in his REGIMEN luxuries delivered by PARACHUTE from an air express.

CLAM, CLAMAT (claim), from *clamare, clamatus:* to call, to cry out.

| claim | clamor | proclamation | clamorous | RECLAMATION | DECLAMATION |
| exclaim | exclamation | reclaim | ACCLAIM | CLAIMANT | DECLAIM |
| proclaim | | | | | EXCLAMATORY |

366

## Change the Name of Dear Old Arkansas?

Senator Foghorn had won the ____1____ prize at his high school commencement, and never forgot it. His style was ____2____ and ____3____. In fact the ____4____ mark was his favorite form of PUNCTUATION. He would ____5____ at the drop of a hat, even at dinner parties. On the floor of the Senate, he set up an equally loud ____6____ over a pension ____7____ or a ____8____ bill affecting three Western states. Another senator once remarked sourly that if they could only ____9____ and condense the verbal fog which Foghorn engendered, they could irrigate all Montana with it.

DIGN (digni, deign, daint, dain), from *dignus:* worthy.

dignity     disdain     dignify     disdainful   DIGNITARY     CONDIGN
dainty      indignation indignant   indignity    DAINTINESS

## Refugee De Luxe

This pompous and ____1____ old POUTER pigeon felt he was being subjected to ____2____s if he had to walk two blocks or carry a small parcel home. He had been some kind of minor ____3____ at a Ruritanian court, and his ____4____ knew no bounds if the doorman forgot his title. He stood on his ____5____, which was about all he had left to stand on, his legs having shrunk to mere PIPESTEMS. Not so the rest of him, for he loved pastry and all sorts of ____6____s.

CAPIT (cipit, cipic, capt, chatt, catt), from *caput, capitis:* the head.

captain   chapter    precipitate CHATTEL         PRECIPITATION   PRECIPITANT
cattle    capitalist precipitous CAPITULATION RECAPITULATION OCCIPITAL
capital                                          CAPITALISM

## Wall Street Mystery

Why the stock market should take such a ____1____ drop when production was rising, savings were huge, demand for goods immense, and dividends high, is a mystery. Is ____2____ under COMPULSION to ____3____ a crisis? Is it close to its last ____4____ as the Marxists claim? Certainly the chief factors in the downward turn of the market are psychological. But if these violent swings continue, we'll be going back to barter, and be using ____5____ for money once more—which, at the present price of steaks, is not so hard to imagine. ____6____s of finance should not even think of ____7____ to such PESSIMISM. It's up to ____8____ to save the system, in their role as managers. And this calls for a ____9____ of fundamental principles, as well as a REVAMPING of FISCAL policies.

**DAT**, from *dare, datus:* to give, do, plan, yield, put.

| | | | | | |
|---|---|---|---|---|---|
| add | surrender | editorial | EDIT | ANTEDATE | ABSCOND |
| date | tradition | perdition | DATUM | EXTRADITION | EDITORSHIP |
| addition | edition | RENDEZVOUS | DATA | DATIVE | EXTRADITE |
| render | editor | TRADITIONAL | | | |

## Underground News

The ____1____ of the underground sheet wrote as he fought, toughly. A ____2____ soon grew up around him. Give him a few scraps of ____3____, and he'd RECONSTRUCT a story. If a whole ____4____ of the paper was captured and burned, he'd rewrite the ____5____ VERBATIM, ____6____ the news from a few scrappy notes, and have a complete run on the streets by nightfall. When a traitor ____7____ed with the paper's funds, he wrote a doubletalk story suggesting methods for "____8____ing" the offender from headquarters; and it wasn't long before the spy had a forced ____9____ with an underground TRIBUNAL. His epitaph appeared in the paper surrounded by a black border.

**CUR, CURAT**, from *curare, curatus:* to take care of, care for, heal.

| | | | | | |
|---|---|---|---|---|---|
| sure | procure | security | accuracy | CURATE | INACCURATE |
| secure | assurance | accurate | reassure | CURATOR | INSECURITY |
| cure | insurance | surety | | | |

## Spending Money to Keep It

The ____1____ of the museum to his horror found the accounts inaccurate; but he was relieved to discover that the error was in bookkeeping, not in the actual state of the funds, which were ____2____. He decided to hire a more expensive ACCOUNTANT, in the interest of ____3____; and he put him under ____4____ bond.

**FORM**, from *forma:* figure, shape, appearance.

| | | | | |
|---|---|---|---|---|
| form | conform | reformation | CONFORMATION | FORMULARY |
| inform | deform | transformation | FORMULATION | REFORMATORY |
| information | formal | deformity | INFORMER | FORMALISM |
| uniform | formation | formality | CONFORMABLE | INFORMALITY |
| reform | formula | formulate | | |
| transform | informal | REFORMER | | |
| | | UNIFORMITY | | |

## Is Your Etiquette Showing?

ETIQUETTE is always in danger of becoming ____1____ without content. Too much ____2____ and too close ____3____ to rigid rules is indeed apt to freeze social life into the mold of ____4____. There is no sovereign

_____5_____ for good manners, and anyone who tries to _____6_____ such a code runs the hazards which even Chesterfield did not wholly CIRCUMVENE. Mere _____7_____ out of Emily Post is sufficient for arranging the forks, but not for effecting the subtle _____8_____ of outward gestures into inward feeling required for putting a company into high good humor. Here that measured _____9_____ which is the desirable end result of all social _____10_____s is the requisite.

FER, LAT (lay) from *ferre, latus:* to bear, carry.

| | | | | | |
|---|---|---|---|---|---|
| difference | refer | translate | defer | REFERENDUM | TRANSFERENCE |
| different | relate | ferry | fertility | SUPERLATIVE | ABLATIVE |
| offer | relation | reference | infer | CONIFEROUS | FLORIFEROUS |
| suffer | relative | fertilize | proffer | REFEREE | FRUCTIFEROUS |
| delay | confer | preference | translation | VOCIFEROUS | ILLATIVE |
| elate | conference | prelate | inference | CORRELATION | OBLATE |
| prefer | fertile | sufferance | DEFERENCE | PESTIFEROUS | PROLATE |
| differ | transfer | circumference | | | |

## The Dialecticians

The conference was exasperated at these newcomers to the international scene, who took nothing on _____1_____, but in the most _____2_____ and _____3_____ manner worried every proposal to death with their DIALECTIC. They made interminable _____4_____s, insisting on constant _____5_____s to earlier documents, and showed endless _____6_____ of resource in HAGGLING over minor points of procedure. They orated for three hours at a time, and it then took six hours to translate their HARANGUES. They would not cut across a circle if there was a chance to go around its _____7_____, and they showed a positive _____8_____ for going off at TANGENTS. _____9_____ them a concession or a compromise, and they were suspicious of it. They had no _____10_____ toward tradition, in fact despised it on principle; but they were facile and ready at erecting their own prejudices into eternal principles, from which they would not abate one jot. In fact, they reminded the delegates of American NEGOTIATORS in the days when the Republic was young—brash, TENDENTIOUS, their dignity easily offended, and great STICKLERS for the letter of the law.

EQU (equi), from *aequus:* equal, just.

| | | | | | |
|---|---|---|---|---|---|
| equal | unequal | adequate | equatorial | EQUITABLE | EQUINOCTIAL |
| equality | equator | equation | INEQUALITY | EQUIVOCAL | EQUANIMITY |
| equity | equivalent | inadequate | EQUABLE | EQUINOX | COEQUAL |
| | | EQUIVALENCE | | | |

## Doubletalker

He was ADEPT at making _____1_____ statements, and if confronted later with a DISCREPANCY between his words and his actions, he was quite

_____2_____ to twisting his own earlier remarks. In fact, his ____3____ when thus caught out was astonishing to colleagues who had more precise notions of ____4____. Had he been a GEOGRAPHER he would have had a globe with a shifting ____5____, and the ____6____ storms would have come at whatever time of year suited his convenience. As it was, his CO-WORKERS came to feel that there was not much ____7____ in any verbal ____8____ he devised, and they expected in dealings with him to come out on the ____9____ —and losing—side of the deal.

FRANG, FRACT, FRACTUR, from *frangere, fractus:* to break.

| | | | | | |
|---|---|---|---|---|---|
| frail | frailty | fracture | FRACTIONAL | FRANGIBLE | IRREFRAGABLE |
| fraction | suffrage | infringe | INFRACTION | IRREFRANGIBLE | REFRANGIBLE |
| fragment | fragile | REFRACTORY | REFRACTION | INFRINGEMENT | |

## Reductio ad Absurdum

This ____1____ group had purged and expelled its ____2____ members for various minor ____3____ of the supposedly ____4____ truths of party doctrine. As a result, many ____5____s appeared in the ____6____ structure of the party. Finally this small remaining ____7____ was so split that they had to divide their journalistic organ into three sections: Right, Left, and Center.

HAB, HABIT (ab, habitu, hibit) from *habere, habitus:* to have, hold.

| | | | | | |
|---|---|---|---|---|---|
| able | enable | prohibit | prohibition | INHIBIT | HABILIMENT |
| debt | exhibit | exhibition | habitual | HABITAT | REHABILITATION |
| habit | inhabit | habitation | disable | INHIBITION | PROHIBITIVE |
| ability | inhabitant | debtor | habitable | DEBILITY | |

## Paul's Parodies

The characters in Elliott Paul's amusing detective story PARODIES have few ____1____s. They constantly behave as if they were at a Beaux Arts ball, and the ____2____ of culture and wardrobe alike rest lightly on them. Their ____3____ liquor INTAKE is fantastic, yet drink seems to have no ____4____ effect on them. They ____5____ great RESOURCEFULNESS in fighting, and Miss Montana in particular shoots French THUGS with an ____6____ of *sang froid* that does credit to her training in the Great Open Spaces.

GER, GEST, GESTUR (gist, gistr, jest), from *genere, gestus:* to bear, or carry on, perform.

| | | | | | |
|---|---|---|---|---|---|
| register | gesture | digestion | indigestion | BELLIGERENT | GESTICULATION |
| suggest | suggestion | digestive | registration | CONGEST | GERUND |
| jest | digest | indigestible | congestion | JESTER | CONGERIES |
| | | | VICEGERENT | | |

## The Joker

Medieval banquets were spared the stale stories of a toastmaster, lifted out of Bennett Cerf's borrowings (without quotes) from Winchell and Lyons. Instead, a professional ____1____ produced a ____2____ of ____3____s designed to aid ____4____, not impede it. His ____5____s and antics were exaggerated in STYLIZED fashion, with ____6____s of both HARLEQUIN and clown. And he LAMPOONED his betters, acting always as a licensed ____7____ of the Devil, talking BAWDY so that everybody could join in who wished, as the mead and ale flowed more freely.

GRAT (gratu, grati, grai, gre), from *gratus:* pleasing, deserving thanks, thankful; *gratis,* by favor, without reward.

| | | | | | |
|---|---|---|---|---|---|
| grace | disgrace | gratification | gratify | GRACELESS | GRATUITY |
| agree | gracious | disagreeable | disagree | DISAGREEMENT | INGRATITUDE |
| agreeable | grateful | congratulation | gratitude | INGRATE | |

## Division of the Powers

Cleveland remarked that every appointment he made yielded him ten enemies and one ____1____. Indeed, most seasoned politicians in the top office are ____2____ when they encounter ____3____ for favors done. But if they're wise, they never ____4____ themselves until their course is run; for toward the end of a second term, the ____5____ and RANCOROUS hostility of Congress toward a President is PROVERBIAL. ____6____ between the two arms of government is the expected thing; and anything a President gets from Congress in that period is in the nature of a ____7____, flung to him with a snarl.

MAN (manu, main), from *manus:* the hand.

| | | | | | |
|---|---|---|---|---|---|
| manner | manifest | manuscript | MANEUVER | MANACLE | AMANUENSIS |
| maintain | manual | emancipation | MANIPULATE | MANICURE | MANUMISSION |
| manage | manure | manifestation | MANUFACTORY | MANIFESTO | BIMANOUS |
| | | QUADRUMANAL | | | |

## The Best People Didn't Like Him

Jefferson tired of acting as his own ____1____, copying all the foreign correspondence of the State Department into a letter book. He finally ____2____ed to have Congress grant him one clerk, but the FEDERALISTS in the Senate tried to block his appointment of Freneau, the poet, as too violently JACOBITE. Always Jefferson's efforts to strike off the shackles and ____3____ from the mind aroused opposition. Even his ____4____ of his slaves in his will was objected to, after his death. But to Jefferson the Declaration was no mere ____5____; it was also a way of life and action.

**MITT, MISS** (mit, mis), from *mittere, missu:* to send, cast, throw, let go.

| promise | commit | remit | intermittent | admittance | REMISS |
|---|---|---|---|---|---|
| admit | committee | compromise | remittance | EMISSARY | DEMISE |
| permit | submit | surmise | submissive | INTERMIT | COMMISSARY |
| dismiss | omit | emit | transmit | MISSILE | MANUMIT |
| commission | mission | | | MISSIVE | TRANSMIT |

## The Worms Turn

The faculty sent him to the CHANCELLOR as their ____1____ on behalf of the two instructors who had been ____2____ed, OSTENSIBLY for reasons of economy. The Chancellor's sense of humor, at best ____3____, was not working when he told his secretary "to ____4____ the faculty's walking delegate to come in." He didn't actually heave any ____5____s at the professor's head, but he looked as if he were about to explode. "I've already looked at this impertinent ____6____ your committee sent in," he roared, "what else do they want to say?" "My ____7____ from them is simply to tell you orally what they thought it more tactful not to put in writing: that they think you're dead wrong, even from the point of view of your own interest," the professor said coolly. "What, they think I've been ____8____ in my duty—," the Chancellor almost gasped. "It's simply that you'd do better to save the money on supplies, buildings and grounds OUTLAYS, and the like, rather than taking it out of the hides of your staff." "You seem to think I can take more grub out of the ____9____ than there is in it," said the Chancellor, thus reminding the professor none too gently that he was one of the 1500 retired generals of World War II. But he SIMMERED down, no longer ____10____ing blue rays, and after meeting with the faculty's executive ____11____, he ____12____d the case by granting the two professors involved nominal SABBATICALS at half pay—and they both landed jobs at twice their current salaries.

**JUNG, JUNCT, JUNCTUR** (join, joint, jointur), from *jungere, junctur:* to bind, connect, unite.

| join | conjunction | adjunct | CONJUGAL | DISJOIN | DISJUNCTION |
|---|---|---|---|---|---|
| joint | injunction | conjugate | JOINER | CONJOIN | JOINTER |
| adjoin | conjugation | REJOIN | JUNCTURE | CONJUNCTIVE | CONJUNCTURE |
| enjoin | junction | SUBJUNCTIVE | SUBJUGATE | JOINTLY | DISJOINTED |

## Tripping Over the Terms

One reason grammar's hard is that there are so many technical terms to master. The ____1____ is laid upon the student to study the ____2____ of verbs. Words that serve as CONNECTIVES are ____3____s; certain other relationships are ____4____, a very subtle distinction in logic. A verb expressing a condition contrary to fact must be in the ____5____ mode, now gradually vanishing. Once the student is properly ____6____ by these stern necessities of TERMINOLOGY, he has little energy left to form the language habits and patterns which would make grammar come alive for him. He gets at best a ____7____ view of the whole process by which language functions.

LEG, LECT, LECTUR (lig, less), from *legere, lectus:* to read, gather, choose.

| | | | | | |
|---|---|---|---|---|---|
| lesson | collection | coil | recollect | legacy | ELIGIBLE |
| collect | election | legend | colleague | collector | LEGIBLE |
| elect | lecture | selection | cull | INTELLIGIBLE | PREDILECTION |
| neglect | legion | dialect | intellect | ELEGANCE | DIALECTICS |
| | LEGIBILITY | | ILLEGIBLE | INTELLIGIBILITY | |

## Bibliomaniac

This BIBLIOMANIAC had an odd ____1____ for picking books on the basis of their ____2____. He liked big type and wide margins. He cared little about ____3____ or ____4____ of style. He would as readily read a ____5____ as a ____6____, if the former appeared in more ____7____ type. As a result his ____8____ was a strange one, containing among other items a DE LUXE edition of Lenin's ____9____ printed on rag instead of on the usual butcher paper; and the DOMINICAN translation of AQUINAS, on VELLUM, apparently stolen from a monastery library.

PAR,[2] PARAT (ver, pair), from *parare, paratus:* to see, to get ready, or make ready.

| | | | | | |
|---|---|---|---|---|---|
| prepare | repair | separation | apparatus | REPARATION | IRREPARABLE |
| several | preparation | sever | preparatory | DISSEVER | SEPARABLE |

## Hero in the Laboratory

Only the courageous PHYSICIST's quick action in ____1____ more widely the two small masses of PLUTONIUM prevented irreparable damage. Some slip had occurred in the ____2____ arrangements, and the blue EMA-NATION showed that they were too close, and that it was imperative to ____3____them. Once an inch closer, they would have been ____4____ ____ed, but by FISSION.

MOV, MOT (mo), from *movere, motus:* to move.

| | | | | | |
|---|---|---|---|---|---|
| moment | remove | remote | mob | commotion | MOMENTUM |
| move | motive | emotion | movable | removal | MOTIF |
| automobile | movement | locomotive | promotion | immovable | MOVIE |
| motion | motor | | | MOMENTOUS | MOBILIZE |

[2] Do not confuse with *par,* equal.

## Rabblerouser

His speech gathered more and more ____1____. He was ____2____ing the ____3____s of the audience and for no good. I began to wish the chairs were not ____4____, and as the crowd began restless and aimless ____5____, I decided we'd have to start a counter ____6____. The RABBLEROUSER kept recurring to his main ____7____, that there was a lot of money in California, and every man Jack there should get his share, and fast. He was steamed up like a ____8____, and it looked as if there'd be no stopping him. But luckily some loggers blew into the back of the hall who spotted him as a onetime fink in the woods. They rushed the platform and broke up the meeting without any waste ____9____.

NOT, from *noscere, notus,* or *gnoscere, gnotus:* to know.

| | | | | | |
|---|---|---|---|---|---|
| note | notion | ignoble | notary | COGNITION | CONNOTE |
| notice | ignorance | denote | NOTATION | INCOGNITO | CONNOTATION |
| noble | notable | notorious | COGNIZANCE | ANNOTATION | DENOTATION |
| ignorant | notify | recognition | | | |

## Word Pictures

Chinese picture-writing is a ____1____ SCRIPT, though ____2____ly hard to learn. It is perhaps better at expressing poetic ____3____s than at rendering the exact ____4____s of words which are so necessary in Western science. But in Chinese, the character not only ____5____s the idea, but illustrates it GRAPHICALLY at the same time—which Blake could do in English only by INTERWEAVING his copper engravings and paintings with his text. No great Chinese CHIROGRAPHER could remain ____6____. His brush strokes identified him. What would we not give for a HOLOGRAPH copy of Li Po's poems, permitting ____7____ of his very AUTOGRAPH style!

PET, PETIT (petu, peat), from *petere, petitus:* to ask, to seek, to rush at, to fly to.

| | | | | | |
|---|---|---|---|---|---|
| repeat | competition | compete | impetuous | IMPETUS | PETULANT |
| appetite | repetition | competitor | competent | INCOMPETENT | CENTRIPETAL |
| petition | | | | | REPETITIVE |

## Collective Open Shop

The spirit of ____1____ gave an immense ____2____ to work in the plant. A new type of ____3____ pump was needed, and it was invented. Many processes were so broken down that they could be performed by the ____4____ techniques of the assembly line. ____5____ craftsmen and ____6____ grumblers were quickly weeded out and shipped to Siberia or the Arctic North.

PAND, PANS, PASS (pac); from *pandere, pansus* or *passus:* to spread, step.

| pass | compass | passenger | expand | expansion | EXPANSE |
|------|---------|-----------|--------|-----------|---------|
| pace | passage | surpass | trespass | encompass | EXPANSIVE |
| | | PASSABLE | | | |

## Universal Man

What the mind of man could ____1____, da Vinci's embraced. He ____2____ed the frontiers of TECHNOLOGY and of art. He had ____3____ ing skill as a DRAUGHTSMAN, and used it alike in preparing the CARTOONS for his painting, in ANATOMICAL drawing, and in enginering design.

MOD (modi), from *modus:* measure, manner, fashion.

| model | modest | commodity | commodious | moderator | COMMODE |
|-------|--------|-----------|------------|-----------|---------|
| modern | moderate | modify | modification | modulation | MODICUM |
| mode | accommodation | | | MODISH | MODAL |

## Selling to Music

She decided to open her first branch in Dallas, next to New York the best outlet for ____1____ furniture and DÉCOR. She found ____2____s for a ____3____ SALON, which she decorated in the same ____4____ as her New York shop, using, however, Southern pine instead of Philippine mahogany, a ____5____ which seemed an appropriate concession to Texan sensibilities. She installed a chamber orchestra in a musicians' gallery, but she had them play Southern ballads, using John Powell's and Annabel Buchanan's ____6____ arrangements. Her shop became the ____7____ thing with all the social BELLWETHERS of Dallas. Her rivals, who at first thought she had acted without a ____8____ of sense, began to follow suit. Only they had cowboy singers, who drew their numbers from John Lomax's collection.

PORT, PORTAT, from *portare, portatus:* to carry, convey, bear long.

| important | sport | transport | export | purport | DEPORTATION |
|-----------|-------|-----------|--------|---------|-------------|
| report | support | porter | deportment | importation | DISPORT |
| port | import | transportation | portable | EXPORTATION | COMPORT |
| | | | DEPORT | | |

## Filibusterer—New Style

He sailed into ____1____ on an old rusty tramp Liberty ship, one of two he owned. He rented an office and set up what was OSTENSIBLY an ____2____-____3____ business, but the officials of the banana republic, who got their cut, knew it was really smuggling. He had a big launch, supposedly for personal ____4____ around the harbor and upriver. Its compartments held an armory of easily ____5____ artillery, tommy guns mostly. When he got too handy with these while landing a drug CONSIGN- MENT, and shot about half the republic's REVENUERS, and, by accident, four of his own ____6____s, the officials had had enough of this FILIBUSTERER. They didn't issue a ____7____ order, they just ran him out of the country, on the grounds that he was upsetting the good-neighbor policy.

PLAC, PLACIT (pleas, plais, plead, plea), from *placere, placitus:* to please.

| | | | | | |
|---|---|---|---|---|---|
| please | pleasure | plea | pleasing | implacable | COMPLAISANCE |
| pleasant | plead | placid | complacent | PLEASANTRY | PLACATE |

## The Office Egotist

His facility and ADROITNESS perhaps justified a certain ____1____ in his manner, but this EGOTIST had a kind of ____2____ ruthlessness and arro- gance when his slightest opinion was challenged, that made him decidedly an unpleasant person. His ____3____es were heavy-handed and humor- less, and all in all he was unbeloved, but far too ____4____ ever to guess it.

PLIC, PLICAT, PLICIT (ple, pil, ply, ploy, play, plex), from *plicare, plicatus:* to fold, bend, turn.

| | | | | | |
|---|---|---|---|---|---|
| reply | multiply | complex | supple | MULTIPLICITY | REPLICA |
| simple | employee | employer | complication | COMPLICITY | PLEXUS |
| apply | simplicity | imply | PLIANT | DUPLICITY | PLIABLE |
| employ | comply | EXPLICIT | IMPLICATION | supplication | MISAPPLY |
| ply | application | DUPLEX | IMPLICIT | multiplication | DEPLOY |
| display | plait | simplify | | | |

## Rationalization

He started out as a parlor SOCIALIST, wobbled into weak-kneed LIBERAL- ISM, and wound up in advertising. He had a ____1____ and ____2____ mind, which lent itself easily to the necessary ____3____es of the HUCK- STERING trade. He understood the ____4____s of his activities, but never let them become too ____5____ in his thinking about himself. He tried to avoid developing ____6____es about his sell-out by CORRALLING the ac- counts calling for INFORMATIONAL advertising. It seemed to lessen his ____7____ in the business if he kept away from ads based on fear motive, or on social stigma—bad-breath accounts, they were called around the agency. The ____8____ of his outside interests helped to keep him from feeling like a three-____9____ scoundrel. At night, in his DUPLEX, he used to ____10____ his thoughts about going into public service.

**SENT, SENS** (senti, sensu), from *sentire, sensus:* to feel, think, perceive.

| | | | | | |
|---|---|---|---|---|---|
| assent | nonsense | resent | sense | SENSIBILITY | sentence |
| consent | nonsensical | RESENTFUL | senseless | sensual | SENTENTIOUS |
| dissent | PRESENTIMENT | scent | sensible | sensuous | sentiment |
| | | UNSENTIMENTAL | | | |

## Sermons and Soda Water the Day After

The ____1____ advice of ASCETICS and saints counseling against ____2____ delights has had little effect on the average ____3____ man. He does not ____4____ in theory, only in practice. Ignoring finer ____5____es he goes on his ____6____ way, savoring the ____7____s, joys, and diversions of the primrose path. He may have a ____8____ of sorrow and regret, but it seems ____9____ to yield to such gloomy worries, until he gets a hangover.

**PART** (port, parti, par, pars), from *pars, partis:* a piece, portion, share.

| | | | | | |
|---|---|---|---|---|---|
| part | particular | partner | apartment | particle | COUNTERPART |
| party | portion | proportion | departure | impartial | APPORTION |
| apart | department | impart | partial | partition | PARSE |
| depart | parcel | | | compartment | PARTITIVE |

## The Soul of Wit

The Dean read out a fancy new piece of legislation. "It won't ____1____," the old math professor called out, and there was a roar of laughter. Nobody had noticed the dangling "whether" until he spoke. He had been educated before knowledge was walled off in ____2____s. He had no ____3____ in the faculty, and was much beloved, perhaps because he distributed his JIBES quite ____4____ly, and without a ____5____ of RANCOR. Also he had a fine sense of ____6____, and his wit ____7____ed flavor to his one-sentence speeches.

**PREHEND, PREHENS** (prign, prent, pris, priz), from *prehendere, prehensus:* to seize, lay hold of.

| | | | | |
|---|---|---|---|---|
| apprehend | APPRISAL | enterprise | prize | REPRISAL |
| apprehension | comprehend | IMPREGNABLE | REPREHEND | surprise |
| apprentice | COMPREHENSION | PREHENSILE | REPREHENSIBLE | SURPRISAL |
| APPRISE | comprise | prison | REPREHENSION | |

## Tax Dodger Extraordinary

The proprietor of this restaurant chain not only had a ____1____ grasp. He also lived up to Mark Twain's definition of a MARSUPIAL: an animal with a large pouch. And what went into the pouch, the owner didn't like to let out—even for income tax. How people could pay taxes so blithely, was beyond his ____2____. When the Treasury was ____3____d of his original views on this subject, it naturally felt them slightly ____4____, and decided on ____5____s. Although he had shown rare ____6____ in cooking up two sets of books, with the aid of an ____7____ who didn't get much of a payoff, his position proved far from ____8____. In fact he was ____9____ed, forced to DISGORGE, fined heavy penalties, and sent to ____10____ for several years.

RAP, RAPT, RAPTUR (rav, rept), from *rapere, raptus:* to seize, snatch, hurry away.

| | | | | | |
|---|---|---|---|---|---|
| rapid | rapine | rapt | ravage | ravenous | RAVISHING |
| rapids | RAPACIOUS | rapturous | raven | RAVINE | SURREPTITIOUS |

### Sharks

The big five in the combine were as ____1____ as hungry COYOTES. Their appetite for money was ____2____, and what they could not ____3____ by direct means, they got by ____4____ methods. They short-changed the foreign outfits, with which they had RECIPROCAL arrangements. If any of their victims were reported as hungry, they said, "Let the ____5____ feed 'em."

RUPT, RUPTUR (rout, rut), from *rumpere, ruptus:* to break, destroy, burst.

| | | | | | |
|---|---|---|---|---|---|
| abrupt | corruption | eruption | interrupt | rout | routine |
| bankrupt | DISRUPT | INCORRUPTIBLE | IRRUPTION | route | RUPTURE |
| corrupt | | | | | RUT |

### Eighth Wonder of the World

The ____1____ of the Mexican volcano, Paracutín, which started as a mere anthill, and grew to a 1500-foot cone in a year, ____2____ed life in nearby villages. The black ash and lava put to ____3____ all plant life for twenty miles around. Numerous ____4____ occurred in the side of the main cone, and eventually these smaller mouths threw up cones of their own.

SAL, SALT (sali, sili, sail, sult, sault), from *salire, saltus:* to leap, rush, issue suddenly forth.

| | | | | | |
|---|---|---|---|---|---|
| assail | exult | exultation | RESILIENT | RESULTANT | SALIENT |
| assault | EXULTANT | RESILIENCE | result | SALACIOUS | salmon |
| DESULTORY | | | | | SALTATION |

### The Joyous Crusader

La Guardia made a FRONTAL ____1____ on evil in the metropolis. He banned ____2____ magazines, drove out the madams, and scotched gambling. There was nothing ____3____ about his methods. He showed posi-

tive ____4____ in battling sin, and explained his ____5____ moves on
the air. Any ____6____ backfire merely roused his scorn, and he showed
remarkable ____7____ whenever he had a setback, as he did when he
ordered raids on bingo games in church parlors.

REG, RECT (roy, rig, regi, ress, recti), from *regere, rectus:* to rule, direct,
arrange.

| | | | | | |
|---|---|---|---|---|---|
| address | direct | INCORRIGIBLE | REALIST | regal | resource |
| correct | direction | INSURGENT | reality | REGIMEN | resurrection |
| CORRECTIVE | director | insurrection | rectify | regiment | ruler |
| dress | DIRECTORY | irregular | RECTITUDE | REGNANT | source |
| dressing | erect | real | rector | reign | REGIME |
| dressy | erection | realty | redress | regular | IRREGULARITY |

## Forced Exit

What started as an ____1____ turned into a ____2____ revolution. Its
____3____ were crafty ____4____. They knew that the General was
____5____, and that he would be merciless to ____6____. So they had to
win, and end his ____7____ once and for all. There could be no compromise. They imposed a severe ____8____ on their forces, and showed a
degree of ____9____ about property and women unusual in revolutions in
that part of the world. They tried to avoid ____10____ that would set sections of the populace against them. So they finally ended the tyrant's
____11____ beyond any possibility of its ____12____.

SED, SESS (see, sidu, siz, sid) from *sedere, sessus:* to sit.

| | | | | | |
|---|---|---|---|---|---|
| ASSESS | ASSIZE | possess | preside | reside | resident |
| assiduous | INSIDIOUS | PREPOSSESS | president | residue | RESIDUARY |
| | | SEDENTARY | | | |

## Exertion Is for Servants

There was a certain ____1____ charm about the ____2____ way of life
of the old style Chinese MANDARINS. They were ____3____ LEGATEES of a
long poetic tradition celebrating the quiet life without exertion. They were
____4____ in cultivating the art of doing nothing gracefully. The last of
the great mandarins, Wu Ting Fang, while presiding at a Chinese-American
banquet in Peiping, the first one at which dancing went on between
courses, asked the American Ambassador, "Why do you go to all this exertion? Why not have the servants do it for you?"

SIGN, from *signum:* a sign.

| | | | | | |
|---|---|---|---|---|---|
| assign | COUNTERSIGN | design | resignation | UNDESIGNED | signature |
| assignment | CONSIGNMENT | designer | sign | UNDERSIGNED | signify |
| ASSIGNATION | DESIGNATION | resign | signal | significance | |
| consign | INSIGNIFICANCE | resigned | signet | SIGNIFICATION | |

379

## V-Sign

The opening bars of Beethoven's Fifth Symphony, starting out as the theme
____1____ on BBC programs broadcast to the undergrounds in occupied
countries, became a kind of musical ____2____ for the resistance movements. The Roman numeral for five is V, so this music came to ____3____
Victory, and was EQUATED with the V-____4____. It acquired increasing
____5____ as the war went on.

STA, STAT, SIST (st, stet), from *stare, status:* to stand; intensive, *sisto,
sistere,* to (cause to) stand.

| | | | | |
|---|---|---|---|---|
| arrest | constitution | insist | RESTATE | stationery |
| ARMISTICE | contrast | instance | rest | statuary |
| assist | desist | instant | RESTITUTION | statue |
| assistance | destitute | INSTATE | SOLSTICE | statute |
| consist | distance | INSTITUTION | RESTIVE | subsist |
| circumstance | distant | irresistible | stable | substance |
| CIRCUMSTANTIAL | EQUIDISTANT | OBSTETRICS | STANCHION | substantial |
| consistency | establish | obstacle | stanza | SUBSTANTIVE |
| constable | estate | persist | state | SUBSTITUTION |
| constant | exist | PROSTITUTION | stately | superstition |
| constitute | existence | REINSTATE | statement | TRANSUBSTAN- |
| constituent | extant | resist | station | TIATION |
| | INCONSISTENCY | resistance | stationary | |

## Nature of the Comic

It's hard to say just what comedy ____1____s of. Certainly it is no
____2____ thing, but varies from place to place, and from one period to
another. Shakespeare, who should know, said that the prosperity of a jest
lies in the ear of him that hears it. The evidence is more than ____3____,
indeed, that comedy thus depends a lot upon prepared ground in the mind
of the listener. A story about footballers dancing a "BALLET moose" in a
varsity show isn't funny to children who never heard of a ballet, let alone
the Ballet Russe, and who don't know what a moose is. The ____4____ is
often made that the COMIC depends on sudden INCONGRUITY or ____5____.
But not all incongruities are funny, only those that show a particular kind
of crack in the smooth wall of normal, ____6____ reality. We feel amused
when an ____7____ wolf's hide turns up as a lady's fur coat. Jokes at the
expense of an ____8____ —the church, for instance—are laughable if
we don't like it; but make us very ____9____ if we admire it. We develop
a high ____10____ to contrive gags and worn out wheezes. Yet Rabelais
or Mark Twain could re-work these old ones into witcracks that would

make an Indian ____11____ laugh. In their hands, some very dull dross
underwent a ____12____ into high though still profane wit.

STRING, STRICT, STRICTURE (strain, straint, strait, stren), from
*stringere, strictus:* to bind, draw tight, filter.

| | | | | | |
|---|---|---|---|---|---|
| ASTRINGENT | CONSTRICTOR | distressing | restraint | STRAINER | strict |
| constrain | DISTRAIN | district | restrict | strait | STRICTNESS |
| CONSTRAINT | distress | restrain | strain | STRAITEN | STRICTURE |
| CONSTRICT | | | | | restriction |

## Tragic Wit

Swift's wit was ____1____. His ____2____ on British landlords' INHU-
MANITY to the poor of Ireland were ____3____ing to many of his friends,
who felt ____4____ed to urge him to put some ____5____s on his wit,
lest more forcible ____6____s be imposed on his person.

SEQU, SECUT (sec, sequi, su, sect, suit), from *sequi, seculus:* to follow.

| | | | | | |
|---|---|---|---|---|---|
| CONSECUTION | ensue | OBSEQUIES | prosecution | second | sue |
| consecutive | execution | obsequious | PROSECUTOR | secondary | suit |
| consequence | executive | persecute | pursue | sect | suitable |
| consequently | executor | persecution | PURSUANCE | SECTARY | suite |
| | | prosecute | pursuit | SECTARIAN | suitor |

## Shades of Red

The bitterest disputes in politics are the ____1____ wrangles of the left.
Factions ____2____ each other, or if one is in power, it ____3____s DIS-
SENTERS if it can catch them, and ____4____s them even into foreign countries. No matter how ____5____ly heretics make their submission, they are
LIQUIDATED. Nor does the ____6____ end with their ____7____ and
____8____. They are still EXCORIATED in the histories prepared by official
order, and held up as an awful example to other ____9____ who have so
far escaped purging.

SERV,[3] SERVAT, from *servare, servatus:* to save, protect, give heed to.

| | | | | | |
|---|---|---|---|---|---|
| conserve | CONSERVATORY | observance | preserve | reservation | reservoir |
| observe | conservation | observation | preserver | PRESERVATIVE | unobserved |
| observer | conservative | preservation | reserve | reservedness | UNRESERVED |

## Joe Miller's Nemesis

This publisher was devoted to the cause of ____1____. He ____2____ed
all the jokes he heard his friends tell, and made enemies of the columnists
by EXPROPRIATING their best *bons mots* without acknowledgment. None of

[3] Do not confuse with "to serve" from *servio, servire.*

their hunting ____3____s were safe from his hawk-eyed ____4____. To be sure, he applied the ____5____ of his wit to their often ____6____ and straggling phrases. But they tired of having him drain off their ____7____ of humor without paying any water-right. They abused him without ____8____, keeping score on his borrowings, and finally proved his NEMESIS by POPULARIZING his name as a new synonym for PLAGIARISM. Had they known enough, they would have called him a *Gehirnfresser*.

TEN, TENT (tin, tinu, tain), from *tenere, tentus:* to hold.

| | | | | | |
|---|---|---|---|---|---|
| ABSTAIN | contentment | detain | lieutenant | retinue | tenant |
| ABSTINENCE | continual | discontent | maintain | sustain | tenement |
| appertain | continue | entertain | obtain | sustenance | TENURE |
| content | continent | impertinent | pertain | TENABLE | UNTENABLE |
| | countenance | incontinent | retain | TENACIOUS | CONTINENCE |

## Scotching a Common Error

The Puritans, says Grierson, were not remarkable for either ____1____ or ____2____. The only ____3____ view as to the origin of the term Puritanism is that it arose from their doctrine of the need for purifying church worship of Romish customs. Any other ETYMOLOGY is ____4____; yet the erroneous view as to its meaning has been held with great ____5____.

TANG, TACT (ting, tag, tigu, tain, teg, tegr, tactus, tast), from *tangere, tactus:* to touch, to reach, to handle.

| | | | | | |
|---|---|---|---|---|---|
| attain | contain | CONTINGENT | INTEGER | TACTFUL | TANGIBLE |
| ATTAINMENT | contagion | disintegrate | INTEGRAL | TACTILE | taste |
| contact | contagious | INTACT | INTEGRATION | TACTUAL | TASTELESS |
| CONTACTUAL | CONTIGUOUS | integrity | tact | TANGENT | TANGENTIAL |

## Way of the Digressor

His mind was always going off at ____1____s. Yet so persuasive was his voice, and his enthusiasm was so ____2____ that he carried his listeners with him into these BYPATHS which were not even ____3____ to the subject in hand. His personal ____4____ was so great that his hearers were scarcely aware of his ____5____ing effect on their reasoning. His ____6____ was never affected, and he kept his GENIALITY no matter how far afield his ____7____ habits of discourse might lead him.

TEND, TENS, TENT, from *tendere, tensus,* or *tentus:* to stretch, strive, try.

| | | | | | |
|---|---|---|---|---|---|
| attend | DISTENSION | INTENDANT | portend | SUBTEND | tendon |
| attendant | extend | INTENSIVE | PORTENT | superintend | TENSE |
| attention | extension | intent | pretend | superintendent | TENSION |
| contend | extensive | intention | PRETENDER | tend | TENSILE |
| contention | extent | OSTENSIBLE | pretense | tendency | tent |
| DISTEND | intend | OSTENTATION | | | |

382

## The Shabby Duke

The Duke of Rutland not only avoided ____1____ and ____2____ in his way of life; he was often positively shabby when he pursued his researches in the Reading Room of the British Museum. But his learning was as ____3____ as his wardrobe was meager. Yet he showed no ____4____ toward pride of ERUDITION. If the rest of the House of Lords should suddenly become equally learned, it might ____5____ a counterrevolution in the British social scheme, with the aristocracy regaining by its brains what it lost through its INFLEXIBILITY.

**VOC** (voice, vou), from *vox, vocis:* voice.

| | | | | | |
|---|---|---|---|---|---|
| advocate | CONVOKE | IRREVOCABLE | revoke | VOCABLE | voice |
| AVOCATION | invoke | provocation | UNIVOCAL | vocation | vouch |
| convocation | EQUIVOCATION | provoke | vocal | VOCIFEROUS | vowel |

## Stormy Petrel

War was at once his ____1____ and his ____2____. He ____3____d the Deity on all occasions. There was never any ____4____ in his talk, and his command of profane ____5____s was unequaled in the Army, even by the top sergeants to whom the general was closely akin in temper. ____6____ as he was, he realized that his tongue was a worse danger to him than the Germans; but he could not curb it. Off the battlefield he was like Nelson away from his QUARTERDECK: a liability to peace and order, but a great addition to the gaiety of nations.

**UT, US, USUR** (usu), from *uti, usus:* to use.

| | | | | | |
|---|---|---|---|---|---|
| abuse | disuse | usage | useless | usury | utility |
| ABUSIVE | misuse | use | usual | utensil | UTILITARIAN |
| PERUSAL | peruse | useful | | | |

## Taking Interest No Sin after A.D. 1550

The EXACTION of any interest whatever was regarded as ____1____ by the MEDIEVAL Church. It was a sin against nature, because gold and silver did not grow by natural increase. The Fathers and Doctors leveled ____2____ language at anyone who exacted interest. A ____3____ of the canon law as it then stood is instructive. However, by GLOSSARIAL reinterpretation the canon lawyers, following the rise of CAPITALISM, brought the law into harmony with actual ____4____. They made taking interest a sin only if the rate was over 10 per cent.

**VEN, VENT, VENTU** (veni, venu, ventu), from *venire, ventus:* to come.

| | | | | |
|---|---|---|---|---|
| CONTRAVENE | covenant | convent | event | invent | revenue |
| adventure | advent | convention | EVENTUALLY | INVENTIVE | SUPERVENE |
| avenue | convene | CONVENTUAL | intervene | INVENTORY | venture |
| CIRCUMVENT | convenient | | | prevent | VENUE |

## *Volpone; or How to Out-Fox a White-Collar Union*

The problem was to ____1____ the union without ____2____ing the Wagner Act. He showed a good deal of ____3____ness in the ____4____. He ____5____ed some doubtful Thomases from joining, by sending his loyal stooges to work on them. It was noised around that there would be a drop in ____6____, and next in size of staff. "Loyal" employees got out circulars to this effect. Luck ____7____d on his behalf: several union members took jobs elsewhere; others left to get married. When the union came to take ____8____ of its chances in an election, it found it no longer had a majority. So the ____9____ of UNIONISM in this office was put off, perhaps forever.

**VID, VIS** (vey, vic, view), from *videre, visus:* to see.

| | | | | | |
|---|---|---|---|---|---|
| advice | PREVISION | prudent | revise | supervision | view |
| evidence | providence | PURVEY | REVISIT | SURVEILLANCE | visage |
| advise | PROVIDENT | review | SUPERVISE | survey | visit |
| evident | provision | | | SURVEYING | VISITANT |

## *Inquisition*

All members of the Embassy staff were kept under close ____1____. Any who had ____2____s of the wrong political complexion found his life more closely ____3____d, and it required no SUPERHUMAN ____4____ for him to realize that he would soon be shipped back to the United States. The Ambassador soon turned on him a ____5____ as forbidding as the Escorial walls, and made careful ____6____ to neutralize his actions. The more ____7____ followed the course so well described by Blake in the line, "Sneaking submission can always live."

**SPEC, SPIC, SPECT** (spici, speci, spy, spi), from *specere (spicere), spictus:* to look at.

| | | | | |
|---|---|---|---|---|
| aspect | ESPIONAGE | perspective | RETROSPECT | spectacles |
| AUSPICES | expect | PERSPICACITY | RETROSPECTION | spectator |
| AUSPICIOUS | expectant | PERSPICUITY | special | speculation |
| CIRCUMSPECT | expectation | prospect | SPECIFICATION | spice |
| CIRCUMSPECTION | INAUSPICIOUS | prospective | SPECIFY | spy |
| DESPICABLE | inspect | respect | specimen | suspicion |
| especial | inspection | respectable | SPECIOUS | |
| ESPIAL | introspective | respective | spectacle | |

384

## Office of Social Swank

The OSS made ____1____ more than respectable, it gave it glamor. Under high-toned social ____2____ from the very start, it showed rare ____3____ in setting ____4____s for its feminine CONTINGENT. Family background and money were ____5____ly desirable attributes. Many an elegant ____6____ of the GENUS DEBUTANTE fought the war in the old red brick building in Washington. The agency did not engage in much ____7____ activity; it was all for action. It liked ____8____ in its AIDES, and did not encourage too much ____9____ habit of mind. The ____10____ of so much youth and beauty saving the Army and Navy Intelligence Services from mistakes they might otherwise have made, was indeed edifying. Yet in ____11____ there may be a few doubts; if so, these did not penetrate to Hollywood, which put its most fetching glamor girls right into the OSS films, where they could pass ____12____ as well up to the wartime standard of PULCHRITUDE in the actual agency.

ANSWERS

AG:
1. agency  2. ambiguity  3. variegated  4. litigation  5. manager
6. actor  7. castigated  8. agent  9. management  10. prodigal
11. cogent  12. agitation  13. synagogue  14. mitigate  15. actuated

APT:
1. inept  2. apt  3. attitudes  4. aptitude  5. adaptability

CERN:
1. discernment  2. indiscretions  3. secretive  4. indiscreet  5. discernible

ART:
1. artistic  2. artless  3. artful  4. artistries  5. artillery
6. inert  7. artistry  8. inertia  9. inertly  10. artifacts
11. artisans

AUD:
1. audiences  2. audible  3. inaudible  4. obeisance  5. auditors
6. audits  7. auditions

CAN:
1. accent  2. enchantment  3. cantata  4. chant  5. canticle
6. recant  7. accentuated  8. cant

CAP:
1. occupation  2. conceit  3. deceive  4. deception  5. captivity
6. susceptible  7. participant  8. receptions  9. capacity  10. emancipation
11. municipal  12. precepts  13. acceptable  14. participle  15. incipient

COR:
1. concordance     2. discord

CRED:
1. creed        2. incredible    3. incredulous    4. credulity    5. discredit
6. credence     7. credit

CED:
1. process      2. succeeded     3. conceded    4. ancestor    5. recess
6. cessation    7. precedents

CURR:
1. courier      2. precursor     3. recurred    4. excursion    5. cursory
6. concurred

CLAUS:
1. recluse      2. secluded      3. cloistered    4. precluded    5. include

CLAM:
1. declamation  2. clamorous  3. exclamatory  4. exclamation  5. declaim
6. clamor       7. claim      8. reclamation  9. reclaim

DIGN:
1. disdainful   2. indignities   3. dignitary    4. indignation    5. dignity
6. dainties

CAPIT:
1. precipitate  2. capitalism    3. precipitate  4. chapter        5. cattle
6. captains     7. capitulation  8. capitalists  9. recapitulation

DAT:
1. editor    2. tradition    3. data          4. edition      5. editorials
6. edit      7. absconded    8. "extraditing"  9. rendezvous

CUR:
1. curator      2. secure        3. security      4. surety

FORM:
1. form      2. uniformity 3. conformity    4. formalism    5. formula
6. formulate 7. information 8. transformation 9. informality 10. forms

FER, LAT:
1. sufferance 2. pestiferous    3. vociferous  4. delays     5. references
6. fertility  7. circumference  8. preference  9. proffer    10. deference

EQU:
1. equivocal   2. equal          3. equanimity  4. equity     5. equator
6. equinoctial 7. equivalence    8. equation    9. unequal

FRANG:
1. fractional  2. refractory  3. infractions  4. irrefragable  5. fractures
6. fragile  7. fragment

HAB:
1. inhibitions  2. habiliments  3. habitual  4. debilitating  5. exhibit
6. exhibition

GER:
1. jester  2. congeries  3. jests  4. digestion  5. gesticulations
6. suggestions  7. vicegerent

GRAT:
1. ingrate  2. grateful  3. gratitude  4. congratulate  5. graceless
6. disagreement  7. gratuity

MAN:
1. amanuensis 2. maneuvered 3. manacles 4. manumission 5. manifesto

MITT:
1. emissary  2. dismissed  3. intermittent 4. permit  5. missiles
6. missive  7. commission 8. remiss  9. commissary 10. emitting
11. committee 12. compromised

JUNG:
1. injunction 2. conjugation 3. conjunctions 4. disjunctive 5. subjunctive
6. subjugated 7. disjointed

LEG:
1. predilection  2. legibility  3. intelligibility  4. elegance  5. lecture
6. legend  7. legible  8. collection  9. dialectics

PAR:
1. separating  2. preparatory  3. sever  4. dissevered

MOV:
1. momentum 2. mobilizing 3. emotions  4. movable 5. movements
6. commotion 7. motif  8. locomotive 9. motion

NOT:
1. noble  2. notoriously 3. connotations 4. denotations 5. denotes
6. incognito 7. recognition

PET:
1. competition 2. impetus 3. centripetal 4. repetitive 5. incompetent
6. petulant

PAND:
1. encompass 2. expanded 3. surpassing

MOD:
1. modern 2. accommodations 3. commodious 4. mode 5. modification
6. modal 7. modish 8. modicum

PORT:
1. port 2. export 3. import 4. transportation 5. portable
6. porters 7. deportation

PLAC:
1. complacency 2. implacable 3. pleasantries 4. complacent

PLIC:
1. pliant 2. supple 3. duplicities 4. implications 5. explicit
6. complexes 7. complicity 8. multiplicity 9. ply 10. deploy

SENT:
1. sententious 2. sensuous 3. sensual 4. dissent 5. sensibilities
6. unsentimental 7. scents 8. presentiment 9. senseless

PART:
1. parse 2. compartments 3. counterpart 4. impartially 5. particle
6. proportion 7. imparted

PREHEND:
1. prehensile 2. comprehension 3. apprised 4. reprehensible 5. reprisals
6. enterprise 7. apprentice 8. impregnable 9. apprehended 10. prison

RAP:
1. rapacious 2. ravenous 3. ravage 4. surreptitious 5. ravens

RUPT:
1. eruption 2. disrupted 3. rout 4. ruptures

SAL:
1. onslaught 2. salacious 3. desultory 4. exultation 5. salient
6. resultant 7. resilience

REG:
1. insurrection 2. real 3. directors 4. realists 5. incorrigible
6. insurgents 7. regime 8. regimen 9. rectitude 10. irregularities
11. reign 12. resurrection

SED:
1. insidious 2. sedentary 3. residuary 4. assiduous

SIGN:
1. signature 2. countersign 3. signify 4. sign 5. significance

STA:
1. consists 2. stationary 3. circumstantial 4. statement 5. contrast
6. stable 7. irresistible 8. institution 9. restive 10. resistance
11. statue 12. transubstantiation

388

STRING:
1. astringent  2. strictures  3. distressing  4. constrained  5. constriction
6. constraints

SEQU:
1. sectarian  2. persecute  3. prosecutes  4. pursues  5. obsequiously
6. persecution  7. execution  8. obsequies  9. sectaries

SERV:
1. conservation  2. conserved  3. preserves  4. observation  5. preservative
6. unreserved  7. reservoir  8. reservation

TEN:
1. abstinence  2. continence  3. tenable  4. untenable  5. tenacity

TANG:
1. tangents  2. contagious  3. contiguous  4. integrity  5. disintegrating
6. taste  7. tangential

TEND:
1. ostentation  2. pretence  3. extensive  4. tendency  5. portend

VOC:
1. vocation  2. avocation  3. invoked  4. equivocation  5. vocables
6. vociferous

UT:
1. usury  2. abusive  3. perusal  4. usage

VEN:
1. circumvent  2. contravening  3. inventiveness  4. venture  5. prevented
6. revenue  7. intervened  8. inventory  9. advent

VID:
1. surveillance  2. visitants  3. supervised  4. prevision  5. visage
6. provision  7. prudent

SPEC:
1. espionage  2. auspices  3. perspicacity  4. specifications
5. especially  6. specimen  7. introspective  8. circumspection
9. speculative  10. spectacle  11. retrospect  12. inspection

### Your Last Trial Run

Here are 100 words of Latin or Greek derivation, most of which have
not so far occurred in the text of this book. Try your hand at analyzing
them to determine the literal meaning; then, by what you know of the

principles of meaning-change, trace the way each word has acquired its present sense. The number following each word indicates the Thorndike frequency number.

| | | |
|---|---|---|
| ALLEVIATE [15] | CONDUCTIVITY [20] | DISINTEGRATION [17] |
| ANTARCTIC [11] | CONFIGURATION [18] | DISSEMINATION [18] |
| ANTHOLOGY [18] | CONSTITUTIONALITY [18] | |
| ANTITHESIS [16] | CONSUMMATION [12] | ERADICATE [ 9] |
| APATHETIC [16] | CONTRADISTINCTION [16] | EUPHONY [19] |
| APHORISM [16] | CONVALESCENCE [17] | EXCURSIVE [16] |
| ARCHAEOLOGY [20] | CONVERGENCE [20] | EXODUS [12] |
| ASSIDUITY [15] | CONVOLUTION [14] | EXPECTANCY [12] |
| ATHEIST [10] | CRITERION [15] | EXPULSION [12] |
| AUGMENTATION [16] | CUMULATIVE [16] | EXTRACTION [15] |
| AUTONOMY [19] | CUNEIFORM [19] | EXTRADITION [16] |
| AVOCATION [18] | | |
| | DEBILITY [16] | FACETIOUS [15] |
| BINOMIAL [20] | DECADENCE [16] | FATUOUS [20] |
| | DECLAMATION [15] | FELONIOUS [20] |
| CALORIMETER [20] | DECLINATION [15] | FELICITOUS [18] |
| CELERITY [15] | DECOMPOSITION [13] | |
| CENTRIFUGAL [13] | DECOROUS [16] | KALEIDOSCOPE [17] |
| CIRCULATORY [16] | DECREPITUDE [16] | |
| CIRCUMLOCUTION [20] | DELIQUESCENT [20] | METAMORPHOSIS [ 8] |
| CIRCUMNAVIGATE [13] | DEMORALIZATION [16] | METROPOLITAN [10] |
| COADJUTOR [15] | DEPRECIATION [11] | MONOLITH [20] |
| COEFFICIENT [19] | DESPONDENCE [17] | |
| COGNITION [18] | DIAGNOSIS [15] | PERIPATETIC [20] |
| COMMISERATION [12] | DISCOMFITURE [12] | PERIPHERY [19] |
| | DISINCLINATION [18] | STEREOTYPE [12] |

*Over 20*

| | | |
|---|---|---|
| ANTHROPOMORPHIC | HELIOGRAPH | APOCRYPHAL |
| PLANISPHERE | HELIOTROPE | APOTHEOSIS |
| STRATOSPHERE | AGORAPHOBIA | ARCHIEPISCOPAL |
| MISOGYNIST | CLAUSTROPHOBIA | AURICULAR |
| PSEUDONYM | AEROLITE | BEATITUDE |
| HEPTARCHY | MICROCOSM | CONSANGUINITY |
| PETROGRAPHY | HECATOMB | EQUIVOCATION |
| PERICARDIUM | GASTRONOMY | EVANESCENT |
| ORTHOGRAPHY | NECROPOLIS | FACTITIOUS |
| ICHTHYOLOGY | OMNISCIENCE | HYPERBOLE |
| | BIPED | |

# Comprehensive Vocabulary-Level Test

This test is in two parts. Part I gives you one hundred clues to words which have occurred in earlier sections of this book and in the examples from the Word-Analyzer. Part II is a multiple-choice quiz. Add your correct answers for both sections and rate yourself according to the Comprehensive Scoring Key.

## PART I

1. a sudden stroke to change regimes (four letters)
2. a noisy ghost: p_____
3. the CUR_____ of the museum
4. They FORM_____ed plans for the invasion.
5. familiar with many languages (eight letters)
6. act or process of spreading out from a center: r_____
7. beginner; raw recruit (four letters)
8. disgusting; smelly
9. uncharged particle in the atom
10. an unrealistic, fanciful notion
11. composed of many syllables
12. calmness of mind: EQU_____ty
13. a gift; a tip: GRAT_____
14. secretary: ___MAN_____
15. special vocabulary of the underworld (five letters)
16. esoteric language of a trade or profession (six letters)
17. another word for "strumpet": h_____
18. the intelligent ones; "eggheads"
19. a ten-letter synonym for "dried": _____HYDR___
20. a five-letter equivalent for "precipitous"
21. overly critical
22. simultaneous feelings of love and hate toward the same person: ambi_____
23. "Cite" and "sight" are HOMO_____s.
24. placing two items side by side: ___POS___
25. a man in his eighties: _____arian
26. a woman in her seventies: _____arian
27. the science that studies ESP: ___PSYCH___
28. word of opposite meaning
29. something that limits: STRICT_____
30. touching: ___TIG___
31. going off at a TANG_____

32. mental keenness:____SPIC____
33. secret, stealthy: ____REP____
34. cranky: c_____ous
35. deprived of a chartered right: dis_____
36. sudden outburst: s_____
37. pertaining to the skin: c_____
38. excessively; more than usually (twelve letters)
39. deviations from the norm: a_____tions
40. something out of its time: ____CHRON____
41. cut short: t_____
42. beyond repair: ____PAR____
43. deep-seated enmity: r_____
44. reputed; supposed: p_____
45. Israeli collective farm: k_____
46. word combining "chuckle" and "snort"
47. disguised: ____NIT____
48. authoritative statement: DICT_____
49. drives to distraction: be_____s
50. division within a religious group: s_____
51. juggle election districts for political advantage
52. mystical state of oblivion: n_____
53. small structure with open sides: k_____
54. able to read and write: LIT_____
55. irritable: PET_____
56. occurring at intervals: ____MITT____
57. choral composition: CANT_____
58. degree earned by Ph.D.
59. name of the whale in *Moby Dick*
60. a musical term meaning "many-voiced": poly_____
61. exaggerated mode of expression: h_____
62. science combining physics and astronomy: ASTRO_____
63. Japanese stock broker: k_____
64. the moon: s_____ of the earth
65. fear and hatred of foreigners: ____PHOB____
66. a word from the Greek KRYPTOS
67. the S_____ic method of debate
68. territory enclosed within a foreign territory
69. resurrected itself from ashes: p_____
70. the universe in miniature: m_____
71. living space: L_____
72. Russian playwright: C_____
73. rejoicing: j_____
74. broken up: FRAG_____
75. study of church art: e_____OLOGY

76. inborn: in_____
77. giving political jobs to relatives: n_____
78. capacity to adjust: ____APT____
79. a polite word for "graft": ____QUISIT____
80. the curve traversed by a proJECTile: ____JECT____
81. one who studies ARTifacts of older civilizations: ARCHE_____
82. International GEO_____ Year
83. polysyllabic jargon: g_____
84. legal grace period: m_____
85. austere in living: a_____
86. prediction based on present knowledge: ex_____
87. having a harsh manner: c_____ty
88. showy: fl_____
89. "He had a PLIant and supPLE mind, which lent itself easily to the necessary ____PLICIT____ of the huckstering trade."
90. The judge could not find ____CED____s that could help him decide the case.
91. the ____FRAG____ truths of this philosophy
92. a de luxe edition of Lenin's ____LECT____ printed on rag
93. given to excessive moralizing: SENT_____
94. hero of a play: ____AGON____
95. fear of open spaces _____PHOBIA
96. beyond the physical: meta_____
97. a "heating through": dia_____
98. a word nearly alike in meaning: syn_____
99. direct opposite: anti_____
100. forerunner: ____CURS____

1. coup
2. poltergeist
3. curator
4. formulated
5. polyglot
6. radiation
7. tyro
8. noisome
9. neutron
10. chimera
11. polysyllabic
12. equanimity
13. gratuity
14. amanuensis
15. argot
16. jargon
17. harlot
18. intelligentsia
19. dehydrated
20. steep
21. hypercritical
22. ambivalence
23. homophones
24. juxtaposition
25. octogenarian
26. septuagenarian
27. parapsychology
28. antonym
29. stricture
30. contiguous
31. tangent
32. perspicacity
33. surreptitious
34. cantankerous
35. disenfranchised
36. spate
37. cutaneous
38. inordinately
39. aberrations

| | | |
|---|---|---|
| 40. anachronism | 61. hyperbole | 81. archeologist |
| 41. truncated | 62. astrophysics | 82. geophysical |
| 42. irreparable | 63. kabuya | 83. gobbledygook |
| 43. rancor | 64. satellite | 84. moratorium |
| 44. putative | 65. xenophobia | 85. ascetic |
| 45. kibbutz | 66. cryptic | 86. extrapolation |
| 46. chortle | 67. Socratic | 87. crusty |
| 47. incognito | 68. enclave | 88. flamboyant |
| 48. dictum | 69. phoenix | 89. duplicities |
| 49. bedevils | 70. microcosm | 90. precedents |
| 50. schism | 71. lebensraum | 91. irrefragable |
| 51. gerrymander | 72. Chekhov | 92. dialectics |
| 52. nirvana | 73. jubilation | 93. sententious |
| 53. kiosk | 74. fragmented | 94. protagonist |
| 54. literate | 75. ecclesiology | 95. agoraphobia |
| 55. petulant | 76. innate | 96. metaphysical |
| 56. intermittent | 77. nepotism | 97. diathermy |
| 57. cantata | 78. adaptability | 98. synonym |
| 58. doctorate | 79. perquisites | 99. antithesis |
| 59. Moby Dick | 80. trajectory | 100. precursor |
| 60. polyphonic | | |

## PART II

Of the four alternative equivalents given for each entry in the test, pick the one closest in meaning to the key word, and put its number in the parentheses in front of the key word.

1. (   ) noisome a) clamorous b) smelly c) appalling d) rascal
2. (   ) canto a) half gallop b) singer c) section of long poem d) drinking vessel
3. (   ) hogshead a) top of barrel b) a chest c) cask of certain content d) profane term of abuse
4. (   ) turbid a) muddy b) upset c) swirling d) crowded
5. (   ) definitive a) meaning b) conclusive 3) part of speech d) small
6. (   ) ingenuous a) clever b) embryonic c) naïvely frank d) genius
7. (   ) doughty a) brave and bold b) full of dough c) sullen d) questioning
8. (   ) incongruous a) out of place b) not running c) not apparent d) representing
9. (   ) expostulating a) after the fact b) theorizing c) post-mortem d) earnestly protesting
10. (   ) proscribe a) write a prescription b) outlaw c) write a letter for d) write a recommendation for

11. (  ) hypothesis a) proven assertion b) tentative assumption c) term paper d) law of nature
12. (  ) phlegmatic a) jolly b) irritable c) unresponsive d) thoughtful
13. (  ) fortuitous a) accidental b) planned c) courageous d) defensive
14. (  ) paradox a) seeming contradiction b) virtuous person c) doxy d) doctrine
15. (  ) dissemination a) insertion b) expulsion c) originality d) dispersion
16. (  ) helot a) mischievous girl b) strumpet c) serf d) satanic
17. (  ) stoic a) lover of good food b) teacher of Plato c) one who denies feeling d) worshipper of beauty
18. (  ) concomitant a) in a coma b) committed c) fawning follower d) accompanying
19. (  ) ascetic a) artistic b) aesthetic c) austere in living d) sterile
20. (  ) ebullient a) pertaining to bullion b) bull market c) joyful d) downhearted
21. (  ) cognizance a) awareness b) state of disguise c) of a similar nature d) meditation
22. (  ) succinct a) smelly b) compact c) verbose d) sweet-tasting
23. (  ) cryptic a) clear b) hidden c) caustic d) brief
24. (  ) antithesis a) that which precedes b) direct opposite c) term paper d) apposite
25. (  ) surreptitious a) repeated b) disreputable c) stealthy d) reptilian
26. (  ) dictum a) ruler b) prediction c) addiction d) authoritative statement
27. (  ) phaëton a) ghost b) kind of fairy c) carriage d) ancient ruler
28. (  ) repertoire a) valise b) works that a musician, actor, or company is ready to perform c) witty backchat d) assistant conductor
29. (  ) beatitude a) point of view b) blessed saying c) saintliness d) raising to sainthood
30. (  ) complaisance a) a compliment b) fatuous acquiescence c) a lovely meadow d) self-satisfaction
31. (  ) shard a) iron-clad hoofs b) fragment of pottery c) tough d) point
32. (  ) kinetic a) egotistic b) wavy c) pertaining to motion d) attractive
33. (  ) chantry a) sea song b) chapel for singing Masses c) music d) wizardry
34. (  ) imminence a) quality of being outstanding b) height c) state of threatening d) cliff

35. (  ) rigmarole a) conveyance b) overturn a wagon c) arranging ropes on mast d) nonsensical sequence of statement
36. (  ) subtrahend a) lower tendency b) number to take away from another c) underground stream d) drift below
37. (  ) shibboleth a) denunciation b) catchword c) sound made by reptile d) keepsake
38. (  ) enzyme a) commissioned officer b) flag c) gland-produced catalytic agent d) a paste
39. (  ) ambivalent a) wailing b) tricky c) double-valued d) symmetrical
40. (  ) catalyst a) invert b) one who classifies books c) stone-throwing device d) reaction agent itself unchanged
41. (  ) dysgenic a) noninheritable b) biologically deficient c) kingly family d) regenerative
42. (  ) pasquinade a) volley of shots b) ornament c) satiric verse d) column
43. (  ) polyglot a) saturated b) familiar with many languages c) polyphonic d) spread out
44. (  ) argot a) special vocabulary of the underworld b) fleet of ships c) regional accent d) mold for metal
45. (  ) putative a) punished b) supposed c) calculated d) rotten
46. (  ) stricture a) edifice b) striking c) something that limits d) authority
47. (  ) perquisites a) gratuities b) inquiries c) requests d) necessary conditions
48. (  ) precursor a) forerunner b) descendant c) anathema d) concurrent
49. (  ) acronym a) a word of opposite meaning b) synonym c) one of two or more words having the same meaning d) a word formed from the initial letters of other words
50. (  ) troglodyte a) amphibious reptile b) man of learning c) cave-dweller d) recluse
51. (  ) bemused a) entranced b) tricked c) amused d) quieted
52. (  ) permissive a) long letter b) recalcitrant c) indulgent d) long lasting
53. (  ) neophyte a) master b) tyro c) new word d) law of physics
54. (  ) alleviate a) rise up b) humor c) make worse d) ease
55. (  ) perspicuity a) density b) clarity c) cryptic quality d) broadmindedness
56. (  ) dissonance a) harmony b) discord c) resonance d) assonance
57. (  ) phonetician a) charlatan b) citizen of Phoenicia c) historian d) expert on speech sounds

58. (   ) chimera a) small monarchy b) collection of bells c) anthology d) fantastic notion
59. (   ) equivocation a) long speech b) doubletalk c) equal time d) extra job
60. (   ) inordinate a) not working b) in order c) excessive d) ordained
61. (   ) truncated a) cut short b) short cut c) packed away d) added
62. (   ) antimony a) conflicting testimony b) antibody c) alimony d) metalloid element
63. (   ) raffish a) clever b) disreputable c) refuse d) roughage
64. (   ) prurience a) virtue b) lewdness c) state of purge d) diseased skin
65. (   ) idyllic a) Platonic b) pastoral c) ideal d) idle
66. (   ) spate a) spittle b) to spite c) sudden outburst d) irritability
67. (   ) polemics a) direct opposites b) art of argumentation c) furry-footed rodents d) antibodies
68. (   ) incognito a) disguised b) unveiled c) recognized d) incommunicado
69. (   ) augury a) omen b) halo c) boring tool d) induct into office
70. (   ) equanimity a) animated b) pertaining to water c) split personality d) calmness of mind
71. (   ) protean a) mutable b) prodigious c) food element d) in favor of
72. (   ) perfunctory a) in the manner of b) official c) mechanical d) dying
73. (   ) sycophants a) jazz musicians b) sidekicks c) fawning followers d) mental abnormalities
74. (   ) xenophobia a) fear of water b) fear of high places c) fear of foreigners d) fear of closed spaces
75. (   ) pastiche a) pastry b) a paste c) mixture of styles d) a rural scene
76. (   ) synapse a) nerve ending b) conference of churches c) symposium d) abridgment
77. (   ) concatenation a) conference b) feline chorus c) state of being close-linked d) state of harmony
78. (   ) cartel a) a French dance b) a small carriage c) price-fixing combine d) unconditional authority
79. (   ) artifacts a) craftsmen b) tricks c) substitutions d) simple man-made objects
80. (   ) quid pro quo a) in the meantime b) unacceptable person c) overpowering force d) one thing in return for another

81. (   ) microcosm  a) germ  b) universe in miniature  c) reduced in size  d) Milky Way
82. (   ) philippic  a) offhand  b) crass materialist  c) delaying maneuver  d) bitter speech
83. (   ) nihilism  a) philosophy of negativism  b) belief in free will  c) anarchism  d) humanism
84. (   ) generalist  a) leader of an Army  b) a vague thinker  c) tabulation  d) versatile person
85. (   ) voluntarist  a) believer in free will  b) do-gooder  c) charitable offering  d) determinist
86. (   ) ontological  a) study of word origins  b) pertaining to the study of insects  c) of the nature of being  d) well-reasoned
87. (   ) extrapolation  a) movement of the poles  b) polarity  c) prediction based on present knowledge  d) insertion
88. (   ) apocryphal  a) hypocritical  b) fabricated  c) awe-inspiring  d) pithy
89. (   ) anachronistic  a) synchronized  b) antigovernment  c) upbeat  d) out of its time
90. (   ) cantilevered  a) sung in a group  b) improvised  c) tilted  d) projected beam supported at one end
91. (   ) ecclesiology  a) religious cant  b) recondite  c) study of organisms and their environments  d) study of church art
92. (   ) historiography  a) geography combined with history  b) writing of history  c) study of artifacts  d) study of the graphic arts
93. (   ) tergiversation  a) idle chatter  b) equivocation  c) charity  d) nagging
94. (   ) megalopolis  a) huge lollipop  b) monument  c) greater metropolitan area  d) feelings of omnipotence
95. (   ) spatiography  a) astronaut's memoirs  b) geography of space  c) science of measurement  d) handwriting
96. (   ) anthropomorphic  a) pertaining to the study of man  b) shapeless  c) pertaining to drugs  d) ascribing human attributes to nonhuman things
97. (   ) ichthyologist  a) one who studies fishes  b) one who smashes idols  c) Eskimo  d) one who studies fossils
98. (   ) misogynist  a) one who gives rubdowns  b) obstetrician  c) one who enjoys punishment  d) woman hater
99. (   ) peripatetic  a) at the external boundary  b) pertaining to human suffering  c) walking about  d) pertaining to the reversal in drama
100. (   ) deliquescent  a) melting away  b) behind in an obligation  c) pertaining to wayward youths  d) very lovely

| | | | | |
|---|---|---|---|---|
| 1. (b) | 21. (a) | 41. (b) | 61. (a) | 81. (b) |
| 2. (c) | 22. (b) | 42. (c) | 62. (d) | 82. (d) |
| 3. (c) | 23. (b) | 43. (b) | 63. (b) | 83. (a) |
| 4. (a) | 24. (b) | 44. (a) | 64. (b) | 84. (d) |
| 5. (b) | 25. (c) | 45. (b) | 65. (b) | 85. (a) |
| 6. (c) | 26. (d) | 46. (c) | 66. (c) | 86. (c) |
| 7. (a) | 27. (c) | 47. (a) | 67. (b) | 87. (c) |
| 8. (a) | 28. (b) | 48. (a) | 68. (a) | 88. (b) |
| 9. (d) | 29. (b) | 49. (d) | 69. (a) | 89. (d) |
| 10. (b) | 30. (b) | 50. (c) | 70. (d) | 90. (d) |
| 11. (b) | 31. (b) | 51. (a) | 71. (a) | 91. (d) |
| 12. (c) | 32. (c) | 52. (c) | 72. (c) | 92. (b) |
| 13. (a) | 33. (b) | 53. (b) | 73. (c) | 93. (b) |
| 14. (a) | 34. (c) | 54. (d) | 74. (c) | 94. (c) |
| 15. (d) | 35. (d) | 55. (b) | 75. (c) | 95. (b) |
| 16. (c) | 36. (b) | 56. (b) | 76. (a) | 96. (d) |
| 17. (c) | 37. (b) | 57. (d) | 77. (c) | 97. (a) |
| 18. (d) | 38. (c) | 58. (d) | 78. (c) | 98. (d) |
| 19. (c) | 39. (c) | 59. (b) | 79. (d) | 99. (c) |
| 20. (c) | 40. (d) | 60. (c) | 80. (d) | 100. (a) |

COMPREHENSIVE SCORING KEY

PART I —CORRECT ANSWERS    _____

PART II—CORRECT ANSWERS    _____

        TOTAL    _____

195–200 right—Ph.D.
181–194 right—Master's degree
161–180 right—College graduate
136–160 right—College freshman level
               (Above average)
100–135 right—Average American

Under 100 right—Substandard

**If your rating was less than Ph. D. level, reread the book and do the quizzes again. Adding to your vocabulary is a lifelong process. Keep working at the techniques you've learned in this book.**

# General Index

Note: See also Word Index, page 409.

402

**403**

405

406

word(s) (*cont.*)
proper adjectives, 254
proper names as, 249–265
radiation of, 183–186
relatives *see* synonyms
rewriters, 47–49
scholars, 49–50
shrinking *see* words, specialization
of meaning of
slang *see* slang
specialization of meaning of, 175,
177–179
stretching *see* words, generalization
of meaning of
substandard, 63
technical, 63, 291–341

word(s) (*cont.*)
transference of meaning of, 186–187
tricky *see* wordplay
uncommon, 3–4, 356–358
wheels of meaning and, 184–186
working, 37–58, 120–122
*See also* dictionaries; doubletalk;
folk etymology; macaronic lingo;
quizzes; radio; television; wordplay
*Words and Their Ways in English
Speech* (Greenough), quoted, 264
Wu Ting Fang, 27–28

Zabel, William, 188

# Word Index

[Note: The words in this index consist of those printed in small capitals in the text to show that they lie in the range beyond the ten thousand commonest in the Thorndike count, plus most of the words and phrases printed in italics or enclosed in quotation marks. The latter include technical terms; informal words (slang, argot, etc.); malapropisms; dictionary labels; "confusion" words (homonyms, homophones, homographs, etc.); words from cultural history; words, such as *theory* and *hypothesis,* that illustrate discrimination of meanings; culturally determined expressions, such as *executive front* and *credit-cardmanship;* common words, such as *humor, wit, angle, line, thing, action,* etc., that have acquired special meanings; and other words emphasized in the text. See also General Index, page 401, for a general index to the book.]

archeology, 143, 390
archetype, 154
archiepiscopal, 390
Archimedes, 123
archipelago, 154
architrave, 154
archives, 53, 154, 198
ardent, 198
argosy, 251
argot, 4, 5, 35, 246, 275, 290, 393, 396
argumentative, 178
Arian, 259
Ariosto, 258
Aristophanic, 260
Aristotelian, 254
Aristotle, 265
armada, 251
armadillo, 109, 111
armistice, 380
arrondissement, 354
artichoke, 277
articulation, 51, 232
artifact, 356, 363, 393
artificer, 363
artificial satellite, 6
artistry, 363
artless, 363
asbestos, 50, 156, 165
ascendancy, 265
ascension, 65, 95
ascetic, 95, 101, 103, 107, 212, 314, 377, 394, 395
ascribe, 150
asepsis, 327
asininity, 32
asp, 109, 111
asparagus, 25
asperity, 217, 247
asperse, 217
aspersion, 46
assemblage, 46
assess, 379
asseverate, 140
assiduity, 390
assignation, 379
assize, 379
assuage, 308

assumption, 78, 125, 210, 213, 215, 247
aster, 154
asterisk, 154
asteroid, 154
astigmatism, 327
astral, 154
astringent, 381
astrionics, 154, 349
astrogation, 154
astrolabe, 154, 330
astrology, 143, 154
astronaut, 6, 95, 96, 104, 154
astronautics, 6, 90, 154, 314
astronavigation, 6
astronavigator, 6
astronomical, 219
astronomical unit, 337
astronomy, 154
astrophobia, 142
astrophysics, 154, 349, 394
astro station, 6
astute, 175
Athanasian, 259
atheist, 390
atmospheric braking, 337
atom, 153
atomic, 291, 314
atomizer, 285
atom-splitting, 153
atonal, 57
atrium, 157
atrocious, 189
atrociously, 233
atrocities, 273
attaché, 95, 103, 109, 110, 111
attainment, 382
Attic, 260
atypical, 43
audiovisual, 120, 134
audit, 363
audition, 363
auditorium, 363
auditory, 363
auger, 140
augmentation, 390
augury, 95, 104, 397
Augustinian, 259
aura, 157, 249, 332
auricle, 40

auricular, 390
auspices, 384
auspicious, 99, 106, 384
austerity, 95, 103
authenticating, 52, 99, 106
authoritarian, 116, 129, 166, 229
authoritative, 229, 271
autobiographical, 65
autocratic, 95, 103
autograph, 144, 374
automate, 97, 104
automatically, 201
automation, 90, 97, 104, 297, 300
automatize, 153
automotivated, 93, 102
autonomy, 390
autosacrifice, 16
avant-garde, 65, 354
avid, 81
avocation, 383, 390
avow, 140
avowal, 92, 101
axiom, 216, 332
aye, 62
Azoic, 155
azote, 155

Babbitt, 245, 250, 258
Babel, 163
bacchanal, 258
bacchanalis, 93, 102, 116
Bach, 67
bach, 346
backbite, 219
backbiting, 92, 101, 217
backwoods, 284
Baconian, 254, 255
bacteriology, 143
badface, 273
badinage, 286
baggage-smasher, 269
bailiff, 140
balance, 202
balance of payments, 297

balance of power, 309, 310
baleful, 100, 106
ballet, 40, 380
ballistic, 65
Balzacian, 261
bambino, 31
bamboo, 29, 31
banal, 273
banana-head, 347
bang, 276
banister, 352
banjo, 200
bank, 297
banshee, 141
Barabbas, 251
barber, 299
barge, 221
barnacles, 327
barodontalgia, 349
barometer, 155
baroque, 233
barosinusitis, 349
barotitis, 349
barotraumatic, 349
barrister, 178
barrow, 285
baseborn, 201
basing point, 296
bastion, 100, 107, 343
baton, 48
bawd, 16, 17, 109, 110
bawdy, 371
bawl out, 219
Bayreuth, 67
bazaar, 41, 53
bazoo, 263
bazooka, 263
bearish, 297
beast, 347
beasties, 62
beat, 47, 98, 105, 346
beat it, 207, 282
beatitude, 355, 390, 395
beat movement, 98, 105
beatnik, 62, 130
Becket, à, Thomas, St., 357
Becky Sharp, 258
bedevils, 97, 98, 105, 394
bedlam, 6, 251, 264, 290
bedridden, 149

circumscribe, 51,
150
circumspect, 202,
384
circumspection,
384
circumstantial,
212, 380
circumvene, 369
circumvent, 384
cite, 38, 39
citified, 201
claimant, 366
clairvoyance, 231
clambake, 12
clandestine, 212,
239, 246
clarity, 92, 101
classes, 192, 193,
357
classified, 180, 181,
304
class struggle, 298
claustrophobia,
142, 390
clearinghouse, 297
clemency, 95, 104,
139
clichés, 273
clientele, 109, 111
climactic, 65
clincher, 61
cloak-and-suiter,
16
closure, 366
cloture, 92, 101
coadjutor, 146,
157, 390
coagulation, 139,
324
coalition, 121
coaxial, 317
cobbler, 299
cocoanuts, 278
coed, 151
coefficient, 390
coequal, 369
coerce, 65, 93, 102
coerced, 115
coercion, 100, 107
coercive, 93, 102
cogent, 136, 344,
362
cogitate, 335, 362
cogitated, 60
cognition, 374, 390
cognizance, 93,
102, 115, 374,
395
coherer, 329

cohesiveness, 109,
112
coiffure, 131, 132
cold-gas jets, 337
cole, 90
coleslaw, 25
collaboration, 357
collapsibles, 121
collateral, 297
collective owner-
ship, 298
collision course,
347
collocations, 332
collop, 90
colloquial, 60, 76,
151, 260
colloquialism, 5,
358
colonialism, 122,
305, 307
colonized, 174
colonnade, 95, 103
colossal, 189
colossi, 305
colossus, 157
coma, 41, 225
combat fatigue,
350
come, 206
comebacks, 286
comedy, 22
come off it, 130
comeuppance, 119,
161
comfit, 148
comic, 258, 260,
266, 380
comma, 41
commandeer, 46,
56
commandeered,
96, 104
command guid-
ance, 317
commerce, 202,
297
commiseration, 390
commissars, 333
commissary, 372
commitments, 92,
101
commode, 375
Common Market,
121
commonty, 22, 23
communicant, 235
communism, 152,
190, 191, 192,
193, 238, 297,

298
Communist, 178,
306
communistic, 298
community, 22
compact, 350
compactness, 136
compatible, 130
compendium, 157,
231
compensatory, 109
compile, 80, 244
complacency, 99,
106, 260
complacent, 268
complaisance, 376,
395
complaisant, 201
complement, 39
complex, 228, 314
complicity, 376
compliment, 39
complimentary,
283
comport, 375
composite, 149,
197
compost, 149
comprehensible,
311
comprehension,
24, 95, 104,
120, 324, 377
compulsion, 367
computations, 316
computers:
analogue, 316
ballistics, 337
digital, 316
electronic, 316,
317
comstockery, 259
conbobberation,
269
concatenation, 51,
232, 340, 397
concept, 125, 130
concern, 177
conchology, 143
conciliate, 233
conciliation, 137
conciliatory, 92,
101
concision, 261
conclave, 95, 103
concoct, 229
concocting, 128,
334
concomitant, 65,
139, 172, 183,

395
concordance, 365
concourse, 224
concretize, 347
concur, 366
concurrent, 127
concussion, 51
condensation, 77
condescension, 93,
102
condign, 367
condish, 12
condottieri, 253
conduce, 150
conducible, 150
conducive, 150
conductivity, 390
conductor, 285
confab, 99, 106
confabulate, 65
confection, 148
confessional, 261
confidante, 251
configuration, 390
conflagration, 46
confluctions, 266
conformable, 368
conformation, 368
confrontation, 92,
101, 137, 308
congeries, 370
congest, 370
coniferous, 369
conjecture, 78,
125, 210, 213,
215, 216, 246,
247
conjugate, 89
conjoin, 372
conjugal, 372
conjunction, 278
conjunctive, 372
conjuncture, 372
conjure, 65
conk, 61
connectives, 372
connoisseur, 99,
226
connotation, 137,
190, 195, 198,
201, 374
connote, 374
cons, 165
consanguinity, 327,
390
conscript, 150
consecution, 381
conservatory, 381
consignment, 376,
379

415

data processing, 316
date, 61
dative, 368
datum, 368
deal off the arm, 277
debentures, 284
debile, 29
debility, 370, 390
debris, 93, 102, 127
debut, 146
debutante, 385
decadence, 390
decalogue, 143
de-canined, 221
decant, 43
decelerate, 337
decentralization, 97, 105
decibel, 95, 103
declaim, 366
declamation, 366, 390
declination, 155, 329, 390
décolletage, 15
decomposition, 149, 330, 390
décor, 375
decorous, 390
decorum, 158, 275, 344
decrepitude, 390
decry, 218
deduce, 150
deducible, 150
deduct, 150
deduction, 80, 150
deep-freeze, 130
de facto, 146, 309, 310, 352
defamation, 218
defame, 217
deference, 369
deferential, 95, 103
deficit, 96, 104, 122
definitive, 93, 102, 115, 271, 394
deflated, 219
deflect, 140
deftness, 99, 106
defunct, 50, 152
degeneracy, 140
dehydrate, 47, 55, 58, 155, 393
de jure, 309
delectable, 99, 106

delegation, 202
deliberative, 308
delightful, 189
delimit, 154, 206, 227, 244
delineate, 140
deliquescence, 140
deliquescent, 390, 398
delirium, 147, 158
delusion, 128
de luxe, 373
demi-devil, 128
demijohn, 263
demimonde, 16, 26, 35
demise, 372
democracy, 138, 190, 191, 192, 193, 358
demonology, 144
demoralization, 390
demos, 154
Demosthenes, 249
demotic, 154
dendrology, 144
denigrate, 50
denigratory, 222
denotation, 206, 244, 374
denotative, 190
denouement, 47, 58, 141
de novo, 309
denti-perforate, 16
denunciatory, 345
deny, 197
deploy, 304, 376
deport, 375
deportation, 375
deposition, 149
depository, 68, 149
deprecate, 65
depreciate, 218, 219
depreciation, 294, 390
depressed areas, 349
depression, 45
depressurizing, 80
deprivation, 326
derisive, 24
derivation, 25, 329
derivative, 63, 147, 148
derogate, 218
derogatory, 71, 130, 188, 201,

219
descant, 43
description, 150
descriptivists, 220
Desdemona, 67, 122, 128, 129
desecrate, 140
desegregate, 96, 104
desegregation, 92, 101, 121
desiccated, 95, 104
desideratum, 158
design stresses, 337
designation, 379
despicable, 384
despondence, 390
desultory, 378
détente, 93, 94, 102, 309, 310, 352
deterioration, 140
determinists, 100, 106
detonating, 141
detonation, 140
detour, 205
detract, 218
detraction, 217
detractors, 23, 218
detritus, 158
deuce, 276
deus ex machina, 146, 354
devastation, 93, 94, 103
developer, 122
deviant, 291
deviate, 141
deviation, 140, 329
devilish, 199
devious, 129
devotee, 224
dghtr, 12
diabetes, 166
diabolical, 128, 134, 199
diabolically, 235
diagnosing, 233
diagnosis, 24, 166, 390
Dial., 76
dialect, 4, 5, 62, 76, 210
dialectical, 86, 94
dialectics, 65, 178, 195, 305, 369, 373, 394
dialogue, 144
diametrically, 50

diapason, 166
diaphanous, 228
diathermy, 152, 394
diatribe, 65, 218
Dickensian, 261
dictator, 146, 158
dictatorial, 229
dictatorship of the proletariat, 307, 358
diction, 108
dictograph, 144
dictum, 48, 96, 104, 146, 158, 255, 394, 395
dielectric, 155, 329
differentiate, 76
diffraction, 329
digit, 316
dignitary, 257, 367
digraph, 144
dilemma, 100, 107, 166, 203
dilettante, 226
dinkus, 29
dinosaur, 230
directive, 64, 151, 181, 304
directory, 379
direct taxation, 297
disaffection, 148
disallowed, 285
disapprobation, 189, 195
disbursement, 109, 111
discernible, 363
discernment, 231
disclaimer, 94, 103
discombobulated, 269
discomfited, 236
discomfiture, 390
discordant, 229
discrepancy, 369
discrepant, 229
discriminating, 112
discrimination, 46, 74, 86, 90, 92, 101, 134, 206, 217, 222, 231, 294
discriminatory, 97, 105
discs, 316
discursive, 366
disenfranchised, 92, 102, 115, 340, 393

disestablished, 264
disgorge, 378
disgruntled, 109, 110
disinclination, 390
disintegrate, 51, 140, 233
disintegration, 390
disjoin, 372
disjointed, 372
disjunction, 372
dismissed, 219
disparage, 216, 217, 219
disparagement, 217, 225
disparity, 96, 104, 229
dispassionate, 193
dispiriting, 95, 104
disport, 375
disputants, 136, 304
disrupt, 378
disseminating, 132
dissemination, 390, 395
dissenter, 96, 104
dissever, 373
dissidents, 109, 110, 115
dissipation, 19
dissociate, 43
dissolute, 43
dissonance, 58, 396
dissonant, 43
distend, 382
distension, 382
distillation, 324, 329
distortion, 329
distrain, 381
distressed areas, 349
distribution, 298
distribution of wealth, 297
dive, 284
divergence, 9
diversification, 312
divination, 81, 86, 231
division of labor, 297
divisiveness, 92, 101
docile, 239
doctor, 197
doctorate, 109, 112, 394

doctrinaire, 229
documentary, 121
dodge, 277
Dogberry, 274
dogma, 24, 166, 192
dogmatic, 64, 229
doily, 140
dole, 198
doll, 275, 276
dolled up, 286
dolor, 158
domesticated, 145
domicile, 50
Dominican, 373
donate, 46
Don Giovanni, 67, 123, 126, 127, 134
Don Juan, 245, 257
donna, 274
Don Quixote, 126
Doppler effect, 329
Doppler shift, 336, 337
dosages, 224
Dostoevsky, 122, 134
double-domes, 270
double entendre, 227
double entente, 227
doubletalk, 246, 247, 347, 357
double-think, 347, 357
doughty, 97, 105, 394
dowager, 22
downdrafts, 366
Downing Street, 309
downtrodden, 119
doxology, 144
doxy, 16, 17, 34
draftees, 237
draft resolution, 308
drag racing, 349
dramatize, 120
dramaturgy, 155
draughtsman, 375
dressed up to the nines, 286
drollery, 109, 111
dromedaries, 29
dromond, 116
drums, 316

dry goods, 275
ducal, 150
ducat, 150
duchy, 150
duck a date, 269
duckets, 278
ductible, 150
ductile, 80
ductless, 9
duffer, 286
dummy, 274
duo-lingual, 26
duplex, 376
duplicity, 128, 376, 394
durable goods, 296
durance vile, 100, 106
Dürrenmatt, Friedrich, 67
dustbin, 63, 285
dust-up, 285
dynamic, 11, 80, 192, 211
dynamics, 80, 155, 329
dynamo, 155
dynamometer, 155
dynasties, 137
dyne, 155
dysbarism, 349
dysfunction, 166
dysgenic, 9, 340, 396

eatable, 200
eateria, 273
eaves-dripper, 18
ebullience, 311
ebullient, 65, 96, 100, 104, 106, 395
ebullition, 100
ecclesiastical, 217
ecclesiology, 109, 112, 394, 398
ecdysiast, 54, 65
ecdysis, 54
echelon, 65
echoic, 203
eclectic, 65, 336, 340
eclogue, 144
ecology, 326
economic, 298
economics, 89, 137, 293, 297
ecstasy, 314
ecstatically, 109, 111

ectoplasm, 234
ecumenical, 95, 103, 121, 238
edge, 293
edible, 200
edict, 8
edit, 368
editorialists, 218
editorializing, 301
editorship, 368
EDP, 316
educe, 150
effect, 40
efficacious, 136
effrontery, 18, 35
eftsoons, 62
Egeria, 251
egghead, 119, 270, 346
egotist, 376
egotistic, 9
Einstein, Albert, 123
Einsteinian, 254
elaborate, 199
elaboration, 208
elasticity, 329
elector, 146
electoral, 302
electorate, 92, 101
Electr., 63
electrification, 330
electrified, 329
electrocardiogram, 65
electrode, 329
electrojet, 155
electroluminescence, 312
electrolysis, 329, 330
electromagnetic, 328
electromagnetism, 314
electromotive, 314
electron, 153, 155, 166, 238, 315, 329
electronics, 90, 155, 314, 315, 316, 317
electroplating, 329
electroscope, 329
electrostatic, 109, 111, 155
eleemosynary, 29
elegance, 373
elephantiasis, 326
elephantine, 230

417

eligible, 373
Eliot, T. S., 357
elite, 109, 112,
    299, 311
eloquent, 93, 102
elusive, 37, 40, 56,
    58, 118, 140,
    253
emaciated, 50
emanation, 178,
    291, 373
emasculated, 94,
    103
embassy, 309, 310
embezzles, 198
embody, 234
embolism, 122
embryo, 328
embryonic, 324
emilyposting, 259
emissary, 372
emotional, 265
empathy, 9, 128
empiric, 230
empiricism, 255
empiricists, 152
emporia, 202
emulation, 51
enamored, 274
encephalogram, 13
enchanting, 189
enclave, 65, 182,
    195, 394
enclosure, 317
encomium, 140
encrusted, 225
encumbered, 48
encyclicals, 229
encyclopedic, 74,
    86
endocrine, 9
endowed, 200
end-product, 295
endued, 200
Endymion, 67, 123
energize, 223
engineer, 189
enigma, 166
enlightenment, 11
enmeshed, 129
enormous, 230
enquiry, 137
en rapport, 309,
    310
enraptured, 127
en regle, 309
ensemble, 80
ensilage, 326
entente, 309, 310,
    352

enterprisers, 293
enthralling, 100,
    107
entity, 153, 343
entomology, 144
entourage, 95, 103
entrepreneurs, 302
envisage, 235
envision, 235
enwrap, 201
enzyme, 9, 58, 340,
    396
ephemeral, 237
epicedian, 29
epicure, 29
epicurean, 236,
    249, 267
epidermis, 326
epigram, 41, 236,
    246
epigrammatic, 200
epigraph, 41
epilogue, 144
epithet, 32
epitome, 166, 223,
    249, 253
epizootic, 155
epoch, 65
equable, 369
equanimity, 100,
    106, 369, 393,
    397
equated, 380
equidistant, 380
equilibrium, 158,
    202
equine-visaged,
    197
equinoctial, 80,
    369
equinox, 158, 328,
    369
equipment, 293
equitable, 369
equivalence, 331,
    369
equivocal, 369
equivocation, 49,
    57, 86, 139,
    227, 247, 383,
    390, 397
eradicate, 390
erg, 155
ergometer, 155
eristic, 232, 247
erroneous, 63
Ersatz, 237
erubescence, 50
erubescent, 57
erudite, 65, 116,

134, 220
erudition, 51, 383
escalation, 90, 312
escalator clause,
    122, 300, 350
eschatology, 144
esculations, 30
esophagus, 166
esoteric, 17
espial, 384
espionage, 93, 102,
    384
esthetic, 109, 112
esurient, 140
ethics, 252, 344
ethnic, 88, 109,
    110, 122
ethnological, 116
ethnology, 144
ethos, 187
etiquette, 259, 368
etymologist, 2, 35,
    359
etymology, 25, 68,
    74, 77, 144,
    275, 382
Euclid, 328
eugenics, 327
eulogize, 46, 56
eulogized, 256
eulogy, 144
euphemism, 65, 96,
    104, 188, 195
euphonious, 155
euphony, 155, 203,
    390
euphuism, 258
eureka, 166
Euripidean, 260
euthanasia, 65,
    116, 117
evade, 139
evaluation, 299
evanescent, 237,
    390
eventually, 384
eviscerated, 228
evocation, 109, 112
evolve, 94, 103,
    192, 194
exacerbate, 93,
    102
exaction, 383
exaggerate, 30
exaggeration, 166
example, 200
excerpts, 305
exclamatory, 189,
    366
excoriate, 65, 218,

381
excretion, 363
excursive, 390
exec, 12
execrate, 217
executive front,
    298
executors, 252
exemplification,
    148
exemption, 92, 96,
    102, 104
exhibitionist, 283
exhortation, 49
exigency, 48, 362
existential, 138
existentialism, 152
existentialist, 100,
    106, 109, 112,
    115
exodus, 166, 390
exonerate, 46
exorbitant, 127,
    128
exorcise, 99, 106,
    352
exotic, 99, 106
expanse, 375
expansive, 375
expatriate, 46
expectancy, 390
expectorate, 50
expectorating, 57
expedient, 304
expertize, 304, 347
explicit, 93, 102,
    376
explicitly, 99, 106
explicitness, 227
explosion, 346
exponent, 136, 149
exportation, 375
expositor, 149, 158,
    235
expostulate, 51, 65
expostulating, 100,
    106, 394
expropriating, 381
expropriation, 358
expulsion, 390
expurgate, 259
extant, 65
extempore, 23, 158
extension, 190
externalize, 234
extraction, 390
extradite, 368
extradition, 368,
    390
extrapolation, 6,

hemophilia, 65
Henry, O., 290
Henry, Patrick, 123
hep, 12, 54
heparin, 65
hepster, 54
heptarchy, 390
herbals, 328
herculean, 51, 230
heretical, 9
Herodias, 259, 290
heterodoxy, 212
heterogeneity, 116, 129, 132
heterogeneous, 66, 218
hexameter, 155
hiatus, 158
hidalgos, 230
hide-a-woo, 11
hierarchy, 95, 103, 154
hieroglyphics, 28
hi-fi, 95, 104, 317
highbrow, 59, 165, 270
highfalutin, 93, 94, 102
high-grade merchandise, 278
high-muck-a-muck, 25
hike, 48
hip, 54
hipper, 98, 105
Hippo, 259
Hippocrates, 134
Hippocratic, 116
Hippocratic oath, 123
hipster, 54
hire-purchase system, 285
His Nibs, 275
histology, 144
historiography, 109, 112, 398
hit-and-run, 62
hitched, 98, 105
hiu muckamuck, 25
h.o., 12
hoarding, 284
hoary, 274
hoax, 94, 103
hobble, 206
hobgoblins, 142
hobo, 240, 284
hogshead, 394
hoi polloi, 160
Holinshed, 67

holler copper, 277
Hollywood, 195
Hollywooden, 260
holocaust, 46, 66
Holofernes, 259
holograph, 144, 374
Homeric, 260
homicidal, 23
homogeneous, 155
homograph, 31, 38, 86, 144, 155
homologue, 155
homologous, 155
homomorphy, 155
homonym, 31, 38, 86, 155
homophone, 22, 31, 38, 58, 66, 68, 393
homunculus, 328
honeysuckle, 23
honk, 98
hoofer, 277
hooked, 130
Horatian, 260
hormones, 147, 328
horrible, 189, 194
hors d'oeuvre, 229
horse-faced, 197
horse-peculator, 29
hospice, 264
hostel, 264
hot, 7, 188, 198
hot-rodding, 349
hotter than a stove, 277
howl, 98
howler, 23
huckstering, 376
hucksters, 364
hullabaloo, 230
humanism, 50, 325
humanist, 109, 112, 115, 265
humanistic, 109, 112
humanitarian, 66
humbug, 25, 96, 104
humor, 72, 82, 265, 266, 267
humorous, 63, 76
humours, 72, 265, 266, 267
humus, 158, 324
hurdle, 7, 97, 207
hurls, 200
hurtles, 200
husbondage, 11

Huxley, Aldous, 123
hybrid, 154
hybridization, 327
hydrant, 155
hydrated, 158
hydro, 155
hydrocarbon, 319
hydrodynamics, 155
hydrometer, 155
hydrophobia, 66, 142, 155
hydroponics, 66, 155, 337, 338, 340
hydrostatic, 155
hydrostatics, 22
hydrotherapy, 233
hygrometer, 116, 117
hyperbole, 66, 166, 189, 195, 390, 394
hypercritical, 41, 58, 393
hypersensitivity, 261
hyphenate, 68
hypnosis, 327
hypocrisy, 30
hypocritical, 41
hypostatize, 234
hypothesis, 78, 79, 118, 124, 125, 133, 134, 210, 213, 214, 215, 216, 246, 247, 395
hypothetical, 124
hysteria, 166, 190
hysterics, 22, 30

Iago, 122, 128, 129
ibex, 29
Ibsen, 357
ichneumon, 166
ichthyologist, 398
ichthyology, 390
iconoclasm, 140
icons, 29
idea, 190
idealist, 93, 102
identity, 200
ideological, 93, 94, 99, 102, 106
ideologists, 192
ideology, 90, 92, 102

idiocracy, 155
idiocy, 155
idiom, 155, 196
idiomatic, 155
idiomorphic, 155
idiosyncrasy, 155
idyl, 40
idyllic, 109, 112, 116, 397
ignitron, 153
illative, 369
illegible, 22, 30, 373
illegitimate, 20
illicit, 268
Illit., 76
illiteracy, 131, 132
illiterate, 20, 22, 29, 63
illogical, 144
illusive, 40
illustrative, 82, 120, 222
image, 180, 347
imagery, 99, 106, 236
immanent, 41, 56
immeasurably, 300
imminence, 9, 395
immoral, 258
immune, 93, 98, 102, 105
impact, 302, 355
impartiality, 302
impassivity, 302
impeccable, 66, 221
impedimenta, 48, 158
impenetrable, 255
imperfection, 148, 291
imperialism, 191, 193
imperialists, 306
imperious, 95, 104
imperium, 145
impetus, 158, 374
impinge, 109, 124, 268
implement, 304
implicate, 46
implication, 182, 201, 212, 376
implicit, 249, 376
impost, 149
impostor, 230
impregnable, 377
impresario, 66, 97, 105, 115

421

liana, 116
liar, 31
libbard, 90
libel, 217
liberalism, 376
liberation, 305, 306, 358
libidinous, 50
libido, 314
lichee, 66
lichen, 40
lickspittle, 221
lictor, 146, 149, 159
lie-ins, 350
lift, 272, 284
liftoff, 349
like a bat out of hell, 267
limbeck, 62
limbo, 279
limpid, 228
line, 68, 69, 177, 190
line-of-sight transmission, 337, 338
liner, 62
lingo, 5, 97
linguistic, 99, 220
linguistics, 273
Lin Yu Tang, 260
liquidated, 239, 381
liquidation, 96, 104, 293
liquidity, 312
lit, 7, 188, 270
literate, 99, 109, 111, 394
lithograph, 144
litigation, 362
litre, 43
litterbug, 347
littoral, 40
lit up like a cathedral, 267
lobbying, 302
loch, 63
locum tenens, 51, 237
locus, 187
locutions, 207
lodestone, 329
loftily, 19
logarithms, 144
logic, 144
logistical, 14
logistics, 14, 86, 144

logogram, 144
logograph, 144
logotype, 144
logroll, 284
loogan, 276
looped, 270
loot, 136, 138
lope, 207, 226
loquacious, 50
loran, 292
lorn, 90
Lothario, 258
lour, 90
lousy, 1, 82, 83, 129, 188
lousy crumb, 130
low-end, 295
loyalty, 190, 191
lubricator, 159
lucidity, 227
Lucifer, 251
Lucretian, 260
Luftwaffe, 351
lukewarm, 259
lupine, 197
lush, 270
lusty, 12
lusus naturae, 291
lynch, 251
Lyndonized, 347
lyre, 31
lyric, 30
lyrical, 311


macabre, 66
macadam, 66, 108, 251
macaronic, 21, 26, 35, 66
macaronis, 282
Macbeth, 122
Macedon, 249
Machiavelli, 123
Machiavellian, 290
Machiavellianism, 253
machinations, 128
MacLeish, Archibald, 123
macro, 348
macrocosm, 348
macroeconomic, 348
macroscopic, 348
macroscopic particles, 337
madras, 251
mag, 12
magisterial, 229

magistral, 229
magna cum laude, 146, 354
magnanimity, 260
magnanimous, 89
magnate, 41
magnetic amplifiers, 315
magnetic fields, 337
magnetic memory units, 315
magnetic observations, 335
magnetometer, 66
magnificent, 189, 194, 199
mahouts, 363
main drag, 276
majority whip, 302
malapropism, 21, 22, 35, 195
malcontents, 350
malediction, 154
malign, 89, 216, 217
malignity, 128, 134, 217
malnutrition, 223
Malthusian, 67, 254, 297
maltreatment, 140
man, 119, 273
manacle, 371
manageable, 362
managerial lag, 298
mandarin, 141, 379
mandate, 93, 94, 103
mandatory, 96, 104, 140
mandolin, 200
maneuver, 92, 93, 102, 232, 371
mania, 147, 159
Manichean, 259
manicure, 371
manifesto, 371
manipulate, 80, 371
manipulation, 128, 275
manipulator, 159
manufactory, 148, 371
manumission, 371
manumit, 372
manuscript, 151

marathon, 153, 169
margin, 293
marginal, 93, 103, 297
marital, 93, 102
Marjoribanks, 264
marker, 277
market, 297
marketable, 92, 101
Marlowe, Christopher, 123
marquisette, 90
marriage counselors, 350
marsupial, 377
marvelous, 189
marvy, 189
Marxian, 69, 254
Marxism, 297, 298, 305
Marxism-Leninism, 305, 306
masers, 315
masquerade, 285
masses, 192, 193
masseuses, 109, 110
massive, 144
mass ratio, 337
materialize, 234
matey, 285
Math., 63
mathematical, 68
matrimony, 21, 258
matrix, 147, 159, 356
matter, 177, 202
mattresses, 30
matzoth, 66, 109, 111
Maud, 269
mausoleum, 251
maverick, 303
mawkishness, 99, 106
mazel tov, 351
mazuma, 276
McCoy (the real), 283
mean, 346
meander, 206
meandering, 199, 240
meaningful, 355
measurable, 293
mec, 61, 62
Mecca, 251
Med., 63
media, 17, 90

mythology, 144
mythos, 179

Nabokov, Vladimir, 67
nadir, 47
naïve, 201
naïveté, 93, 102
naphtha, 156, 166
narcissism, 66
narcissistic, 100, 106
Narcissus, 251, 290
nard, 90
narrators, 222
natch, 273
national liberation movement, 306
naturalists, 152
naturalized, 244
naturopaths, 43, 231
nausea, 147, 160
nauseating, 189
naval, 63
navigating, 198
Nebuchadnezzar, 259
nebula, 160
necromantic, 48
necrophobia, 142
necropolis, 390
negates, 212
negatron, 66
negotiators, 369
nemesis, 166, 251, 382
Neocene, 155
neolithic, 155
neologism, 144, 155, 195
neologists, 188
neology, 155
neon, 155
neophyte, 86, 155, 396
neoplasm, 155
nepotism, 66, 303, 340, 394
nervous, 211
Nestor, 255, 257, 258
neurological, 316
neurologist, 233
neurones, 326
neurosurgeon, 121
neuter, 160
neutron, 9, 35, 333, 393

New Deal, 303
New Frontier, 303
newsies, 273
Newton, Isaac, Sir, 123
Newtonian, 254, 332
Ngo Dinh Diem, 67
Nicene, 259
nicotine, 263, 313
Nietzschean, 254
Nigeria, 67
nihilism, 398
nihilistic, 116, 118, 134
nil, 160
nirvana, 66, 109, 110, 115, 394
niter, 160
nixed, 259
Nkrumah, Kwame, 67
nob, 346
nobles, 300
noggin, 276
noisome, 9, 35, 86, 393, 394
no kiddin', 130
nom de guerre, 234
nom de plume, 234
nomenclature, 284
nominal, 98, 105
nonadjacent, 223
nonce, 269
nonconformist, 100, 107, 348
nondescript, 151
nondurable goods, 296
nonsensical, 24
nonstandard, 60, 63, 188
noodle-twister, 269
norm, 117
nosey-parker, 285
nostalgia, 99, 106, 143
nostrum, 160, 193
notation, 374
novelty, 89
nuances, 109, 111, 222
nuclear, 90, 224
nuclear fission, 154
nucleonics, 66
nucleus, 177, 326
nude, 201
nullifies, 212
number, 316

numerically, 331
numerology, 141
nunciature, 95, 103
nuncio, 309
nut, 129, 130
nutrient, 338
nuts, 346
nutty as a fruit-cake, 268
nyctophobia, 142
nylon, 318

Oakley, Annie, 283, 289
obdurate, 89
obeisance, 363
objectify, 234
objectional, 18
objective, 187
objurgate, 217
oblate, 369
obliquity, 169
obliterate, 22
obloquy, 216
obscene, 63
obscenity, 13, 66, 109, 111
obsequies, 381
obsidian, 109, 110
obsolete, 62, 76, 173, 235
obstetrics, 380
obstreperous, 235
O'Casey, Sean, 67
occipital, 367
occupancy, 127, 128
occupation, 202
occupational neurosis, 350
octogenarian, 64, 86, 393
octopus, 23, 160
octuplets, 18
oddballs, 130
oddities, 25, 96
odium, 160
odyssey, 249
oecumenical, 238
oenological, 99, 106
offbeat, 62
off his nut, 276
officialese, 303
ohm, 251
oiled, 270
oil lobby, 302
old do-re-mi, 276

old equalizer, 276
Old Nobadaddy, 258
old warm squati-voo, 277
oligarchy, 154
omega, 166
omnibus, 66, 92, 101, 120, 190, 195
omniscience, 390
omnivorous, 140
once in a coon's age, 276
onerous, 247
one-upmanship, 347
on fire, 11
on ice, 269
onomatopoeia, 11
onslaught, 141
on the button, 130
on-the-job training, 350
on the snatch, 276
ontological, 109, 112, 115, 398
onyx, 166
o.o., 12
operational, 310
ophthalmia, 166
opium, 147
opportunism, 307
opprobrium, 160
optimistic, 51
option, 297
oracular, 22, 229
oratorical, 260
orbit, 337, 338
    parking, 336
    satellite, 335
    synchronous, 334
orbital refueling, 335
orbital speed, 337
orbiting, 121
orchid, 230
ordeal, 211
order, 184
orientation, 326
Orlando, 258
ornate, 97, 105, 212, 233
ornithology 144
Orpheus, 123
orthography, 144, 390
Orwell, George, 123
Orwellian, 311

428

principle, 216
pristine, 116
private capitalistic system, 298
private property, 297
probability, 224
probe, 349
  deep-space, 335
  lunar, 349
  space, 312, 349
  Venus, 349
proboscis, 161
process, 304
proclivities, 275
proconsul, 146, 161
procrastinator, 190, 195, 250
proctor, 146, 161
procurator, 146, 161, 355
production, 297, 298
  cost of, 297
profanation, 140
profane, 63
profanity, 216, 222
proficient, 148
profile, 101, 107
profit, 297
profiteering, 127, 128, 297
profusion, 357
prognosticate, 51
prognostication, 288
programmer, 316
programming, 349
progression, 97, 105
prohibitive, 370
projectile, 137
projection, 314
Project Mercury, 312
prolate, 369
proletarian, 298, 340
proletarian internationalism, 306
proletariat, 119, 134, 298
prolific, 147
prolix, 161
prologue, 144
Prometheus, 331
promiscuity, 109, 110

promote, 278
promulgated, 332, 336
propaganda, 146, 161
propagandists, 92, 102
propitiate, 233
proposition, 177, 190, 210
propound, 149
proprietary, 127, 128
pros, 165
proscribe, 150, 172, 394
prosecutor, 381
prospector, 161
prostitution, 380
protagonist, 109, 112, 138, 154, 172, 394
protean, 100, 106, 227, 247, 397
protégée, 93, 102
protocol, 14, 155
protomartyr, 155
proton, 155, 238, 330, 340
protonotary, 155
prototype, 155
protozoan, 155
Proustian, 261
proverbial, 371
provident, 384
providential, 22
provisional, 212
provocative, 267
provost, 9
prurience, 109, 111, 397
prussic, 263
psalmody, 355
psalter, 167, 355
pseudo, 233, 257, 330
pseudonym, 234, 390
psyche, 155, 167
psychiatrist, 66, 233
psychiatry, 90, 155, 333
psychoanalysis, 155
psychoanalyst, 142, 233
psychodrama, 155
psychological, 71, 244, 265

psychology, 8, 71, 144, 190, 265
psychometrical, 333
psychopathologist, 233
psychosis, 155
psychosomatic, 155
psychosomatics, 350
psychosurgery, 155
psychotherapist, 233
psychotherapy, 155
public accommodations, 350
pulchritude, 385
pun, 21, 27
punctilio, 66, 218
punctuation, 367
pungency, 109, 110
punning, 270
purchasing power, 297
purists, 244
pursuance, 381
pursuivant, 90
purvey, 384
put, 206
putative, 93, 102, 115, 394, 396
put down, 285
putrefaction, 22, 148
put the blast on, 277
put the finger on, 62
put the lug on, 278
put the old sleeve on, 277
Puzzle Palace, 303
pyre, 231
pyrites, 156, 167
pyrography, 144
python, 167
pyx, 90, 167

quadrant, 66, 330
quadrumanal, 371
quaestor, 146, 161
Quai d'Orsay, 309
quail, 270
qualm, 139
quandary, 22
quarterdeck, 383
quasi, 161, 238

queller, 50
quickie, 347, 350
quid pro quo, 146, 309, 340, 352, 397
quietus, 161
quip, 235
quire, 40
quirk, 24, 36, 266
quisling, 251
quixotic, 249, 290
quondam, 161
quorum, 146, 161
quota, 89, 146, 161, 295

Rabelaisian, 261, 275
rabblerouser, 374
rabble-rousing, 61, 92, 101
raceme, 90
rachitic, 141
racism, 305, 307
racket, 60, 61, 130
raconteur, 66
racy, 354
radar, 292, 340
radiation, 90, 178, 291, 324, 330, 338, 393
  cosmic, 337
  infrared, 337
  secondary, 337
  solar, 337
  trapped, 337
radionics, 66
radio telescopes, 357
raffish, 397
raffishly, 109, 111
rail at, 219
rajah, 231
rally, 61
ramifications, 215, 247
ramifying, 144
ramjet, 335
ramshackle, 94, 103
rancor, 27, 93, 102, 128, 161, 377, 394
rancorous, 371
random, 116
random-tandem, 116
random, 199
range, 184
rank, 184

ranting, 258
rapacious, 378
rapprochement,
     66, 309, 310,
     352
raspberry, 59, 60
rationalizations,
     93, 102
rat race, 347
rats, 300, 302
ratted, 130
raucous, 109, 141
ravin, 90
ravine, 378
ravishing, 378
rayon, 313
razz, 59, 60, 343
razzberry, 59
reactionary, 251
reaction vector,
     337
reactor, 92, 101
real gone, 346
realist, 379
realize, 234
rebukes, 219
recalcitrant, 239
recant, 222, 364
recantation, 364
recapitulation, 367
recession, 90, 304
recipient, 364
reciprocal, 183,
     195, 378
reclamation, 366
recluse, 366
reconnaissance, 66
reconstruct, 368
reconversion, 296
recorder, 365
recoupment, 99,
     106
recriminations, 305
rectitude, 379
rectum, 147, 161
recurrence, 179
red, 178
redeem, 358
redeploy, 93, 103
refection, 148
referee, 369
referendum, 146,
     161, 369
reflux, 147, 161
reformatory, 368
reformer, 368
reformism, 307
refraction, 370
refractory, 239,
     370

refrangible, 370
regard, 177
regenerative, 9
regime, 47, 66,
     230, 379
regimen, 146, 147,
     162, 366, 379
regional, 137
regnant, 379
regress, 140
regrettable inci-
     dent, 308
rehabilitation, 370
reify, 234
reinforcement, 314
reinstate, 380
rejiggering, 302
rejoin, 372
rejuvenator, 147,
     162
relativism, 344
relativity, 125
relaxation of ten-
     sion, 308
relay station, 337
relegated, 343
relentless, 301
relict, 50
religion, 193
relocated, 127
relocating, 334
reminiscences, 127
remiss, 372
remorseless, 260
Renaissance, 43,
     81, 258
rendezvous, 95,
     104, 239, 368
renovated, 95, 104,
     127
rentier, 297
reparation, 373
repellent, 318
repertoire, 395
repertory, 99, 106
repetitious, 273
repetitiousness,
     197
repetitive, 374
replica, 162, 376
reprehend, 377
reprehensible, 377
reprehension, 377
repression, 314
reprieve, 201
reprisal, 377
repudiate, 46
re-refer, 151
rescript, 151
researcher, 223

resentful, 377
residuary, 379
residues, 165
resign, 11
resilience, 51, 378
resins, 318
resistor, 315
resonance, 126,
     127, 324
resourceful, 257
resourcefulness,
     222, 370
respectability, 270
restate, 380
restaurateur, 98,
     105
restitution, 380
restive, 380
restructuring, 129
resultant, 378
resumption, 43
resurgence, 43
retainer, 44, 58
retention, 44
reticence, 44
reticulated, 224
retina, 147, 162
retinue, 88
retorts, 286
retract, 222
retribution, 166
retrospect, 384
retrospection, 384
revamping, 367
revelatory, 83
reveler, 258
revenant, 225
revenuers, 376
revisionism, 152,
     307
revisit, 384
revitalized, 350
revolution, 358
revolutionary
     movement,
     305
revolutionists, 274
rewrite, 223
rhubarb, 269
ribaldry, 222
ride, 207
ridic, 346
riding the air, 299
rig, 274
right wing, 303
rigmarole, 109,
     110, 396
rigorous, 237
Rimski-Korsakov,
     67

ring-tailed roarers,
     282
rise, 284
rive, 90
robot, 257
robust, 260, 271
robustness, 260
rock, 276
rockabilly, 98, 105
rocket:
     atomic-powered,
     337
     multistage, 335
     pyrotechnics,
     337
     retro-, 335
     satellite, 6
     second-stage,
     336, 337
     shuttle, 337
     space, 6
     step-, 335
     step-, chemi-
     cally-fueled,
     335
rocket-braking,
     335
rocket engine, 6
rocket propellant,
     335
rocket propulsion,
     335
rocketry, 337
rococo, 233
rodded up, 277
rodomontade, 257
roentgens, 337
roistering, 97, 98,
     105
rood, 90
Rooseveltian, 254
Roscoe, John, 276
rostrum, 146, 162
Rotarian, 258
roulette, 179
rous, 207
royalties, 295
rubberneckers, 62
rubbing out, 268
Rubicon, 252, 290
ruefully, 117
rug rank, 273
rumble, 286
ruminant, 23, 140
rumpscuttle, 274
run, 179, 206
runic, 331
runnel, 90
run-out powder,
     276

social evolution, 298
socialism, 138, 297
Socialist, 298, 306, 376
socialite, 13, 54, 94, 103, 107
social security, 350
sociohistorical, 325
sociological, 127, 129
sociology, 89
sockeroo, 12
socko, 12
Socratic, 193, 195, 249, 290, 394
soft-drink set, 12
sol, 162
solar cells, 337
solar energy, 337
solar engine, 6
solar panel, 337
solar plasma, 337
solar radiation, 337
solar satellite, 337
solar solstice, 330
solar wind, 337
soldiering, 300
solecisms, 344
solemn commitments, 308
solid-state, 315, 340
soliloquies, 187
soliloquize, 66
solstice, 380
somnolent, 50
sonar, 100, 106, 292, 340
sonic, 337
soothsayer, 355
sophisticated, 98, 105, 260
sophisticates, 25
sophistication, 182
Sophoclean, 260
sored up at, 276
sortie, 141
soused, 270
sovereignty, 308
spacecraft:
    altitude-stabilized, 337
    spin-stabilized, 337
space medicine, 349
space rocket, 6
space ship, 6

space shots, 346
space station, 6, 335, 337
spanner, 285
sparrow grass, 25
sparsely, 94, 103
spate, 92, 101, 109, 112, 393, 397
spate of allegations, 308
spatiography, 349, 398
spearheaded, 90
specialization, 175, 195
specification, 294, 384
specify, 384
specious, 41, 384
spectroscope, 138, 155, 172
spectroscopic measurements, 335
spectrum, 90
speculation, 210, 297
speculator, 162
speech center, 129
speed-up, 300
speleological, 143
speleology, 143
spelunker, 143
Spengler, 123
Spenglerian, 245, 254
sperm, 328
spermatozoon, 167
spheroid, 155
Spinoza, 67
spiritualists, 234
splay, 90
splendid, 189
splice, 121
spliced, 134
splinter groups, 343
split-level, 350
splittism, 152
spondulicks, 275
sponge, 221
sponsor, 146, 162
spoonerism, 21, 24
spoony, 275
sporadic, 51
sport, 291
sprung, 62
sputnik, 25, 173, 354
sputum, 147, 162

squadristi, 352
squadrons, 364
squalid, 99, 106
squalor, 109, 110
square, 1, 6, 59, 61, 62, 66, 119, 130, 273, 286, 346
squat, 173, 284
squawker, 274
squeal, 201
squeeze, 136
squib, 217, 251
squiffed, 270
stabilization, 294
staccato, 66
stadium, 162
stages, 338
    booster, 337
    fifth, 337
    first-step-rocket, 337
staging, 337
Stalinist, 254
stamina, 162
stanchion, 90, 380
standard, 61, 188
Stanislavsky, 67
state, 177
static, 211
statisticians, 224
status, 146, 162
status symbol, 347
steals, 198
steam winches, 122
steapsin, 90
steatopygous, 6, 108
steering jets, 335
stenographer, 144
stentorian, 141, 235
stereo, 317
    super-stereo, 317
stereophonic, 312
stereoscope, 155
stereotype, 260, 390
sterility, 326
sterilization, 326
sternum, 147, 162
stethoscope, 155
stewed, 270
stichomancy, 81
sticklers, 369
stiff, 240, 270
stifflicated, 269
stigma, 167

stimulus, 326
stingy, 136, 138, 171
stipule, 90
stirk, 274
stockpile, 93, 94, 103, 296
stockpiling, 312
Stoic, 395
stoical, 252, 267, 290
stolid, 99, 106
stoma, 90, 167
stomate, 90
stowaway, 140
strainer, 381
straiten, 381
strata, 162, 273
stratagems, 237
strategically, 109, 111, 317
stratosphere, 390
stretch, 59, 61, 62
stretch-out, 300
strictness, 381
stricture, 92, 101, 115, 381, 393, 396
strident, 141, 235
strike, 18, 39
strikebreaking, 300
strontium, 66
strophe, 167
strumpet, 27, 35
strumpetry, 16, 17, 109, 110
stubby, 109, 110
stupor, 147, 162
stylized, 371
stylograph, 144
stylus, 81
stymied, 45
suave, 236
subatomic, 315
subconscious, 24, 142
subjective, 187
subjugate, 372
subjunctive, 372
sublimation, 314
sub rosa, 309, 310
subscribe, 150
subscriber, 151
subscription, 151
subsidy, 293
subsonic, 337
substandard, 60, 63, 188
substantial, 23, 89
substantialize, 234

432

434

435